Case Studies in Diversity

Refugees in America in the 1990s

EDITED BY
DAVID W. HAINES

PRAEGER

Westport, Connecticut
London

Library of Congress Cataloging-in-Publication Data

Case studies in diversity : refugees in America in the 1990s / edited
  by David W. Haines.
       p.   cm.
     Abridged ed. of: Refugees in America in the 1990s. Westport, Conn.:
     Greenwood Press, 1996.
     Includes bibliographical references and index.
     ISBN 0–275–95804–3 (pbk. : alk. paper)
     1. Refugees—United States. I. Haines, David W.
  HV640.4.U54C37   1997
  362.87'0973—dc20   96–44673

British Library Cataloguing in Publication Data is available.

An expanded, hardcover edition of *Case Studies in Diversity: Refugees in
America in the 1990s* is available under the title *Refugees in America in the 1990s:
A Reference Handbook* from the Greenwood Press imprint of Greenwood Publishing
Group, Inc. (ISBN: 0–313–29344–9).

Library of Congress Catalog Card Number: 96–44673
ISBN: 0–275–95804–3

First published in 1997

Praeger Publishers, 88 Post Road West, Westport, CT 06881
An imprint of Greenwood Publishing Group, Inc.

Printed in the United States of America

The paper used in this book complies with the
Permanent Paper Standard issued by the National
Information Standards Organization (Z39.48–1984).

10 9 8 7 6 5 4 3 2 1

To Howard and Grace Haines

Contents

Acknowledgments

This volume is a subset of *Refugees in America in the 1990s: A Reference Handbook*. For both that original effort and this paperback version, particular appreciation goes to Sheila Barrows, Toyo Biddle, Loren Bussert, Barbara Chesnick, Fred Conway, Steve Gold, Linda Gordon, Elzbieta Gozdziak, Beatrice Hackett, Phil Holman, David Howell, Nguyen Manh Hung, Jeff McDonald, Carol Mortland, Karen Rosenblum, and Ann Rynearson. At Greenwood Press, I would like to thank Cynthia Harris, Alan Sturmer, Bridget Austiguy-Preschel, and Susan Badger. Finally, I have benefitted greatly in recent years from the work of the American Anthropological Association's Committee on Refugee Issues and from contact with Richmond, Virginia's resettlement community, particularly Marilyn Breslow, Kathleen Jackson, Jeff Sulik, and Nancy Riddle-moser.

Chapter 1

Introduction

DAVID W. HAINES

This volume provides an overview of the major refugee groups who have come to the United States since the end of the Second World War. It focuses on those who have met the formal, legal criterion of refugee status and on those who have arrived in relatively large numbers.[1] The chapters are drawn from a larger, previously published volume on refugees and reorganized to permit both a comparison of refugee groups and a comparison of the way in which the refugee experience can be studied and interpreted.[2]

It is difficult—and perhaps dangerous—to attempt to summarize the varied origins and experiences of the diverse refugees who have come to the United States. Instead, this introduction suggests some core issues and approaches: First, the key factors in understanding the experience of refugees in the United States; second, the varying approaches that can be taken in examining the experience of particular refugees; third, important emerging issues in understanding the refugee experience at the end of the twentieth century; and fourth, some suggestions about how to approach the book.

Throughout the remainder of this chapter, it is important to remember that the experience of refugees both overlaps and diverges from the experience of other immigrants in terms of their adjustment to the United States and in terms of U.S. response to them both before and after their arrival. As an issue of scale, refugees are only a minor segment of legal immigration to the United States, and legal immigration itself is only part of the overall level of immigration to the United States that has created such sharp public concern in recent years. As an issue of structure, refugees are a special category of people who are admitted to the United States for humanitarian reasons, have often suffered greatly before reaching the United States, and are resettled through an impressive combination of public and private resources.

KEY FACTORS IN UNDERSTANDING THE REFUGEE EXPERIENCE

The resettlement of refugees in the United States over the past fifty years has yielded a rich body of research on a very diverse set of newcomers. This research has benefitted from an unusually broad representation of academic researchers from various disciplines, program and policy analysts, and those providing direct services to refugees. The research—particularly for Cuban and Southeast Asian refugees—is voluminous. In terms of survey data, for example, I suspect that the information available for Southeast Asian refugees is more extensive than for any other immigrant group during its early years in the United States. The research on Cubans, particularly in Miami, is also extensive in amount, sophisticated in analysis, and very influential in sociological theory.

Fifty years into post–war refugee resettlement, thirty-five years into Cuban resettlement, and twenty years into Southeast Asian refugee resettlement, the research on the refugee experience has settled into a general, broadly shared framework. Analysis of the background of refugees continues to focus on core areas of demographic, economic, political, and socio-cultural background and how these are affected by the refugee experiences of flight, asylum, and resettlement—often with the transit to the United States emerging as a distinct layer of its own in the personal histories of refugees. In this multi-disciplinary and conjointly "academic" and "applied" effort, most of us have been forced to incorporate analytic perspectives that we might otherwise have minimized. As a practical research issue, for example, anyone looking for sources on refugees will, at the least, be browsing journals from anthropology, education, geography, history, law, medicine, political science, psychology, sociology, and social work, as well as from such interdisciplinary areas as ethnicity, gender studies, international relations, and migration.

Overall, the research points to six general sets of factors that are essential to understanding the experience of refugees.

First is demographic structure. Cuban and Soviet populations, for example, are relatively old. On the other hand, most Southeast Asian refugee groups are relatively young, but differ markedly in the number of men and women—Vietnamese have an imbalance toward men, while Cambodians have an imbalance toward women. These imbalances have lasting implications for marriage patterns. In terms of families, Southeast Asian refugees have relatively large families, while Cubans and Soviet Jews have relatively small ones. Although both anthropologists and sociologists (who account for the great majority of the authors in this book) have been quick to look at the implications of family size and structure, their approaches are sometimes different. Anthropologists may look to family size as reflecting cultural preferences while sociologists may see family size more as the result of fertility levels, which have a variety of economic as well as social causes.

Second is socio-economic background. Occupational and educational background, in particular, are essential in considering the experience of refugees—both in flight from their home country and in integration into the United States. They bring with them to the United States not only variation in occupational and educational background but also the class structure that is the correlate—if not the source—of that variation. Some of the most sophisticated quantitative analysis is on these subjects, but there has also been considerable field research seeking to examine specific refugee histories or particular work sites in America.

Third is kinship. For example, much has been made of the honor of the Cuban family and the ways in which female employment and intact marriages have contributed to Cuban refugee economic success. The more extended kinship structures of most Southeast Asian refugee populations have permitted both short-term economic strategies based on multiple wage-earners and longer-term strategies based on the economic advancement of the next generation. Again, the approaches vary from survey-based analysis of household structure and earnings to field research on small sets of families to more formal analysis of kinship systems. (My own first foray into refugee research, for example, was an analysis of Vietnamese kinship terminology.)

Fourth are the specific values and expectations that refugees bring with them. American notions of individual initiative, for example, are alien to many refugees who have strong group orientations—usually along kinship lines. In other situations refugees may be more American than Americans: many refugees—particularly those in the East Asian tradition—attach enormous importance to education and thus find more value in American educational institutions than do Americans themselves. These values not only affect refugees' lives, but often become a source of direct concern to them when the values are threatened by the economic and social pressures of life in a new country.

Fifth is the effect of exodus. The decision to flee is a difficult and dangerous one that has severe consequences for the individuals, families, and groups involved. Furthermore, escape involves a dangerous and often contorted passage through the jurisdiction of other nations and frequent stays in countries of asylum and transit—often under international protection. The drownings and assaults against the Southeast Asian "boat people," coupled with extensive stays in difficult camp conditions, are well known. Long and indeterminate stays of Ethiopians in the Sudan, of Afghans in Pakistan, and of eastern Europeans in a variety of transit countries may be less life-threatening, but provide their own dangers and after-effects.

Sixth is the impact of American society. Once in the United Sates, the refugee experience is shaped and often frustrated by the situation of the host society. For example, different refugee groups at different times have found the general economic situation in the United States more or less conducive to their economic incorporation. The specific localities in which refugees settle—only partially as a matter of choice—also affect their incorporation in terms of available housing stock, specific jobs, educational resources, and general community public opinion about them. For refugees, one unique factor involves the special programs aimed to assist them in adjusting to the United States: these programs range from broad, relatively impersonal agency efforts to direct sponsorships by individuals, families, and churches.

Out of these six sets of factors have come various academic analyses aiming to establish what specific factors affect which specific outcomes. For example, there have been extensive arguments about the relative effects of occupational background versus educational background, and of educational background versus English language competence. Over time, however, there has been an increasing attention toward the full range of these factors as they apply to the specific histories of particular refugees. In earlier years, by contrast, there were often overly simplified considerations of refugee adaptation that focussed on single outcome measures (most frequently ''self-sufficiency'') or that lumped together widely different refugee experiences into such questionable categories as ''Indochinese.''

DIVERSE APPROACHES TO THE REFUGEE EXPERIENCE

This generally shared framework can be seen throughout the twelve chapters in this volume. Each of the authors in this volume covers the same basic stages of the refugee experience, from the events that forced exodus, to the complexities of escape and frequent long stays in countries of temporary asylum, to the initial difficulties of adjusting to a new country for which (unlike most immigrants) they have little preparation, to some of the longer-term issues of incorporation into American society—an ''incorporation'' that leaves some at the margins of that society. In the process, the common factors of demographics, socio-economic background, kinship, cultural values, after-effects of exodus, and the impact of American society on the refugees can all be seen.

Yet the authors also take quite different approaches to their subjects. Sometimes the difference reflects the amount of research on particular refugee groups. For Cubans and Vietnamese, for example, there is an enormous range of quantitative and qualitative research. For many other refugees, the existing research is far more limited, forcing the chapter authors to rely more heavily on their own individual research. Some of the difference, however, lies in the approach that the authors take to their subject matter, reflecting their academic and professional backgrounds (which include anthropology, health, history, political science, program administration, and sociology). The authors were encouraged to discuss these particular areas of expertise. Joseph Coleman, for example, discusses the unusual private resettlement program for Cubans with which he was involved, Carol A. Mortland gives added emphasis to the discrepancies between refugee and American views of resettlement based on her broad range of academic research and service provision experience, Mehdi Bozorgmehr continues his examination of the differences between Iranian immigrants and refugees (preferring the term ''exile''), and Pamela A. DeVoe pays particular attention to the spiritual dilemmas of life in America for the Lao.

The most pervasive difference, however, involves the way chapter authors assess the importance of different kinds of information in explaining the refugee experience. Therefore, rather than group the chapters here in terms of region, they are grouped into four parts reflecting whether political, sociological, anthropological, or historical considerations are of central importance.

Part I: Political Approaches includes the two major refugee groups of the post–World War II period. Both the Cubans and Vietnamese are now large, well-established groups in the United States; the progress of both groups is documented in a wide range of quantitative and qualitative research, and is also documented in at least two decennial censuses (three for the Cubans). Both groups are in the United States as the direct result of U.S. confrontation of Communist regimes—regimes that have survived not only that U.S. confrontation but also the subsequent collapse of the Soviet Union. Finally, both groups have been successful in economic terms, have been widely lauded for that success, and have actively promoted that success as part of their image.

In looking at these two groups, both Coleman for the Cubans (Chapter 2), and Nguyen Manh Hung and myself for the Vietnamese (Chapter 3), are able to draw on existing research to address the size and location of these groups and their economic status. Both chapters face similar questions about the politics of exile from societies that are still Communist, including the moral question of how to balance return visits and financial remittances on the one hand, with continued activism on behalf of human rights in the home country on the other. Although both chapters address a wide range of social and economic issues, the discussion frequently returns to politics both in the new country and the old.

Part II: Sociological Approaches includes chapters by Steven J. Gold on Soviet Jews (Chapter 4) and Mehdi Bozorgmehr on Iranians (Chapter 5). Both chapters share several core features. Although both discuss the home country situation, that discussion is relatively brief. Instead, both focus on the current situation of Iranians and Soviet Jews, concentrate on economic status and incorporation, and tend to rely on quantitative data. Both also opt not to use the label "refugee," instead choosing "emigré" (Soviet Jews) and "exile" (Iranians). The reasons for doing so are based largely on self-identification, but also have some legal implications in the Iranian case: many of the Iranians are not refugees in the formal, legal sense.

In discussing Soviet Jews, Gold provides a brief overview of exodus routes, then turns to three main subjects: demographic patterns, economic issues, and relations with the host society—including the interaction between the refugees and the existing Jewish community. Throughout he draws on his own research and the considerable quantitative data that exists for Soviet refugees. Like Gold, Bozorgmehr provides a brief introduction to the home country, but quickly turns to the situation in the United States. Also like Gold, he focuses on the specific details of the economic situation largely through quantitative data, and then concludes with a discussion of integration that focuses on Iranian ethnicity. His comments on Iranian diversity and the differential ways in which particular Iranian groups (Muslim, Jew, Baha'i, and Christian) integrate with existing American groups is an interesting complement to Gold's discussion of Soviet Jews' interaction with the American Jewish community.

The four chapters in Part III: Anthropological Approaches provide a more extensive discussion of the home country situation, with an emphasis on developing a cultural overview of the societies from which the refugees came. In dealing with the situation of refugees in the United States, the emphasis is less on quantitative data and more on qualitative discussions of life, based on a broad range of research fieldwork and program involvement. Life in the United States is considered in terms of cultural continuities and discontinuities, and in terms of the core anthropological understanding of social life: particularly the importance of looking at the interaction of the sexes and the generations. DeVoe, for example, begins Chapter 6 with a discussion of the topography of Laos, and then provides a succinct history of Laos and its refugee exodus. She then turns to the initial resettlement of Lao refugees combining a discussion of employment, housing, and neighborhoods with the issue of education and its effects on the different generations. As she turns to longer-range issues, the core anthropological concern with cultural continuities and discontinuities emerges as she focuses on the role of Buddhism, strains on relations between men and women, and the attempt by the Lao to maintain a balance of old traditions and new American realities.

Juliene G. Lipson and Patricia A. Omidian also begin their discussion of Afghan refugees in Chapter 7 with the topographical basics and the historical factors leading to exodus. They then must confront the complexity in Afghan exodus, the long periods of temporary asylum in Pakistan, and the uncertainty of events in the home country—uncertainty which continues to disrupt Afghans' lives in the United States. In looking at resettlement, they discuss such issues as finances, job opportunities, educational limitations, and neighborhood problems. As they turn to longer-range issues of resettlement, they choose to organize that discussion in terms of the basic anthropological structures of social life: men versus women, and older versus younger generations.

In Chapter 8, Timothy Dunnigan, Douglas P. Olney, Miles A. McNall, and Marline A. Spring address the situation of the Hmong, a major highland group from Laos who, along with the ethnic Lao discussed by DeVoe, comprise the vast majority of refugees from Laos. Like DeVoe, they begin with the situation in Laos, tracing the events that led to the Hmong exodus. Like Lipson and Omidian, they also must confront the long and often debilitating periods of time spent in temporary asylum. As they turn to resettlement, they provide sequential discussions of kinship, religion, economic adaptation, education, marriage and fertility, and community politics. Like the other anthropologists, they return to the issue of cultural continuity and change in their conclusion, with a particular emphasis on continuity in the structure and process of Hmong kinship.

Carol A. Mortland provides the final chapter in Part III. She starts with a description of Cambodia, tracing it from the earliest archaeological records through the American war to the holocaust that occurred in the late 1970s. Although true to the political events of that period, she continues to focus on the cultural core of Cambodian society which for her, as for DeVoe on the Lao, is intertwined with Buddhism. She sorts out the various refugee flows and the issues of asylum in Thailand, and then turns to resettlement in the United States, structuring her presentation into two separate sections: "Resettlement American Style," and "Resettlement Cambodian Style."

The final four chapters take a more historical approach to the situation of refugees in the United States. In Part IV, the historical sections are expanded in two ways. First, the attention to historical detail for the home country is more extensive than in the other chapters. Second, that commitment to historical detail continues in the consideration of refugees in the United States. The past is not an issue of international politics, as is central to the Cuban or Vietnamese cases, is not a short background to understanding current social and societal relationships, as is the case in the sociological chapters, and is not even an extended discussion to explain and convey certain distinct continuities, as it is in the anthropological approaches. Rather, the inventory of past events is part of a continuing flow of events in which the experience of refugees is embedded and from which it cannot be extricated.

In Chapter 10, Elzbieta M. Gozdziak painstakingly traces the historical roots of Eastern Europe and the specific historical events that have created and molded particular ethnic groups as majorities in some countries and minorities in others. This consideration of background takes up a major portion of her chapter. However, even when the subject turns to refugees in the United States, the commitment to historical detail remains. Thus she traces the history of immigration to the United States, particularly from Poland and Hungary, and how the new emigrés fit and do not fit into that existing history of immigration.

In a similar way, John K. Whitmore carefully traces the history of the Chinese in Cambodia and Vietnam since the seventeenth century in Chapter 11. The social organization of the Chinese in both countries receives a particularly coherent rendering, as does the economic centrality of the Chinese during the French colonial period. His discussion of resettlement turns for a time to discussion of some largely quantitative research that emphasizes the strong cultural basis for educational achievement among these refugees. At the end he returns to the more detailed consideration of the course of Chinese incorporation in the United States, particularly in the development of specific economic relationships in particular American cities based on long-established relations of kinship, region, and economics.

In Chapter 12, Frederick J. Conway and Susan Buchanan Stafford also devote the majority of their attention to historical issues. Haiti's political and cultural history is described in some detail, as is the shifting course of U.S. response to Haiti and Haitian refugees. Their discussion of resettlement shares many of the concerns of other chapters: employment, education, community, and ethnic identity. In addition, as with the Cubans, the experience of Haitians in America is tied closely to the historical events in a nearby homeland. As important, however, is the way in which the Haitian refugee experience in America is tied into the history of American refugee policy and eventually into the history of race relations in the United States.

In Chapter 13, Tekle M. Woldemikael is also intent on a clear identification of the historical events that brought Ethiopians and Eritreans to the United States, the circumstances that keep them in the United States, and the events that shape their identity as ethnic, national, and racial groups in the United States. As his chapter indicates, it is not possible to understand the experience of Eritrean and Ethiopian refugees in America without understanding the turbulent and complex history of the now separate Ethiopia and Eritrea and the varied independence movements that created them. Woldemikael also shows the dilemmas in ethnic identity that occur as Ethiopians and Eritreans, and more especially their children, are co-opted into the American structure of race relations. His chapter provides a provocative ending point for the book as it shows how forcefully the internal divisions of American society can permeate the experience of refugees in America.

EMERGING ISSUES

Much of the analysis of refugees in the United States continues to be concerned with issues of early resettlement (particularly employment, income, and household self-sufficiency) and the longer-range issues of incorporation into American society (particularly generational changes in the way different groups are absorbed into American society). With a well-established second generation, the "aging" of the original population, and the changes in the global political order in the 1990s, however, some new issues emerge in the consideration of refugees in America. Four merit particular attention: the reconstruction of relations with the home country; the realignment of political and social attitudes toward both home and new country; the construction and reconstruction of spiritual identity; and the intertwining of the refugee experience—real and perceived—with changes in American immigration policy and the self-identity of the larger society.

The Home Country

For almost all refugees, relations between the United States and their home countries are now more extensive than would have been imaginable a decade ago. Refugees have tended to be very sharply separated from their countries of origin by virtue of flight and the events leading to it. This rupture with the home country was one of the major factors which distinguished them from other immigrants, but it no longer seems automatic or final. The sharp physical divide between Eastern and Western Europe has dissolved and in Asia, a still-

Communist Vietnam welcomes back large numbers of its overseas refugee population as visitors, lures them as investors, and reaps the benefits of remittances that are approaching a $1 billion annual figure. Thus although the gap remains sharp for some countries, such as Iran and Afghanistan, most refugees have options for at least temporary return, must begin to address the issue of possible long-term return, and are—at the very least—a part of an increasingly reconnected diaspora.

Realigning Attitudes

Because of this potential reconnection to the home country, their increasing time in the United States, and changes in the United States itself, refugee social and political attitudes must also shift. Life in the new country has lost some of its luster for many refugees. The political freedom offered to the parents, for example, reemerges as the social freedom of children from their parents; it is far less appealing to them in that guise. The practical issues of resettlement often remain unresolved: imbalanced sex ratios keep men or women single; lack of job skills and English competence leave some refugees marginalized; and life in the neighborhood draws refugees into racial and class distinctions that are alien, physically dangerous, and culturally unraveling. The task of establishing a viable economic and social life in America thus continues to be arduous. How are refugees to balance that task with their responsibilities to support their relatives remaining in the home country (through remittances and sponsorship), to help rebuild the country (through investment of time or money), and to push for human rights advances (through political activity and withholding of financial support)?

Spiritual Identity

Almost inevitably, refugees—like immigrants—face challenges to their spiritual and religious views. The religious views and practices of Soviet Jews have received considerable attention, particularly as the views of the emigrés and the receiving community often diverge, causing frustration on both sides. In other cases, refugees must recreate their religious institutions: new Buddhist temples and Catholic churches for Southeast Asian refugees are a staple of the resettlement story. Different problems emerge for minority groups within a refugee population. Southeast Asian Christians are often cut off from their compatriots because of their religion, particularly when religion is woven into the core of ethnic identity—as with Buddhism for the Khmer or traditional spirits for the Hmong. Furthermore, the residue of a holocaust (for the Khmer) and the practical difficulties of a new life (for the Lao) may call into question basic religious tenets even of those who retain their traditional beliefs. For the former, Mortland notes how Khmer Buddhists are left with unanswerable questions about how a holocaust could have been created by Buddhists; for the latter, DeVoe notes the limitation of opportunities to accrue Buddhist merit in the United States, but the increased opportunities to accrue "demerit."

The Evolution of American Society

Finally, the refugee experience exists within American social and political history. Currently, for example, refugees are caught up in the broader rise of anti-immigrant sentiment and legislation in the United States. Their position is an anomalous one: they are a small part of the legal immigrant stream and a very small part of the combined legal and illegal immigrant stream. They are in many ways the closest of current immigrants to the venerable "huddled masses yearning to breathe free," and they are also generally the least prepared for a new life in the United States. Refugees find themselves in a changing America, and in changing economic, ethnic, and racial mixes in particular localities and workplaces. They are a part of a joint history that includes themselves, the extensive network of people and services directed toward them, the communities in which they settle, and the other immigrants who are reshaping American society and Americans' perceptions of that society. Just as refugees are witnesses to many of the crucial international events (and horrors) of the second half of the twentieth century, so also are they important witnesses to this continuing transformation of America.

SUGGESTIONS FOR APPROACHING THE BOOK

Although all the chapters in this book started with the same general outline, the extraordinary cultural and historical diversity of the refugees, the wide range in research available on particular groups, and the varied disciplinary backgrounds of the authors combine to create a complicated overall picture. Some suggestions on how to approach the book may thus be of value.

First, the history of refugees in the United States is closely linked to the history of the U.S. opposition to Communist regimes. Thus one good place to start is with the chapters on Cubans and Vietnamese. These chapters can then be supplemented by a consideration of Soviet Jews. The chapter on Haitians is a useful counterpoint in showing how inconsistent American policy can be when anti-Communism is not a clear factor in refugee exodus. These chapters provide the core of a political understanding of refugee policy and programs over the last thirty-five years.

Second, particular aspects of refugee resettlement can be examined by looking at selected sections of all or some of the chapters. All the chapters follow a rough framework of introduction, historical background, flight and transit, initial resettlement, longer-term adaptation, and future prospects. Although the exact section headings vary, and the experience of groups (and approach of the authors) may make equivalent sections longer or shorter, it is indeed possible to compare, for example, the structure of exodus and transit for the different groups, or even authors' summary "prospects" statements on these groups at the ends of the chapters.

Third, the explicit organization of the book can be used to look at how people look at the refugee experience. Although the division among political, sociological, anthropological, and historical approaches is neither sharp nor complete, nevertheless it permits a consideration of options in approaching the complex story of refugees in the United States. An initial approach might be to try one chapter from each section (perhaps Vietnamese, Iranian, Khmer, and Ethiopian/ Eritrean) to sample the different emphases, and then to consider what is gained—and what lost—as authors decide how much limited space to allocate to different stages of the refugee experience (for example, discrimination in home country, exodus), to different specific topics (for example, religion, kinship, employment), and to different specific methods (for example, survey data, census data, interview material, personal observation).

Fourth, the book can be used as a sampler of recent research on refugees. All the authors have been directly involved in refugee research or policy, and many have been responsible for path-breaking work. The book thus provides a starting point for a more theoretical consideration of the refugee experience and the policies and programs designed to shape that experience after arrival in America. As a starting point, for example, one could look at: Whitmore's comments on the Institute for Social Research (ISR) studies on refugees, education, and cultural values (which go well beyond his specific discussion of ethnic Chinese), Mortland's counterposing of the refugee and recipient society views of resettlement, Bozorgmehr's sorting out of the sociological meaning of exile within the enormously diverse Iranian population, and Woldemikael's concise presentation of the tension between ethnicity and race for Ethiopians and Eritreans.

Fifth, and finally, the book can be used as a starting point for examining both the broader history of America as a nation of immigrants and the wider role of America as an actor in the international area. As a nation of immigrants, the United States has developed an unusually high degree of social and cultural diversity that has both fueled its economic and intellectual development and been a periodic basis for nativist rejection of those from other countries. As an actor in the international arena, America's willingness to provide assistance to refugees overseas, and back that up with admission of refugees to the United States for resettlement,[3] continues to define and document the American moral— and often religious—commitment to human rights.

NOTES

1. With the Refugee Act of 1980, the United States accepted the formal United Nations definition of "refugee," specifying that a refugee is:

Any person who is outside any country of such person's nationality or, in the case of a person having no nationality, is outside any country in which such person has habitually resided, and who is unable or unwilling to return to, and is unable or unwilling to avail himself or herself of the protection of, that country because of persecution or a well-founded fear of persecution on account of race, religion, nationality, membership in a particular social group, or political opinion.

U.S. law also includes an equivalent definition for people remaining in their countries of origin who are nevertheless subject to persecution or a well-founded fear thereof.

In U.S. government terminology, a "refugee" is distinguished from an "asylee" since the former designation applies to those whose legal status is determined *before* arrival in the United States and the latter applies to those whose legal status is determined *after* arrival based on applications for asylum—applications that have sharply varying rates of success depending on the applicant's country of origin. To further complicate matters, the United States created a new "entrant" status for Cubans and Haitians arriving in 1980. That status is discussed in the chapter on Haitians by Conway and Stafford.

It is also the case that people from a particular country arrive in the United States with different legal statuses. Some may be refugees, others may be legal immigrants (either temporary or permanent), and yet others may be undocumented or "illegal" immigrants. The mix of refugees and non-refugee immigrants can be seen most clearly in the discussions of Iranians by Mehdi Bozorgmehr in Chapter 5 and Eastern Europeans by Elzbieta M. Gozdziak in Chapter 10.

In sorting out the legal definitions of "refugee" and the actual numbers of refugees coming to the United States, the core government sources are the annual reports of the Office of Refugee Resettlement (of the U.S. Department of Health and Human Services) and the Immigration and Naturalization Service (of the U.S. Department of Justice). The non-governmental U.S. Committee for Refugees in Washington, D.C. produces an annual yearbook and a monthly newsletter, both of which provide solid overviews and data on refugees in the United States and throughout the world. Concise summaries of U.S. law on refugees are provided by Philip Holman and Linda Gordon in their chapters in *Refugees in America in the 1990s: A Reference Handbook* (see note 2).

2. The larger, hardcover edition of this book (*Refugees in America in the 1990s: A Reference Handbook*. Westport, CT: Greenwood Press, 1996) includes an additional seven chapters: an introduction to the U.S. refugee program, an overview of basic patterns in refugee adjustment, a review of available statistics on refugee admission and adjustment of status, a consideration of public opinion on refugees, an overview of the global refugee situation, a review of documentary films on refugees, and an annotated introduction to some 200 basic academic books and articles on refugees. The size of that reference volume precluded a complete paperback edition.

3. Although this book is more comprehensive than other existing sources on refugees in the United States, some refugees are not included. For example, there are many situations in which the number of refugees from a particular country is small, or at least much smaller than for the groups represented here. Perhaps more importantly, this book does not address the numerous people who have fled to the United States clandestinely or who have overstayed their initial legal period because of fears for their safety if they were to return to their home country. Even if they are finally granted asylum, their experience differs in important ways from those whose transit to the United States is as formally accepted refugees.

Part I

Political
Approaches

Chapter 2

Cubans

JOSEPH COLEMAN

The refugee experience is distinct from that of other immigrants. Refugees do not initially expect to remain permanently in their countries of asylum, and are not—again at least initially—oriented toward fully integrating into them. Instead, they arrive in their new countries in what they hope will be a temporary absence from their own home countries.[1] This sense of temporary absence is particularly important in understanding Cuban refugees. The extreme geographical proximity of Cuba and the United States, and the long-intertwined political histories make for a closeness that has often been oppressive for Cubans but has also kept alive the direct involvement of Cuban refugees in events in the home country and the possibility of return. For exiles in America, the traditional Cuban view of the United States as a sort of dominating "monster" remains important. José Martí, Cuban's revolutionary writer and poet around the turn of the century, believed that it was difficult—perhaps impossible—to live with the "monster in its lair." That view persists today.

This chapter addresses the homeland from which the Cuban refugees fled, how they left, their resettlement in the United States, and their general situation as exiles in America. It begins, however, with a consideration of the emotional importance of Cuba to the revolution and to those who fled from it.

THE LOVED LAND

In the middle of the last century, J. G. Cantero wrote in his book *Los ingenios de Cuba* (The sugar mills of Cuba) that his country's soil was "the favorite of Providence" and that people would know of that preferment if they saw and felt Cuba's "copious and clear rivers, the state and variations of its benign and humid atmosphere, and above all the vivifying warmth of its tropical sun" (quoted in Williams 1984:363–364).[2] Cantero continued, noting the "majestic sight of the sun as it appears over the hills from which it bathes with its gilded rays the emerald fields covered with the transparent dew of the morning gently stirs the soul, elevating it to the sublime Creator of such a splendid picture."[3] Similarly, in the late 1980s a middle-aged Cuban refugee woman living in Florida told how she had been sent away to school in the United States when she was six years old to learn English. Then, when she was ten, Castro came to power, and she went into exile. "I had two exiles," she said. "I was sent away twice from the best place in the world." The two vignettes give some sense of what many Cuban refugees think and feel about their country. Such attachment remains an important and continuing part of their refugee experience. It is not too much of an exaggeration to say that for most Cubans, home is always Cuba.

Cuba itself, however, is ruled by a more ideological vision summed up in the phrase *Fidel-patria-revolution.* The triad (with *patria* best translated here as "motherland" or "homeland") has been a rhetorical and symbolic basis for the Cuban revolution from the beginning. The phrase is still invoked regularly in Cuba, although there has been substantial loss of credibility in all three of the terms. Castro still affirms that he and the revolution can and must continue to protect *patria* and that the complete triad still has important meaning for the Cuban people and still provides them support. Others have suggested (e.g., Pérez-Stable 1993:11) that, in contrast, Cuba is no longer "in revolution" and that the transformation of Cuban society essentially began and ended in the 1960s.

Whether the revolution succeeded or failed, or whether it continues or ended decades ago, many Cubans have left, and many more continue to try to leave. Those who left first in 1959 and came to the United States were those who had been wealthy and influential in the pre-Castro society. They were followed by persons from the middle economic classes and eventually the lower economic strata—who were a significant component of the 1980 Mariel boat exodus. Over time, it is probably fair to say that the balance shifted from those who had been politically persecuted or threatened to include at least some who fled because of material deprivation.

HOME

The story of Cuban refugees in the United States is the story of events in Cuba as much as it is of a new life in America. Cuba became a Spanish colony in 1511, and its capital—Havana—has been an important and cosmopolitan city for almost 500 years. One early effect of the Spanish control, and of the several European diseases they introduced, was the virtual disappearance of native peoples from the island in that first century. Since that time, the population has been divided between those of Spanish descent and those descended from the hundreds of thousands of slaves imported from Africa to work in the sugar plantations and mills. Significant immigration from Spain in the early 1900s served to maintain large numbers of those with Spanish rather than African origins.

By the 1990s, Cuba's population was about 11 million people, with an annual growth rate of only around 1 percent. About 57 percent of the population is mulatto, 37 percent is white, and 11 percent is black.[4] Life expectancy is about 78 years for women and 74 for men. Literacy is high (95 percent for men and 93 percent for women), and infant mortality is low (about 11 per 1,000 live births—lower than in parts of the United States). The Cubans are generally a healthy and well-educated people. Medical care and public health have been strongly supported by the government. Educational opportunities for Cubans have also been extensive under Castro. As in many other socialist countries, technical and scientific subjects have been strongly emphasized, and the arts and humanities are heavily conditioned by socialist ideology. Similarly, the written language, fiction as well as nonfiction, has taken on much of the abstract, dull, and propagandistic characteristics of socialist discourse.

The country as a whole remains relatively underpopulated with its population spread over a territory about one third larger than South Carolina and slightly smaller than Pennsylvania. (In European terms, Cuba is substantially larger than Austria and about the size of Belgium, the Netherlands, and Switzerland combined.) The country is very narrow in parts but quite long east to west. Its 750-mile length is approximately the distance from Chicago to New York. At least as important as its own internal structure, however, is its geographic location: about equidistant from Florida and Mexico and commanding access to the Gulf of Mexico. Its location encouraged many in American government and politics to view it as a part of America's natural jurisdiction. Indeed, there was at times a belief that Cuba would eventually become a state.[5]

The Cuban experience with the United States has long-standing economic, social, and cultural aspects, and often involves sharp contrasts. In cultural terms, for example, Cubans are a passionate people, and the contents of their beliefs and passions are as varied as they are strongly held. They thus wonder at the strange, unemotional, undemonstrative ways of most Americans. Joan Didion, for example, notes Cuban attitudes toward Ted Koppel and his guests on *Nightline*. They were, she notes, "a constant source of novelty and derision" for well-educated, cultured Cubans. The term *Nightline* became a kind of shorthand description for powerful American leaders who lacked passion. Cubans watched with wonder as Americans "with very opposing points of view" talked "completely without passion" and "without any gestures at all" (Didion 1987:78–79). "Speaking from the heart," by contrast, is a commonly heard phrase in the Cuban enclave, and the expression represents a habit of mind among Cubans that they see as quite different from American manners.

In political terms, it is difficult even to separate the Cuban from the American. The Spanish-American War is perhaps the most telling junction of Cuban and U.S. history.[6] For the United States the war began in the summer of 1898. However, it was Cuba's second war of independence: It had begun for them in

1895 and ended very quickly after U.S. troops arrived. Americans remember Teddy Roosevelt and the Rough Riders at San Juan Hill, but most Cubans remember that their own forces already controlled the countryside when the Americans arrived. By 1898 the Cuban Army of Liberation had forced Spain to "concentrate in cities," and when the United States attacked, "there was nowhere to retreat" (Rudolph 1985:21).

After the war, Cuba's independence was shaped by American intentions, good and bad. Cubans were considered by the United States to need a strong hand if they were to become democratic, rational, and capitalist. This attitude was typified in the Platt Amendment of 1901. This amendment (to a U.S. military appropriations bill) contained several clauses that were forced into the new Cuban constitution. Under its terms, Cuba was required to accept as legitimate all acts of the military government of the United States that had been installed there; had to permit the United States to purchase or lease land it needed for "coaling and naval stations" (thus, the beginning of the Guantánamo Naval Base); and was required to allow the United States to intervene at any time to "preserve Cuban independence" or "to support a government capable of protecting life, property, and individual liberties" (Rudolph 1985:21). Although the Platt Amendment may have been intended by the United States as a relatively benevolent (if permanent) restriction on Cuba's independence, it was, from the Cuban perspective, an enormous humiliation. Elihu Root, secretary of war early in the century and a major force behind the Platt Amendment, briskly spelled out the nature of the relationship. Although he recognized that Cuba was "technically a foreign country," it "occupies an intermediate position, since we have required it to become part of our political and military system" (Paterson 1994:5).

Although the verbal stances of later American leaders were softened, Root's description of the relationship remained essentially correct until Fidel Castro. Castro's emphasis on achieving true independence from the United States helps explain the extent of his support among middle-class Cubans. Before Castro, under the dictatorship of Fulgencio Batista, there was widespread corruption as well as "profound inequalities" between the urban and rural sectors in Cuba (Pérez-Stable 1993:6). Castro often spoke of the revolution that would rectify such injustices, but, at least in the beginning, that revolution was not so much for communism as against the United States. For many reasons (see, for example, Paterson 1994), relations between the two countries worsened to the point that as President Dwight Eisenhower was preparing to leave office in December 1960, he broke diplomatic ties with the Castro government. By then Cuba had nationalized almost all American businesses, and also many belonging to Cuban entrepreneurs, who would soon become refugees. The attempted invasion by Cuban exiles at Playa Giron on the Bay of Pigs in the spring of 1961 made relations even worse. (The handling of the Bay of Pigs invasion also alienated many Cuban exiles who believed, often with a continuing sense of deep betrayal, that the American support had been inadequate.)

In December 1961 Castro proclaimed that Cuba was now a Communist state. In the following year, Cuba was expelled from the Organization of American States, which had also voted for a political and economic blockade of Cuba. The United States instituted a trade embargo, which has remained in effect at some level ever since. Castro in turn moved closer to the Soviet Union. In the fall of 1962, Russia began to place missiles and atomic warheads on the island, and the Cuban Missile Crisis followed. Communism and anti-Americanism remained pillars of the revolution from then on. Even in the late 1980s, as Eastern Europe was leaving the fold and the Soviet Union itself was beginning to collapse, Castro forcefully restated his own commitment to communism. At the same time, he moved against, and eventually executed, more than a dozen top military and government officials (including the revolutionary hero General Arnaldo Ochoa) who were accused of involvement in drug trafficking and ill-specified violations of national security.[7]

Three decades after the revolution, Castro remains central not only to Cuba but to the views and hopes of Cubans in America. For the exiles, the views are negative. Alina Fernandez Revuelta, Castro's refugee daughter (born out of wedlock), was asked if her father was a dictator. "That's not the right word," she said. "I looked it up once. A dictator is someone granted absolute but temporary powers in an emergency." She thought her father was a tyrant instead. "A tyrant," she explained, is an "absolute ruler unrestrained by law, who usurps people's rights" (Oppenheimer 1992:282). For others, the views are positive. There is a widespread perception across many countries of a sense of selflessness in Cuba, a generous spirit, and an enviable strength of character. A middle-class Dominican from Santo Domingo (personal communication), for example, said that he and many Latins still believe that U.S. foreign policy is driven almost entirely by material considerations, which are amoral and sometimes immoral. "I think," he continued, "Cuba has always been the one country almost everyone in Latin America admires. I mean, here we have this small, poor country, resisting and standing against the greatest power on earth!"

LEAVING HOME

After Castro took power and after it became clear that the influence of the upper economic classes would count for much less in the new regime than originally thought, the large-scale emigration of the wealthy and the near-wealthy began.[8] It was clear that the new regime, whatever political label it deserved at the time, was moving toward the egalitarian ideal of a new society for the *Hombre Nuevo* (New Man) it wished to develop. It was also clear that there would be a major distribution of wealth from rich to poor and from cities, notably Havana, to the countryside. For those who left at this time, it was relatively easy to bring much of their wealth with them. There were few restrictions or controls on those who wished to leave, or on their money.

The number of departures is not exactly known. Approximately 200,000 left for the United States in the early period that followed the exit of Batista and his immediate circle. Perhaps another 200,000 fled to other countries at the same time. The departure of the wealthiest Cubans was quickly followed by that of large numbers from the professional and managerial classes. This first wave of emigration slowed with the imposition of the trade embargo in 1962 and ended with the Cuban Missile Crisis later that year. By that time, Castro and his government had made a solid start in their attempt to reshape Cuba and its people through a system of pervasive education, rewriting of history, and constant exposure of individuals to group meetings and public events at which central themes were repeated.

The next major wave of emigration began in the fall of 1965 after the Cuban economy had deteriorated seriously. The political pressures on Cuba from the poor state of its economy (before Russian aid reached massive levels), and on the United States from rumors of chaotic, unimpeded exits from Cuba, were strong enough to bring the Cuban and U.S. governments to agreement on what became the so-called Freedom Flights, from the airport at Veradero in Cuba to Miami. Those who left were almost all close relatives of Cubans already living in the United States. The flights ended in 1973, after about 300,000 people on several thousand flights had been admitted to the United States (Portes and Stepick 1993:103–104). From then until the late 1970s, probably less than 40,000 Cubans were admitted to the United States. A large majority of these came from so-called third countries (i.e., did not come directly from Cuba) and were admitted as parolees rather than as refugees (see Gordon, this volume; Holman, this volume). Many were service workers, domestic servants, gardeners, hairdressers, taxi drivers, and others who had been employed by those in the wealthy economic classes who had exited Cuba earlier. In the late 1970s, in a brief warming between the administration of President Jimmy Carter and the Cuban government, Cuba released some 3,000 political prisoners and permitted them to travel to the United States. Including their accompanying family members, a total of between 10,000 and 15,000 people were admitted.

Then in early 1980 came the boat exodus from the port of Mariel, during which more than 120,000 Cubans came to the United States. Those trying to leave were assailed by those determined to stay. It was a time when "people turned against people, friends against friends." There were now many *actos de repudio*, staged mass acts of repudiation in front of the homes of people who were leaving Cuba. People began to "turn on each other like vicious animals, repeating the slogans" (Geldof 1991:302). As one Mariel refugee noted, Cuba had allowed nearly 100,000 Cuban exiles to return for visits in the late 1970s. Before that, she had been taught that they were all *gusanos* (worms) who had abandoned the *patria* (their country in the most spiritual sense). Now the Cuban government said the refugees were to be welcomed. The joke began to run through Cuba that the worms had turned into butterflies. It was no longer important, it seemed, that the visitors had left the country, or that they were capitalists. "They had many dollars to spend" (Geldof 1991:301); it seemed that it "really didn't have to do with ideology, it had to do with money." The myth and magic of the revolution were necessarily tarnished.

The general disillusionment and weak economy that brought on the Mariel exodus were followed by a more sharply deteriorating economy in the late 1980s and early 1990s as communism became weaker in the Soviet Union and Eastern Europe.[9] The economy was further weakened when President Bill Clinton tightened the existing embargo in 1993. Yet as communism elsewhere became less potent, Castro reaffirmed his commitment to the system and instituted what he called a "time of special sacrifice," a period of severe material restrictions for the Cuban people. One observer noted in 1990 that urban Cubans "who are dragging themselves through the day may be asked ('like Cambodians' they say indignantly) to go out and work in the fields" (Williams 1990:32).

In the summer of 1994, departures from Cuba increased greatly. By July, as many as 2,000 people a day were attempting the boat trip. In all of 1993, by way of comparison, only 3,000 to 4,000 had made the trip. In September 1994, President Clinton made the first of two profoundly significant changes in Cuban refugee policy: First, he ended the 30-year practice of giving refugee status to almost every Cuban who reached U.S. territorial waters or landed on U.S. soil. Cuba in turn agreed to "deter" those attempting to leave. Then in May 1995, Clinton took the second step. Apparently without consulting the Cuban refugee community, which had heretofore been a significant force in shaping U.S.-Cuban policy, he ordered the repatriation of Cubans seeking to enter the United States. At the same time, he determined that the United States would admit most of those who had been detained at the Guantánamo Naval Base since mid-1994. Any new attempts to reach the United States would be rebuffed, although the possibility of making refugee determinations in particular cases remained.

These changes in policy were criticized by many. The U.S. Committee for Refugees noted in its 1995 *World Refugee Survey* that "the recent policy shift by the Clinton Administration resulting in the near-automatic return of Cuban rafters to Cuba violates the right of Cubans to flee their country and seek asylum from persecution." The policy change "sets a dangerous example for other countries throughout the world who may make similar decisions to keep would-be refugees at bay" (news release, May 31, 1995). Human Rights Watch (news release, May 26, 1995) charged that Cuba was renewing its crackdowns on human rights activists, that it still had many hundreds of political prisoners, and that it had—following its deterrence agreement with the United States—recriminalized attempted exits from the country.

RESETTLEMENT

The resettlement of Cuban refugees has been a joint public and private sector responsibility. Many Cuban refugees have come to the United States to reunite with relatives, and thus unrelated volunteer sponsors have been rare. Still, each publicly funded refugee has at least a formal sponsorship from a voluntary agency responsible for ensuring that the initial "reception and placement" services funded by the U.S. Department of State have been provided. In many cases, an agency's only responsibility is monitoring to determine that the required services have been performed by the families receiving the refugees.

Beyond that general pattern, however, the resettlement of Cubans has involved a series of important precedents that have shaped the experience not only of Cuban refugees but also of U.S. resettlement efforts in general. When the United States began accepting and resettling Cuban refugees at the end of the 1950s, for example, it set a new precedent by paying for the majority of resettlement costs. Never before had the federal government been so involved in the financial costs of bringing refugees to America or of assisting them in learning to live in a new country. Indeed, the previous assumption had been that refugees "do it themselves" with the help of some private groups and volunteer sponsors. Despite the continuing importance of private and voluntary agency contributions, this new pattern of federal government support would become the standard for all refugees.

The Cuban refugee program set another important precedent: the provision of impact aid for localities providing services to refugees, particularly education. The large number of well-educated, successful Cuban parents expected and received high-quality educational resources for their children, including perhaps the first large-scale example of bilingual education for immigrant children. The effort was somewhat different from that later developed for other immigrant groups. Cuban parents did not believe their children needed bilingual support for learning or for living in their "own" culture; instead, they simply wanted education in Spanish because they thought their children were entitled to it. Unlike the situation for other groups, there was not much question whether Cuban children would learn English. A high percentage of the second generation became fluent, or very close to it, in both English and Spanish. For education and other impact aid, the federal government and the state of Florida have been engaged for many years in (usually polite) discussions about the extent of resettlement costs for Cubans and who should pay what portion of them. By the 1980s there was acceptance by Florida that the federal government would no longer pay 100 percent of all the costs of refugee "impact," though it would continue to pay some of those costs.

Another critical aspect of Cuban resettlement, both for Cubans and for government programs for all refugees, was the dense congregation of Cubans in Florida (see Table 2.1) and particularly in Miami (see Table 2.2). Not only was the result a transformed Miami and an unusually successful economic enclave but also a federal refugee program that thereafter was geared toward broader dispersal of refugees. Subsequent resettlement of Cubans away from Miami was supported by the federal government, and dispersal became a major, continuing policy issue in the later resettlement of Southeast Asian refugees. The issue of dense settlement reemerged in Miami with the 1980 Mariel boat exodus. Part of the sensitivity involved a segment of the arrivals who were either felons or

Table 2.1
Cubans by Selected States, 1990

State	Cuban Population	% of Total
Florida	674,052	64.57%
New Jersey	85,378	8.18%
New York	74,345	7.12%
California	71,977	6.89%
Illinois	18,204	1.74%
Texas	18,195	1.74%
Louisiana	8,569	0.82%
Massachusetts	8,106	0.78%
Georgia	7,818	0.75%
Pennsylvania	7,485	0.72%
Total: Top 10 States	974,129	93.31%
Total: United States	1,043,932	100.00%

Note: Ethnicity is self-assessed.
Source: U.S. Bureau of the Census 1992.

mentally ill–perhaps 5,000 to 10,000 of the 120,000 entrants. (Higher estimates include additional people jailed for political offenses.) The Mariel exodus was also an important precedent in its inclusion of refugees who had long lived under a Communist system. The arrivals were indeed "new Cubans" who had lived much—sometimes all—of their lives under the Castro regime. They arrived only to find the relatively weak condition of the U.S. economy in 1980. Both Americans and the old Cubans had very strong reactions to the Mariel exodus, although the former focused on the gross numbers of people who entered, while the latter concentrated more on the nature of the individuals and on the years of experience separating the Marielitos from earlier arrivals. A decade later, similar dilemmas would appear for Southeast Asian refugees.

Finally, and coming full circle, the Cuban resettlement is also unique because Cubans are the only recent refugee group to have been admitted to the United States in significant numbers under a privately funded admissions and resettlement system. The program began in 1988 and was administered by the Cuban American National Foundation and the federal government. (Several other groups had very small numbers admitted under the private program.) In the five years that the Cuban program functioned, almost 10,000 Cubans came to the United States from third countries[10] at almost no cost to federal, state, or local

Table 2.2
Cubans by Selected Urban Areas, 1990

Urbanized Area	Cuban Population	% of Total
Atlanta	5,227	0.5%
Boston	5,143	0.5%
Chicago	16,593	1.6%
Ft. Lauderdale	23,307	2.2%
Houston	7,496	0.7%
Las Vegas	5,531	0.5%
Los Angeles	52,437	5.0%
Miami	560,508	53.7%
New Orleans	5,891	0.6%
New York (metro)	150,021	14.4%
Orlando	9,006	0.9%
Philadelphia	5,257	0.5%
Tampa	30,846	3.0%
Washington, D.C.	8,564	0.8%
West Palm Beach	14,491	1.4%
Total: 15 Urban Areas	900,318	86.2%
Total: United States	1,043,932	

Notes: Ethnicity is self-assessed. Urban areas follow census definitions. Percentages do not add up exactly because of rounding.

Source: U.S. Bureau of the Census 1992.

governments. There was a separate allocation of admission numbers for the unfunded program. Refugees in this program had to meet the U.S. statutory definition of refugee, not be firmly resettled in another country, and be otherwise eligible for admission under immigration statutes and refugee program criteria. The program required that the private sector bear admission and resettlement costs for the first two years, or until the refugee attained permanent resident status, whichever came first. In addition, cases were prepared by privately paid staff for adjudication by immigration officers. As in the larger admissions program, the Immigration and Naturalization Service determined refugee status and eligibility for admission to the United States.

Unlike those who administered the regular refugee programs, Cuban Foundation staff were required to verify that the individual sponsors (who were mostly relatives of the refugees) had sufficient financial resources to prevent the refugees from qualifying for welfare assistance, Medicaid, or government refugee service programs. Federal, state, and local government officials were alerted to the specially altered immigration documents these refugees were given, which advised that the bearer was admitted under a special program and that if the refugee attempted to obtain government assistance or services, the foundation should be contacted. The program worked remarkably well, but it was not continued—in part because the government felt that the mainstream refugee program was capable of handling the reduced number of refugees it planned to admit. During the years the program operated, refugees were admitted to the United States from many countries in Latin America and the Caribbean, from Western Europe, and from Canada. A small number were also admitted from Russia.

INTEGRATION

Cubans have not been typical of either refugees or immigrants to the United States. They have not wanted to or had to make many of the accommodations to American society that other newcomers have faced. To a remarkable extent, they have been able, if they wished, to live independently and separately. This, along with the considerable knowledge of America that they often brought, helps explain the lack of culture shock and disruption they have experienced. The integration of Cubans has thus been less an integration into mainstream American society than an integration into a Cuban community that happens to be located in America.

The exact number of Cuban refugees who have come to the United States is difficult to reconstruct from government records. Gordon (this volume) estimates 735,000 refugees from Cuba and an additional 206,000 immigrants, for a total of 941,000 by the end of fiscal year (FY) 1994. The 1990 census provides a figure of 1,043,932 self-designated Cubans (see Tables 2.1 and 2.2, U.S. Bureau of the Census 1992). A separate estimate for foreign-born Cubans that year was 736,971 (U.S. Bureau of the Census 1993a). The population is concentrated in Florida (65 percent of the Cuban population), with sizable, though far smaller, numbers in New Jersey (8 percent of the total), New York (7 percent), and California (7 percent). The concentration by urban areas is equally impressive. Miami has about 54 percent of the total Cuban population, followed distantly by the New York metropolitan area (14 percent of the total) and Los Angeles (5 percent).

Census data from 1990 also provide some useful, general comparative information on the Cuban population in America. Comparison with the general U.S. population and the general Hispanic population (see Table 2.3) shows a relatively older population. Cubans had a median age of 38.9 years, well above that of the general U.S. population (33.0 years) and far above that of the general Hispanic population (25.6 years). The census data also suggest the frequently noted strength of the Cuban family. For example, 79 percent of Cuban family

Table 2.3
Selected Characteristics of Cubans, 1990

	Cuban	Hispanic	U.S.
Under age 16	16.1%	31.4%	22.9%
Median age	38.90	25.60	33.00
5 & older who don't speak English well	48.6%	39.4%	6.1%
Labor force participation (age 16 & up)			
All	65.0%	67.5%	65.3%
Female	55.6%	55.9%	56.8%
Per capita income	$13,786	$8,400	$14,420
% below poverty	14.6%	25.3%	13.1%
% of households with 2 or more workers	60.6%	57.6%	58.9%
% of family households with 2 parents	78.1%	69.9%	79.5%
% under 18 in 2-parent households	71.5%	66.0%	73.0%
% in linguistically isolated households	28.6%	23.8%	3.5%

Notes: Ethnicity is self-assessed. See source for exact definitions of variables.
Source: U.S. Bureau of the Census 1993b.

households included both parents (compared to 80 percent for the general U.S. population but 70 percent for the general Hispanic population), and 72 percent of the Cubans under age 18 lived in two-parent households (compared to 73 percent for the general U.S. population but only 66 percent for the general Hispanic population). The economic importance of the Cuban family is evidenced by the percentage of households with two or more workers: for Cubans the figure was 61 percent, compared to 59 percent for the U.S. population and 58 percent for the Hispanic population.

Somewhat surprisingly, the census data also indicate a population that does not rate its English-language ability as very high (see Garcia and Diaz 1992; Resnick 1988). When respondents were asked to assess their ability, 49 percent of Cubans said that they did not speak it "very well," versus 39 percent of Hispanics overall. By Bureau of the Census calculations, 29 percent of Cubans lived in linguistically isolated households, again a figure higher than that for Hispanics in general (24 percent). Despite their self-perceived lack of English ability, however, Cubans had a per capita income ($13,786) well above that for Hispanics ($8,400) and only slightly less than that of the general U.S. population ($14,420).

These census data also support the long-standing view of Cubans as a relatively old population with a strong family structure and an ethnic community strong enough to make the use of English less of a necessity than it has been for most immigrant and refugee groups. The data also support the more general notion, common in both the popular media and the academic literature, of Cubans as a success story, particularly that Cubans are more successful in a shorter period of time than other immigrants. Much of this difference reflects the great confidence Cubans have in themselves as a successful and cultured people. They expect to succeed, and often do. The image of Cuban success does not go unchallenged, however. The situation of many Cubans fails to match the image of success (e.g., Jorge and Moncarz 1987),[11] and the success itself has some negative consequences. Many non-Cubans, particularly in Miami, believe that Cubans have succeeded too rapidly and with too little gratitude to the United States. They did, after all, receive considerable public assistance in their early years in the United States.[12]

The impressive success of Cubans in the United States is not, however, necessarily an indication of their commitment to, or full integration into, American society. Many Cubans, particularly those born and raised in Cuba, are still in exile. The Spanish term used by the refugees is *el exilio*. The term has a long history and has been used by Cubans of many political positions for over 150 years. Cuba always remains close: emotionally, politically, and geographically. This closeness is reflected in the way Cubans construct their identity in the United States. Williams (1991:31) describes Cuban-Americans as "America's most restless immigrant group" who are "not quite sure on which side of the hyphen to hang their identities—and their future." This ambivalence reflects again the profound, enduring emotional link with Cuba. A poll conducted in the early 1990s asked members of various immigrant groups if the "old country" was better. The Cubans were "virtually alone" in saying that it was—and many of them "remain obsessed with events back in Cuba" (31).

A later survey of second-generation immigrant children in the Miami schools (Portes and Zhou 1994) indicated the continuing strength of a Cuban identity. Less than a fifth of all the Hispanic children identified themselves as non-hyphenated Americans. For Cuban students, "Cuban" alone was the most frequent choice, followed by "Cuban-American" and an occasional selection of

"Hispanic." (The proportion of Cubans choosing "Cuban" was highest among those children from high-status families who attended private schools.) By way of contrast, Nicaraguans chose the label "Hispanic" almost as often as they chose "Nicaraguan." On the basis of the survey, the researchers suggest the Cuban experience is best understood as one of "paced, selective assimilation" (30–31).[13]

The strong political influence of the relatively conservative refugee community is a final distinctive feature of the Cuban experience in the United States. Cubans' political activism and influence are unique among recently arrived refugees in this country and were instrumental for decades in maintaining the U.S. government's concern over Cuba. Castro's arrogance, spirit, and independence were offensive to both Washington and Cuban refugee conservatives, although for somewhat different reasons. To Washington, Castro was a tool of worldwide communism and one that was too close to the United States. To the Cuban refugees, however, he was the despised ruler of their country. Despite their internal differences, Cubans—at least in foreign policy—have been united, consistent, and effective. Particularly in Florida, the Cuban voting bloc has been tremendously important.

Central to that political effort has been the Cuban American National Foundation, the most powerful conservative Cuban organization in the United States. After some loosening in U.S.-Cuban relations in the late 1980s, the election of Ronald Reagan shortly after the Mariel boat lift provided a particularly opportune time for the foundation. It is still not entirely clear whether the Cubans found Washington or Washington found the Cubans. Anticommunism was one of the prime bases of the Reagan administration, and many of the administration's appointees were determined that no more "Mariels" would happen. Thus, just as the conservative Cubans were ready to exercise the power they had been building, the Reagan administration was ready for them. That influence continued under the Bush administration. One result was the program of private resettlement for Cubans from third countries. With the end of the cold war, and the shift to a Democratic administration, however, the "umbilical cord" (Booth 1994) was broken. As Cuba's outside support lessened, so did American concern about Cuba. Within the Cuban community in America there began to be more consideration of the possibility of normalizing relations with Cuba, but as one commentator (Booth 1994) noted, based on a survey of the refugees, over half favored both a U.S. invasion of Cuba and talks with Castro: "[A]side from the people in the organized groups, there is a feeling among Cubans to say yes to anything that might work. Yes to invasion. Yes to negotiations."

CONCLUSION

Nineteenth-century Cuban historian Luis Estévez y Romero said of Cuba's relations with the United States, "[P]oor Cuba always hopeful, always disappointed," and David Rieff (1993:115) adds, "and always ambivalent towards the United States.'' For Cubans in America, the ambivalence is doubled since they must construct an identity that hinges both on events in Cuba and on their own current lives in America.

Many believe that whatever happens to Castro, Cuba will participate more fully in the international ''free market system.'' Without Soviet aid, this has become inevitable. Even those sympathetic to the revolution foresee change. Hildita, Che Guevara's daughter, for example, said of the revolution: ''The dream is not dead. It's dormant, frozen in time. Capitalism has regenerated itself over the years. It has adopted new forms. But communism has failed to keep up with the times. There is no such thing as neocommunism. That's what I would like. Communism with a human face'' (Oppenheimer 1992:277–278). Others sympathetic to Castro see not only a poor economy but a breakdown in socialism as the ''second economy''—capitalistic and noncentralized—expands and becomes more entrenched. Ironically, these changes may result in economic improvements that strengthen the Castro regime.

In America, the general picture of Cuban refugees remains one of impressive individual economic advances; strong, traditional family structures; and the creation of a uniquely effective social, political, and economic enclave—an enclave that has transformed south Florida.[14] Whether that success in America implies Americanization remains an unresolved question. There is also the broader question of what role the Cuban community in America could and would play in a post-Communist Cuba. Geldof (1991:306) notes the comments of Mirta Ojita, a successful Marielita, who believes that when there is change in Cuba, ''it will come from the inside. And I'm hoping that some of the people here in Miami will not have a lot of influence once we all go back to Cuba. . . . Most will not go back, except to visit, to open businesses, to buy a place in Veradero. But they will not live there, or help put the country back together.'' More forcefully, Maria Elena Cruz, the poet and dissident, has said, ''First we were a Spanish colony. Then, we became an American colony. Then, we became a Soviet colony. The last thing we need now is to become a colony of Miami's Cuban exiles'' (Oppenheimer 1992:329).

NOTES

1. In recent years the classical model of refugees as people with compelling reasons to flee persecution has been diluted. Many refugees have been classified by both the government and the public as simply another category of immigrant. The failure to distinguish them is due in part at least to decisions to admit persons who seem not to have fled from clear and severe persecution. To say this is not to say that it is easy to separate political persecution from the economic and other causes for emigration, but it is to say that the rigor with which the classic political definition has been applied in the United States and in other refugee-receiving countries does vary significantly from one time period to another and from group to group.

2. Cantero was the owner of an *ingenio,* a mechanized but labor-intensive sugar

refinery. The term has many other (related) meanings in Cuban Spanish, such as a talented or creative person, a wit, a kind of cleverness and sharpness, or a cutter (human or otherwise). The word's meanings sum up an important part of the Cuban national character.

3. Cantero omitted mention of the rich red-brown earth that in many parts of Cuba makes other colors even more brilliant by contrast.

4. Hutchinson's Encyclopedia, CompuServe Information Service. The racial categories follow the original. Other observers note instead that the Cuban population is divided between whites and mulattoes.

5. Why Cuba did not become a state is a complex and interesting question. Many (perhaps most) Cubans and at least some North Americans believe that it did, from time to time, become a state in all but name. José Martí, the early champion of Cuban independence and a gifted writer, who is "claimed" by both the Cuban Left and Right, said that Cubans had a kind of "geographic fatalism" (quoted by Geldof 1991:xvi).

6. Palmer (1956:622) might describe it as "Imperialism as Crusade." Imperialism rose from many different motives: Commercial, financial, and political ones were combined with humanitarian and religious ones.

7. As one scholar put it, "[T]he summer of 1989 notoriously highlighted the pitfalls of charismatic authority and the weaknesses of Cuban institutions, especially the Communist party" (Péréz-Stable 1993:164). Ochoa, a heavily-medaled hero of Cuba, and a close associate of Castro for many years, was arrested, tried, and then executed, along with the other officials, on charges of drug trafficking and not-clearly-laid-out violations of national security. Many who have looked at the affair believe there was reason to conclude Ochoa's actions had been approved or at least disregarded "at the highest levels of government" (Pérez-Stable 1993:164–165). Andres Oppenheimer (1992), in what is probably the most controversial part of his book, provides a great deal of attention to the Ochoa affair.

It seemed clear to refugees in Miami and to people inside Cuba that whatever the exact degree of complicity, the leadership had to have had substantial involvement for acts on the order of the offenses to have been committed. The affair was a serious blow to solidarity between the leadership and the people of Cuba and, if anything, a greater blow to the charismatic authority of Castro. Many refugees in the United States cheered, at the same time they were cheering the beginning of loss of support to Cuba from the Soviet Union and its Eastern European allies. Weakness and corruption at the top of government were out in the open and out on the street. Castro and Cuba were not the same thereafter.

8. "Without question," wrote Lynn Bender (1973:271), Cuba's most successful export from the very beginning of the Castro regime was not sugar or revolution but the "physical removal of its domestic enemies."

9. For a sympathetic account of the Cuban economy at the time, see Deere (1991).

10. The practice of emigration to third countries, other than the United States, usually—but not always—with the intention of reaching the United States ultimately, began soon after the revolution and has continued to the present. The U.S. government has welcomed this relatively small but significant movement of Cubans away from its shores and tried regularly through the years to prevent the later entry of these emigrants to the United States. At least some of those who traveled to third countries such as Spain or Venezuela did so thinking they had assurances from U.S. officials that they would in time be admitted to America.

For many years U.S. government policy prevailed, but in the late 1980s, the Cuban American National Foundation began a resettlement program for third country refugees that was accomplished without federal government funds for most of the approximately five years it existed. The program demonstrated, among other things, that many of those who had gone to third countries met both the refugee definition and the U.S. federal government requirement that they not be "firmly resettled" in those third countries. Many of the governments involved had not extended the benefits of permanent residency to the Cubans—such benefits being, in brief, the measure of "firm resettlement."

11. The Mariel exodus in 1980 raised a serious challenge to this image of success and also raised anew the question of Cubans exceeding the resources of Miami. Neither problem was as serious as originally feared. The differences turned out to be less economic than social. Rieff (1993:67–68) quotes a student at Miami-Dade Community College, speaking to the Cubans in his class who had grown up in the United States about what they—the long residents—thought of Cuba, "You're all like some guy who's in love with a girl who doesn't want nothing to do with him. You dream about her and write her name down over and over again, and pretty soon you've made her up, 'cause she's nothing like what you imagine. Well, I'm here to tell you, neither is Cuba!" For general discussions of the "Mariel" Cubans and their effects on Miami, see Bach, Bach, and Triplett (1981), Card (1990), Portes and Jensen (1989), and De la Campa (1994).

12. The Cuban use of significant amounts of public assistance in their early years in the United States reflected the federal government's decision to use public funds for resettlement. There was only a small federal bureaucracy administering the 100 percent reimbursement of costs to local government jurisdictions. Despite a general feeling that the federal government was giving Cuban refugees some sort of special status, reimbursement was not always obtained by state and local government. The author, for example, became, many years ago, the administrator of the Cuban program in a local jurisdiction outside Florida and found there were few rules for determining the eligibility of Cubans for the fully federally financed welfare and Medicaid programs. For Medicaid, the Cuban program had such low visibility and had been given such low priority by the agency that no request for the available 100 percent reimbursement of costs had been made for at least three years.

13. Another kind of example of this continuing Cuban identity occurred at the very end of the 1980s. When it began to become clear to Cubans in the United States that communism in the Soviet Union and Eastern Europe was severely weakened, and indeed disappearing in some countries, many refugees essentially stopped spending money. Some put their houses on the market. Seeing that Cuba was rapidly losing its support and believing this meant the early fall of Castro, they wanted to have the resources to return home quickly.

14. For discussions of the transformation of Miami, see Croucher (1994), Rieff (1987, 1993), Pérez-Stable and Uriarte (1993), Portes and Stepick (1993), and Lamphere, Stepick, and Grenier (1994).

REFERENCES

Bach, Robert L., Jennifer B. Bach, and Timothy Triplett. 1981. The Flotilla Entrants: Latest and Most Controversial. *Cuban Studies* 11:29–48.

Bender, Lynn Darrell. 1973. The Cuban Exiles: An Analytical Sketch. *Journal of Latin American Studies* 5:271–278.

Booth, William. 1994. Cuban Exiles Find Their "Umbilical Cord" to Washington Has Broken. *Washington Post,* June 18.

Card, David. 1990. The Impact of the Mariel Boatlift on the Miami Labor Market. *Industrial and Labor Relations Review* 43(2):245–257.

Croucher, Sheila. 1994. Mandela in Miami: The Globalization of Ethnicity in an American City. *Journal of Developing Societies* 10(2):186–202.

De la Campa, Roman. 1994. The Latin Diaspora in the United States: Sojourns from a Cuban Past. *Public Culture* 6(2):293–317.

Deere, Carmen Diana. 1991. Cuba's Struggle for Self-Sufficiency. *Monthly Review* 43(July–August):55–74.

Didion, Joan. 1987. *Miami.* New York: Simon and Schuster.

Franklin, Jane. 1993. The Cuba Obsession. *Progressive* (July):18–22.

Garcia, Ricardo L., and Carlos F. Diaz. 1992. The Status and Use of Spanish and English among Hispanic Youth in Dade County (Miami) Florida: A Sociolinguistic Study, 1989–1991. *Language and Education* 6(1):13–32.

Geldof, Lynn. 1991. *Cubans: Voices of Change.* New York: St. Martin's Press.

Haines, David W., Editor. 1985. *Refugees in the United States: A Reference Handbook.* Westport, Connecticut: Greenwood Press.

Jorge, Antonio, and Raul Moncarz. 1987. The Golden Cage Cubans in Miami. *International Migration* 25(3):267–282.

Koont, Sinan. 1994. Cuba: An Island against All Odds. *Monthly Review* 46:1–19.

Lamphere, Louise, Alex Stepick, and Guillermo Grenier, Editors. 1994. *Newcomers in the Workplace: Immigrants and the Restructuring of the U.S. Economy.* Philadelphia: Temple University Press.

Oppenheimer, Andres. 1992. *Castro's Final Hour: The Secret Story behind the Coming Downfall of Communist Cuba.* New York: Simon and Schuster.

Palmer, R. R. 1956. *A History of the Modern World.* New York: Alfred A. Knopf.

Paterson, Thomas G. 1994. *Contesting Castro: The United States and the Triumph of the Cuban Revolution.* New York: Oxford University Press.

Pérez-Stable, Marifeli. 1993. *The Cuban Revolution: Origins, Course, and Legacy.* New York: Oxford University Press.

Pérez-Stable, Marifeli, and Miren Uriarte. 1993. Cubans and the Changing Economy of Miami. In *Latinos in a Changing U.S. Economy.* Edited by Rebecca Morales and Frank Bonilla. Newbury Park, California: Sage Publications. Pp. 133–159.

Portes, Alejandro, and L. Jensen. 1989. The Enclave and the Entrants: Patterns of Ethnic Enterprise in Miami before and after Mariel. *American Sociological Review* 54: 929–949.

Portes, Alejandro, and Alex Stepick. 1993. *City on the Edge: The Transformation of Miami.* Berkeley: University of California Press.

Portes, Alejandro, and Min Zhou. 1994. Should Immigrants Assimilate? *The Public Interest* 116 (summer 1994):18–33.

Resnick, Melvyn C. 1988. Beyond the Ethnic Community: Spanish Language Roles and Maintenance in Miami. *International Journal of the Sociology of Language* 69: 89–104.

Rieff, David. 1987. *Going to Miami: Exiles, Tourists, and Refugees in the New America.* Boston: Little, Brown.

———. 1993. *The Exile: Cuba in the Heart of Miami.* New York: Simon and Schuster.

Rudolph, James D., Editor. 1985. *Cuba: A Country Study* (Foreign Affairs Studies, The American University). Washington, D.C.: U.S. Government Printing Office.

U.S. Bureau of the Census. 1992. *Census of Population. General Population Characteristics—United States.* (1990 CP-1-1). Washington, D.C.

———. 1993a. *The Foreign Born Population of the United States.* (CP-3-1). Washington, D.C.

———. 1993b. *Persons of Hispanic Origin in the United States.* (CP-3-3). Washington, D.C.

U.S. Committee for Refugees. 1995. *World Refugee Survey.* Washington, D.C.

White, Robert. 1989. Review of Dominguez, Jorge L. *To Make the World Safe for Revolution. Commonweal* (May 19, 1989):304–305.

Williams, Eric. 1984. *From Columbus to Castro: The History of the Caribbean, 1492–1969.* New York: Vintage Press.

———. 1990. The Self-Laceration of Cuba. *The Economist* 316:31–32.

———. 1991. Show Me the Way to Go Home. *The Economist* 321:31.

Chapter 3

Vietnamese

NGUYEN MANH HUNG AND
DAVID W. HAINES

Refugees from Vietnam constitute the second largest group of people ever formally accepted as refugees by the United States. Like the Cubans—the largest group—they play a major part in the history of the cold war. Their status as refugees from communism, and from Communist countries that the United States has directly confronted, is key to their history. For both Cuba and Vietnam, cold war–based conflicts have been particularly personal, either through extensive economic sanctions and abortive military action with the Cubans or through direct military involvement, withdrawal, and subsequent economic sanctions with the Vietnamese. The resettlement of refugees from both countries has thus been both a major humanitarian effort and an important political mechanism for showing continuing support to anti-Communist elements in both societies.

By the mid-1990s, formal support for accepting refugees from both countries was winding down. The number of refugees from Vietnam was still significant, but most were arriving through the Orderly Departure Program and involved two populations of particular importance to the United States: Amerasian children and reeducation camp survivors. In particular, 1994 was an important milestone for refugees from both Vietnam and Cuba. For Vietnam, the lifting of the trade embargo raised further possibilities for interaction with the home country; for Cuba, the United States discontinued its long-standing practice of automatically granting refugee status to those fleeing from Cuba and instead determined to classify them as a special kind of immigrant to be handled through formal processing in Cuba.

The movement of refugees from Vietnam has been extensive, complicated, and often dramatic. Refugees have come from a variety of social, religious, and ethnic backgrounds. Many were well educated and familiar with American and Western society; others were minimally educated and rural in origin. Some were government officials, military officers, businessmen, doctors, and teachers; others were farmers, fishers, and common soldiers. Many were swept up in a mass exodus as the Republic of Vietnam crumbled in April 1975; others left in later years through harrowing boat escapes; yet others came out in the relative safety of an orderly departure program, but after years of confinement in so-called reeducation camps. Some were able to bring family members with them or gradually reconstruct their families over time; others had to face a difficult adjustment to an alien society alone. For all, however, the loss of homeland and the ordeals of adapting to a rapidly changing new society remain acute despite some remarkable successes in surviving and adapting to a new life in America. They all have, as James Freeman (1989) aptly entitled his collection of Vietnamese refugees' stories, "hearts of sorrow."

This chapter focuses on these Vietnamese refugees, their origins, the factors that underlay their exodus, their journey to the United States, and their experience adapting to American society. The chapter begins with a brief status report on a group that has rapidly become one of America's largest Asian-origin populations and then turns to the history of this major group of American newcomers.

VIETNAMESE-AMERICANS IN THE 1990s

With the great influx of refugees in the second half of the 1970s, it was quickly clear that the Vietnamese would become a major segment of America's Asian-origin population. By the time of the 1980 census, they were already the sixth largest Asian-origin group (U.S. Bureau of the Census 1983), and the estimates were that they would be the fourth largest by 1985 (Gardner, Robey, and Smith 1985:5). Like most other Asian-origin populations (except Asian Indians), they were concentrated on the West Coast, although they were less concentrated there than other groups, and had a sizable representation in southern states where other Asian-origin groups were noticeably absent. The Vietnamese refugees were different in many ways from the established Asian-origin groups, with a much lower average age, much larger households, and lower educational levels. Compared with other Asian-origin groups, they were also much more frequently below the poverty line in terms of household income, though much of this reflected the recency of their arrival.

The early snapshot of Vietnamese refugee adaptation provided by the 1980 census showed an important new Asian-origin population that shared some of the characteristics that had made other Asian-origin groups relatively successful in recent American history but also a population that might face additional difficulties. By the time of the 1990 census, the expectations about increased size had been realized, with Vietnamese then over 600,000,[1] with particular concentration in California (see Table 3.1). Comparative information continued to suggest that despite similarities with other Asian-origin groups, particularly others who were arriving as immigrants, relatively large household size and

Table 3.1
Vietnamese by Selected States, 1990

State	Vietnamese Population	% of Total
California	280,223	45.60%
Texas	69,634	11.33%
Virginia	20,693	3.37%
Washington	18,696	3.04%
Louisiana	17,598	2.86%
Florida	16,346	2.66%
Pennsylvania	15,887	2.59%
Massachusetts	15,449	2.51%
New York	15,555	2.53%
Illinois	10,309	1.68%
Total: Top 10 States	480,390	78.17%
Total: United States	614,547	100.00%

Note: Ethnicity is self-assessed.
Source: U.S. Bureau of the Census 1992.

some limitations in education and English-language competence posed continuing problems. However, the data also indicated the relative advantage that Vietnamese had over other Southeast Asian refugee groups. This confirmed what virtually all research since 1975 had indicated about the relatively high educational levels of Vietnamese and their relative economic success in the United States compared with refugees from Cambodia and Laos (e.g., Gordon 1989b; Dunning and Greenbaum 1982; Caplan, Whitmore, and Bui 1985; Aames et al. 1977; Kim and Nicassio 1980; Rumbaut 1989).

By the time 20 years had passed since the fall of Saigon, the virtual end of Vietnamese refugee resettlement in the United States had thus left a sizable new Asian-origin population that shared much of the demographic profile of other Asian immigrants, particularly in settlement patterns and a rapid rise in business ownership (O'Hare 1992:37), appeared relatively well advantaged compared with other Southeast Asian refugee groups, and was progressing rapidly in adjusting to American society—although that process was clearly far from complete. The Vietnamese refugee population was also one that had emerged in the public media and in a broad range of research as one with some distinctive features. Three merit particular notice.

First, Vietnamese refugees had taken the task of adapting to American society very seriously, both individually and as a community. "Success" and the hard work needed to achieve it were staples of the Vietnamese refugee experience in America and were widely noted in the academic and popular press. That focus on success yielded some startling individual success stories within the first decade of resettlement: a concert violist, the first West Point female cadet, an astronaut, and some impressive entrepreneurs. Perhaps more important, much of that effort toward success was directed at education. Vietnamese valedictorians were common and pointedly lauded for their success. Vietnamese students flooded colleges and universities, with a strong emphasis on science and engineering where the prospects for a return on effort were likely to be highest.

Second, the emphases on success and education were wound into the core institution of Vietnamese life: the family. Nathan Caplan, John Whitmore, and their colleagues have emphasized the interlinked importance of family and education among Southeast Asian refugees (Caplan, Whitmore, and Bui 1985; Whitmore, Trautmann, and Caplan 1989; Caplan, Choy, and Whitmore 1991). Based on some of the best available survey data, they have identified the value of education as a pervasive cultural value that affects Southeast Asian refugees of all classes. Although they argue that this linkage exists for all Southeast Asian refugees, there is little argument that, if anything, it is most pervasive among the Vietnamese who, unlike those from Cambodia and Laos, have for millennia absorbed the classic East Asian emphasis on the value—even moral imperative—of education.

Third, as with America's other largest formal refugee group, the Cubans, the Vietnamese refugees have been highly political. Despite their commitment to achieving success in America and on American terms, they were quick to raise objections when they perceived inaccurate portrayals of Vietnam and of the Vietnam War (Nguyen Manh Hung 1984a, 1984b). In the 1980s, the release of *Vietnam: A Television History* was particularly painful to them since it raised concern among Vietnamese parents about negative stereotypes of the Vietnam War that were being used in educational situations. With losses in the war so much more severe than those of majority Americans, it was not possible for the Vietnamese to accept the dismissive way in which the Republic of Vietnam was often treated by the American media. A decade later in the 1990s, the increasing frequency of return visits to Vietnam and the increased opportunity for economic interaction represented by the end of the trade embargo raised anew the dilemmas of being in exile by virtue of political stands taken in the increasingly distant past.

By the mid-1990s, after 20 years of refugee exodus and resettlement, the Vietnamese were thus the second largest political refugee group ever formally accepted for resettlement in America, a major component of America's Asian-origin population, a group with both impressive successes and continuing problems in adjustment, and a people who emphasized the importance of success, were strongly family oriented, and had continuing political uneasiness (and sometimes fractiousness) about their status as exiles and their relationship with a changing—but still Communist—homeland. A fuller understanding of their experience hinges on a review of the political history of Vietnam, the patterns of their escape and transit to the United States, and the details of their encounter with a new society.

THE VIETNAMESE REFUGEES: WHO ARE THEY?

The Vietnamese refugees are the result—the fallout—of the Vietnam War. They came halfway around the world from a very old civilization to a very young country. Vietnamese think of themselves as descendants of the mythical King Hung, who founded the country more than 4,000 years ago. Recorded history traces the establishment of the kingdom of Nam Viet, a small country in the south of China, to the year 208 B.C. The over 2,000 years of Vietnam's subsequent history have been ones of continuous resistance to foreign domination and expansion to the south. In 111 B.C., China annexed Vietnam and ruled it for more than a thousand years. Although China succeeded in leaving a lasting cultural influence on Vietnamese society, the Vietnamese still retained their own distinct cultural and political identities. Chinese rule was interrupted by revolts, and in A.D 939, Vietnam finally succeeded in regaining its independence. In the thirteenth century, after defeating the invading armies of Kublai Khan, the Vietnamese began to move southward. They annexed the kingdom of Champa in 1471 and gained control over the Mekong Delta by the mideighteenth century. From a small country based in the Red River Delta, the location of Hanoi, Vietnam had expanded to a length of 1,300 miles from north to south, although only 100 miles wide at its narrowest in central Vietnam, near the former border between the northern and southern parts of the country.

As the European powers began their colonial expansion in Asia, Vietnam came under the sway of the French. The French established their first outposts in 1858 in Tourane (now Da Nang) and 1859 in Saigon. The inroads continued, and 25 years later in 1884, France was able to force the Vietnamese emperor to acknowledge French control of the entire country.[2] That control was imposed very differently in the north, central, and south of the country, amplifying regional differences that remain significant to this day. Although the court succumbed to French pressure, resistance against French rule, led by scholar-patriots and members of the imperial family, continued. Throughout the late nineteenth century, resistance was traditionalist with an emphasis on the pre-French political and cultural structure and the need to return to it. In the early twentieth century, spurred by Japanese military victory in the Russo-Japanese War of 1904–1905, more change-oriented opposition to the French developed under the leadership of Phan Boi Chau and Phan Chu Trinh.

The first formal, modern nationalist party, the Viet Nam Quoc Dan Dang (VNQDD), emerged in the 1920s. The aborted uprising at Yen Bay in 1930, a critical milestone in Vietnamese political history, led to the execution of its leaders and thus to its demise as the dominant anti-French force. It was into this vacuum that the Indochinese Communist Party (ICP) moved. As the French hold on Vietnam weakened in the early stages of World War II, the ICP in 1941 formed a broader resistance organization: the Viet Nam Doc Lap Dong Minh Hoi (Vietnam Independence League), known as the Viet Minh. In March 1945, Japanese forces overthrew the French colonial government in Vietnam and encouraged Emperor Bao Dai to declare Vietnam independent from France, which he did. Six months later, Japan surrendered to the Allies, and Viet Minh partisans seized their opportunity, took control of Hanoi, and set up a provisional government with Ho Chi Minh as president. Emperor Bao Dai abdicated in favor of the new government and was in turn immediately appointed its supreme adviser. In the South, government authority was exercised through the Provisional Executive Committee of the South, a coalition of various competing nationalist groups. Viet Minh control over this committee, unlike the situation in the North, remained precarious.

On September 12, 1945, British forces arrived in Saigon to disarm the Japanese. They permitted the French to stage a coup against the Committee of the South and to reestablish French control of the South before the British departed in January 1946. At roughly the same time, Chinese troops moved into the North to disarm the Japanese. With them came the leaders of two other organizations (the VNQDD and the Viet Nam Cach Menh Dong Minh Hoi—Vietnam Revolutionary League) that had organized the fight against French colonialism from their bases in China. Joining forces with their comrades at home, they demanded a share of government leadership. The ICP was officially dissolved, and a new coalition government was formed to cope with the return of the French. In March 1946, the new government (headed by Ho Chi Minh) signed an agreement with France, giving France unhampered access to North Vietnam in return for French recognition of Vietnam as ''a free state . . . belonging to the Indochinese Federation and to the French Union.'' The nationalists immediately accused the Communists of being too compromising on Vietnam's independence. The Communists used the breathing spell given by this agreement to move against their opposition. Caught between the Communists and the French, prominent nationalist leaders, one by one, left the government and went into self-imposed exile. In December 1946, the French provoked an incident in Hanoi to move against the Viet Minh. The colonial war began.

After the Chinese Communists took control of mainland China, the Viet Minh openly acknowledged its Communist ties. The ICP was reconstituted as the Vietnam Workers' Party, and the Democratic Republic of Vietnam established diplomatic relations with China and Russia. At the same time, the French, unable to defeat the Viet Minh on the battlefield, attempted a political solution. They agreed to the return of ex-Emperor Bao Dai who, as ''head of state,'' would have authority over the internal affairs of a unified Vietnam, while France still retained control over foreign relations and defense. France now could claim that it was at the front line of the cold war, helping a nationalist government in its struggle against communism. The United States moved to accord diplomatic recognition to the Bao Dai government and increased its financial support to the French military effort in Vietnam. The colonial war in Vietnam took on new dimensions: communism versus nationalism and totalitarianism versus democracy.

The war lasted eight years. In 1954, after the French were defeated at Dien Bien Phu, an international agreement ending the Vietnam War was signed in Geneva. Vietnam was divided at the seventeenth parallel; the North came under the control of the Communists, and the South belonged to the nationalists. The Final Declaration, which the United States and the Bao Dai government refused to sign, provided for national elections to be held in 1956 to reunify the country. In June, a new set of agreements was signed between France and Vietnam, providing the basis for genuine independence. Ngo Dinh Diem was appointed prime minister with full power but returned from exile to find South Vietnam in a state of near chaos. He began to take control of the armed forces, arranged for the withdrawal of French troops, and made significant strides toward reintegrating the country. In 1956, a new constitution was proclaimed, and Diem was subsequently elected president of the Republic of Vietnam. Among other accomplishments, his government was able to resettle nearly a million refugees who fled south from the Communist regime in the North. Many of these same people were among those who left Vietnam 20 years later when Saigon fell to that same Communist regime.

The elections originally planned for 1956 to reunify the country, as specified by the Geneva Final Declaration, did not take place. The result was renewed war. In 1959, the first Republic of Vietnam government post was attacked by guerrillas. In 1960, the National Front for the Liberation of South Vietnam (NFLSVN) was formed to lead the war against the government. The Front was tightly controlled by the Vietnam Worker's Party through its Central Office for South Viet Nam (COSVN). The United States was committed to help Diem mount a counterinsurgency campaign against the rebels. In 1962, the U.S. Military Assistance Command was established, and antiguerrilla special forces were sent to Vietnam. As the war progressed, Diem became increasingly authoritarian and was finally overthrown in 1963 by the military in a coup d'état, to which the United States acquiesced. The 1963 coup was followed by a period of political instability and military setbacks in South Vietnam. To stop this deterioration, the United States decided to send troops to South Vietnam and began to bomb North Vietnam. China and Russia, in turn, poured massive aid into North Vietnam, and the Socialist Republic of Vietnam increased its infiltration into South Vietnam. The war escalated. On Tet (the lunar New Year) in 1968, the Front launched a general offensive in several major cities. It was a costly campaign to the Front in terms of human lives, but it turned out to be a major political victory for them. The United States, knowing it could not win a quick military victory, decided to disengage. Troop withdrawal, "Vietnamization," and diplomatic negotiation began. In 1973, a cease-fire agreement was concluded in Paris. It provided for the total withdrawal of U.S. combat forces but not for the withdrawal of North Vietnamese forces. U.S. aid to South Vietnam was subsequently reduced, and Vietnamization could thus not proceed as originally planned. By 1975, the correlation of forces was utterly in favor of the Communists. Under the probing attack of Communist forces, President Thieu decided to redeploy South Vietnamese forces to defensible areas away from Central Vietnam. The withdrawal, originally from Pleiku and then from Hue, turned into a rout.

As Communist forces advanced toward Saigon, an American-organized evacuation was hastily implemented. The operation was able to evacuate approximately 130,000 Vietnamese but did not succeed in bringing out many Vietnamese who would be endangered by a Communist victory.[3] Hundreds of thousands of Vietnamese who grew up with the idea that they were fighting for a good cause alongside a committed ally were left to face an uncertain future. Within months after the Communist victory, that future became a more certain one: banishment from employment, loss of property, denial of access to education for children, and imprisonment in "reeducation" camps. Many of those left behind to this fate would eventually escape, but the path would be a long, painful, and often deadly one.

WHY DID THEY LEAVE?

Vietnamese refugees left their homeland for a variety of reasons. In 1975, most left because of the fear of communism and their fate under the new regime: possible imprisonment or even execution, and expected loss of social status and political freedom. Those leaving in later years had a different mix of reasons. Ethnic Chinese, for example, left because of racial and economic discrimination; some were even forced or "asked" to leave by a government worried that they would become a fifth column for Chinese action against Vietnam. These ethnic Chinese included those who had lived in North Vietnam for generations and those who clearly belonged to the working class. Religious leaders and their followers (both Catholics and Buddhists) left to avoid religious discrimination and persecution. Some left in panic, particularly in 1975; others left because life had become hard and unbearable to them and held no future for their children. It became common for Vietnamese parents to sacrifice everything in order to enable their children to escape the country, which helps explain why children and young people were such a major segment of those escaping by boat in the late 1970s.

Although economic hardship became one of the reasons for escape, it was rarely the root or sole cause for risking the dangers of departure.[4] Many people, especially those who were released from reeducation camps and those who were associated with the former government or with the American war efforts, suffered severe discrimination, and that discrimination had economic consequences. They did not get sufficient rations for necessities from government stores; they could not get jobs; their children were deprived of the opportunity to enter colleges and universities; and they were forced to go to the new economic zones, where their life became so hopeless that many came back to the cities to lead an illegal, barely subsistent life. The economic hardships they endured were thus very much the result of discrimination on political and social grounds. Such discrimination, and its often severe economic consequences, continued to fuel the refugee exodus that was at its peak in the late 1970s and continued sporadically through the 1980s. Conflict and warfare in Indochina (for example, the Sino-Vietnamese conflict and border war of 1979, the Cambodian invasion of 1979), political repression, worsening general economic and social conditions, and tales of a good life abroad have also been factors in that exodus.

THE FLOW OF REFUGEES FROM VIETNAM

By 1995, the total number of Indochinese refugees had amounted to nearly 2 million—about half of whom eventually came to the United States. Approximately 200,000 left during 1975 itself, and there were scattered escapes in the two years after that. The most extensive exodus, however, took place between March 1978, when the Vietnamese government began to enforce its socialist economic policy, particularly against ethnic Chinese who resided in Cholon (Saigon's sister city), and July 1979, when, under international pressure at the United Nations Geneva Conference on Indochinese Refugees, the Vietnamese government pledged to take "firm and effective measures" to stop the flow of refugees for a "reasonable period."[5] In order to understand this massive exodus, it is necessary to distinguish four general types of exodus from Vietnam, all of which had their own unique features. There have been first-wave refugees, second-wave refugees, escapees, and orderly departures.

The first-wave refugees left Vietnam during the spring of 1975 as Communist forces advanced toward Saigon and the United States began to airlift its nonessential employees out of Vietnam. This evacuation was organized by the U.S. government. Leaving before April 29 were Vietnamese dependents of U.S. servicemen and government workers,[6] people who worked for foreign companies and were not within draft age, people with connections to the Americans who organized the airlift, those sponsored by Vietnamese-Americans already living in the United States, and those who could talk or bribe their way into the U.S. processing center at Tan Son Nhat airport just outside of Saigon. Leaving in panic on April 29 itself, the day when U.S. military and civilian personnel were requested to leave within 24 hours, were those who could arrange to be at one of several designated locations in the city, could get into the American embassy itself, or could reach waiting barges on the Saigon River.

The first-wave refugees who left before April 29 (and a few who left on that date) boarded planes at Tan Son Nhat airport and were flown to Clark Air Base in the Philippines. Those who left on April 29 were flown by helicopters or taken by barges to waiting naval ships that carried them to Subic Bay in the Philippines. From the Philippines, refugees were flown to Guam and then to one of four refugee camps in the United States (Camp Pendleton in California, Fort Chaffee in Arkansas, Eglin Air Base in Florida, and Fort Indiantown Gap in Pennsylvania), where they waited for security clearance and sponsors to get them out of camps. Although this evacuation was in many respects admirably executed, it failed in its initial, prime objective of evacuating all Vietnamese whose lives would be endangered by the Communist takeover.

The second-wave refugees left Vietnam during the 1978-1979 period, at the height of the Sino-Vietnamese conflict. Resenting ethnic Chinese control of private business in South Vietnam, and fearing the possibility of a Chinese fifth column in Vietnam, the Vietnamese government clamped down on Chinese in business and forced them to leave the country. This evacuation was organized—although unofficially—by the Vietnamese authorities and was therefore labeled by refugees as "unofficial departure." People who wanted to go had to register and pay in gold for a place on a boat. This was done through an intermediary called the organizer. When all the arrangements were made, they were told to assemble at a designated location, where they were brought to the waiting boat. Security agents would then escort their boat out of Vietnam's territorial waters. Second-wave refugees were predominantly ethnic Chinese, about 250,000 of whom went to China. But there were many ethnic Vietnamese who were able to buy false papers and register themselves as Chinese for the purpose of "unofficial departure."

The escapees, on the other hand, plotted their own departures. They were a continuing factor from 1975 on. Although a few took the land road through Kampuchea into Thailand, the majority took to the sea. They pooled resources to buy boats and gasoline for their trip; recruited a navigator (usually a former navy man); forged their papers; bribed local security agents; and left clandestinely, usually in the darkness of night, for the sea in small, unsafe boats. Their departure was the riskiest, and if caught by the authorities, they would be imprisoned. Once on the high seas, they fell prey to the sea and to the pirates who roamed the Gulf of Thailand.

The combination of these two flows during the late 1970s—second-wave "unofficial departures" and clandestine escapees—resulted in the "boat people" crisis that engaged world attention and action. Except for those Chinese and Vietnamese who found a place on the few "big boats" and arrived promptly and safely at ports of destination, most second-wave refugees shared the same risks as the escapees once they were on the high seas. Even if they survived the angry waves, mechanical failure, the lack of food and water, multiple robberies, assaults, and rapes, they still had to suffer humiliation, mistreatment, and internment in countries of first asylum. It is estimated that half the boat people were drowned at sea or killed during their journey in search of freedom and compassion (see Grant et al. 1979; USCR 1984). Both second-wave refugees and escapees landed in countries neighboring Vietnam where they lived in makeshift camps and began a long wait to be screened for acceptance by countries willing to resettle them permanently.

The final type of exit involves the Orderly Departure Program. That program was the result of the 1979 Memorandum of Understanding between Vietnam and the United Nations High Commissioner for Refugees (UNHCR), which was endorsed by all the major resettlement countries (including the United States). The Orderly Departure Program was initially mostly for those with family ties to people already living abroad, but the United States also accepted former employees of its mission in Vietnam and other Vietnamese who were closely associated with the U.S. effort in Vietnam before 1975. Their departure was the safest way out of the country but was not always easy to arrange. Entry permits from the country of destination and exit visas from the Vietnamese government had to be obtained. The waiting period was usually long, from two to five or more years, depending on one's connections, circumstances, luck, bribery, policies of each government, and the current status of U.S./Vietnamese relations. Although the program experienced ups and downs, it quickly became a major channel for Vietnamese exit.[7]

In subsequent years, the Orderly Departure Program has also been the vehicle for U.S. efforts to help two particular groups of Vietnamese. First, in December 1987, the United States recognized a special responsibility for Amerasian children. The situation of these children was particularly harsh after the American withdrawal. They, and their families, were subject to both official and popular abuse. Frequently they were reduced to a tenuous life on the streets. Since that time, a significant number of Amerasian children have been brought to the United States.[8] Second, in 1989 the United States made a broad offer to resettle those who had been placed in reeducation camps. This group of Vietnamese refugees had faced years of debilitating life in the camps and severe discrimination when they were released. Facing a new life in America would be particularly difficult for them because of their age and a long backlog of health and emotional problems resulting from up to 20 years of severe deprivation, as well as a culture gap that had developed between them and family members who had preceded them to the United States.

VIETNAMESE REFUGEES IN THE UNITED STATES

By 1995, the United States had received well over a million refugees from Indochina. Vietnamese refugees accounted for about two thirds of that total by nationality. In addition, some 200,000 Vietnamese arrived as immigrants, most through the Orderly Departure Program (ODP) (see Table 3.2). These refugees are a mixed group in terms of their background and in terms of their stage of resettlement. A large number of Vietnamese refugees are professionals, graduated from major universities and military academies in Europe and North America, and are familiar with the Western way of life. Others come from rural areas, have a much more traditional outlook, and lack much experience with urban, Westernized society. The initial, first-wave refugees tended to be more urban and professional in background, better educated, and more fluent in English;

Table 3.2
Vietnamese Arrivals by Fiscal Year

Year	Refugees	Immigrants	Total
1975	125,000	3,039	128,039
1976	3,200	4,230	7,430
1977	1,900	4,629	6,529
1978	11,100	1,890	12,990
1979	44,500	6,365	50,865
1980	95,200	4,104	99,304
1981	86,100	1,714	87,814
1982	42,600	2,452	45,052
1983	22,819	2,790	25,609
1984	24,856	4,878	29,734
1985	25,222	4,661	29,883
1986	21,700	5,514	27,214
1987	19,656	3,170	22,826
1988	17,571	3,922	21,493
1989	21,924	15,251	37,175
1990	27,796	27,677	55,473
1991	28,385	32,165	60,550
1992	26,856	40,213	67,069
1993	31,405	22,342	53,747
1994	34,110	10,400	44,510
Total	711,900	201,406	913,306

Notes: Immigrants include Amerasians and many of those arriving through the ODP. Chinese from
   Vietnam are included.

Sources: Gordon (1987) for refugees and immigrants through 1982; ORR (1995) for refugees thereafter; annual statistical yearbooks of the U.S. Immigration and Naturalization Service for arriving immigrants thereafter.

those coming later tended to be more frequently ethnic Chinese, more often
from rural backgrounds, with lower English proficiency, and with fewer skills
directly transferrable to an industrialized economy. Perhaps as important as their
higher skill levels, earlier arrivals have had a longer time to adjust to the United
States, faced better economic conditions on arrival in the United States, and
survived a relatively smooth escape from Vietnam that limited at least their
physical ordeal. Those coming later as boat refugees arrived as the United States
was entering a serious recession in the early 1980s, bore the aftereffects of a
dangerous escape and frequent long periods in camps, and faced a society whose
compassion toward refugees was contracting. Those arriving recently, particu-

larly such groups as Amerasians and reeducation camp survivors, face not only one of America's periodic surges of antiimmigrant sentiment but also a 20-year history of severe discrimination in their home country that has left both emotional and physical scars.

Vietnamese refugees have resettled in every state and many territories of the United States. Despite the initial government attempt to disperse them throughout the country, secondary migration has led to heavy concentration of refugees in a few states. By 1980, over two thirds of Indochinese refugees were living in only nine states (California, Illinois, Louisiana, Minnesota, Oregon, Pennsylvania, Texas, Virginia, and Washington). California had a third of the refugees, followed by Texas (10 percent) and Washington (4 percent). By 1990, the California figure had risen to nearly half (45 percent). California has been the major magnet for secondary migration of Vietnamese refugees, but it has not been the only one. Secondary migration has been prompted by a variety of causes that may create geographical clusters: climate, employment opportunities, reunification with relatives, accessibility to social services, and the pull of established ethnic communities. For example, Vietnamese refugees in Louisiana are predominantly Catholic, and the nation's capital area (including Washington, D.C., northern Virginia, and suburban Maryland) has a larger number of professionals working for international organizations and for federal and local governments. California and Texas have a large number of entertainers, writers, journalists, English as a Second Language teachers, and blue-collar workers. Ethnic Chinese have tended to concentrate in California and New York where they work in restaurants, grocery stores, retail sales, and commercial real estate. Southern California, with its warm climate, large population of Vietnamese refugees, thriving Vietnamese business community along Bolsa Avenue, major Vietnamese-language newspapers, and the possibility of leading a social life similar to that at home, has been called by Vietnamese "the refugees' capital."

The concentration of Vietnamese refugees in particular areas is significant (see Table 14.3) and has consequences. Large numbers of new arrivals, for example, may strain local resources. Geographic concentration also provides the basis for the development of functioning ethnic enclaves that have both positive and negative aspects. On the positive side, such enclaves provide uprooted refugees with a sense of identity and belonging. The enclave is a particularly effective mechanism for facilitating the exchange of information and mutual help, thereby aiding the resettlement process, reducing anxiety and mental distress, and providing vital employment and business-related information. The enclave has important economic functions in nurturing ethnic businesses by providing both an ethnic and "tourist" clientele. The disadvantaged who cannot function effectively in mainstream American society may also find a protective, navigable environment within the enclave. On the negative side, the formation and persistence of ethnic enclaves may lead to the development of a social ghetto, which provides a source of instability, ethnic conflict, and a shelter for criminals. This has largely been avoided in the Vietnamese experience in Amer-

Table 3.3
Vietnamese by Selected Urban Areas, 1990

Urban Area	Vietnamese Population	% of Total
Atlanta	5,541	0.90%
Boston	9,476	1.54%
Chicago	7,648	1.24%
Dallas/Ft. Worth	19,380	3.15%
Denver	5,867	0.95%
Houston	32,492	5.29%
Los Angeles	136,586	22.23%
Minneapolis/St. Paul	7,676	1.25%
New Orleans	11,274	1.83%
New York	14,967	2.44%
Philadelphia	10,061	1.64%
Portland/Vancouver	8,082	1.32%
Riverside/San Bernardino	7,586	1.23%
Sacramento	9,464	1.54%
San Diego	21,004	3.42%
San Francisco/Oakland	28,760	4.68%
San Jose	54,115	8.81%
Seattle	12,516	2.04%
Stockton	6,756	1.10%
Washington, D.C.	22,976	3.74%
Total: 20 Urban Areas	432,227	70.33%
Total: United States	614,547	

Notes: Ethnicity is self-assessed. Urban areas follow census definitions. Percentages do not add up exactly because of rounding.

Source: U.S. Bureau of the Census 1992.

ica, but antiimmigrant sentiments in America have often forced immigrant groups in on themselves, exacerbating such negative aspects of ethnic enclaves.

Economically, Vietnamese refugees have generally made a rapid adjustment to American society. Although persistent dependence on income support is still found among the youngest and the oldest refugees, and among those with little education and little English-language competence, labor force participation and employment rates of Vietnamese refugees do improve over time. The experience of early arrivals was particularly impressive. By 1982, those arriving from 1975 to 1977 were in the labor force at a higher rate than the general U.S. population:

72.1 percent for those who entered the United States in 1975 and 74.3 percent for those who entered the United States in 1976–1977, compared to 64.1 percent for the general U.S. population (ORR 1983). An extensive 1980 survey (Dunning and Greenbaum 1982; Dunning 1989) showed the predictable positive correlations between labor force participation, on the one hand, and the level of education, use of English, and length of residence of the refugees, on the other.

The experience of later arrivals has not been as uniformly positive but compares favorably with other recent arrivals to the United States. Employment continues to increase over time in the United States, and reliance on public support declines. Families continue to pool the returns from low-wage jobs, thus transforming them into workable household incomes. When possible, refugees move into jobs that pay better, even though these jobs are usually also relatively low status. Jobs in the electrical and electronic industries and in the machine trades are a particularly common option, but even such dangerous jobs as meatpacking (Stull, Broadway, and Erickson 1992) have attracted Vietnamese refugees because of their increased wages. Many other refugees have turned to setting up their own businesses. Bureau of the Census surveys of minority-owned businesses in the 1980s, for example, show a threefold increase in the number of Vietnamese businesses per 1,000 Vietnamese refugees from 1982 to 1987 (O'Hare 1992:37). Most of these have been family businesses that cater principally to ethnic clients (restaurants, laundries, grocery stores, hair salons, and tailor shops). Some Vietnamese have become involved in car dealerships, insurance, sales, and real estate; others have opened medical and dental offices; a few are engaged in wholesale, import-export, and manufacturing.

Behind an appearance of economic success, problems remain. Some Vietnamese refugees have difficulty in finding any jobs; many have difficulty finding good jobs. The U.S. economy is being restructured in ways that frequently eliminate the semiskilled manual jobs that would be most advantageous for a population with limited language skills. The option of setting up a business, even with the cost savings that result from the labor of family members, remains a risky proposition. The initial economic success of the Vietnamese refugees may thus have built-in limits. Upward mobility may be, as it has been for other immigrants at other times, effectively blocked (Gold and Kibria 1993; Haines 1987).

Even when economic progress is adequate, other problems endure. The situation of middle-aged and older refugees who were most active in the war and the government of the Republic of Vietnam deserves particular note. They do not appear to have fared as well in social and psychological adjustment as in economic terms. Most have not made a conscious effort to integrate themselves into American society, join professional organizations only when they have to, and infrequently interact socially with other Americans. Their social friends are predominantly Vietnamese. Even those with good jobs in mainstream American society lead a dual life—one in the office among their American coworkers and another at home and during off-hours among their Vietnamese compatriots. This phenomenon is prevalent especially among the educated and Westernized elements, for they have felt not only a loss of status but also a loss of motivation. Two early surveys of Vietnamese refugees provide useful information. One (Dunning and Greenbaum 1982) indicated that although 13 percent of Vietnamese refugees interviewed saw an improvement in their lives, about two thirds rated their lives as less satisfying than they had been in Vietnam. This discrepancy between economic success and psychological well-being is also supported by a survey of Vietnamese living in the southern Gulf Coast and in northern California (Starr et al. 1979; Roberts and Starr 1989). The findings show that economic success and psychological well-being are not consistently related among Vietnamese refugees and that the refugees who had greater educational attainment, higher social status, greater English proficiency, and a less traditional Vietnamese outlook—people generally thought of as better equipped for adjustment—tended to have higher incomes but also show greater strain from the process.

One important factor for these refugees is a "Vietnam syndrome" similar to the one experienced by American veterans of the Vietnam War. The syndrome causes withdrawal, a pessimistic outlook, and a negative attitude toward social participation. These refugees felt betrayed when South Vietnam was lost to the Communists and also believed that the U.S.-organized evacuation in 1975 was not actually meant to include them. They see the version of Vietnamese history prevalent in the American media and intellectual circles as distorted, unfair to them personally, and unfair to the cause in which they believed and for which they fought. They see themselves as losers and believe that there is no use in explaining the complexity of the Vietnam War to people who do not understand it or who refuse to accept their viewpoint.

This Vietnam syndrome is felt most acutely by former Vietnamese soldiers, especially by those who bore the brunt of the fighting and did not know why they had to withdraw during the last month of the war without having a chance to fight. It is also experienced by some generals who feel guilty about their performance during the last critical days of the war—and by Vietnamese who have arrived in the United States after having spent years in Communist reeducation camps. The Vietnam syndrome has often found a more active outlet among the former military than among the educated and the professionals who are doing better economically. Many of the former military, for example, have joined the various resistance movements, hoping one day to liberate Vietnam from the Communist regime. For these people, their presence in the United States is only temporary; their future is not in the United States but in a liberated Vietnam. Many of them also participate in activities against slanted histories of the Vietnam War, against human rights violations by the Hanoi government, and in commemoration of "National Shame Day" as the April 30 anniversary of the fall of Saigon is designated. Leaders of these movements know well the difficulty of their task but believe that the effort has an immediate beneficial effect in restoring a sense of self-confidence and self-respect to the refugees regarding their role in the war and their historical heritage.[9]

The situation of reeducation camp survivors is yet more difficult. Those who spent long years in the camps find it extremely difficult to adjust both to conditions in a new country and to the changing situation in Vietnam. Even reunion with relatives already resettled in the United States can be painful. Wives have become financially independent and have adopted different ways of thought and behavior. Some have even started new families after waiting for years with little hope of their husband's release. Their children were often too young when they left Vietnam to have any understanding of their father's trauma, may not have any appreciation for his political views, and often behave in ways that appear uncommunicative and disrespectful. Even with former colleagues, the experience of the camp survivors is difficult as they confront new gaps in status, financial situation, and political outlook. The trauma can be severe, leading even to suicide: Surviving the expected cruel treatment of enemies does not prepare them for the unexpected disappointment with their family and friends. For those who endure and attempt to create a new life in America—against such odds—a new kind of bravery is required.

Various other segments of the Vietnamese refugee population also face problems. The elderly, for example, often cannot compete effectively in the labor market; they usually cannot drive and thus have no independent means to get to a job, which is a particularly severe problem in southern California. Their traditional outlook and lack of English proficiency limit their ability to function effectively in the mainstream society. Although they may become more dependent on their children, their children are likely to have less and less time for them. There is little comfort in the company of their grandchildren, who tend to speak English more fluently than Vietnamese and to have a much more American outlook. For the older refugees who feel isolated in a changing family environment and in a strange world beyond the family, the need for peer support is obvious. Places of worship (such as Buddhist temples) and mutual assistance associations (such as Vietnamese senior citizens associations) can provide them with friendship and assistance. Participation in social and cultural activities of these organizations can be vital to a sense of self-worth and fortify them in their role as bearers of Vietnamese culture and tradition.

Vietnamese women have also had to adapt to changing circumstances. Many have to abandon a traditional role in the family and become wage earners—and often become the sole or primary wage earner. They may not be well prepared to cope with an unfamiliar Western world of work or with sullen husbands who find it hard to adjust simultaneously to their loss of status and to the changing role and behavior of their wives. This can cause serious tension in the family, can affect the welfare of the children, and sometimes leads to marital separation or divorce. On the whole, the Vietnamese family, which emphasizes the group over the individual, has weathered such storms of change. Vietnamese women, suggests Nazli Kibria (1990, 1993; cf. Tran and Nguyen 1994; Haines 1988), may believe that the "patriarchal" aspects of husband/wife roles need adjusting but seem to be committed to renegotiating roles without actually rupturing them. In addition, the more extended family, in which relatives live together and pool their resources, has helped many Vietnamese refugees to achieve economic self-sufficiency in a relatively short time.

If the adult refugees are faced with difficulties in their social and psychological adjustment, they can find much solace in their children. Despite the disruptions of resettlement, the temptations of a consumer society, and what many view as the poor influence of undisciplined American children, Vietnamese children are doing well in schools. Many Vietnamese have been valedictorians in their graduating classes. Others have graduated from colleges and universities and are pursuing careers in government and in the private sectors. A noticeable pattern among first-generation Vietnamese students has been their overwhelming concentration in science and engineering over the humanities. Kerry Penning (1992), for example, looked at courses of study pursued by Vietnamese in three Orange County community colleges and found Vietnamese about three times as likely to be in science, technology, and business areas as were other students. He, like others, stresses both the rationality of such an approach and the extent to which such a choice is an explicit family strategy toward enhancing the prospects of future generations. Again, it is the family that emerges as perhaps the key factor in identifying an improved future for Vietnamese in the United States and in mobilizing its members toward that goal.

BEYOND INITIAL RESETTLEMENT

The U.S. government and the voluntary agencies did a remarkable job in resettling a large influx of Vietnamese refugees into the United States in the aftermath of an unpopular war. This success was made possible by the traditional American compassion for refugees, by core features of Vietnamese society (a cohesive family structure, a capability to accommodate to change that is based on a turbulent history), and by important themes in Vietnamese culture (the need to live in harmony with nature, a high value placed on education).

Becoming economically self-sufficient has been, from the government's point of view, the immediate goal for newly arrived refugees. For most Vietnamese refugees, given some time for orientation to American society and some English-language and vocational training, this has been possible—despite a public welfare system that does not always provide an ideal combination of incentives and disincentives for beginning work at minimum-wage jobs. Many Vietnamese refugees have done much better than simple survival; others, through their children, will see a future move upward from what for now remains a bleak economic situation. As Vietnamese refugees have moved beyond the issues of minimal economic survival, they have become more active participants in a variety of American institutions, both "mainstream" and minority. Their future has become linked, sometimes in unpredictable ways, with that of other refugees, other immigrants, and other minorities. When Los Angeles exploded in race riots, for example, the Vietnamese were easily confused with other Asians, particularly the Koreans, who were the objects of much violence. Increased interaction inevitably leads to both cooperation and conflict, especially conflict between the refugees and people at the lower rungs of the social ladder who may feel their own position threatened by the newcomers. Government cannot legislate away such conflict, but civic leaders, both American and Vietnamese, and the opinion makers can at least minimize its impact by avoiding the temptation to exaggerate, distort, and stereotype.

Just as the Vietnamese became a more established part of the American scene, however, relations with the home country began changing. Increasing return visits to Vietnam by Vietnamese and by Americans, the loosening of economic restrictions within Vietnam, and the end in 1994 of the ban on economic relations between Vietnam and the United States began to make the divide between Vietnam and Vietnamese abroad less complete. One major refugee assistance organization, for example, turned its attention to economic assistance projects in Vietnam as one aspect of a broadened vision of Vietnam, and overseas Vietnamese linked together in at least some common causes. Vietnam became increasingly available to Vietnamese refugees in the United States, and the refugees became increasingly important to the Vietnamese government. An important political shift occurred. In the late 1970s and early 1980s, when the wounds of the war were still fresh and the Vietnamese occupation of Cambodia provided an opportunity for the resistance movement to develop international connections, anti-Communist activists among the refugees favored a military solution through the overthrow of the Communist regime in Vietnam. That position received considerable support from the Vietnamese refugees in the United States. However, the arrest and execution of resistance leaders who attempted to enter Vietnam from Laos, the withdrawal of Vietnamese troops from Cambodia, the reestablishment of relations between Vietnam and the Association of Southeast Asian Nations (ASEAN), and the collapse of Communist regimes in the Soviet Union and Eastern Europe all contributed to a shift away from military solutions toward political solutions. The resulting demands for human rights observation and democratization in Vietnam were effective enough that the Vietnamese government came to warn against the "scheme of peaceful evolution."

Nevertheless, there were significant changes in Vietnam. The government began economic renovation in 1986. It subsequently moved away from a centrally planned economy, made serious efforts to attract foreign investment, and attempted to involve overseas Vietnamese in the reconstruction of the country. By 1995 Vietnam was at peace with its neighbors, had established a liaison office in Washington, and had begun to shed much of its socialist dogma. Vietnamese refugees were divided in their response to that effort. Some advocated no cooperation with the regime until it became fully democratic and fully observant of essential human rights; others wished to cooperate in economic and technical areas to induce further change in government policy. Opponents of cooperation lost some ground as the overseas Vietnamese increased their visits to Vietnam and their financial support to relatives still in Vietnam. The visits and assistance to relatives, however, did not reflect direct support of the regime or a willingness to deal with it on a long-term basis. Although the support to relatives was about $750 million each year by middecade, the cumulative amount formally invested was less than $100 million—and even that money was devoted to trade and quick turn-around schemes rather than long-term investment. The overseas Vietnamese, more than other foreign investors, appeared to remain too skeptical about the sincerity of the regime to part with investment capital for more than a short period of time. At middecade the distance between the refugees and Vietnam had lessened, but the remaining gap was a formidable one.

NOTES

1. Published reports from the census provide two distinct ways to count Vietnamese. First is the count by country of birth (U.S. Bureau of the Census 1993b). Counts by country of birth only include those who are foreign born, thus missing: (a) children born in the United States (a considerable number); (b) children born in refugee camps (again, a considerable number); and (c) anybody else of Vietnamese extraction who might have been born outside Vietnam (presumably a very small number). The second is by self-reported ethnicity or race (U.S. Bureau of the Census 1993a). This number will include those missed by the foreign-born count and will also exclude those people from Vietnam who do not consider themselves ethnically Vietnamese (e.g., Chinese-Vietnamese who would classify themselves as "Chinese" rather than "Vietnamese"). In the text, this second, ethnic self-reporting figure is used.

2. The early French rule is portrayed vividly by Osborne (1969). Woodside's (1971) book on Vietnam and the Chinese model provides the classic introduction to the resurgent Vietnamese state during the early nineteenth century.

3. The photographs of the last helicopters leaving from the roof of the American embassy are well known. However, there were a variety of other escape routes, including earlier flights from Tan Son Nhat airport and various boats from Saigon and other harbors. Gail Kelly (1977) provides a particularly good description of the various escape routes in 1975 and the way in which this initial "wave" of Vietnamese refugees was resettled to the United States. Although many of those leaving were high-ranking military and government officials and their families, a very broad, if erratic, cross section of Vietnamese society also escaped at this time.

4. Interviews with recently arrived refugees who escaped from Vietnam after being released from "reeducation camps" about the reasons for their dangerous escape invariably provide an answer like: "We knew the chance of making it to safety was only ten percent, but we'd rather die than live with 'them.' "

5. Until spring 1978, the flow of refugees from Vietnam was about 2,000 to 5,000 per month. Mass exodus began in March 1978 (22,000), rose sharply in April (62,000), maintained that level through early 1979: May (60,000) and June (60,000) 1979. By August, however, the flow was down to 6,000. United Nations High Commissioner for

Refugees (UNHCR) data on refugee arrivals in Thailand indicate a total number of arrivals of 34,316 in 1977, doubling to 69,140 in 1978, peaking at 200,000 in 1979, and declining to 113,867 in 1980 and to 43,260 in 1981. (UNHCR figures for Thailand include both those fleeing by sea and the "land" people coming out from Cambodia and Laos during the same period.)

6. The term *dependents* was interpreted loosely to include not only spouse and children but also the spouse's parents, brothers, sisters, and sometimes other relatives. This made it possible for many Vietnamese who, through friendship or bribery, could pass themselves as spouses or dependents of U.S. citizens to get a place on the planes.

7. The Vietnamese government was willing to participate in the Orderly Departure Program for two main reasons: First, the plight of the boat people and international pressure during the 1978–1979 period forced Hanoi to put a tight control on clandestine escapes by boat and relax its control on legal exits. Second, Hanoi hoped a liberal emigration policy might help to improve its relations with Western nations, especially with the United States, at a time when Hanoi was diplomatically isolated because of its invasion of Cambodia.

8. See Kelly (1992) for comments on Amerasian children's lives in Vietnam; Ashabranner and Ashabranner (1987) for comments on unaccompanied refugee children, including Amerasians, in the United States; Mortland and England (1987) for a very good analysis of Vietnamese youth in foster care (with Caucasian families); and GAO (1994) for a more formal review of the Amerasian resettlement program.

9. A different type of active political participation can be found among younger Vietnamese and people who are concerned about their long-term role in the United States. Citizenship has been acquired by many. Especially in areas of dense concentrations, ad hoc and permanent groups have been formed to work in support of legislation or political candidates.

REFERENCES

Aames, Jacqueline, Ronald Aames, John Jung, and Edward Karabenick. 1977. *Indochinese Refugee Self-sufficiency in California: A Survey and Analysis of the Vietnamese, Cambodians, and Lao and the Agencies that Serve Them.* Report Submitted to the State Department of Health, State of California.

Ashabranner, Brent, and Melissa Ashabranner. 1987. *Into a Strange Land: Unaccompanied Refugee Youth in America.* New York: Dodd, Mead, and Company.

Caplan, Nathan, Marcella H. Choy, and John K. Whitmore. 1991. *Children of the Boat People: A Study of Educational Success.* Ann Arbor: University of Michigan Press.

Caplan, Nathan, John K. Whitmore, and Quang L. Bui. 1985. *Southeast Asian Refugee Self-Sufficiency Study: Final Report.* Ann Arbor, Michigan: Institute for Social Research.

Dunning, Bruce B. 1989. Vietnamese in America: The Adaptation of the 1975–79 Arrivals. In *Refugees as Immigrants.* Edited by David W. Haines. Totowa, New Jersey: Rowman and Littlefield. Pp. 55–85.

Dunning, Bruce, and Joshua Greenbaum. 1982. *A Systematic Survey of the Social, Psychological, and Economic Adaptation of Vietnamese Refugees Representing Five Entry Cohorts, 1975–1979.* Washington, D.C.: Bureau of Social Science Research, Inc.

Freeman, James A. 1989. *Hearts of Sorrow: Vietnamese-American Lives*. Stanford: Stanford University Press.

Gardner, Robert W., Bryant Robey, and Peter C. Smith. 1985. Asian Americans: Growth, Change, and Diversity. *Population Bulletin* 40(4).

Gold, Steve, and Nazli Kibria. 1993. Vietnamese Refugees and Blocked Mobility. *Asian and Pacific Migration Journal* 2(1):27–56.

Gordon, Linda W. 1987. Southeast Asian Refuge Migration to the United States. In *Pacific Bridges: The New Immigration from Asia and the Pacific Islands*. Edited by James T. Fawcett and Benjamin V. Cariño. Staten Island, New York: Center for Migration Studies. Pp. 153–173.

———. 1989a. The Missing Children: Mortality and Fertility in a Southeast Asian Refugee Population. *International Migration Review* 22(2):219–237.

———. 1989b. National Surveys of Southeast Asian Refugees: Methods, Findings, Issues. In *Refugees as Immigrants*. Edited by David W. Haines. Totowa, New Jersey: Rowman and Littlefield. Pp. 24–39.

Grant, Bruce, et al. 1979. *The Boat People: An "Age" Investigation*. New York: Penguin Books.

Haines, David W. 1987. Patterns in Southeast Asian Refugee Employment. *Ethnic Groups* 7:39–63.

———. 1988. Kinship in Vietnamese Refugee Resettlement: A Review of the U.S. Experience. *Journal of Comparative Family Studies* 19(1):1–16.

Kelly, Gail Paradise. 1977. *From Vietnam to America: A Chronicle of the Vietnamese Immigration to the United States*. Boulder, Colorado: Westview Press.

Kelly, Katie. 1992. *A Year in Saigon*. New York: Simon and Schuster.

Kibria, Nazli. 1990. Power, Patriarchy, and Gender Conflict in the Vietnamese Immigrant Community. *Gender and Society* 4(1):9–24.

———. 1993. *Family Tightrope*. Princeton, New Jersey: Princeton University Press.

Kim, Young Yun, and Perry M. Nicassio. 1980. *Research Proiect on Indochinese Refugees in the State of Illinois*. (5 vols.). Chicago: Travelers Aid Society of Metropolitan Chicago.

Le Ngoan. 1994. Profile of the Vietnamese American Community. National Congress of Vietnamese in America.

Mortland, Carol, and Maura G. England. 1987. Vietnamese Youth in American Foster Care. *Social Work* 32(3):240–245.

Nguyen Manh Hung. 1984a. Refugee Scholars and Vietnamese Studies in the United States: 1975–1982. *Amerasia Journal* 11(1):89–99.

———. 1984b. "Vietnam: A Television History": A Case Study in Perceptual Conflict between the American Media and the Vietnamese Expatriates. *World Affairs* 142(2):71–84.

Office of Refugee Resettlement (ORR). 1983. *Report to the Congress: Refugee Resettlement Program*. Washington, D.C.: U.S. Department of Health and Human Services.

———. 1995. *Report to the Congress: Refugee Resettlement Program*. Washington, D.C.: U.S. Department of Health and Human Services.

O'Hare, William P. 1992. America's Minorities–the Demographics of Diversity. *Population Bulletin* 47(4).

Osborne, Milton E. 1969. *The French Presence in Cochinchina and Cambodia*. Ithaca, New York: Cornell University Press.

Penning, Kerry. 1992. Tradition and Pragmatism: An Exploration into the Career Aspirations of Vietnamese Refugee College Students. In *Selected Papers on Refugee
Issues.* Edited by Pamela A. DeVoe. Washington, D.C.: American Anthropological Association. Pp. 89–99.

Roberts, Alden E., and Paul D. Starr. 1989. Differential Reference Group Assimilation
among Vietnamese Refugees. In *Refugees as Immigrants.* Edited by David W.
Haines. Totowa, New Jersey: Rowman and Littlefield. Pp. 40–54.

Rumbaut, Rubén G. 1989. Portraits, Patterns, and Predictors of the Refugee Adaptation
Process. In *Refugees as Immigrants.* Edited by David W. Haines. Totowa, New
Jersey: Rowman and Littlefield. Pp. 138–182.

Starr, Paul D., Alden Roberts, Rebecca LeNoir, and Nguyen Ngoc Thai. 1979. Adaptation
and Stress among Vietnamese Refugees: Preliminary Considerations. In *Proceedings of the First Annual Conference on Indochinese Refugees.* Fairfax, Virginia:
George Mason University. Pp. 110–127.

Stull, Donald D., Michael J. Broadway, and Ken C. Erickson. 1992. The Price of a Good
Steak: Beef Packing and Its Consequences for Garden City, Kansas. In *Structur-
ing Diversity.* Edited by Louise Lamphere. Chicago: University of Chicago Press.
Pp. 35–64.

Tran, Thanh V., and Thang D. Nguyen. 1994. Gender and Satisfaction with the Host
Society among Indochinese Refugees. *International Migration Review* 28(2):
323–337.

U.S. Bureau of the Census. 1983. *Asian and Pacific Islander Population by State: 1980.*
Washington, D.C.: Department of Commerce.

———. 1992. *1990 Census of Population. General Population Charactersitics—United
States.* Washington, D.C.

———. 1993a. *Asians and Pacific Islanders in the United States.* (CP 3-5). Washington,
D.C.

———. 1993b. *The Foreign Born Population of the United States.* (CP 3-1). Washington, D.C.

U.S. Committee for Refugees (USCR). 1984. *Vietnamese Boat People: Pirates' Vulnerable Prey.* New York: American Council for Nationalities Service.

U.S. General Accounting Office (GAO). 1994. *Vietnamese Amerasian Resettlement: Education, Employment, and Family Outcomes in the United States.* Washington,
D.C.

Whitmore, John, Marcella Trautmann, and Nathan Caplan. 1989. The Socio-Cultural
Basis for the Economic and Educational Success of Southeast Asian Refugees.
In *Refugees as Immigrants.* Edited by David W. Haines. Totowa, New Jersey:
Rowman and Littlefield. Pp. 121–137.

Woodside, Alexander B. 1971. *Vietnam and the Chinese Model.* Cambridge: Harvard
University Press.

Part II

Sociological Approaches

Chapter 4

Soviet Jews

STEVEN J. GOLD

After three decades of emigration, there are now sizable communities of Jews from the former USSR in several nations and three continents, including Western Europe (some 40,000 live in Germany), North America, and Israel (Tress 1994). While the greatest number of émigrés reside in Israel, since the mid-1960s, almost 325,000 Jews from the former Soviet Union have settled in the United States (HIAS 1995). From 1988 to the present, persons from the former Soviet Union have been the largest refugee nationality to enter the United States (Littman 1992). Further, Soviet Jews[1] constitute the most numerous group of Jewish immigrants to enter the nation since the 1920s. Members of this population are notable for their high levels of skill and education, the intact status of their families, the extensive resettlement services they receive from both Jewish and government agencies, and—among Jewish migrants—their minimal premigration exposure to formalized Jewish training.[2] As educated Europeans who receive ample advocacy and support from a well established community of native-born coethnics, Soviet Jewish émigrés enjoy excellent prospects for a relatively smooth and rapid merger into the American middle class. In this, Soviet Jews are dramatically distinct from other major refugee groups of the period since 1980.

The presence of one third of a million émigrés is the result of enormous efforts expended by the American Jewish community over the last 25 years and, accordingly, represents the successful culmination of a campaign to save Soviet Jewry. However, despite their status as religious refugees and the generous support they have received from American coethnics, Jews from the former Soviet Union have been less religious and more Russian in their style of adaptation to the United States than was expected by the host community. Drawing upon their high levels of skill, Soviet Jews' economic adjustment to the United States has been a story of success. In contrast, their patterns of communal adaptation have generally reflected their own independent values and prerogatives rather than the model of rapid amalgamation planned for them by the American Jewish community.

EXODUS

As educated Caucasians exiting a relatively peaceful part of the world, Jews from the former Soviet Union may seem to have little reason to flee from their homeland. However, their historical and contemporary experience as Soviet Jews gives them ample reason to exit while the opportunity is available.

As an oppressed group under the czars, Jews played an important role in the Russian Revolution. However, from Joseph Stalin's time through the 1980s, the Soviet government maintained policies to limit Jews' influence in the nation's government and bureaucracy. Such steps were taken as part of an effort to discourage religion and extend control over all bases of power in the USSR. For example, between 1937 and 1974, the number of Jewish deputies in the Supreme Soviet was reduced from 47 to 6 (Simon 1985a: 8). Further, Soviet purges—from the show trials of the 1920s to the "Doctor's Plot" of the post–World War II era—included disproportionate numbers of Jewish victims (Chesler 1974; Simon 1985b).

Prior to the 1960s, the Soviet system offered Jews access to higher education because technical experts were required for the nation's military and industrial development. Soon, however, this path was restricted. "As Khrushchev pointedly indicated, 'we' no longer need the Jews because we have 'our own' experts" (Jacobs and Frankel-Paul 1981: 5). In 1960, Jews accounted for 3.2 percent of the students enrolled in higher education in the USSR. By 1971, the figure was less than 2 percent (Simon 1985b: 183). An electronics engineer described his confrontation with anti-Jewish quotas imposed by the Soviet bureaucracy:

I wanted to continue my education and get a promotion in my field. But as a Jew, I could not go above a certain level. It's not so much anti-Semitism among the people I worked with—I had good relations. But my bosses were limited with what they could do. It was Brezhnev time—it was State anti-Semitism. It wasn't much from the people. This is what is so outrageous—is that it's a State anti-Semitism, they just impose it. (Gold 1992: 33–34)

Anti-Zionism, a major plank in Soviet foreign policy from the 1960s onward, had dire consequences for Russian Jews. Articles condemning Israel appeared with increasing frequency in the official Soviet media after the 1967 Arab-Israeli war and thus gave government sanction to anti-Semitic attacks. "Getting the hint," ambitious officials would carry out personal projects of harassing, demoting, or refusing to hire Jews as a means of currying favor with superiors

(Gold 1992). Finally, while nearly all Soviet Jews confronted institutional discrimination, direct prejudice was also common, especially for those living in the Ukraine. An émigré from Odessa described the rampant anti-Semitism Jews encountered in Kiev during the 1970s:

When I came to Kiev, I took a bus usually from railway station or from airport. And I would ask myself, "How long will it take before I hear something about Jews?" Usually, it took 15 or 20 minutes and I would hear something already. These anti-Semitic feelings and thoughts, it's first place for them. Their anti-Semitic feelings and anti-Semitic conversations and everything, for them it's problem number one. (Gold 1992: 34)

As of the mid-1990s, the climate in the former USSR—characterized by impending economic crisis, social disorder, a revival of intolerant churches, and the rise of ultranationalism—appears to be a textbook example of a setting ripe for anti-Semitic outbreaks (Gitelman 1992). As Communist Party control of ideology has been replaced by freedom of expression, Jews have enjoyed greater access to communication and religious participation. At the same time, however, anti-Semites have also become increasingly open, active, and virulent. For example, in 1992, the Russian Nationalist Party published a manifesto featuring its 75 slogans. Of these, 52 were explicitly anti-Semitic or anti-Zionist (Gitelman 1992). In the 1990s, Vladimir Zhirinovsky, the leader of Russia's Liberal Democratic Party, became an important political force. His many anti-Semitic remarks have given Jews and other ethnic minorities cause for concern (Ingram: 1994: 8A). In 1994, he told the UN Correspondents' Association that "the majority of new business structures" in the former USSR "are headed mostly by Jews" and "most of the money is criminal." Accordingly, as of the mid-1990s, many Jews in the former Soviet Union still hoped to leave for the United States, Israel, or other Western nations (Brym 1993).

The post–World War II exit of Jews from the USSR has been shaped by a complex configuration of political relations between the United States, the USSR, and Israel. Prior to the 1970s, there was little Jewish emigration; during the entire decade of the 1960s, only 2,465 persons entered the United States from the USSR (Chiswick 1993: 262). However, during the late 1970s, and then a decade later in the late 1980s and early 1990s, thousands of Jews were able to leave. Peak years of entry into the United States were 1979, when 28,794 arrived, and 1992, when 45,888 Jews from the former Soviet Union entered (ORR 1990; HIAS 1995) (see Table 4.1).

Leaving the Soviet Union is only half of the story of migration. Once they exit, Soviet Jews must decide on a place to settle. The two major choices are the United States and Israel. There has long been a debate over who should be able to choose Soviet Jews' country of refuge. Prior to its downfall, the Soviet government permitted Jews to exit for either of two reasons. The first was family unification—allowing Soviet citizens to join relatives in other nations. This affected relatively few. The second reason for exit was the law of return. Since

Table 4.1
Soviet Jewish Refugee Arrivals by Calendar Year

Year	Number	As % of Prior Year
1965	12	
1966	36	300%
1967	72	200%
1968	92	128%
1969	156	170%
1970	135	87%
1971	214	159%
1972	453	212%
1973	1,449	320%
1974	3,490	241%
1975	5,250	150%
1976	5,512	105%
1977	6,842	124%
1978	12,265	179%
1979	28,794	235%
1980	15,461	54%
1981	6,980	45%
1982	1,327	19%
1983	887	67%
1984	489	55%
1985	570	117%
1986	641	112%
1987	3,811	595%
1988	10,576	278%
1989	36,738	347%
1990	31,283	85%
1991	34,715	111%
1992	45,888	132%
1993	35,581	78%
1994	32,622	92%
Total	322,341	

Source: Hebrew Immigrant Aid Society (HIAS) program information.

Jews' passports were stamped with "Jew" instead of the Soviet republic where they were born, they were allowed to go to Israel. Initially, the majority of Soviet Jews granted exit visas settled in Israel. However, from 1976 to 1989, at least half opted instead to dwell in the United States. Before the glasnost era, the official destination of all Jewish émigrés was Israel. Upon exiting the USSR, a large fraction "dropped out" as they applied for, and were almost always given refugee status by, the United States. By the late 1980s, less than 10 percent each year chose Israel (Gold 1994; Woo 1989).

Jews from the former Soviet Union cite several reasons for prefering the United States over Israel. These include greater economic opportunity, as well as a higher level of national security and no compulsory military service. (For a group who paid a great human price in World War II, the latter considerations are of major significance.) In addition, émigrés often assert that they feel more comfortable in the secular and pluralistic United States than in Israel, which they describe as "an Orthodox country."[3] Finally, Russian Jews are accustomed to identifying with a big nation and so prefer exchanging one superpower for another, as opposed to moving to a tiny country, which for many has a total population surpassed by that of their former city of residence.

From the early 1970s to the late 1980s, Soviet Jews coming to the United States would spend about a month in Italy while their resettlement applications were processed. After October 1, 1989, the United States no longer accepted Soviets who sought to enter the United States with Israeli visas (Woo 1989; Tress 1991). Instead, Jews who wished to enter the United States applied directly to the U.S. embassy in Moscow. The number of Soviet refugees permitted to enter the United States (Jewish and otherwise) is limited to 50,000 a year. As of 1995, priority is given to selected groups of former Soviets that the United States Congress has identified as likely targets of persecution. These include Jews, Evangelical Christians, Ukrainian Catholics, and followers of the Ukrainian Autocephalous Orthodox Church. Eligible persons with close, legal-resident relatives (parent, spouse, children, siblings, grandparents, and grandchildren) in the United States are granted priority for entry. Members of these denominations who have immediate U.S. citizen relatives (parent, spouse, or unmarried minor child) must apply as immigrants rather than refugees.

DEMOGRAPHIC INFORMATION

From 1965 through the end of 1994, HIAS resettled 322,341 Soviet Jews (HIAS 1995). (See Table 4.1.) The greatest number come from Russia and Ukrainia, which also have the largest Jewish populations among the former Soviet Republics. However, while Russia has the largest number of Jews, Ukrainia is the major source of émigrés. Of the 194,047 Soviet Jews who entered the United States between 1980 and May 1993, 42 percent (81,421) were Ukrainians, 24 percent (46,391) were from Russia, 13 percent (24,437) were Byelorussians, 6 percent (12,591) were Uzbeckis, 6 percent (11,113) were Mol-

Table 4.2
Origins of Soviet Jewish Refugees by Year of Arrival

Republic	1980-1989		1990-1993		1980-1993	
Ukraine	32,850	43.0%	48,571	41.3%	81,421	42.0%
Russia	20,237	26.5%	26,154	22.2%	46,391	23.9%
Byelorussia	10,419	13.7%	14,018	11.9%	24,437	12.6%
Moldavia	3,376	4.4%	7,737	6.6%	11,113	5.7%
Latvia	2,313	3.0%	2,173	1.8%	4,486	2.3%
Uzbekistan	3,111	4.1%	9,480	8.1%	12,591	6.5%
Azerbaijan	1,608	2.1%	3,107	2.6%	4,715	2.4%
Other	2,405	3.2%	3,632	3.1%	6,037	3.1%
Unknown	10	0.0%	2,846	2.4%	2,856	1.5%
Total	76,329	100.0%	117,718	100.0%	194,047	100.0%

Note: 1993 figures are through May.
Source: HIAS 1991, 1993.

davians, 2 percent (4,715) were from Azerbaijan, and 2 percent (4,486) were Latvians. The remainder (4 percent) came from other Soviet Republics or had unknown origins (HIAS 1993)[4] (see Table 4.2).

In terms of their patterns of settlement, state-level data from the 1990 census reveal that 30 percent of USSR-born American residents live in New York, 23 percent in California, 6 percent each in New Jersey and Illinois, and 5 percent each in Florida, Pennsylvania, and Massachusetts. Hence, 80 percent of those born in the Soviet Union reside in seven states. It should be noted that because federal statistics tabulate only the nationality and not the religion of refugees, there is no way of knowing what proportion of these are Jews. For example, Los Angeles is the major point of settlement for Soviet Armenians. Analysis of the 1990 census reveals that only 33 percent of post–1965 former Soviet residents in Los Angeles County *are not* of Armenian ethnicity. In contrast, only about 500 of the more than 60,000 former Soviets in New York City are of Armenian ethnicity[5] (see Table 4.3).

Key Characteristics: Age and Family Patterns

Three sociodemographic features of the Soviet émigré population are crucial for understanding their adaptation to the United States: their age; their intact, multigenerational families; and the class and culture-based patterns of interaction and support maintained within these social units.

Table 4.3
Location of Persons Born in the USSR, 1990

State	% of Total
New York	30%
California	23%
Illinois	6%
New Jersey	6%
Massachusetts	5%
Florida	5%
Pennsylvania	5%
Total	80%

Source: U.S. Bureau of the Census 1993.

Soviet Jews are the oldest refugee group entering the United States. Kosmin's 1989 study of Soviet Jews who had been in the United States at least 8 years found their median age to be 49. Of those entering the United States during 1991, 34 percent were over 50 and 15 percent were over age 65. About 18 percent of 1991 entrants were of school age. In fiscal year 1986, entering Soviet refugees' average age was 37, with women's median age being 41.4 years. However, since 1990, the median age has declined. For purposes of comparison, the average age of all immigrants entering the United States in 1991 was about 29 years (Kosmin 1990; ORR 1987; HIAS 1993).

The significant number of elderly among the Soviet Jewish population yields distinct patterns of adjustment. Refugee families experience problems because the elderly have difficulties learning English, finding employment, and making their way in the United States. At the same time, elderly émigrés help with child care and provide a strong sense of community as they congregate on streets, in parks, and in community centers in neighborhoods where they settle (Orleck 1987). Finally, since elderly émigrés are beyond working age, it is they who most commonly rely on government assistance for a considerable period after their arrival. In contrast, younger émigrés make rapid progress in their efforts to be self-supporting (see below).

Soviet Jewish families are often intact, have few children, and frequently include three generations. Because Soviet Jewish families are often extended and small in size, they are able to devote ample resources to child rearing—a pattern retained from the former USSR, where deep involvement across generations was typical and required for child rearing, since women as well as men worked outside of the home (Simon and Brooks 1983: 57; Markowitz 1994:

154–157). Prior to 1989, Soviet emigration policy worked to ensure the emigration of intact, multigenerational families by encouraging or even mandating the exit of elderly émigrés along with their more youthful offspring (Drachman and Halberstadt 1992). Since that time, family preferences and U.S. immigration policy have furthered this pattern of family unification (Gold 1994).

Additional evidence of the intact nature of émigré families involves high rates of matrimony. According to the 1990 census, 80 percent of post-1965 employed Russian male immigrants between the ages of 24 and 65 were married. This marriage rate exceeds that of all post-1965 male immigrants in the same age range by 17 percent (Chiswick 1995: 29). Thus, family composition, cultural orientation, and immigration regulations have all reinforced the Soviet Jewish family's ability to function as a source of support and stability for émigrés in America.

Soviet émigré families reveal many patterns that facilitate their smooth adjustment to American society. However, they also manifest certain characteristics that hinder adaptation. For example, in the Soviet Union, parents were highly involved in their childrens' lives, while the peer group—a central force in American adolescents' socialization—had relatively little influence (Shlapentokh 1984). This was especially the case among Jewish families, because parents felt their efforts were necessary to shield children from anti-Semitism and ensure chances for success. Carried over to the United States, parents' desire to protect children sometimes fosters excessive dependence and prevents émigré youth from establishing social relationships, developing a sense of autonomy, and dealing with American life on their own terms (Markowitz 1994; Hulewat 1981; Kozulin and Venger 1993).

Further, while generational conflicts exist among all immigrant families, such problems are aggravated among highly skilled Soviet Jews. The unprecedented ability of certain émigrés to adjust to America quickly widens the gaps in levels of adaptation that may exist within a single immigrant family (Gold 1989). For example, Sasha, a 35-year-old émigré, was making $30,000 a year as a computer programmer two years after his 1982 arrival in the United States. His position contrasted dramatically with that of his parents who knew almost no English, did not drive, and were unemployed. Consequently, Sasha had to provide their economic support, translation, and transportation in addition to managing his own career and family life. To offer the parents some independence, the family resided in a Russian-speaking neighborhood far from his job, thus requiring Sasha to make an 80-mile commute. He summarized his relationship with his dependent parents: "With my parents, it's not that they are just from a different country, they are from a different world. There are so many things they just don't understand. I have to take care of them. But I have my own life too" (Gold 1992: 70).

Becoming Americans: Language and Citizenship

Soviet émigrés (with the exception of the elderly) tend to make excellent progress with language acquisition. While about 50 percent spoke no English on arrival, within a few years, upwards of two thirds or more rate themselves as "good, very good, or excellent" at the English language. Between 50 and 70 percent have taken English classes (Simon 1985a; Kosmin 1990; Federation 1985). According to the 1990 census, 78.5 percent of employed, post-1965 Russian male immigrants to the United States speak English "well," "very well," or exclusively (Chiswick 1995: 29).

Soviets show a higher propensity to naturalize and do so more rapidly than the other major refugee groups (Cubans and Southeast Asians) who have entered the United States since 1975. From 1980 through 1991, almost 60,000 persons born in the USSR became citizens. This represents about 57 percent of those who arrived in the United States between 1975 and 1985 as refugees (ORR 1993: 61). The former Soviets' rapid naturalization provides members of this group with opportunities for political participation, eligibility for jobs and scholarships, and a higher priority ranking when assisting relatives to gain entry into the United States.[6]

EMPLOYMENT AND ECONOMIC FACTORS

When analyzing the economic progress of refugee groups, three main issues must be considered. First, one must evaluate the population's ability to find jobs. The second issue involves the level of income produced. Ideally, earnings should permit a refugee to survive without reliance on government benefits. Finally, if a refugee group is to achieve integration into the host society, prospects for economic mobility should exist. It is generally accepted that the first job a refugee finds in the United States may not be an ideal position. Nevertheless, employment itself does yield rewards in the form of income, work experience, and cultural orientation. As time passes, however, refugee workers should have the potential for promotion in order to increase their earnings, receive appropriate remuneration for their skills, and attain some level of occupational satisfaction. While many of these issues are determined by the economic environment within which a refugee seeks work, resettlement services and language, job training, and job placement programs can contribute to a group's positive economic integration.

As a result of their education, skills, and the benefits they receive, Jews from the former Soviet Union tend to do relatively well in the States after a short period of adjustment. Simon and Brooks (1983), in a nationwide sample, found their average educational level to be 13.5 years, a figure that exceeds the average for the U.S. population by a year and is among the very highest of all immigrant groups entering the country (Gold 1992: 43). Data from the 1990 census are consistent with Simon and Brooks' estimate. For employed male post-1965 Russian immigrants between 24 and 65 years of age, nationwide, the educational level was 14.8 years (Chiswick 1995: 29). Average education was above 13 years for Soviet-born persons in both New York City and Los Angeles. Fifty-eight percent of former Soviets in New York City and 72 percent in Los Angeles County had 1 or more years of college.

Soviet Jewish émigrés receive economic rewards for their high levels of education. The 1990 census revealed that employed Soviet men residing in New York City who arrived in the United States between 1975 and 1981 were making approximately $32,000 annually in 1990, while their counterparts in Los Angeles were making over $43,000. For purposes of comparison, the average earnings for all employed foreign-born men was about $26,000 in New York and $24,000 in Los Angeles in 1990; while employed, native-born white men in New York and Los Angeles earned approximately $46,000.

Employed Soviet women who entered the United States between 1975 and 1981 made about $22,500 in New York and approximately $26,000 in Los Angeles. Their earnings were consistently between 58 percent and 72 percent of those of employed Soviet men who arrived at the same time. For purposes of comparison, the average earnings for employed, foreign-born women were $19,000 in New York and $16,400 in Los Angeles in 1990; while employed, native-born white women earned about $31,000 in New York and $26,000 in Los Angeles in 1990. As might be expected, recently arrived Soviet men and women made much less in 1990 than those émigrés with longer tenure in the United States.

While the average income of former Soviets suggests a generally successful merger into the American middle class, the economic adjustment of this population covers a wide range, from poverty to significant wealth. For example, about 30 percent of those who had been in the United States for a year or less in June 1991 were receiving cash assistance. Kosmin found that among émigrés in the United States eight years or more in 1989, 42 percent of those households in New York and 36 percent of those in Los Angeles were making less than $20,000 per household. In contrast, 8 percent of former Soviets in New York and 16 percent of those in Los Angeles had a household income of $60,000 or more in 1989 (ORR 1992: A-18, 19; Kosmin 1990: 24–25).

Labor Force Participation

Labor force participation rates for Soviet Jews in the United States are generally quite high, with nearly 70 percent of working-age émigrés employed full- or part-time. Between 10 percent and 28 percent are seeking work, depending on the year of the survey and the part of the country sampled. With the large numbers arriving since 1990 and the depressed economic conditions they encounter in many receiving communities, a sizable fraction of recent arrivals are underemployed (Krautman 1990; Gold 1994: 20).

The 1990 census determined that the labor force participation rate for Soviet immigrant men in New York City was 76 percent, and 57 percent for women. Excluding recent arrivals, the labor force participation rate was 89 percent for men and 68 percent for women. Roughly similar trends were evident in Los Angeles, where the labor force participation rate for Soviet immigrant men was 79 percent and 63 percent for women. Excluding recent arrivals, the labor force participation rate in Los Angeles County was 88 percent for men and 71 percent for women. With the exception of those in the United States three years or less in 1990, unemployment rates were quite low, less than 7 percent for men or women in New York and Los Angeles. Between 32 and 59 percent of working-age women were not in the labor force.

One economic asset of the Soviet Jews over natives or other immigrant groups is the unusually high number of women with professional and technical skills. Sixty-seven percent of Soviet Jewish women in the United States were engineers, technicians, or other kinds of professionals prior to migration. In contrast, only 16.5 percent of American women work in these occupations (Simon 1985a: 17; Simon, Shelly, and Scheiderman 1986; Eckles et al. 1982: 29; U.S. Bureau of the Census 1984: 216). According to the 1990 census, 29 percent of post-1965 Soviet émigré women in New York City and 26 percent of émigré women in Los Angeles County work as professionals in the United States. The very high level of women's education and professional experience is one of the most noteworthy aspects of the Soviet Jewish population. In fact, the total number of women workers with former employment as "Professionals" or "Engineers" exceeds that of men (HIAS 1993; Gold 1994: 52).

Use of Cash Assistance

According to the Office of Refugee Resettlement (ORR), in 1986, about 26 percent of Soviet refugees were supported by cash assistance. This figure includes some Armenians and others as well as Jews (ORR 1987: 34–35). Data from the 1990 census show that 14 percent of Soviet-born men and 13 percent of Soviet-born women in New York City, and 7 percent of Soviet-born men and 11 percent of women in Los Angeles County, were on supplemental security income (SSI), Aid to Families with Dependent Children (AFDC), or General Relief in 1990. However, excluding recent arrivals, use of cash assistance declined to 5 percent for men and 10 percent for women in New York, and 5 percent for men and 9 percent for women in Los Angeles. Hence, once settled, refugees are able to reduce their use of government assistance.

According to data produced by the HIAS Matching Grant Department, the self-sufficiency rate for Soviet Jews in the United States after four months was 24.6 percent for those arriving in 1990, 23.8 percent for those entering in 1991, and 18.3 percent for those arriving in 1992. In general, it appears that émigrés arriving in smaller cities had a better chance of being self-supporting after four months than those who settled in larger cities. For example, in Baltimore there was an 80-percent-plus rate of self-sufficiency among Soviet Jews within four months of arrival in the years 1989 to 1992. In contrast, in Los Angeles émigrés had a four-mouth self-sufficiency rate between 22 and 11 percent for the same years, and in New York the largest point of settlement for the four-month self-sufficiency rate was about 5 percent after 1989. In addition to community size, other factors, such as the state-determined availability of public assistance, might also influence self-sufficiency rates. The fact that New York and California have much more generous benefit programs than does Maryland may partly explain the higher rates of self-sufficiency evident in Baltimore versus Los Angeles and New York (Gold 1994: 48–49).

The combination of large numbers of émigrés entering the United States and the recession of the early 1990s made initial job finding difficult for former Soviets. However, Soviets are noted for their rapid rates of exit from RCA (refugee cash assistance), which actually improved between 1990 and 1991, despite the generally sluggish economic conditions of the period. To quote from the 1993 Office of Refugee Resettlement *Report to the Congress:* "The RCA utilization rate for the Soviets is the lowest of any large group (28 percent) and represents a dramatic decrease from the previous year (50 percent), when a surge of arrivals in the winter and early spring of 1991 contributed to heavy RCA utilization" (ORR 1993:24). The high skill levels of émigrés, their motivation to find work, and the assistance provided them by agencies and community members can be credited with this impressive performance.

Areas of Employment

According to these statistics, Soviet Jews in the United States appear to be finding jobs and are earning a good living, considering their short stay in the United States. One problem they confront, however, is an inability to meet their previous level of occupational prestige. For example, a study of New York's Soviet Jewish community found that while 66 percent had professional, technical, and managerial occupations in the USSR, only half of these, 33 percent, found similar jobs in the United States (Federation 1985).

Soviet Jews experience problems in finding appropriate American jobs because of their lack of job-related licenses and certification, their limited English-language skills, and the incompatibility between certain Soviet and American occupations. For example, there are few American job opportunities for classical accordion players, coaches of sports seldom played in the United States, or engineers who formerly designed tundra-friendly (and by U.S. standards, hopelessly outdated) structures for the Siberian oil industry. Agency data reveal that a large fraction of formerly professional Soviet Jews are able to adapt to the U.S. economy by finding jobs in the skilled trades, bookkeeping and accounting, computer programming, and technical fields (Federation 1985).

The literature on Soviet Jewish émigrés includes several accounts of self-employment. Former Soviets gravitate toward several enterprises including engineering companies, restaurants and grocery stores, retail trade, and construction and real estate. In the 1980s, taxi companies in New York and Los Angeles included many Soviets, but émigrés often leave this risky enterprise after only a few years (Russell 1985).

Data from the 1990 census suggest that a sizable fraction of Soviets are involved in small business. In New York, 15 percent were self-employed (21 percent of men and 8 percent of women) with higher rates in Los Angeles, where 25 percent (33 percent of men and 17 percent of women) were self-employed. When compared with census data among various migrant groups, the Los Angeles figure puts Soviet Jews among those groups with the very highest rates of self-employment. This is an impressive finding, considering that as refugees from a Communist nation Soviet Jews lack two of the most essential resources for entrepreneurship—business experience and investment capital. On the other hand, high rates of entrepreneurship are common to Jewish immigrants to the United States. Their involvement in self-employment resonates with a literature that identifies entrepreneurship as a viable adjustment strategy for migrant groups (Gold 1992; Kestin 1985; Lubin 1985; Orleck 1987; Portes and Rumbaut 1990).

While many Soviets are becoming self-employed, others are entering white-collar and professional occupations. This pattern is consistent with that revealed by other highly skilled, educated, and English-speaking migrant groups such as Indians and Filipinos. Finally, it should be noted that various professions, such as doctor, dentist, and engineer (ones that involve a significant proportion of Soviet Jews) are often practiced independently and hence constitute both professional work *and* self-employment (Gold 1988; Mangiafico 1988: Portes and Rumbaut 1990).

INTERACTIONS WITH RESETTLEMENT ACTIVITIES AND SCHOOLS

Soviet Jews in the United States enjoy perhaps the most well-funded and professionally staffed resettlement system ever devoted to immigrants and refugees (Eckles et al. 1982; Gold 1994). Nearly all Soviet Jews have been resettled by the Hebrew Immigration Aid Society. The HIAS model of resettlement combines centralized policymaking, administration, and data collection with local-level service provision, thus giving each community the flexibility required to help clients according to local conditions and needs. For example, HIAS mandates certain program standards, such as reunion with relatives and "earliest appropriate job placement" in order to "avoid fostering reliance on public and private institutions." However, actual service provision is carried out by a team of local professionals in coordination with family members and community volunteers. "Consequently, the nature of programs developed within each community are often unique to that community's specific environment" (ORR 1993: C-10,11).

Compared with the refugee resettlement systems devoted to other ethnic and nationality groups, Soviet Jews' agencies are highly centralized and integrated, long established, well funded, and few in number. They enjoy a level of government and private funding per refugee that is considerably greater than that allocated for other groups. For example, during the early 1980s, the federal government gave each VOLAG (voluntary agency) $525 per Southeast Asian refugee. In contrast, Soviet Jews' resettlement agencies, which had access to nongovernment funds provided by Jewish charities, received $1,000 per refugee. Additional funding was made available by combining communal and governmental funds via a federal matching grant program (Eckles et al. 1982; HIAS 1991, 1993). In fiscal year 1992, the Council of Jewish Federations received almost $34 million in matching grants to resettle almost 34,000 refugees of whom 90 percent were Soviets (HIAS 1991).

Depending on the community of settlement, services to Soviet Jews are available from several coordinated agencies. Intake services, vocational and language training, and health care are often accessible from public agencies and community colleges or adult schools. The Jewish Family and Children's Service provides counseling, financial aid, and case management. The Jewish Vocational Service offers job placement and occasionally job training. Jewish Community Centers and Young Men's and Women's Hebrew Associations (YMHAs/YWHAs) deliver social and recreational activities; the Bureau of Jewish Education contributes a variety of religious and cultural activities. Because of the constitutional separation of church and state, resettlement activities with religious content may not be supported with governmental funds.

Several synagogues, Jewish camps, and Jewish day schools have developed programs on their own or in consort with Jewish federations to welcome émigré families. In accordance with matching grant requirements, anchor families—established relatives of recently arrived émigrés—are expected to deliver certain benefits as well, valued at approximately $400 per refugee in Los Angeles during 1993. Resettlement agencies provide services for both immediate needs such as housing and health care as well as longer-term concerns of religious education, social integration, recreation, and cultural enrichment.

Finally, while the services available to Soviet émigrés may vary according to the Jewish agencies resettling them, benefits available through state and local sources also impact clients. For example, due to state regulations, a refugee family of four living in California in 1989 would be eligible for $734 monthly in AFDC benefits. The same family living in Texas would receive a maximum of $221. Further, while two-parent, indigent families are eligible for AFDC in California, they are not in Texas (Rumbaut 1989: 103).

Feelings about Agencies

Soviet Jews generally have positive evaluations of the services they receive in resettlement. Gitelman (1985: 62) found that 80.4 percent of émigrés to the United States rated their resettlement agencies as working ''very well; well; or not badly'' (versus 44.3 percent for Soviet Jews in Israel). A New York–based study found that 71 percent of émigrés had a positive impression of NYANA (New York Association for New Americans) (their major resettlement agency), while only 29 percent had a negative impression (Federation 1985: 39). Nevertheless, émigrés also confront difficulties in adjusting to the United States. According to several studies, the major problems encountered by Soviet Jews in the United States are what Simon, Shelly, and Schneiderman (1986) call ''bread and butter issues.'' They include (in rank order) learning English, finding a job, earning enough money, and missing family and friends.

Unlike most immigrants who have little experience in obtaining government services, former Soviets come from a society where substantially more of life's necessities are distributed by government agencies than is the case in the United States. Accordingly, a unique problem that former Soviets confront is relearning ways of interacting with agencies in a dramatically different social context. A fairly large amount of literature has addressed Soviets' confrontations with this change in areas of service provision involving cash assistance, physical and mental health, job placement, and community socialization (Gold 1987, 1992; Markowitz 1993; Drachman and Halberstadt 1992; Ivry 1992).

Culture-based conflicts in several areas of service delivery are challenging to resettlement staff and clients alike. Moreover, since difficult interactions involving job placement, religious socialization, and mental health service provision account for a large proportion of the relations between Soviet Jews and American Jewish agencies, the two communities often develop their images of each other in a hostile setting that overwhelms the goodwill with which both parties initially regard one another.

Children's Academic Adjustment

School-aged émigrés are generally well educated and tend to excel in U.S. schools. For example, in a 1991 comparison of the 12 largest immigrant groups in the New York City public schools (grades 3–12) who had been in the country three years or less, students from the former USSR ranked first in reading scores, second in math, and fifth in English. Their reading and math scores were much higher than all students in the New York schools, including the native born. In addition, their mean increase in score over the previous year was the highest of all groups in both reading and English, and among the highest in math (New York City Public Schools 1991).

However, because of their lack of English skills and knowledge about the American educational system, émigré students experience frustration in attempting to achieve their goals. Schools in the former USSR are generally more rigorous and accelerated than their American counterparts, with students attending a 10-year (since the 1990s, 11-year) rather than 12-year system. Soviet students begin studying advanced subjects such as calculus and biology before Americans and consequently are years ahead of Americans of the same age.

Because of the lack of structural congruency between the two educational systems, Russian students are frequently required to repeat earlier work. Many
émigré students find this to be destructive to the high levels of achievement
motivation they initially bring to the United States (Gold and Tuan 1993).

SOCIAL ORGANIZATION

Soviet Jews have much interaction with each other but form few organized
community activities (Orleck 1987; Markowitz 1991; Gorbis 1992). Their communities are often geographically concentrated, allowing the many aged émigrés
to interact easily. Many ethnic businesses direct their goods and services to
émigrés. Various publications, especially *Novoye Russkoye Slovo* (New York)
and *Panorama* (Los Angeles), are available as well as Russian language television and radio.

While their communities are marked by divisions based in ideology, region
of origin, educational level, occupation, and other factors, Jews from the former
Soviet Union, especially the great majority from the European Republics, have
many social similarities. They tend to be educated, urbanized, and Russian
speaking and share many common values. Émigrés rely on frequent interaction
for both a social life and obtaining important information and resources. In
contrast, it appears that Soviet Jews do not form a great number of close relations with American Jews or gentiles. One reason for this is the rather broad
cultural and linguistic gap between émigrés and American Jews.

For example, while American Jews tend to be Democrats, most Soviet Jews
are politically to the right and, when naturalized, join the Republican Party (Gold
1992; Noonan 1988; Markowitz 1993; Lipset 1990). A journalist described Jews
from the former Soviet Union as "a community that is staunchly conservative
Republican and is quite puzzled by the left leaning liberalism of American
Jews" (Frumkin 1993: 17).

Resistance to Organization

Émigrés generally avoid formal organizations. This is both because they lack
experience in creating voluntary associations and because in the USSR such
entities were imposed by government bureaucrats rather than voluntarily created
by members. Consequently, émigrés assumed that persons who took leadership
roles in communal activities did so only in order to obtain some personal benefit.
According to a report on Soviet Jewish émigré organizations, émigrés "developed a very strong negative attitude toward such organizations and activities"
and "the figure of the social activist acquired a permanent negative classification
in the minds of many new immigrants" (Ilyin and Kagan 1991: 5).

As a result, the creation of formal organizations among this group has been
difficult. Studies on both coasts describe émigrés' difficulties in creating viable
associations (Gold 1992; Markowitz 1993). Nevertheless, several types of formal

organizations have been identified. First are broad-based groups that seek to unite all Russian Jews or "new Americans"; second are veterans associations; and third are professional associations. Another type involves leisure and cultural activities such as sports teams and musical groups. Finally, Chabad has organized synagogues for Russian speakers in several localities (Freedman 1993). According to Ilyin and Kagan's (1991) report on Soviet émigré associations, in different ways, these organizations seek to help newcomers adapt to the United States, to retain Russian-language culture, and to develop a Jewish identity. These organizations vary widely in terms of their emphasis on a Russian or Jewish cultural orientation, their financial well-being, stability, and relations with American Jewish groups.

While émigrés have not developed an extensive network of formalized ethnic organizations, this does not always mean that they seek to avoid each other. Rather, reports continually emphasize Soviet Jews' deep social involvements and their immersion in an extensive array of informal networks that provides for both practical needs as well as a culturally rich social life (Markowitz 1993). For example, nightclubs that offer a lavish variety of Russian-style food and drink and feature entertainers versed in Russian, Jewish, and American popular music have become the centers of Soviet Jewish communities throughout the United States. These settings provide an environment where flashily dressed émigrés spend long evenings in celebration of religious and secular events in a style that combines their Russian, Jewish, and American identities. Former Soviets have also established networks within which they pursue a very wide variety of activities and interests ranging from literature, art, and poetry to politics, sports, various professions, and entrepreneurship (Gold 1992; Markowitz 1993; Simon 1985a).

Finally, when considering Soviet Jews' community patterns, it should be noted that the high levels of skill they possess together with the many benefits they receive from the Jewish community and the U.S. government may reduce their need to create mutual aid associations of the type common among other migrant communities, including earlier cohorts of Russian Jews. Consequently, by their very existence, resettlement services offer a disincentive to group formation.

JEWISH IDENTITY AND BEHAVIOR

Jewish identity is a complex issue for Soviet émigrés. While they have little formal Jewish education (only 4 percent had one year prior to migration), at the same time many appear to have deep feelings of connectedness and strong ethnic or national identification as Jews (Kosmin 1990; Markowitz 1988). The Soviet émigré population is marked by generational variation in religious experience. Three generations of Soviet émigrés in the United States—the elderly, the middle-aged, and the young—have each had a different experience with Judaism (Orbach 1980; Freedman 1993). The elderly are often familiar with traditional

Eastern European Judaism that they learned from their parents or before the Stalinist restrictions of the 1930s. Middle-aged Soviet Jews grew up in an atheistic environment that encouraged the assimilation of Jews. Consequently, their minimal experience of Judaism is secular. Finally, émigré children frequently have had some exposure to contemporary Judaism, since numerous religious activities and scholarships to Jewish camps, schools, and the like, are made available as part of their resettlement program. So the meaning and experience of Jewish identity for each generation on Russian Jews are so different that they offer only limited potential for family unification. It is paradoxical that Soviet Jews—religious refugees—are troubled by problems of religious unification (Hyfler 1991).

A major question in the realm of émigrés' Jewish identity involves the ways through which sentiments are manifested in behavior. A study conducted by the Federation of Jewish Philanthropies in New York noted that these feelings are often strongest when associated with distant, abstract, and symbolic elements of Jewishness and are much weaker when émigrés confront actual, face-to-face participation in organized Jewish life. Perhaps because of their origins in the anti-Semitic USSR, émigrés maintain a private and personal approach to Judaism that does not lend itself to participation in organized Jewish activities (Federation 1985: 24).

A number of surveys have explored Soviet Jews' involvement in Jewish rituals and behaviors and found them to be roughly similar to those of American Jews'. Émigrés who have been in the United States longer and are financially better off tend to be more involved in Jewish life (Kosmin 1990; Krautman 1990). In general, Jewish identification among émigrés is secular or nationalistic rather than religious. Kosmin found that over 60 percent of émigrés surveyed felt that the meaning of being Jewish in America was "cultural" or "nationality," while less than 30 percent felt it was "religious" (Federation 1985: 21; Kosmin 1990: 35).

Despite their lower levels of Jewish education, émigrés from the former Soviet Union are in various ways more "ethnic" (in terms of their involvement with coethnic persons, networks, and outlooks) than many American Jews. This point is illuminated by the work of sociologist Herbert Gans, who describes assimilated, third-plus generation American white ethnics (notably Jews) as maintaining "symbolic ethnicity" through self-selected, identity-related expressive behaviors. This is contrasted with the more extensive reliance on ethnic communities and networks for the fulfillment of basic needs as maintained by first-generation groups such as the Soviets (Gans 1979).

Soviet émigrés' strong ethnic ties are suggested by the responses to several questions in the 1990–1991 New York Jewish Population Study. For example, Jews from the former Soviet Union have higher rates of Yiddish competence, membership in Jewish Community Centers and Young Men's and Women's Hebrew Associations, and reading Jewish publications than all New York Jews. They are much more likely to have close friends or immediate family living in

Table 4.4
Ethnic Ties: All Jews versus Post-1965 Soviet Arrivals

Question	Response	All	Soviet
Do you speak Yiddish?	Yes	38%	42%
Have you or any member of your household been a dues-paying member of a YMHA or Jewish Community Center within the past 12 months?	Yes	15%	17%
Do you regularly read any Jewish publications?	Yes	41%	49%
Do you or your spouse have any close friends or immediate family living in Israel?	Yes	46%	83%
Of the people you consider your closest friends, would you say that:	Few or none are Jews	6%	0.20%
	Most, almost all, or all are Jewish	66%	96%
When it comes to a crisis, Jews can only depend on other Jews:	Disagree	47%	25%
	Agree	50%	68%

Source: Horowitz 1993.

Israel than all New York Jews, exceed all New York Jews by 30 percent in terms of asserting that most or all of their closest friends are Jewish, and much more strongly believe that when it comes to a crisis, Jews can only depend on other Jews. Finally, Jews from the former USSR have more negative views of Jewish-Gentile intermarriage, even when the non-Jewish spouse converts to Judaism, than do all New York Jews. These measures suggest that despite Russian émigrés' lower rates of Jewish education and religiosity than American Jews, they are more involved with other Jews in certain ways than are members of the larger community (see Table 4.4).

Jewish Socialization

The Jewish community's resettlement system encourages Soviet émigrés to plan their adjustment to the United States in accordance with the values of

American Jewish life. Some émigrés have responded favorably to such pro-gramming. They have joined synagogues, sent their children to Jewish day schools and camps, participated in Jewish community activities, and raised funds for Jewish philanthropies. National and New York–based surveys have deter-mined that around 40 percent of Soviet Jews belong to synagogues—roughly the same proportion as members of the larger community (Kosmin 1990; Ho-rowitz 1993). In addition, anecdotal evidence suggests that religious amalga-mation is taking place. For example, the Chabad Russian Center of Los Angeles hosted 4,000 émigrés for its Yom Kippur services in 1993, while the Beth Shalom People's Temple in Brooklyn, New York, has attracted some 500 Soviet Jewish members (Estulin 1993; Ruby 1993).

In general, however, émigrés are only selectively concerned with American Jewish activities. Some émigrés remain unaffiliated because their most imme-diate priorities in the United States are finding jobs and getting their families established. Others avoid involvement with American Jewish institutions be-cause they resent the condescending way in which they are sometimes ap-proached by staff who, in one article, were urged "to create a Jewish need in him [the Soviet émigré] just as we would with a child, while at the same time understanding that he is no child" (Goldberg 1981: 161). Conflicts involving religious and cultural socialization for Soviet émigrés were most notable during the early years of resettlement (prior to the mid-1980s) when media exposure to the image of the pious refusenik made most American Jews assume that Soviet Jews would be both religious and anti-Soviet.

Just as émigrés sometimes resist efforts at religious training, most also retain a strong "Russian" identity. While Soviet Jews generally dislike communism, many retain a feeling of attachment to the culture, language, cuisine, literature, landscape, and way of life of their homeland and are unwilling to abandon these traditions in favor of Americanisms. When Americans approach former Soviets with strident criticisms of Russia and clear expectations that they should forsake their background, émigrés become alienated. Consequently, just as many Soviet Jews resisted the German-American Jews' assimilation programs early this cen-tury, so do today's former Soviets often dislike Americanization activities (Howe 1976; Mindel, Habenstein, and Wright 1988).

By the late 1980s, official acknowledgment was finally given to the fact that most Soviet Jews were not religiously active. Initial hopes for rapid religious assimilation were replaced by a more realistic acknowledgment of Soviet émi-grés' secular and ethnic rather than religious identification (Carp 1990). An American rabbi who works with Soviet Jews reflected on this realization: "One of the disappointments that many rabbis felt was that most of the Soviet Jews did not find a need to express their Jewishness. We should have understood this, because they come from a secular, atheistic country, but it was difficult to ac-cept" (Barber 1987: 41).

CONCLUSIONS

The patterns of economic and social adaptation and the political outlooks of Soviet Jewish émigrés appear to be fairly clear. Skilled, educated, and availed of excellent services, émigrés have achieved an enviable economic record. While they learn English quickly, most prefer to interact among themselves in an informal context that emphasizes their own language and culture. Identifying as Jews, most are not highly religious but maintain certain forms of ethnic attachment to their community that exceeds that of American Jews.

Accordingly, what remains to be seen is the degree to which these émigrés will become involved with Jewish life in the future, either on their own terms or in consort with the American Jewish community. While the general consensus regarding former Soviet Jews' communal and religious lives suggests that they are neither highly organized nor religiously involved, that image is beginning to be challenged as a number of reports reveal that groups of émigrés in various communities throughout the United States are creating organizations and becoming absorbed in Jewish life.

As today's émigrés often point out, Jews from the former Soviet Union are drastically different from the cohort of their coethnic countrymen who entered the United States from Russia almost a century ago. The early group were relatively unskilled and immersed in the collective folkways of Eastern European Judaism (Yiddishkeit). In contrast, today's contingent are religiously untrained, politically conservative, individualistic in outlook, and by and large, sophisticated urban professionals. Nevertheless both migrant communities cared deeply about the traditions of their European way of life and, while grateful to America for the opportunities and freedom it offered, strongly guarded their independence from established Jews, who they saw as overzealously planning their Americanization.

NOTES

1. While the Soviet Union no longer exists, the term *Soviet Jews* will be used interchangeably with *Jews from the former Soviet Union*. The less clumsy *Russian Jews* (a term often used by émigrés themselves) will not be used because most émigrés actually came from the Ukraine.

2. For this article, data on Soviet émigrés from the 1990 census (5 percent public use microdata sample) were drawn from the two largest locations of their settlement, New York City and Los Angeles County. These two locations accounted for over 50 percent of post-1965 migrants from the USSR tabulated in the 1980 census. A comparison of descriptive statistics of these two populations shows a very high degree of similarity. Since Armenians are a significant non-Jewish refugee group that has entered the United States from the former USSR since 1965, persons who claimed that they had Armenian ancestry or spoke Armenian at home were excluded from our analysis, as well as from

figures cited from Chiswick (1995). Additional data are from computer runs from *The 1991 New York Jewish Population Study* (Horowitz 1993).

3. According to the 1990–1991 Jewish Population Study of New York, the fraction of former Soviet Jews who have seriously considered living in Israel exceeds the rate of all Jewish New Yorkers by only 11 percent (30 percent of post-1965 Jewish immigrants from the former Soviet Union have considered living in Israel, while 19 percent of the entire Jewish community has done so).

4. Figures for 1990 entrants are unavailable and hence are not included in this tabulation.

5. According to the 1990 census, 41,995 persons born in the USSR have migrated to Los Angeles County from 1965 to 1990. Of these, 28,267 (67 percent) were Armenians (i.e., they reported Armenian ancestry or spoke Armenian at home). In contrast, of the 60,044 post-1965 émigrés from the former USSR in New York City, only 543 (1 percent) were Armenian.

6. According to the 1990–1991 Jewish Population Study of New York, 33 percent of post-1965 Jews born in the former Soviet Union are registered to vote.

REFERENCES

Barber, Jennifer. 1987. The Soviet Jews of Washington Heights. *New York Affairs* 10 (1):34–43.

Brym, Robert J. 1993. The Emigration Potential of Jews in the Former Soviet Union. *East European Jewish Affairs* 23(2):9–24.

Carp, Joel M. 1990. Absorbing Jews Jewishly: Professional Responsibility for Jewishly Absorbing New Immigrants in Their New Communities. *Journal of Jewish Communal Service* 66(4):366–374.

Chesler, Evan. 1974. *The Russian Jewry Reader.* New York: Behrman House Inc.

Chiswick, Barry. 1993. Soviet Jews in the United States: An Analysis of Their Linguistic and Economic Adjustment. *International Migration Review* 27:260–285.

———. 1995 Soviet Jews in the United States: Language and Labor Market Adjustments Revisited. Department of Economics, University of Illinois at Chicago, Mimeographed.

Dorf, Nina, and Fay Katlin. 1983. The Soviet Jewish Immigrant Client: Beyond Resettlement. *Journal of Jewish Communal Service* 60(2):146–154.

Drachman, Diane, and Anna Halberstadt. 1992. A Stage of Migration Framework as Applied to Recent Soviet Emigres. In *Social Work with Immigrants and Refugees.* Edited by Angela Shen Ryan. New York: Haworth Press. Pp. 63–78.

Eckles, Timothy J., Lawrence S. Lewin, David S. North, and Danguole J. Spakevicius. 1982. *A Portrait in Diversity: Voluntary Agencies and the Office of Refugee Resettlement Matching Grant Program.* Washington, D.C.: Lewin and Associates.

Estulin, Naftoli. 1993. Chabad Russian Immigrant Program and Synagogue. Leaflet, September.

Farber, Bernard, Charles H. Mindel, and Bernard Lazerwitz. 1988. The Jewish American Family. In *Ethnic Families in America.* Edited by Charles H. Mindel, Robert Habenstein, and Roosevelt Wright, Jr. New York: Elsevier. Pp. 400–437.

Federation of Jewish Philanthropies of New York. 1985. Jewish Identification and Affiliation of Soviet Jewish Immigrants in New York City—A Needs Assessment and Planning Study. Unpublished papers.

Frankel-Paul, Ellen, and Dan N. Jacobs. 1981. The New Soviet Migration in Cincinnati. In *Studies in the Third Wave: Recent Migrations of Soviet Jews to the U.S.* Edited by Dan Jacobs and Ellen Frankel-Paul. Boulder: Westview Press. Pp. 77–114.

Freedman, Jenny A. 1993. Soviet Jews, Orthodox Judaism, and the Lubavitcher Hasidim. *East European Jewish Affairs* 1(23):57–77.

Fruchtbaum, Irene, and Rodney Skager. 1989. Influence of Parental Values on Dating Behavior of Young Russian Women: A Cross-Cultural Perspective. UCLA Department of Education. Mimeographed.

Frumkin, Si. 1993. Who Are the Russians? *Jewish Journal* (Los Angeles), November 19–25:17.

Gans, Herbert. 1979. Symbolic Ethnicity: The Future of Ethnic Groups and Cultures in America. *Ethnic and Racial Studies* 2(1):1–20.

Gitelman, Zvi. 1978. Soviet Immigrants and American Absorption Efforts: A Case Study in Detroit. *Journal of Jewish Communal Service* 55(1):77–82.

———. 1985. The Quality of Life in Israel and the United States. In *New Lives: The Adjustment of Soviet Jewish Immigrants in the United States and Israel.* Edited by Rita J. Simon. Lexington, Massachusetts: Lexington Books. Pp. 47–68.

———. 1992. Soviet Jewry: A Global View. Paper presented at Wilstein Institute Board Retreat, University of Judaism, Los Angeles, December 12.

Glazer, Nathan, and Daniel Patrick Moynihan. 1963. *Beyond the Melting Pot.* Cambridge: The MIT Press.

Gold, Steven J. 1987. Dealing with Frustration: A Study of Interactions between Resettlement Staff and Refugees. In *People in Upheaval.* Edited by Scott Morgan and Elizabeth Colson. New York: Center for Migration Studies. Pp. 108–128.

———. 1988. Refugees and Small Business: The Case of Soviet Jews and Vietnamese. *Ethnic and Racial Studies* 11(4):411–438.

———. 1989. Differential Adjustment among New Immigrant Family Members. *Journal of Contemporary Ethnography* 17(4):408–434.

———. 1992. *Refugee Communities: A Comparative Field Study.* Newbury Park, California: Sage Publications.

———. 1994. Soviet Jews in the United States. *American Jewish Yearbook* 1994:3–57.

Gold, Steven, and Mia Tuan. 1993. Jews from the Former U.S.S.R. in the United States. San Francisco: Many Cultures Publishing.

Goldberg, Simcha R. 1981. Jewish Acculturation and the Soviet Immigrant. *Journal of Jewish Communal Service* 57(3):154–163.

Gorbis, Boris Z. 1992. Give Us Your Poor Homeless Organizations: A Review of California's Soviet-Jewish Organizations. In *New Voices: The Integration of Soviet Émigrés and Their Organizations into the Jewish Communal World.* Edited by Madeleine Tress and Deborah Bernick. New York: Council of Jewish Federations. Pp. 17–23.

Gorelick, Sherry. 1981. *City College and the Jewish Poor.* New York: Schocken Books.

Halter, Marilyn. 1995. Ethnicity and the Entrepreneur: Self-Employment among Former Soviet Jewish Refugees. In *New Migrants in the Marketplace.* Amherst, Massachusetts: University of Massachusetts Press. Pp. 43–58.

Hebrew Immigrant Aid Society (HIAS). 1991. *Annual Statistics 1979–1991.* New York: HIAS.

———. 1993. *Annual Statistics 1965–1993.* New York: HIAS.

———. 1995. *Annual Statistics 1965–1994.* New York: HIAS.

Horowitz, Bethamie. 1993. *The 1991 New York Jewish Population Study*. New York: United Jewish Appeal—Federation of Jewish Philanthropies of New York.

Howe, Irving. 1976. *World of Our Fathers*. New York: Bantam Books.

Hulewat, Phillis. 1981. Dynamics of the Soviet Jewish Family: Its Impact on Clinical Practice for the Jewish Family Agency. *Journal of Jewish Communal Service* 58(1):53–60.

Hyfler, Robert. 1991. When Is a Refugee No Longer a Refugee and Other Post-Resettlement Observations. *Journal of Jewish Communal Service* 67:285–288.

Ilyin, Pavel, and Mikaella Kagan. 1991. Finding a Niche in American Jewish Institutional Life—Soviet Jewish Émigré Organizations. Paper presented at the Wilstein Institute for Jewish Policy Studies Conference: Soviet Jewish Acculturation—Beyond Resettlement, Palo Alto, California.

Ingram, Judith. 1994. Zhirinovsky Blames Jews. *Lansing State Journal,* November 10: 8A.

Ivry, Joann. 1992. Paraprofessionals in Refugee Resettlement. In *Social Work with Immigrants and Refugees*. Edited by Angela Shen Ryan. New York: Haworth Press. Pp. 99–117.

Jacobs, Dan N., and Ellen Frankel-Paul, Editors. 1981. *Studies of the Third Wave: Recent Migrations of Soviet Jews to the United States*. Boulder, Colorado: Westview Press.

Jacobson, Gaynor I. 1978. Soviet Jewry: Perspectives on the "Dropout" Issue. *Journal of Jewish Communal Service* 55(1):83–89.

Kestin, Hesh. 1985. Making Cheese from Snow. *Forbes,* July 29: 90–95.

Kosmin, Barry. 1990. *The Class of 1979: The "Acculturation" of Jewish Immigrants from the Soviet Union*. New York: Council of Jewish Federations.

Kozulin, Alex, and Alex Venger. 1993. Psychological and Learning Problems of Immigrant Children from the Former Soviet Union. *Journal of Jewish Communal Service* 69:64–72.

Krautman, Jerry Allan. 1990. A Study of the Acculturation and Jewish Identity of Soviet Jews Emigrating to Los Angeles between 1972 and 1989. Master's thesis, University of Judaism.

Lipset, Seymour Martin. 1990. A Unique People in an Exceptional Country. In *American Pluralism and the Jewish Community*. Edited by Seymour Martin Lipset. New Brunswick, New Jersey: Transaction. Pp. 3–29.

Littman, Mark. 1992. *Monthly Data Report for September 1992*. Washington, D.C.: Office of Refugee Resettlement.

Lubin, Nancy. 1985. Small Business Owners. In *New Lives: The Adjustment of Soviet Jewish Immigrants in the United States and Israel*. Edited by Rita J. Simon. Lexington, Massachusetts: Lexington Books. Pp. 151–164.

Mangiafico, Luciano. 1988. *Contemporary American Immigrants: Patterns of Filipino, Korean, and Chinese Settlement in the United States*. New York: Praeger.

Markowitz, Fran. 1988. Jewish in the USSR, Russian in the USA. In *Persistence and Flexibility: Anthropological Perspectives on the American Jewish Experience*. Edited by Walter P. Zenner. Albany, New York: SUNY Press. Pp. 79–95.

———. 1991. The Not Lost Generation: Family Dynamics and Ethnic Identity among Soviet Adolescent Immigrants in the 1970s. Paper presented at the Wilstein Institute for Jewish Policy Studies Conference, Soviet Jewish Acculturation—Beyond Resettlement, Palo Alto, California.

————. 1993. *A Community in Spite of Itself: Soviet Jewish Émigrés in New York.* Washington, D.C.: Smithsonian Institution Press.

————. 1994. Family Dynamics and the Teenage Immigrant: Creating the Self through the Parents' Image. *Adolescence* 29(113):151–161.

Mindel, Charles H., Robert W. Habenstein, and Roosevelt Wright, Jr. 1988. Family Lifestyles of America's Ethnic Minorities: An Introduction. In *Ethnic Families in America: Patterns and Variations, 3rd Edition.* New York: Elsevier. Pp. 1–14.

New York City Public Schools. 1991. Test Scores of Recent Immigrants and Other Students, Grades 3–12. Mimeographed.

Noonan, Leo. 1988. Russians Go Republican. *The Jewish Journal,* November 18–24:31.

Orbach, Alexander. 1980. The Jewish of Soviet-Jewish Culture: Historical Considerations. *Journal of Jewish Communal Service* 57(3):145–153.

Office of Refugee Resettlement (ORR). 1987. *Report to the Congress: Refugee Resettlement Program.* Washington, D.C.

————. 1990. *Report to the Congress: Refugee Resettlement Program.* Washington, D.C.

————. 1991. *Report to the Congress: Refugee Resettlement Program.* Washington, D.C.

————. 1992. *Report to the Congress: Refugee Resettlement Program.* Washington, D.C.

————. 1993. *Report to the Congress: Refugee Resettlement Program.* Washington, D.C.

Orleck, Annalise. 1987. The Soviet Jews: Life in Brighton Beach, Brooklyn. In *New Immigrants in New York.* Edited by Nancy Foner. New York: Columbia University Press. Pp. 273–304.

Panish, Paul. 1981. *Exit Visa.* New York: McCann and Geoghegan.

Portes, Alejandro, and Rubén Rumbaut. 1990. *Immigrant America: A Portrait.* Berkeley: University of California Press.

Rischin, Moses. 1962. *The Promised City.* Cambridge: Harvard University Press.

Ruby, Walter. 1993. Russian Jews in America. *Jewish World,* April 2–8:16–19.

Rumbaut, Rubén. 1989. The Structure of Refuge: Southeast Asian Refugees in the United States, 1975–1985. *International Review of Comparative Public Policy* 1:97–129.

Russell, Raymond. 1985. *Sharing Ownership in the Workplace.* Albany, New York: SUNY Press.

Schiff, Alvin I. 1980. Language, Culture and the Jewish Acculturation of Soviet Jewish Emigrés. *Journal of Jewish Communal Service* 57(1):44–49.

Schwartz, Larry R. 1980. Soviet Jewish Resettlement: Operationalizing Jewish Consciousness Raising. *Journal of Jewish Communal Service* 57(1):50–55.

Shlapentokh, Vladimir. 1984. *Love, Marriage, and Friendship in the Soviet Union: Ideals and Practices.* New York: Praeger.

Simon, Rita J. 1983. Refugee Families' Adjustment and Aspirations: A Comparison of Soviet Jewish and Vietnamese Immigrants. *Ethnic and Racial Studies* 6(4):492–504.

————, Editor. 1985a. *New Lives: The Adjustment of Soviet Jewish Immigrants in the United States and Israel.* Lexington, Massachusetts: Lexington Books.

————. 1985b. Soviet Jews. In *Refugees in the United States.* Edited by David W. Haines. Westport, Connecticut: Greenwood Press. Pp. 181–193.

Simon, Rita J., and Melanie Brooks. 1983. Soviet Jewish Immigrants' Adjustment in Four United States Cities. *Journal of Jewish Communal Service* 60(1):56–64.

Simon, Rita J., Louise Shelly, and Paul Schneiderman. 1986. Social and Economic Adjustment of Soviet Jewish Women in the United States. In *International Migra-*

tion: The Female Experience. Edited by Rita Simon and Caroline Brettell. Totowa, New Jersey: Rowman and Allenheld. Pp. 76–94.

Tress, Madeleine. 1991. United States Policy toward Soviet Emigration. *Migration* 3/4 (11/12):93–106.

―――. 1994. Research Note: The Soviet-Jewish Refugee Populations in Germany and the United States Compared. New York: HIAS.

Tress, Madeleine, and Deborah Bernick. 1992. New Voices: The Integration of Soviet Emigrés and Their Organizations into the Jewish Communal World. New York: Council of Jewish Federations.

U.S. Bureau of the Census. 1983. *1980 Census of Population, Detailed Population Characteristics,* Part 6, California Section 1. Washington, D.C.

―――. 1984. *Statistical Abstract of the United States.* Washington, D.C.

―――. 1993. *1990 Census of Population, Detailed Population Characteristics.* Washington, D.C.

Wirth, Louis. 1928. *The Ghetto Chicago.* Chicago: University of Chicago Press.

Woo, Elaine. 1989. Anticipated Reunion Turns into a Nightmare for Soviet Emigre. *Los Angeles Times,* November 24:B1, B12.

Chapter 5

Iranians

MEHDI BOZORGMEHR

Right after the bombing in Oklahoma City on April 19, 1995, some Americans blamed Middle Easterners—and more specifically, the Iranian government—for masterminding this terrorist act. Although the terrorists were found to be Americans, the stereotype of the Iranian regime as a sponsor of terrorism endures. The widespread allegations are that Iran is trying to sabotage the delicate Arab-Israelis peace process and to acquire the raw materials and technology to build an atomic bomb. The terrorism stereotype does not stop at "state terrorism" and apply only to the Iranian regime since sometimes Iranians abroad are also perceived as Islamic fundamentalists. As such, the status of Iranians in the United States is precarious in a changing world order, where the alleged threat of Islamic fundamentalism has replaced communism. Ironically, Iranians in the United States have done nothing to perpetuate this stereotype. If anything, many Iranian exiles who arrived in the United States after the revolution are opposed to their government's policies—otherwise, they would have remained in Iran; and those who came to the United States before the revolution would have repatriated instead of staying on in the United States. But most Americans cannot make a distinction between the Iranian regime and Iranians, at least not in times of crisis when they become aware of Iranians among them. Iranians become scapegoats anytime conflict between Iran and the United States rages, which has been incessant in one form or another since the advent of the Islamic Republic of Iran in 1979. This is not unique to Iranians, however, and is often the fate of exiles fleeing revolutions in the Third World (e.g., Cubans and Nicaraguans), where new regimes take a vehemently anti-American position in light of past American support of their overthrown dictatorships. However, unlike the early waves of Cuban "golden exiles" before them, who were both well-to-do and well received in the United States because they opposed socialism, Iranians did not enjoy a favorable reception.

There are two major stereotypes about Iranians in the United States; first, as mentioned above, that they are Islamic fundamentalists; and second, that they are affluent. Drawing on vivid images of Iran in the media, especially during the "Iranian hostage crisis," Americans often think of Iranians in the United States as devout Muslims and sometimes as religious zealots. The stereotype of Iranians as very religious Muslims and extremists is inaccurate since most Iranian Muslims in the United States are secular; indeed, the religious Iranian Muslims have no reason for leaving a strict Muslim society (Sabagh and Bozorgmehr 1994). Moreover, there are many non-Muslim Iranians in the United States, including Christians, Jews, and members of other religious minorities, to whom the Muslim label does not even apply (see Kelley, Friedlander, and Colby 1993).

Although religious diversity is not unique to Iranians, it is perhaps more pronounced among them than many other refugee groups. The Iranian group includes a sizable number of religious minorities because the revolution and its outcome in Iran were Islamic and, as such, a threat to its non-Muslim minorities. Despite Iran's relative religious homogeneity, where about 98 percent of its prerevolution population was Muslim, all of Iran's religious minorities are present in the United States. Iranians are especially diverse in Los Angeles, partly because of their concentration—about one out of every three Iranians in the United States is in Los Angeles—and partly because they are drawn to this metropolitan area by the presence of their non-Iranian coreligionists, especially Christian Armenians and Jews.

The second major stereotype of Iranian exiles is that they are affluent, which, unlike the first one, contains a kernel of truth but generally in terms of high occupational status rather than imported wealth. This stereotype is very much at odds with the image Americans have of refugees as the "wretched refuse of teeming shores," inscribed on the Statue of Liberty. It is one thing to come to the United States poor, start at the bottom, and move up through hard work and perseverance, as so often have the immigrants and refugees of yesteryear; it is quite another to arrive directly and obtain desirable jobs. The image of "rich Iranians" dates back to the oil boom of the mid-1970s, when Iran and other members of the Organization of Petroleum Exporting Countries (OPEC) cartel benefited from skyrocketing oil prices. As one of the richest men in the world, the shah of Iran also perpetuated a superrich image by his grandiose and lavish displays of wealth. At that time, however, the vast majority of Iranians abroad were college and university students. The shah's image was thus at odds with the experience of most Iranian students who had to support themselves or were financially helped by their families in Iran. Of course, the stereotype of rich Iranians was reinforced by the exodus of the Iranian exiles in the late 1970s and early 1980s. This stereotype has gone unchallenged to this day, because contrary to the experience of other initially high-status refugees such as Cubans and

Vietnamese, the refugee flow from Iran has not yielded comparably lower social origins. This is not to say that recent refugees from Iran are not needy and deserving of the U.S. government's refugee assistance programs—but only that due to the problems of exit, cost of travel, and difficulties of obtaining a U.S. visa, poor Iranian refugees simply cannot make it to the United States, as have Cuban and Vietnamese "boat people." This feature sets the Iranian exiles apart from all other exiles in the United States since, as will be shown later, Iranians are one of the highest-status groups, not only compared with other refugees but even compared with economic migrants. That is why the term *exile*, which connotes a higher social class origin than *refugee*, is more appropriate for Iranians and is used frequently in this chapter.[1]

IRAN BEFORE THE REVOLUTION

Given the extreme socioeconomic selectivity and religious diversity of Iranians in the United States, it is important not to generalize from Iranian society to Iranian exiles. Nevertheless, a brief introduction to the social, economic, and political conditions of Iran may help the unfamiliar reader better understand the Iranians' backgrounds.

Direct U.S. influence in Iran dates back at least to the Central Intelligence Agency (CIA)–sponsored coup in 1953, which brought back the late shah to power and deposed Dr. Mohammed Mossadeq, the popular Iranian prime minister who advocated the nationalization of Iranian oil. Thereafter, Iran and the United States established close economic, social, and political ties, which in turn facilitated the movement of Iranians to the United States. The shah's new industrialization drive began in the 1960s and took off in the 1970s with the rising oil revenues. The upper classes of Iranian society disproportionately benefited from the booming economy. Unlike the less-populous oil-producing countries in the Persian Gulf (e.g., Kuwait), Iran had the labor force to operate its emerging industries. But the educational infrastructure was neither well developed nor sufficiently advanced to prepare Iranian students for the technical and managerial tasks. Overseas education was the only alternative as the need for skilled labor grew in Iran, outstripping the supply of universities to educate a burgeoning number of high school graduates. Whereas high incomes and savings made it possible for wealthy Iranians to travel and even invest abroad, even the less privileged sent their sons, but rarely daughters, abroad for higher education to avoid mandatory military conscription. Because of the patriarchal nature of Iranian society, females were less likely than males to be sent to study abroad unsupervised. Although Iranian students went to many countries in pursuit of postsecondary education, their favored destination was the United States. By the late 1970s, Iran had become the premier exporter of foreign students in the world and the largest country of origin of foreign students in the United States (Bozorgmehr and Sabagh 1987). The increasing presence of Americans in Iran, and the dominance of the English language globally, established English as the standard foreign language taught in Iranian high schools. By the time they graduated from high school, a basic familiarity with English directed Iranian high school graduates toward English-speaking countries when seeking higher education. The choices of destinations were narrowed down to advanced industrial countries because Iranian students were mostly interested in technical education such as engineering to prepare them for the rapidly industrializing Iranian economy. The United States was the preferred destination because its extensive college and university system could absorb Iranian students, whereas the extremely competitive English system did not offer similar opportunities. The United States also offered more job opportunities than England did, in case students needed to support themselves or supplement their income. This picture changed drastically after the Iranian revolution caught the world by surprise in 1978–1979.

The Iranian revolution came as a shock, not only to observers abroad but also to the people in Iran themselves. If anything, Iran was experiencing an economic boom in the early 1970s, although there was a sharp economic downturn just prior to the revolution. Thus, the causes of the Iranian exodus were initially more political than economic. Later, as the Islamic ideology and the Muslim clergy dominated the revolutionary process and its outcome, fear of religious persecution for the religious minorities (Jones 1984) and intolerable living conditions for the secular Muslims accounted for their mass flight. To the question, What was your main reason for leaving Iran? one Iranian in Los Angeles answered: "Being a Baha'i I was threatened. They threw acid at me. My son was kidnapped. My house was destroyed. I was imprisoned and lost my job." Another Iranian exile in Los Angeles gave the following answer to why he left Iran: "My life was in danger because I was well known and had close contact with the royal family." Early waves of exiles were drawn from the elites and most modernized segments of Iranian society often for political reasons such as the one mentioned above. The emergence of a theocratic state in Iran, the only one of its kind in the world at present, and its imposition of a strict code of behavior were particularly intolerable for the modernizing Iranian women. The following quote echoes the main reason for this group to leave their homeland: "lack of freedom in Iran, meaning limitations of women's work and activities." Iranian exiles also happened to be mostly educated, an education that was sometimes obtained in the United States and in Europe. Thus, there was no cultural, social, and economic gulf between them and Americans, resulting in little conflict on these grounds. In this sense, once more, Iranians do not fit the image of a typical refugee, that is, one who is poor, illiterate, and observes strikingly different customs, whose very presence creates cultural conflict with Americans.

The conflict between Americans and Iranians in the United States has operated at a political, rather than economic or cultural, level. There was hardly any conflict between Americans and Iranian students who lived in the United States before the Iranian revolution. The conflict started during the revolution around America's support of the late shah. The conflict between Iranians and Americans intensified in 1980–1981 when 52 Americans were taken hostage for 444 days in Iran. This sad event in Iranian-American relations coincided with the massive influx of Iranian exiles into the United States, who soon after arrival faced a presidential decree to deport Iranians who were out of legal status in violation of their visas. This was an unfair targeting and scapegoating of Iranians in the United States who had been persecuted by a regime that they had left behind. U.S.-Iran tensions have continued to the present, as shown by the withdrawal of Conoco's deal with Iran in 1995 due to presidential pressures. Unfortunately, every time these tensions break out as conflicts, Iranians in the United States become scapegoats and suffer the consequences.

EXODUS AND TRANSIT: FROM FOREIGN STUDENTS TO EXILES

Iranian migration to the United States came in two distinctive waves: before and after the Iranian revolution of 1978–1979. As pointed out above, Iranians who emigrated before the revolution were mostly students—although there were also a few economic migrants—while those who have left after the revolution are mainly exiles or political refugees. The consolidation of the Islamic Republic of Iran, on the one hand, and the growth of the Iranian community in the United States, on the other, have sustained the migration of Iranians to the United States. Data from the Immigration and Naturalization Service (INS) and the U.S. Census Bureau tell the same story: Iranian migration to the United States continues unabated, although not at the late 1970s high levels (see Tables 5.1 and 5.2).

From 1950 to 1992, 247,261 Iranians entered the United States as legal immigrants, that is, with a permanent residency visa. Illegal immigration from Iran to the United States is negligible, visa overstayers excepted. Although some of these had immigrant status upon arrival, most were admitted with student visas or as visitors for pleasure and subsequently changed their status to permanent residents. Given the difficulties of obtaining a U.S. visa, it is not surprising that most Iranians are not admitted to the United States directly as immigrants. The data in Table 5.1 further show that there was a sharp increase in the number of Iranian immigrants from 2,730 in the 1950s to 8,895 in the 1960s and 23,230 during 1970–1977. Starting with the Iranian revolution in 1978–1979, and in spite of the closure of the American embassy in Iran, there was a rapid acceleration in the number of immigrants admitted from Iran, reaching an annual average of over 10,000 in the early 1980s. Almost one quarter of all Iranian immigrants first entered the United States as refugees or were classified as asylees after their arrival, which qualifies the Iranian migration as part of an exile or refugee stream. Many of those who have arrived with immigrant visas are refugees from outside the United States. For the first 30 years, from 1950 to 1980, there were only 732 Iranian refugees and asylees, but this number jumped dramatically to 58,381 in the next 12 years, due to the Iranian revolution. The number of refugees/asylees would have been even higher if all Iranians who were exiles in a sociological sense were granted refugee or asylee legal status.

Table 5.1
Iranians Admitted to the United States, 1950–1992

Year	Immigrants	Refugees & Asylees
1950-59	2,730	
1960-69	8,895	
1970-76	18,969	
1977	4,261	732
1978	5,861	
1979	8,476	
1980	10,410	
1981	11,105	366
1982	10,314	701
1983	11,163	1,450
1984	13,807	3,544
1985	16,071	5,420
1986	16,505	6,022
1987	14,426	5,559
1988	15,246	6,895
1989	21,243	8,167
1990	24,977	8,649
1991	19,569	8,515
1992	13,233	3,093
Total	247,261	59,113

Source: Compiled from annual statistical yearbooks of the U.S. Immigration and Naturalization Service.

Of the almost 35,000 Iranian immigrants admitted before the revolution (i.e., 1950–1987), less than half (almost 14,000) were new arrivals (Bozorgmehr and Sabagh 1987; Table 5.1), whereas of a total of 108,694 Iranian immigrants admitted in 1987–1990, one third (30,565) were new arrivals. Thus, the trend among Iranians is toward obtaining permanent residency and settling down in the United States, a trend that has become more pronounced after the revolution. Data reported by the INS, but not shown here because they are no longer an important factor in Iranian migration, indicate that the number of nonimmigrants (mainly students but also visitors) from Iran has dropped precipitously from its peak in 1977–1979.

Iranians who came to the United States before the revolution were mostly students or economic migrants and were very distinctive from the exiles who

Table 5.2
Selected Characteristics of Foreign-Born Iranians, 1990

Characteristic		%
Sex	Male	57%
	Female	43%
Period of immigration	1985-1990	31%
	1980-1984	19%
	1975-1979	34%
	Before 1974	16%
Education*	College or higher	51%
	Some college	20%
	High school diploma	16%
	Some high school	7%
	Elementary school	6%
Occupation**	Higher white-collar	43%
	Lower white-collar	43%
	Blue-collar	14%

Notes:
*Education data are based on Iran-born persons aged 25 and over.
**Employment data are based on Iran-born persons aged 16 and over.
Higher white-collar = Managerial and professional occupations.
Lower white-collar = Technical, sales, clerical, and service occupations.
Blue-collar = Farming, craft, and transportation occupations, plus operators and laborers.
Source: U.S. Bureau of the Census 1993.

arrived after the revolution. Using period of arrival in U.S. census data, we have shown that the characteristics of the Iranian exiles differ from those of immigrants (Sabagh and Bozorgmehr 1987), which in turn affects their social and economic integration. However, the U.S. census data are imperfect for this purpose because the Iranian revolution occurred in 1978–1979, and the census data are reported for the 1975–1980 arrivals, thus resulting in a mixed group of exiles and immigrants. Our survey of Iranians in Los Angeles remedied this problem by asking the respondents about their motivation for leaving Iran. Those who stated that their motivation was either religious and/or political persecution were classified as exiles, and the rest were classified as immigrants. This intragroup comparison showed that less than half of the Iranian householders in Los Angeles (43 percent) were exiles, and over half (57 percent) were immigrants.

Moreover, this classification closely corresponded with the timing of the Iranian revolution. Yet, only one third of the sociologically defined exiles obtained legal refugee/asylee status. Surprisingly, one seventh of immigrants also obtained this status. Clearly, many Iranians could not prove a well-founded fear of persecution despite their original religious and/or political motivations for leaving Iran.[2]

It was relatively easy to acquire a U.S. visa before the seizure of the American embassy in Iran and its indefinite closure. It is now impossible to obtain a U.S. visa directly from Iran since there is no American embassy in that country. After the closure of the American embassy, Iranians have had to go to a third country to receive a visa to come to the United States. For Iranian exiles, the modal pattern has been to enter the United States on a tourist or visitor visa and subsequently to apply for political asylum. Some have applied for refugee status directly from Iran, but this process often has taken much longer. Other more fortunate ones who are immediate relatives of Iranian naturalized citizens have obtained an immigrant visa through the family reunification provisions of American immigration law.

Coming to the United States is becoming less economically feasible for Iranians since the Iranian currency is weak against the dollar, especially on the black market, thus requiring substantial money to finance the long trip. Moreover, the Iranian government levies a fee for leaving Iran and will not allow its citizens to take large amounts of money out. At the same time, given the anti-immigrant, and particularly antirefugee, backlash in Europe, most European countries have clamped down on their immigrant admissions. This is even more of a problem for Iranians because European countries are even more concerned than the United States about the threat of terrorism. Thus, the ultimate objective of Iranians who can afford it is to emigrate to the United States.

Religious minorities, in particular, fled Iran under treacherous conditions, often paying a middleman to get them across the border to neighboring Turkey and Pakistan, which did not require a visa for Iranians. From there, they usually migrated to European countries (Germany, Italy, Spain, Scandinavia) before obtaining a visa to come to the United States. Iranians, especially those who were not allowed to leave the country, recount horror stories about their flight. One such story was even portrayed in the otherwise sensational and stereotypical movie *Not Without My Daughter,* when an American woman tried to escape the wrath of her Iranian husband and leave Iran with her daughter.

Since official data do not report religion, our survey of Iranians in Los Angeles is important for examining the differences in patterns of migration of Muslims and religious minorities. The survey data on Iranians in Los Angeles tell a distinctive story about the exodus of non-Muslim minorities from Iran. While none of the Muslims left Iran for religious reasons, many Baha'is did so since they were singled out by the Islamic Republic for political persecution. Less than half of the Iranians in Los Angeles left Iran for political reasons, though this percentage was higher for Jews than it was for other groups. Combining political and religious reasons, a higher proportion of the more persecuted religious minorities (i.e., Baha'is and Jews) than of the less persecuted minority (Armenians) or the Muslim majority thus become exiles in a sociological sense. Among all Iranians who left Iran for reasons other than political ones, an insignificant segment did so for economic reasons. Similarly, education and family were much more important reasons for leaving Iran than were economic reasons, which shows that Iranians are not economic migrants (Bozorgmehr 1992: Ch. 4).

As far as the stereotypical issue of wealth is concerned, some of the earliest Iranian exiles to the United States managed to bring out considerable capital, although no one knows exactly how much. But many of them had to leave much of their assets behind, often in the form of not readily liquidable real estate. (Iranians invested in fixed assets such as real estate because of the erratic and uncertain economic climate in Iran under the shah.) As in many other refugee streams, the recent Iranian exiles to the United States, many of whom are members of religious minorities in Iran, are not as well-off as the early waves.

INITIAL RESETTLEMENT—WITHOUT A HELPING HAND

Unlike legally defined refugee groups such as Cubans and Vietnamese before them, Iranians for the most part received little help in their migration and resettlement from the U.S. government. Less than one in five of Iranian exiles in Los Angeles received any type of organizational help in moving from Iran to the United States, and those who did were mostly religious minorities from Iran, for example, Jews, who were assisted by international coreligionist organizations such as the Hebrew Immigrant Aid Society (HIAS).

One may argue that many of the Iranians who originally came to the United States as temporary migrants (e.g., students) have become "self-imposed exiles" by changing their mind about returning to Iran. But integration to American society can also bring about a change of mind among sojourners, in addition to the changing conditions in the homeland. Clearly, exiles left Iran more permanently than did the immigrants, which is reflected in their migration pattern. While half of Iranian immigrants migrated alone, only about one third of exiles did so. Moreover, religious minorities from Iran have migrated to the United States more in family units than have the Muslim majority due to the former's precarious status in Iran. Moving with the nuclear family, and even the extended one, has reduced the probability of return to the country of origin for the minorities. When asked about their plans upon arrival in the United States, about two thirds of Iranian exiles in Los Angeles indicated that they planned to stay in the United States permanently, and the rest said they would like to go back to Iran soon or someday. At the time of the survey in 1987–1988, an even greater percentage (83 percent) planned to stay in the United States. Even among Iranian immigrants, less than half (41 percent) of whom had originally planned to stay in the United States, the proportion had increased to 73 percent. Ironically, the main reasons behind change in plans for both exiles and immigrants were identical, namely, the Iranian revolution, political and religious persecution, and the Iran-Iraq war in the 1980s.

INS data on categories of Iranian admissions to the United States and our survey data on Iranians in Los Angeles are consistent in that they both show that, by and large, Iranians arrive in the United States under temporary student and visitor visas (Bozorgmehr 1992; Bozorgmehr and Sabagh 1988). This pattern has changed as Iranians have increasingly become naturalized citizens of the United States and can bring their immediate relatives over through family reunification. Iranian exiles suffered from a major change in the U.S. refugee laws in 1980. U.S. policy shifted from granting outright refugee and parolee status to migrant groups, as it had done with Cubans and Indochinese in the past, to a case-by-case evaluation of an individual migrant. Each applicant for refugee status now has to have proof of persecution beyond reasonable doubt if returned to his/her respective country of origin. Thus, it has become easier to arrive in the United States temporarily and subsequently apply for political asylum than to apply for refugee status from overseas. Iranians have faced serious difficulties in obtaining U.S. visas, especially after the Iranian hostage crisis of 1980–1981. An INS restrictive policy toward Iranians was in effect during those 444 days when Americans were held hostage in Iran. Simply, many more Iranians would migrate to the United States if they could obtain U.S. visas more easily. For instance, fleeing an antagonistic revolutionary regime, Iranian religious minorities in Los Angeles have relied on asylee/refugee visas more so than have Muslims, but the percentages admitted under this visa are low compared with the proportion of these subgroups who are sociological exiles. A lack of correspondence between political/religious reasons for leaving Iran and refugee/asylee visas points to the difficulty of obtaining refugee/asylee visas even among the persecuted Iranian religious minorities. Limited in options to get a U.S. immigrant visa, less than half of Iranians in Los Angeles have had to turn to visitor visas to come to the United States. However, a much higher percentage of religious minorities than Muslims were reclassified as asylees, indicating that religious minorities from Iran were in a better position to prove fear of persecution if returned to Iran than were Muslims.

ECONOMIC INTEGRATION

Immediately after the Iranian revolution in 1980, Iranians were one of the highest-status immigrant groups in the United States, as measured by their levels of education and occupation. At that time, however, Iranians consisted mainly of recent exiles fleeing the revolution and former college students. As such, it was not surprising that Iranians were highly educated professionals and affluent entrepreneurs. Over 15 years after the revolution, it is timely to know whether, and if so how, the arrival of recent refugees has affected the socioeconomic characteristics of Iranians in the United States.

Since the Los Angeles region has the largest concentration of Iranian immigrants in the United States, and the most comprehensive data are available through our survey of Iranians in Los Angeles, I will focus on this metropolitan area. Whenever applicable, however, the characteristics of Iranians in Los Angeles will be compared with their counterparts in the United States. The 1990 U.S. census enumerated about 285,000 Iranians in the United States, of whom 100,000, or 35 percent, were in the Los Angeles metropolitan area (five-county region), and about 80,000, or 28 percent, were in Los Angeles County. The vast majority of Iranians in Los Angeles were foreign born in both 1980 and 1990, mainly due to the influx of new exiles and refugees.

Most discussions of the economic integration of refugees have centered around the difficulty that these migrants face in transferring their skills and, as a result, experiencing more initial downward mobility than economic migrants. However, few studies have collected data on the occupational background of exiles/refugees in order to adequately address this issue, and when they have, the data are not often comparable since the economic structures of refugee sending and receiving countries are vastly different. To correct this problem, we used the U.S. census occupational classification for occupations in Iran and the United States. Although the broad U.S. census classification was also adopted in the Iranian census, it is admittedly less than perfect for the Iranian economy. Nevertheless, it serves a useful function in evaluating the occupational mobility of Iranian exiles and immigrants to the United States. Ultimately, a group's economic well-being should be evaluated in terms of the education and skills that it possesses, and in this sense, it is also important to examine the performance of Iranians in the United States.

According to the 1990 U.S. census, with half of its population 25 years and older holding a bachelor's degree or higher (see Table 5.2), foreign-born Iranians were the third-most highly educated major immigrant group (more than 100,000 persons) in the United States after Asian Indians and Taiwanese. As such, Iranians were the most highly educated group among exile or refugee groups. As Table 5.2 further indicates, less than half of Iranian immigrants and exiles in the United States hold higher white-collar (professional and managerial specialty) occupations. Only 14 percent of Iranians hold blue-collar jobs, but even this low rate is misleading since it contains occupations like hairdressers (a female-dominated Iranian occupation). Insofar as Iranians have opted for self-employment, they have sidestepped the usual problems of transfer of skills that wage and salaried refugees usually face. This is not to suggest that entrepreneurs do not experience downward mobility as their businesses are scaled down and/or are often forced to venture into new and uncharted business territories. Nevertheless, there is some occupational continuity since the refugees could use their entrepreneurial acumen to become established in business and not be at the mercy of employers who might question their knowledge and skills.

Self-employment is also a well-established traditional route to upward mobility. The rate of self-employment is higher among Iranians in the United States (21 percent) than it is among many other groups. But unlike other immigrant groups who turn to self-employment because of disadvantages in the labor market (e.g., language handicaps), the presence of former commercial minorities such as Jews and Armenians and availability of capital partly account for the high self-employment rate of Iranians. The rate of Iranian self-employment is even higher in Los Angeles than it is in the United States as a whole due to the greater presence of Armenians and Jews. Iranians also have a much higher self-employment rate compared with the other groups—33 percent versus 24 percent, 19 percent, and 8 percent for non-Hispanic white, Asian, and Hispanic immigrant males, respectively, in 1990 in Los Angeles.

Like most other groups, the socioeconomic status of Iranian females is lower than males. Still, with 42 percent holding a bachelor's degree and higher, Iranian women in the United States are very highly educated. The most striking feature of the economic integration of Iranian females is their very low rate of labor force participation, which is mainly a carryover from Iran. Yet Iranian women have made great strides toward working outside the home in the United States, as evidenced by a substantial increase in their labor force participation over time. Although part of this is due to the fact that in 1980 many Iranian exiles from the 1978–1979 revolution had just arrived and were not yet in the labor force, as shown to be the case among males, the increase in the labor force participation of females is more substantial than that of the males. The female rate of labor force participation is noticeably higher in the United States than it was in Iran, where even in 1990 it was below 20 percent. But the overall Iranian rate is misleading in light of the extreme selectivity of Iranian immigrant women. Nevertheless, Iranian women are increasingly entering the labor market in the United States (Dallalfar 1994), which has significant effects for the changing sex roles and family life of this population.

Immigrants, such as Iranians, usually concentrate in specific occupations or industries to continue an economic heritage, to have greater opportunities of working with coethnics, to fill a void in the existing economic structure, and to avoid discrimination, among other reasons. To put it more succinctly, immigrants carve out occupational and industrial niches.[3] For Iranians, this pattern of occupational or industrial concentration has more or less persisted over time. Almost all of the top ten Iranian niches in Los Angeles are managerial, professional, and sales—highly desirable and lucrative niches. Remarkably, self-employment levels are very high for many of the niches. Self-employment rates exceed 30 percent, not only for high-status occupations (physicians) but also for blue-collar workers (hairdressers) (Bozorgmehr, Der-Martirosian, and Sabagh in press).

Ultimately, there are two ways to assess the occupational success of Iranians. First, the occupational distribution of Iranians is compared with that of other groups, particularly native-born whites.[4] Second, the earnings of Iranians are compared with those of the native-born white population. But since the two groups differ in characteristics that could influence earnings, we have to consider not only the actual earnings of Iranians but also the earnings they would receive if they had the same characteristics as native-born whites.[5]

In 1990, the occupational distribution of foreign-born Iranians in Los Angeles was most similar to that of native-born whites and least similar to that of native-born blacks.[6] This pattern has persisted since 1980, and holds true for industry with minor modifications. Thus, Iranians in Los Angeles are much more like native whites and Asians than like African-Americans and Hispanics in their occupational and industrial distribution. Since, on the average, native whites and Asians hold better jobs than Hispanics and blacks, occupational dissimilarity is a crude measure of economic well-being for Iranians.

In short, Iranian immigrants and exiles opt for managerial, professional, and entrepreneurial occupations. Whether they are successful, however, is more problematic to establish. Since Iranians have a high degree of professional and entrepreneurial experience, we would expect them to also have higher earnings generally.

Although foreign-born Iranians have relatively high earnings compared with other major foreign-born groups, they are not doing as well compared to native whites, at least not in Los Angeles. Some may argue that these are relatively new immigrants and as such they are expected not to do as well as native whites. If this is the case, then the earlier immigrant cohorts should do relatively better. In general, the longer the length of residence in the United States, the higher the earnings of immigrants. The best way to judge the economic performance of Iranians is to compare their earnings in dollars with the native-born whites, on the assumption that they have similar education, job experience, and so on.[7]

Actual earnings of Iranians are higher than the native whites'. But on the assumption that Iranians have the same characteristics as native whites, their adjusted earnings are lower than the native whites'. This suggests that even though Iranians have higher labor market skills, they are not treated like Anglos or whites despite their racial classification as such. This is also illustrated by the experience of the 1970–1979 Iranian cohort. Comparing the figures for 1980 and 1990, this group does not reap the same economic rewards as do native whites, but nonetheless its earnings have improved during a relatively short ten-year period. The 1970–1979 cohort included high-status exiles from the Iranian revolution, as well as former university students. The most recent immigrant cohort (1980–1990), however, is even more disadvantaged than the earlier cohort due to the influx of less educated and skilled refugees. For instance, among Iranians who immigrated before 1980, 72 percent of males and 42 percent of females aged 25 to 64 had 4 or more years of college education. The corresponding rates for the 1980–1990 cohort are 54 percent for males and 27 percent for females.

Exiles and refugees usually experience downward mobility during the initial phase of resettlement and only later, after improving their English and acquiring occupational skills, may recuperate economically. Iranian immigrants, and especially exiles, have experienced downward social mobility on their first job and even current job compared to Iran. While 45 percent held managerial, executive, and professional specialty jobs in Iran, only 35 percent had similar first occupations and current occupations in Los Angeles by 1987–1988 (Bozorgmehr and Sabagh 1991: table 7). Although the passage of time may help the economic progress of Iranian exiles in the United States, it is doubtful that those who are reaching old age could ever surpass their former occupations.

SOCIAL INTEGRATION

Social integration or *assimilation* refers to the absorption of a minority group into the dominant group. Sociologically speaking, a minority group, such as Iranians, with high levels of education, occupation, and English-language proficiency, is expected to become rapidly integrated into American society. Since Iranians by and large have not assimilated, why do they need and utilize ethnicity, despite their high status and ample resources? Answering this question requires a systematic empirical and analytical explanation, which is beyond the scope of this chapter. True, some Iranians are very assimilated, especially those who arrived much earlier as students, subsequently married Americans, and settled down in places where there are few Iranians. But most, especially the post-revolution exiles who have settled in areas of Iranian concentration such as Los Angeles, New York, and Washington, D.C., have tenaciously resisted integration. One may argue that the difference between these two groups has less to do with their migrant type than with the year of immigration—that is, the earlier arrivals are more assimilated than the later ones. But it is not so much time of arrival as the pattern of migration that accounts for the differences in social integration. Iranian students were well on their way toward assimilation because they had migrated on their own, until they were joined by parents and other relatives or relocated within the United States to be near them. Often having migrated with family members, or reunifying with them soon after, the exiles have maintained close ties with relatives, thus reinforcing their ethnicity. This is particularly the case among religious minorities from Iran, who have sometimes moved as entire families. If timing of arrival cannot fully explain remaining ethnicity, then what can? The economic explanation is that reliance on coethnics confers economic advantages to the group such as information for getting a job or starting a business. Some sociologists have argued that the entrepreneurs or self-employed are more ethnic than their salaried counterparts because the former's coworkers are often coethnics. Since Iranians are very entrepreneurial (Light et al. 1993), it is tempting to accept this explanation. This economic explanation of ethnicity, however, does not fully explain the Iranian experience either. For one, there are many professionals among Iranians who are expected to assimilate rapidly due to their English proficiency and high levels of education, which puts them in direct contact with non-Iranians. Although some Iranian professionals are also self-employed, and as such often work in an ethnic milieu, we would expect professional status to promote integration among those who are not self-employed. But even the latter are often very ethnic, though not nearly as much as the entrepreneurs. Therefore, other non-economic factors must account for the lack of integration of Iranians into the mainstream. Perhaps the most important and relevant one here is exile status, whose effect is both direct and indirect. Exile status, because of its involuntary nature, results in a stronger sense of loss for the homeland (Naficy 1993). Furthermore, exiles also include religious minorities from Iran, who are more solitary than most immigrants.

All indicators of ethnicity point to its maintenance among Iranians, at least in Los Angeles. Intermarriage is traditionally used as the best indicator of assimilation. In other words the higher the rate of intermarriage, the more assimilated the group. With 90 percent of Iranian females married to Iranian males (many in Iran), Iranian immigrants and exiles are very unlikely to have intermarried. Besides marriage in Iran, the sizable presence of endogamous minority groups, notably Jews and Armenians, accounts for the low rate of intermarriage.

The use and maintenance of ethnic language are particularly high among foreign-born Iranians, the majority of whom speak their mother tongues at home despite their facility with English. Although Iranians do not come from a country where English is commonly used, they show a remarkable degree of English proficiency. A good command of English reflects their high level of education, which in many cases was obtained in the United States. Among Los Angeles Iranians who speak a language other than English at home, about 80 percent claim that they speak English well or very well.

Iranians in Los Angeles are highly ethnic partly because they consist of religioethnic minorities, e.g., Armenians and Jews, with a long and well-defined history of minority experience. Among Iranian subgroups, the Muslims are the most assimilated, but even they are not fully assimilated because of their exile status and a strong sense of Iranian nationalism.

In Los Angeles, where all Iranian subgroups are present, the extreme diversity of Iranians results in a much more complex pattern of social integration than most other groups. This pattern is less complex in New York where Iranian Muslims and Jews are the two major subgroups. In both Los Angeles and New York, Iranians have non-Iranian coreligionists, a factor that figured partially in their initial settlement in these two metropolitan regions. Thus, if and when social integration occurs, the first tendency among Iranian subgroups is toward coreligionists of non-Iranian background. This is least likely among Muslims, however, who by the very dint of their secularism and their stronger identification with their nationality than religion are unlikely to mingle with devout non-Iranian Muslims. Thus, their integration, which also happens to be the most rapid of all other major Iranian subgroups, is very similar to the traditional assimilationist path, that is, into mainstream American society.

In the case of religious minorities from Iran, the issue of social integration becomes much more problematic than for Muslims. Of particular importance is the extent to which Armenians and Jews, the two largest religious minorities from Iran, have become integrated within the general community of Los Angeles Armenians or Jews. Data on friendship ties and participation in organizations indicate a lack of integration. The close friends of most first-generation Iranian Jews and Armenians are Iranian coreligionists. Furthermore, they are more likely than the Muslims to define their ethnicity in terms of both their nationality and religion, thus setting them apart from other Iranians. At the same time, however, these groups find themselves struggling with a set of coreligionists who define themselves more in religioethnic than in national-origin terms. Although minorities from Iran might find a congenial coreligionist community, cultural and class differences are pronounced enough to prevent social integration among the first generation.

These first-generation differences, however, are slowly disappearing among the second generation. Thus, less than half of Armenian and Jewish Iranian children, both second- and one-and-a-half generation (i.e., born in Iran and emigrated before the age of ten) have exclusively Iranian coreligionists close friends. These generational differences suggest that as Iranian Jewish and Armenian children grow up, they may move away from the Iranian community and become oriented toward the general Armenian and Jewish-American communities. However, this also depends on whom they marry. Not surprisingly, the first choice of almost all Iranian Jewish and Armenian parents is that their children marry Iranian coreligionists. Surprisingly, however, marrying a non-Iranian Jew or Armenian is the second choice, and marrying an Iranian only a third. The attitudes of young Iranian Jews in Los Angeles toward mate selection suggest that their selection of future husbands and wives very closely corresponds to their parents' wishes (Hanassab 1993).

Discrimination and prejudice are two other key factors that prevent or delay the social integration of Iranians, especially Muslims, into American society. Even in multiethnic Los Angeles, Muslims and other Iranians continue to experience discrimination, although the extent of this has decreased since the Iranian hostage crisis from about a quarter who indicated they experienced discrimination to a tenth. On the other hand, about half indicated that there is prejudice against Iranians. One Muslim Iranian in Los Angeles recounted his worst experience of discrimination during the hostage crisis:

With seven years of professional experience and education I received no responses from any companies to which I was sending my résumé. Then I changed my name from Mohammad to Mike in my résumé and immediately got four responses, including one from a company that had not responded to Mohammad.

Sadly, this experience could have been repeated during the Gulf War and the bombing of the World Trade Center in New York since *Mohammad* is also an Arabic name. The owner of an Iranian fast-food restaurant in Los Angeles told us that during the hostage crisis "some of my customers have regretted having eaten at my restaurant after finding out I was Iranian." Another Iranian summing up the influence of the media on American public opinion toward Iranians said: "The daily behavior of Americans depends on what they said about Iranians on TV the night before."

CONCLUSIONS AND PROSPECTS

Iranian exiles and refugees are different from other contemporary exile and refugee groups in the United States. This is mainly due to the background of Iranians and the historical context of their migration, which in turn have affected their social and economic integration into American society and economy. Iran was a rapidly modernizing and Westernizing society when the revolution broke out in the late 1970s. The Iranian revolution and the establishment of the Islamic Republic of Iran had a dual effect: first, forcing the exodus of the elite and members of religious minorities from Iran; second, discouraging the return of Iranian college and university students who were pursuing a technical education in the United States. These two groups, although sociologically distinctive, were not unrelated. Indeed, many of the exiles were relatives of the students, and this factor accounts for the emergence of the United States as the largest concentration of Iranians in the Western world (Bozorgmehr in press). The combination of former students and elite exiles accounts for the highly educated, entrepreneurial, and professional Iranian community in the United States.

In spite of these characteristics and their corresponding contributions to the American economy and society, Iranians in the United States suffer from discrimination and prejudice because of negative stereotypes associated with the Iranian regime. Despite their high-status occupations and English-language proficiency, Iranian immigrants on the whole are surprisingly unassimilated. This level of ethnicity exceeds expectations for highly educated professionals but is congruent with the experiences of entrepreneurial minorities, who make up a large segment of Iranians. However, the main explanation for the maintenance of ethnicity is the presence of former religious minorities from Iran, who were forced into exile by the Islamic outcome of the Iranian revolution. But even Iranian Muslims are more ethnic than would be expected from their socioeconomic status because many are exiles, whether real or self-imposed, and as such have a strong sense of Iranian nationalism or attachment to the homeland. Given this surprisingly high level of retained ethnicity, it is unlikely that Iranians in the United States will become fully assimilated in the near future. If the children of Iranian Armenians and Jews assimilate, they will do so within the general Armenian and Jewish communities. The assimilationist trajectory of Iranian Muslim children is not clear, but they are likely to move toward middle-class American society.

ACKNOWLEDGMENTS

This chapter is based on research supported in part by grants from the National Science and Russell Sage Foundations. I would like to thank David

Haines, Claudia Der-Martirosian, and especially Georges Sabagh for their comments on drafts of this chapter.

NOTES

1. In this chapter, *exile* is a sociological term based on religious or political motivations for leaving the country of origin; *immigrant* refers to all others, including those whose motivations for emigration are social (e.g., to pursue education) and economic. *Refugee* is a formal legal status obtained from outside the country of refuge, and *asylee* is a formal legal status obtained from within the country of asylum.

2. Whenever data are available, the refugee/immigrant distinction is pointed out in this chapter. Unfortunately, this can be done for Iranians in Los Angeles only, for whom we have survey data. Thus, when Iranians in the United States are mentioned, or when other sources than our survey are used, it means Iranians irrespective of their exile or immigrant status.

3. An *ethnic niche* is an occupational or industrial specialization in which a group is overrepresented by at least 50 percent relative to its size in the labor force.

4. The term *native-born whites* is used to refer to native-born whites excluding the Hispanic population.

5. This analysis was carried out for the Los Angeles region to ensure that all groups face the same opportunity structure.

6. This comparison was done by deriving an index of dissimilarity.

7. These comparisons are made using regression analysis. Only the two most recent immigration cohorts (1980–1989 and 1970–1979) are included in the earnings regressions due to the small sample sizes of the two earliest cohorts (1960–1969 and before 1960). The 1980–1989 cohort consists mostly of refugees, whereas the 1970–1979 cohort includes former students and economic migrants. Because of the generally low level of labor force participation of Iranian females, the results are presented for males only to make the comparisons with other groups meaningful.

REFERENCES

Bozorgmehr, Mehdi. 1992. Internal Ethnicity: Armenian, Bahai, Jewish, and Muslim Iranians in Los Angeles. Unpublished Ph.D dissertation, University of California, Los Angeles.

———. In press. Diaspora in Postrevolutionary Period. *Encyclopedia Iranica.*

Bozorgmehr, Mehdi, Claudia Der-Martirosian, and Georges Sabagh. In press. Middle Easterners: A New Kind of Immigrant. In *Ethnic Los Angeles.* Edited by Roger Waldinger and Mehdi Bozorgmehr. New York: Russell Sage Foundation.

Bozorgmehr, Mehdi, and Georges Sabagh. 1988. High Status Immigrants: A Statistical Profile of Iranians in the United States. *Iranian Studies* 21(3–4):4–34.

———. 1991. Iranian Exiles and Immigrants in Los Angeles. In *Iranian Refugees and Exiles since Khomeini.* Edited by Asghar Fathi. Costa Mesa, California: Mazda Publishers. Pp. 121–144.

Dallalfar, Arlene. 1994. Iranian Women as Immigrant Entrepreneurs. *Gender and Society* 8(4):541–561.

Hanassab, Shideh. 1993. Premarital Attitudes of Young Iranians regarding Mate Selection: Arranged Marriage vs. Inter-Marriage. Unpublished Ph.D. dissertation, University of California, Los Angeles.

Jones, Allen K. 1984. *Iranian Refugees: The Many Faces of Persecution.* Washington, D.C.: U.S. Committee for Refugees.

Kelley, Ron, Jonathan Friedlander, and Anita Colby, Editors. 1993. *Irangeles: Iranians in Los Angeles.* Los Angeles: University of California Press.

Light, Ivan, Georges Sabagh, Mehdi Bozorgmehr, and Claudia Der-Martirosian. 1993. Internal Ethnicity in the Ethnic Economy. *Ethnic and Racial Studies* 16(4):581–597.

Naficy, Hamid. 1993. *The Making of Exile Cultures: Iranian Television in Los Angeles.* Minneapolis: University of Minnesota Press.

Sabagh, Georges, and Mehdi Bozorgmehr. 1987. Are the Characteristics of Exiles Different from Immigrants? *Sociology and Social Research* 71(2):77–84.

———. 1994. Secular Immigrants: Religiosity and Ethnicity among Iranian Muslims in Los Angeles. In *Muslim Communities in North America.* Edited by Yvonne Yazbeck Haddad and Jane Idleman Smith. Albany: State University of New York Press. Pp. 445–473.

U.S. Bureau of the Census. 1993. *1990 Census of Population and Housing: Public Use Microdata Samples.* Washington, D.C.

Part III

Anthropological Approaches

Chapter 6

Lao

PAMELA A. DEVOE

Over the last 20 years, particularly since the late 1970s, about 250,000 refugees from Laos have been resettled in the United States, about half of whom are ethnic Lao. Before coming to this industrial, technologically oriented, Judeo-Christian culture, they were a traditional, wet-rice agricultural group, following Buddhist traditions in their home country of Laos in Southeast Asia. While most Americans know the plight of Vietnamese or Cambodian refugees, few are aware of who the Lao are or even how they became homeless, displaced by the spillover of a war raging in neighboring Vietnam. This chapter will look at where these refugees came from; why they were forced to leave their home area; the initial dilemmas faced by the host country and by the refugees as they coped with a radically different sociocultural environment; and finally, how well they were able to adjust and to survive, sometimes by changing and sometimes through keeping and adapting essential traditional cultural characteristics.

THE HOME COUNTRY: LAOS

Topography and Its Impact

Today the landlocked country of Laos shares borders with Vietnam, Cambodia (Kampuchea), Thailand, Burma, and China. Its 91,425 square miles (Thee 1973:1) are defined in part by the Mekong River and the Mekong's fertile valley on the west side. In the north, however, the boundary wanders through extremely mountainous areas, separating Laos from China, Burma, and Thailand (Dommen 1985:1). It shares its longest border, over 1,300 miles, with Vietnam on the east.

The geographic relief of Laos is hilly and mountainous. Generally speaking, the land slopes from the north to the south and from the east to the west, with narrow river bottoms running between steeply sloped land. The mountain areas are often densely forested, particularly in the north. The south is characterized more by glade forest and savannas. The country's most significant alluvial plains are along the Mekong River. The Plain of Jars, an area of rolling hills, is in the north, and the Bolovens Plateau is in the south (Dommen 1985:2).

Transportation, and therefore intracountry communication, is and always has been problematic. Because of the nature of Laos' rivers, including the Mekong River, navigation is impossible except by small boats (Dommen 1985:2). Further, there are only a handful of major roads tying the country together. When the French left Laos, there were only about 1,500 miles of roads, few of which were completely passable in the rainy season. These roads were considerably expanded by the 1970s, although they still remained limited (Thee 1973:4). The country's major cities all lie along the banks of the Mekong River just across from Thailand, including Luang Prabang and Vientiane.

Ethnicity

Ethnically, while Laos is quite diverse, there are three major divisions (Thee 1973:5): the Thai-Lao group (also known as the Lao Loum, Valley Lao, or Lowland Lao), the Khas (also known as Lao Theung or Highland Lao), and the Sinitic and Tibeto-Burman group (called Lao Soung or Mountaintop Lao). Most refugees we refer to as Lao are members of the Lao Loum or Lowland Lao ethnic group. They came into the area in the sixth or seventh centuries from the southern provinces of China, driving the Lao Theung to the lower ranges of the mountains. Today, the Lowland Lao still occupy the valleys, particularly along the Mekong, where they were later influenced by the Khmer and Indian cultures. The Lao Theung, the descendants of the oldest inhabitants of the country, are concentrated in the central and southern part of Laos. The Lao Soung, a more recent addition to the area, came from South China in the early eighteenth century. Arriving late, they settled in the less populated mountains and hilltops of northern Laos. The best known of this group are the Hmong people, another important refugee group in America. (The Hmong refugees are not referred to by the term *Lao* and are discussed in a separate chapter in this volume.) *Lao* has come to refer only to the Lowland Lao people, and that is how the term will be used here. Occasionally, the term *Laotians* will be used in this chapter to refer to all of the citizens of the country of Laos, regardless of ethnicity.

The French Period

Historically, foreign colonies existed in the larger Laotian cities: Chinese, Vietnamese, Indian, Pakistani, Thai, as well as more recent additions of French and American groups (Thee 1973:5–6). Except for the French and Americans, who dealt with political and military issues, foreigners were traditionally most active as merchants and in the trades.

In the past, the whole of northeastern Thailand, the Mekong River Valleys, and south almost to the Gulf of Siam were ruled periodically by Lao rulers and then by Thai rulers. Before the French colonized the area, Laos was ruled by Thailand. Nevertheless, regardless of the changes in leadership, whether Thai or Lao, the common people lived out their everyday lives largely oblivious to the machinations of their ruling elites. In fact, the ethnic Lao lived and migrated throughout this area without major difficulty (Manich 1967:8–9).

Today there are more ethnic Lao people on the Thai side of the border than in Laos itself. The reason for this lies with French colonialism. In the late 1800s, the French took over both Vietnam and Cambodia. They intended to move into Laos and Thailand as well, but the British interfered, and the French ended up with the area east of the Mekong (which was part of Thailand at the time) (Manich 1967:9–10). Saying that they only wanted to give the area back to the Vietnamese, who also laid claim to the territory based on previous historical suzerainty, France took over Laos. Eventually, they gave a northeastern strip to Vietnam. However, this was not a historically Vietnamese area and had ethnic Thai living there. France then went on to give a southern section of Laos to Cambodia. Again, this section was not Cambodian, since the people there were ethnically Lao and still speak Lao. At the same time, the larger ethnic Lao population was divided by the Mekong River. The majority (six or seven times the number in Laos itself [Toye 1968:46]) ended up in former Laotian lands now subsumed politically by Thailand. The minority left behind in Laos lived on the relatively narrow plains along the eastern side of the Mekong River.

Making matters worse, the French included in Laos territory that had never been under Lao domination. Further, the territory held other ethnic groups with a long history of hostility toward the lowland peoples. These ethnic groups were also split into two different nation-states through French intervention: the Kha tribes in the southern highlands of Laos and their relatives in the central high-lands of Vietnam (Toye 1968:46).

During France's 50-year colonial period in Laos, until the end of World War II, the country stagnated economically and culturally (Thee 1973:10; Toye 1968: 44–45). For example, under French influence, the use of a national Laotian language suffered. Laos became part of French Indochina, and French was the lingua franca of the area (Dommen 1985:1–2). Furthermore, the written script used for Lao was that used for Thai (Manich 1967:7–8). The script was devel-oped in 1283 by King Rama Kamhaeng of Sukhotai and adopted by the Lao and the Thai since both were under his leadership at that time. Because of the French colonial policy of not encouraging the local language, Lao books ceased to be published, and only Thai books were available. Even the Buddhist priests had to study and use Thai since all of their religious books were in Thai.

Being much more oriented toward Vietnam and its people, France used Laos to alleviate population pressures in Vietnam by encouraging Vietnamese to mi-grate into Laos (Toye 1968:44). As a result, most of the Laotian political or public administrative offices were given to Vietnamese rather than Lao. A large portion of urban populations consisted of ethnic Vietnamese rather than local ethnic groups.

Further, while illiteracy was standard for most Lao, the available secondary schools were filled with children of immigrants. For example, in the 1930s, only 52 Lao completed secondary school (there was only one secondary school in the country, and it was in Vientiane) compared with 96 Vietnamese children. Most local Lao education remained the responsibility of the Buddhist temples, with monks as teachers. Out of approximately 160,000 school-age children, less than 13,000 attended schools. Thus, there was little development of a middle class. At the same time, the elite class, with their social standing secure under the French, apparently complied with colonial power without complaint (Toye 1968:60).

As a result, by 1945 when the French left, there were at least 50,000 Vietnamese in Laos, and two thirds of primary and assistant teachers in Laos were Vietnamese (Toye 1968:45). The former tradition of literacy and literature in the Lao language had disappeared. As a symbol of the stagnation France imposed on Laos, one need only look at the roads France built during its colonial period. If roads were built at all, it was only

to facilitate the movement of troops from Vietnam in case of civil emergency; Luang Prabang, Sam Neua, Savannakhet were connected by simple metalled roads with the road and rail system of Vietnam, but were not linked to each other. Thus Sam Neua could be reached from Hanoi by dry-weather road in a day, but it was still several days by mountain trail from Luang Prabang and Vientiane which administered it. (Toye 1968:59–60)

Although the French were ousted from Laos briefly between 1945 and 1946 by the Japanese, after the Japanese were defeated in World War II, the French reasserted their power. Between 1946 and 1954, however, France gradually gave Laos more and more rights of self-government (Thee 1973:11). Finally, in 1954 French rule ended. Still the Laotian peoples were not allowed to work out their own governmental system. For, with the French gone, the United States, afraid that Laos would be taken over by Communist leaders, stepped into the power vacuum and became a dominant intervening power.

By January 1, 1955, the United States Operation Mission opened in Vientiane, and the Royal government became a "tame client of Washington" (Thee 1973: 12). The following years were marked by civil war and unremitting aggression by North Vietnamese armies. Every American president, from Dwight Eisenhower through Richard Nixon, approved the use of U.S. forces in Laos (Thee 1973:379–380). By 1971, the *New York Times* estimated that almost 2 million tons of bombs had been dropped by the United States on Laos (which is comparable to *total* tonnage dropped during World War II). Others within Laos estimated that there were actually 3 million tons of bombs dropped on Laos. At the same time, a Staff Report of Edward Kennedy's Subcommittee to Investigate Problems Connected with Refugees and Escapees noted that the *official* count of Laotian refugees was almost 300,000 people. By 1971, figures indicated that one third of the country's people were homeless. The rate of refugee movement correlated directly with the intensity of U.S. bombings.

During this time, the Lowland Lao, who traditionally lived in the Mekong and other river valleys, were significantly affected by the political situation raging around them (Thee 1973:4–5). First, their population was unevenly distributed throughout the valley areas because of the war and the heavy U.S. bombing. Whole areas were depopulated. Second, refugees were forced from the countryside, as it came under the control of the Pathet Lao, to the cities which were under the control of the Royal government.

The Pathet Lao

The Lao People's Democratic Republic was established in 1975. The Communist takeover of Laos was a by-product of Communist takeovers in Vietnam and Kampuchea (Brown 1982:17–23). In the previous year, 1974, the United States and Thailand withdrew their military forces (in accordance with the Paris cease-fire agreement of February 21, 1973), but up to 40,000 Vietnamese soldiers remained in Laos along the Ho Chi Minh trail. Therefore, within a short time, the Pathet Lao, backed by the North Vietnamese, finally established the Lao People's Democratic Republic, ending their 30-year struggle for power.

A consequence of the Pathet Lao takeover was the 1975 "flight of the commercial and political elite" (Brown 1982:22) across the Mekong River and into Thailand. While a few thousand fled by the time of the Pathet Lao takeover, within the next five years (that is, by the end of 1980) an estimated 300,000 Laotian people, of mixed ethnicity, poured into Thailand as refugees (Van-es-Beeck 1982:324). Among these refugees, thousands had already fled their original homeland areas within Laos as the Pathet Lao took over their villages, only to have to flee again, this time into another country.

Concerned by the large number of people crossing their borders, Thailand took the stand that Laotian peoples fleeing to Thailand from their homeland after May 1975 were illegal immigrants with no protection under the law. Nevertheless, because of the large native Lowland Lao population in Thailand, tens of thousands of Lowland Lao and Sino-Lao refugees were able to "blend" into the largely ethnic Lao-Thai peoples in northeastern Thailand. By illegally purchasing identity documentation, their position within Thailand was assured. Others stayed illegally with no documentation and were easily exploited, often taking work at very low wages (Brown 1982:328). Most Laotians, however, tried to reach refugee camps established within Thailand's borders. Once in the camps, they were under the protection of the United Nations High Commissioner for Refugees—according to the Geneva Convention on Refugees of 1967 and its Protocol (Brown 1982:328). For those Lao refugees who made it to the refugee camps, the wait for resettlement to another country was often several years (Chan 1990:2–3; Crisp 1987; Haines 1985:22–23). Many children grew up only knowing camp experiences and camp life. By the time their families were resettled, these children had little, if any, memory of their home villages and traditional life. Their parents had memories of village life, but these, too, were overlaid with other memories of war, escape, and life interned as refugees in Thai camps.

INITIAL RESETTLEMENT[1]

Employment, Housing, and Neighborhoods

Initially, much of the research carried out with Southeast Asian refugees in the United States, including the Lowland Lao, centered on economic aspects of their adjustment (for example, Bach et al. 1983, 1984; DeVoe and Rynearson 1983; Haines 1987, 1989:14). Much of this early research was driven by governmental concern about how much refugee programs were going to cost and, therefore, how long it took each refugee or refugee family to become economically independent. A major consequence of this governmental concern was to push refugees to become self-sufficient as soon as possible. As a result, people were placed in whatever jobs were available, mostly low-paying, unskilled employment (DeVoe 1982, 1993a, 1993b; Hamilton 1986).

While some of the Lowland Lao who fled Laos were from the local elite, or from high military positions, the majority of Lao refugees coming to the United States were involved in nonmechanized labor, such as wet-rice farmers, or were simple soldiers. They had little or no contact with the technology common in an industrialized society. As the research I conducted over a period of several years in St. Louis, Missouri, indicated, much confusion emanated from this disjointed union of cultures. For example, one employer told of a middle-aged woman brought to him as a potential employee within a few days of her arrival in St. Louis. The employer needed more information to complete her application form. When handed a telephone so that she could call her sponsor to get the necessary information, she just looked uncomprehendingly at the phone, never having used one before. Such unfamiliarity, however, did not deter the refugees from accepting whatever jobs were available to them, nor did it keep them from succeeding in mastering their employment tasks to the satisfaction of their employers.

Further, many Lao refugees came with little or no education, could not read and write in their own language, and had held jobs that were nontransferable to the highly industrialized, urban environment in which they found themselves (Haines 1989:8). Since they were refugees, not immigrants, and therefore, had not had time to prepare for the end destination, a large number of people arrived without speaking English (except for what they were able to learn while in refugee camps). Nevertheless, one study indicated they had the highest rate of employment of all Southeast Asian ethnic groups (Hamilton 1986).

Both I (DeVoe 1982) and Blanchard and Harding (1984) found employers often had positive stereotypes concerning Lao workers. However, I also found (DeVoe 1982, 1993b:52) that employers indiscriminately lumped their Lao employees together with other Southeast Asian refugees, particularly with the Vietnamese who had already started coming into the area in large numbers. For example, most employers interviewed professed to have no trouble communicating with their refugee workers, regardless of their lack of English-language skills. Demonstrating the task to be done was often enough. Sometimes sponsoring agencies would be able to initially provide interpreters for the interview and the first few days on a new job. However, on occasion, employers would find an interpreter among the people already working in the factory or business. Unfortunately, because the employers did not recognize the differences among Southeast Asian refugees, it was not uncommon for employers to put Vietnamese workers with newly hired Lao workers to act as ''interpreters.'' Despite such well-intentioned but misguided arrangements, many Lao managed to become productive workers. Employers often commented on their Southeast Asian workers' high degree of dependability, reliability, and general work ethic. On the other hand, perhaps due to the language difficulty, the employers also had very low expectations for their refugee employees, which affected their chances for job advancement and higher wages.

Besides being unskilled and lacking English, another problem related to employment was that when the Lao refugees came to the United States—especially because they were often lumped together with Vietnamese refugees—women's roles were misunderstood (DeVoe 1993a; Stier 1991). In Laos, women worked as entrepreneurs, as marketers, worked in their own fields, and generally were a significant factor in the family's financial success. Working outside of the home was considered normal and even desirable (Van Esterik 1980). This Lao attitude was counter to what many Americans expected. Among the St. Louis Lao, when Lao families first came to the United States, the adult males were often immediately found some kind of unskilled employment, but the married women, especially if they had children, were left unemployed. Women felt this lack of work not only as an economic handicap (less money in the family) but also as a psychological loss. They missed the interaction that they normally would have shared with fellow workers. Such interaction was all the more a loss since they lived in relatively isolated conditions in urban, multiethnic settings, a sharp contrast to when they were at home in their own villages, surrounded by family and long-term friends. As a result, even with language and literacy problems, the Lao women tried to find outside employment as soon as possible. Such commitment to work helped these struggling families handle some of the economic difficulties they faced but also raised another problem: child care.

Since the normal living pattern in the home country was for young Lao couples to move into or near the wife's family's compound, child care was never an important issue. There was usually another extended family member, grandparent, aunt, or cousin, to watch over the children (see also Zaharlick, Jobrack, and Calip-Dubois [1993:184–187] on family dynamics). In the new American environment, many Lao lived in nuclear families with no other blood relatives in the area. One consequence of this living pattern was that there were no inexpensive, reliable, caring adults to watch the children of working parents. As a result, other older, nonrelative Lao might be hired to care for the children. Sometimes, the children were left to their own devices, often watching television for hours, just as many American children do.

The two most obvious ramifications of these child care patterns are: First, a paid babysitter, even if not given much money, significantly diminishes the family's meager economic resources; and second, the children are overexposed to non-Lao values, behaviors, and ideas through mass media (and at the same time, are underexposed to Lao values, behaviors, and ideas because of their isolation from other Lao adults). As a result, whatever the child care solution, if a relative was not available to care for the children, this became another stressor for the family struggling to cope and survive.

Coincident with the low wages newly arrived refugees were able to make was the limited amount of money the family could allot to housing. This was very clear in St. Louis. People were initially resettled in apartments that had major problems, such as plumbing (so that they often only had cold water even in winter, and where the pipes in the walls burst from time to time) and poor maintenance (where the windows rattled in their frames, allowing the winter winds to chill the rooms' temperatures even more). Besides these physical problems, the housing was often in the more dangerous areas of the city (Rynearson and DeVoe 1984). When families moved from their initial apartments in an effort to find more secure living arrangements, they usually ended up in another poor, relatively unsafe, location. Random crime and violence were everyday concerns. People were robbed in their homes, and a few were attacked on the streets. If one family was attacked, the psychological sense of fear and vulnerability was shared by all within the Lao community as word of the event spread. The country they had come to as a safe haven from danger and the unknown was proving to be problematic, unreliable, and even dangerous. Nevertheless, they did not live their lives as paranoid hermits, hidden away from their surrounding neighbors. The neighboring Lao children played in front of their homes among themselves. Lao adults could often be seen chatting on the streets. Teenagers clustered in small groups outside their apartments. Although Lao of all ages sometimes formed friendships with non-Lao coworkers, fellow students, or fellow Christian church members, these neighborhood street scenes remained largely Lao.

Education and the Generations

Because the primary aim of the various levels of government (and therefore also of the sponsoring agencies) for adult refugees was rapid economical self-sufficiency, any schooling was limited. Most received English-language training until they started to work. However, education programs aimed at helping illiterate Lao refugee adults to read and write in English were few and far between. Adults who wanted to update (or "Americanize" by getting a license or certificate in the United States) their professional credentials, or earn a graduate equivalency degree (GED), or get a post–high school education achieved this on their own, on an ad hoc basis (personal communication with service providers).

Children were immediately enrolled in age-appropriate classes. Although there may not have been a large number of any one ethnic group coming into a particular school system, most refugees were resettled in metropolitan areas. Overall, these urban schools had to teach increased numbers of new multiethnic students with little or no English-language skills (personal communications with educators in the Midwest and the Southwest). While in the late 1970s, schools in certain areas (California and Arizona, for example) had bilingual programs for their Spanish-speaking students, this rapid increase in students speaking diverse languages created the need for another type of educational solution. Public schools responded by developing English as a Second Language programs and classes for their ethnically diverse children. The programs were set up to help students learn English as quickly as possible. Besides programs oriented toward students' needs (i.e., to help them adjust and succeed within the school environment), programs and workshops were also developed to aid teachers now faced with multicultural classrooms. These latter training programs encouraged cultural sensitivity on the part of the teachers and often gave concrete clues of what to expect from students of a particular ethnic background. The results of such training were mixed (e.g., DeVoe 1991, 1994). While teachers often learned to differentiate a Lao from a Cambodian from a Vietnamese from a Chinese student, they tended to overidentify students from these various groups with a certain list of cultural characteristics. This led to a more sophisticated form of ethnic stereotyping and affected the way teachers interpreted an individual student's work; for example, Vietnamese students are superior; Lao boys readily get into trouble; Cambodian parents are not interested in their daughters achieving a high school education. Teachers' efforts at helping some students were hampered because of these preconceived categories: The categories often determined the level and type of assistance given.

An example of one area where the attitudes and expectations of school personnel conflict with those Lao parents is the question of what age constitutes adulthood (personal communication with St. Louis service providers and school administrators and staff). In the home country's rural area, a young girl may be married by the age of 16 years, and boys in their late teens (high school age by American standards) may start to court girls of 13 or 14 years of age (middle-school age in the United States). These older Lao refugee boys may exhibit interest in the girls by hanging around the junior high schools they attend. Such behavior concerns school staff members because the boys are considered too old for the middle-school students, and their interest is interpreted as inappropriate by school personnel. Some Lao parents, who want their girls to take advantage of the education offered in the United States, also are unhappy with this and may take action. In one case, a family sent their child away to live with a relative in another city. To some parents, however, this behavior is not necessarily a problem, and so they do not interfere. Zaharlick, Jobrack and Calip-Dubois (1993) have also found that it is now more acceptable to consider marriage after a young person has graduated from high school. On the other hand, there were cases in St. Louis where parents themselves became a problem when they interpreted schooling past the early or middle teenage years to be excessive compared to the level of education their child would have received at home in Laos and excessive compared to the family's need for another employed worker. Family finances may ultimately determine whether a young person, considered a capable adult by home country standards, will remain in school and graduate with a high school degree.

Nevertheless, the end result of the Lao students' involvement in the American educational system is that they are better able to deal with their surrounding environment than their parents are. The students, even at a young age, often become and remain the family interpreter with non-Lao. This simple act of being the interpreter upsets the balance of power between the parent and the child. This is an issue that will not diminish within the Lao, or any refugee, community. Non-English-speaking adults may never achieve a comfortable level of proficiency with English, thereby giving their children a lifelong advantage over them in access to information, interpretation of such information, and interaction with the larger non-Lao community. Information access plays into the changing dynamics of power relationships and dependency, that is, of role reversal for these two generations.

INTEGRATION

Religion: Spiritual Adjustment Issues[2]

The differences in values, expected behaviors, languages, types of economic subsistence (e.g., nonmechanized agriculture versus industrialization), and even religion (Buddhism versus Christianity) cause considerable stress for arriving refugees. Under these circumstances, people frequently seek support from familiar sources. One of these is religion.

Many Lao refugees attend Christian churches in their American communities. The reason for attendance varies: The church may have sponsored them; they may have been Christian in the camps or in Laos; or they may be responding to active recruitment on the part of a given church. Nevertheless, Lao often do not consider their traditional religious beliefs and Christian religious beliefs to be mutually exclusive. Therefore, a Lao Christian may still feel the need to make *bun* (merit) or may go to a spirit medium to help resolve a problem. Such openness offers them flexibility in their struggle to survive in a stressful environment. On the other hand, such a multireligious approach can also create psychological difficulties.

Having access to a Lao *wat* gives the community a sense of ethnic maintenance and psychological support (Krulfeld 1994). For those Lao communities without a *wat* (Buddhist temple) and resident monks, stress results from *not* being able to carry out prescribed religious duties.

As Theravada Buddhists, Lowland Lao believe in reincarnation: the merit an individual accumulates in a past life determines what this life will be like. For example, a person born with *bun* or merit (somewhat equivalent to the Christian concept of "grace") will be long-lived, successful, and wealthy. Those born lacking *bun* will suffer poverty, sickness, and misfortune (Haarhoff 1973; Hanks 1965). And, of course, what one does and how one behaves in this life will have direct bearing on one's next life (Kaufman 1960; Keyes 1983; Tambiah 1970). Tambiah (1970) suggests that members of the Lao ethnic group in their homeland perceive merit making as having two main aspects: First, it ensures "a rebirth blessed with happiness, prosperity and wealth" (53); and second, it "produces a happy and virtuous state of mind" (53–54). So Tambiah found that villagers viewed merit making as more future oriented (e.g., rebirth) and abstract (e.g., a happy state of mind) than emphasizing immediate practical concerns.

Both in Southeast Asia and in the United States, Lao believe that the best way to make *bun* is through giving food daily, or giving other gifts and money periodically, to the Buddhist monks and the *wat*. Many Lao communities in the United States, such as the one in St. Louis, do not have a Lao *wat*, and therefore, there are no monks living in these communities either. Thus, for these Lao, there is no way for them to adequately make *bun* on a normal, daily basis, as they would in their homeland. One man (personal communication), who attended a Christian church, reflected the feelings of many when he said that if his community had a *wat*, he could go there. As a member, he would give to the monks and the *wat* generally and thus accumulate merit. He added that he could not make merit in a Christian church and that he needed to make merit.

Merit making for the Lao in Southeast Asia performed an important social function. In their native villages, making *bun* was often a communal affair (Keyes 1983). As a communal activity, merit making clearly delimited the critical social group. Village residents shared the responsibility of feeding and caring for the monks in the local *wat*. Another major source of merit making, and concurrently, village solidarity, in Southeast Asia was the special calendrical rites held at the *wat*. These occasions necessitated major collective action on the part of the villagers. Thus, while the benefits of merit making were accrued individually, the *process* served to promote the solidarity of the community.

In St. Louis, at least some Lao expressed a strong need to make *bun* in order to reap its immediate rewards; for example, they would have better health, good employment, and more money—all very concrete, immediate results. The implications of this present-oriented approach are even more serious when one considers that while it is rather difficult for many Lao in the United States to make *bun,* at the same time, they are constantly earning *baap.* (*Baap* can be translated as "demerit.") People make *baap* through bad thoughts and bad behavior. Examples are buying meat to eat and, therefore, having some part in causing another living being's death, and speaking unkindly to or about another person. Thus, while it is easy in America to build demerit (*baap*), at the same time, it is quite difficult to accrue merit (*bun*). A circular problem can result from this constant earning of *baap.* For example, for a community to have one or two residing monks and a *wat* in their community, they must have the financial resources to maintain them. Establishing a *wat* and maintaining monks is a financial drain on the community. Since the local St. Louis Lao perceive themselves as being poor (a sure sign of lacking merit), they cannot raise enough money. Without a temple and monks, they cannot acquire *bun* to counter the accumulating *baap.*

In their home country of Laos, being Buddhist was often equivalent with being Lao (Rutledge 1990:366), and in spite of participation in Christian activities in the United States, Buddhism continues to be an important ethnic identity marker. Krulfeld (1994) worked in a community in Virginia that was able to sponsor several monks and a *wat* in 1980, after only a few years in the United States (see also Ranard 1990). She notes how important this temple was in helping the community cope with their grief and stress, both psychological and spiritual. It gave the Lao, whose homes were geographically dispersed, a concrete sign of communality and solidarity. In many ways the temple and its monks reified their sense of Lao ethnic identity and of the traditional Lao values and behaviors versus those of the surrounding area.

Besides using Buddhism in accumulating *bun,* there is another resource in the Lao informal folk tradition (that is, not specifically Buddhist) for coping with a difficult environment, as well as with the unknown, the unexpected, or the tragic (which can be taken as a result of one's having *baap*). That is, one can have recourse to spirits, or *phii*[3] (Chotisukharat 1971; Tambiah 1970), as well as use of the *baci.* Belief in spirit intercession is a ubiquitous element in traditional Thai and Lao society (Chotisukharat 1971; Gandour and Gandour 1976; Haarhoff 1973; Kaufman 1960; Klausner 1964; LeBar and Suddard 1960; Tambiah 1970; Turton 1972). The spirits, *phii,* range from benevolent, prestigious figures to malevolent, violent beings (Tambiah 1970). The benevolent spirits function through mediums as curing agents and diviners in their homeland. The mediums can be considered a link in a broad-based support system. The *phii* continue to perform their helping functions within the Lao community. The belief in spirit possession may lie dormant until the need for a medium's services arises due to persistent illness or continued misfortune. At that point, particularly if the intervening services of a *wat* and its monks are not available, a medium may be sought to discover if a spirit is the cause of their problems. The following is an example of the use of a medium in St. Louis.

The Lao community in St. Louis had a medium living in the city from 1982 to 1983. Before coming to the area, the spirit medium lived for almost two years with her family as a cultural isolate in a rural American town. During this time, her spirits did not come to her; she attended a Christian church. Since she had a distantly related matrilineal relative in St. Louis, she and her family finally decided to move. During her residency in the St. Louis area, she was very active as a spirit medium. At least once a week, usually more often, the *nang tiam* (as the medium possessed by a spirit was called) was asked to perform healing rites and for divination, for example, for a winning lottery number or an answer to a serious family question.

Many people professed *not* to believe in her, saying that belief in spirit possession was not compatible with being a good Buddhist. When in need, however, these same people turned to the *nang tiam* for help. For example, one member of the Lao Buddhist Association repeatedly brushed aside the existence and activities of the *nang tiam* as not being Buddhist. However, when a woman neighbor became excessively tired and unable to work, and after the services of an American medical doctor proved fruitless, he agreed with the assessment by another Lao that his neighbor's troubles were due to *baap* (which the woman had acquired by not attending the local Laotian New Year celebrations). Since there were no monks available for her to make *bun* to counter her *baap,* this member of the Lao Buddhist Association further agreed with the opinion of other Lao that it might be necessary to bring in the spirit medium to cure the woman.

Thus, at least in this community that had no *wat* but did have a spirit medium present, the medium became a viable alternative in times of stress. While the Lao themselves speak of these two religious traditions as being antagonistic to each other in some respects, the two traditions come out of the same Lao cultural framework, and both reinforce basic concepts (e.g., *bun* and *baap*) and worldviews that are alien to the new urban, mid-American environment. By so doing, these ongoing religious traditions provide a sense of security and solidarity in the face of cultural change.

A third significant religious tradition that can help in times of stress as well as delineate what being Lao is, is the *baci* ceremony, sometimes called the *sukhuan* (which means calling back a person's soul) (Turton 1972). The *baci* is found among many Southeast Asian peoples, but it is especially important to the Lao who have developed a distinctive ceremony combining animist traditions and beliefs with Buddhist traditions (Peachey and Peachey 1983). The *baci* marks all important Lao occasions such as births and marriages, as well as assuring good health and well-being—and even acknowledging a farewell. Originating in animist beliefs that each person has 32 spirits (*kwan*), the *baci* is performed to keep the spirits from leaving or, in the case of illness, to call them back to the sick person. A *baci* often includes recitation of Buddhist Pali scriptures and ends with the symbolic act of tying strings around the wrists of the honored guests.

The *baci* is important to the Lao refugee community in several ways. It can be held with or without Buddhist monks. A religious specialist is not necessary. Thus, the existence of a *wat* in the area is irrelevant to the community's being able to resort to this religious tradition. Furthermore, the *baci,* while not actually a Buddhist tradition, is not considered to be in competition with Buddhism and even incorporates Buddhist scriptures. If Buddhist monks are available, they will perform this rite (Krulfeld 1994). As a part of the informal religious tradition, the *baci* is critical in alleviating stresses from other sources (jobs, health, family). It also serves as a public marker of Lao solidarity.

Gender Relations: Maintenance and Change

Women's positions vis-à-vis men's positions in Laos were economically strong; women were marketers and farmers, earning money for the family. Matrilocality remained the preferred residency pattern after marriage (i.e., the newly married husband and wife lived with or near her parents), and descent was traced through the female line. However, a significant overlay on this strong position of women was a Buddhist tradition that relegated women to a position subservient to men. For example, while men could be monks in search of enlightenment, women could only be nuns who acted as caretakers for the monks. The women had no significant religious role (Kirsch 1982; Krulfeld 1994; Van Esterik 1982). This, plus 50 years of French colonial government and hundreds of years of contact with Chinese, Vietnamese, and Indian cultural elements (all male-dominated cultural traditions), created a complex relationship between the genders. As the Thai (close cousins to the Lowland Lao) say, women are like the back legs of an elephant; men are the front legs (Potter 1977). That is, women are important, even critical, but they are behind the men and follow the men.

In the United States, Lao men complain that women have changed, that they no longer behave toward men as they used to in their home country (Rutledge 1990; Zaharlick, Jobrack, and Calip-Dubois 1993). This is possible and consistent with the impression in the community that there are more divorces in the United States (Rutledge 1990; Zaharlick, Jobrack, and Calip-Dubois 1993) than in Laos. However, given the difficulty of surviving on one income from the low-income jobs people have, it is possible that problems within the family only appear to be greater than they were in the past. Men have had to adapt and adjust in numerous ways, from work to their children's schooling, to available entertainment, to not being able to worship in the traditional, familiar way. As a consequence of these changes, they may have a heightened need for an eye of calm in the storm of change in which they find themselves. Unfortunately, it is not possible for the family to remain unchanged and ever peaceful since the women—pivotal to this scenario—have their own problems and losses to which they must respond and adapt.

There is considerable irony in the new sets of roles of Lao women in the United States. Often Americans think of their culture as being more open, free, supportive, and equal than other cultures, particularly where women are concerned. However, just the opposite is often the experience of Lao women. American society perpetuates greater gender inequalities on them than they left behind in their home country (DeVoe 1993a; Van Esterik 1980, 1982) First, the loss of the extended family, is an emotional burden for the Lao. The everyday consequences of the loss of the extended family are particularly hard for the women (Boserup 1970; Camus-Jacques 1989; DeVoe 1993a:31; Indra 1987; Loescher 1989:24; Montgomery 1991; Spero 1985). By coming to another country, they have effectively severed most or all ties with those who could offer psychological support, guidance, nurturance (Bell 1991; Knudsen 1991), and practical assistance with their family and household responsibilities. This isolation may cause the demoralized and depressed mindset Rumbaut (1989:155–156) found among Southeast Asian women compared to their male counterparts.[4]

Thus, within the home, women do not have their grandmothers, mothers, or even sisters to assist with the everyday domestic tasks of cleaning, cooking, and child care. At the same time, both men and women expect that the women will work and contribute to the family finances. It is not possible for the family to function in the same manner as in the home country. In this time of need, men often can be found helping within the home. In the St. Louis Lao community (Rynearson and DeVoe 1984), when the women worked or went to school, they maintained primary responsibility for home activities, but the men were capable and prepared to assist with domestic activities. On the negative side, because both adults work, the children often lack caregivers with them through the day and become too "Americanized" and apparently lacking in obedience and respect. Men, to whom the traditional extended family (usually matrilineally related) was not as important, do not suffer the same sense of loss at its absence. Men do, nevertheless, see their last bastion of familiarity and comfort, the nuclear family with themselves as head, altered without their desire or permission.

Ethnic Identity

In spite of the stress Lao contend with as refugees and as foreigners trying to adjust to a new sociocultural environment, the majority do not cling to their Lao ethnic identity. They see themselves as Lao-Americans or situationally, as Lao or American (see *Silk Sarongs and City Streets* 1986; Krulfeld 1992). Such ethnic flexibility or nesting of ethnic identity is not uncommon in Southeast Asia (Denton 1976; Rajah 1990). Interestingly, Krulfeld (1994) found that length of residence in the United States was not a factor in ethnic self-identification. One person who had lived in the United States for 15 years reportedly felt completely Lao and was not comfortable with Americans; others who had been in America for a much shorter time felt part of both cultures, Lao and American. Krulfeld also found that while the children were immersed in American culture through school, they identified as Lao-Americans, an identity that was acceptable to most of their parents. Parents did worry, however, that their children would lose their identity as Lao because, according to the parents, the children were quickly losing Lao values and forgetting Lao traditions. The children, however, said they were Lao by descent, so they could not possibly lose their Lao ethnicity. The minority of adults identifying mostly or exclusively as Lao connected negative morals and values with American culture and positive morals and values with their own Lao culture (e.g., obedience and respect for parents and the elderly). Their way of handling the stress of the new environment was to turn more completely toward an idealized traditional Lao culture and identity.

The majority of Lao, however, while maintaining Lao cultural traditions through activities such as dance and religious ceremonies, seem comfortable with the details of everyday American life—with its clothing styles, food, work patterns, housing, and urban life. This attitude allows them to identify as bicultural, as being a part of both cultures, Lao and American, and to forge a new ethnic identity—Lao-American.

CONCLUSIONS AND PROSPECTS

The Lao came to the United States as refugees, often unprepared educationally, socially, economically, and psychologically. They came bearing the scars of their prerefugee and refugee experiences but carrying the hope for a secure, stable, and prosperous life for themselves and their families in America. Since there were few Lao already living in the United States, most refugees settled in urban areas with no Lao community support systems, such as a *wat* or even a simple specialty grocery store selling Lao foods and condiments.

The thrust of aid from the larger American community was directed toward helping Lao adults achieve economic self-sufficiency. Diverse programs were set up to help in this process: English-language training classes, some health care, and job placement services. Schools were expected to be the adjustment vehicle for those 18 years of age and younger. Unless there were problems that interfered with employment or schooling, the Lao were left to their own devices in creating a new sense of self as individuals and as a community. This the Lao did by establishing *wats* if possible, by maintaining other informal traditional beliefs and behaviors, and by banding together to offer each other support in the face of everyday challenges.

After 20 years of resettlement in America, the majority of people appear to identify as Lao and Lao-American. Although parents worry about children maintaining their Lao identity, the children seem to take such an identity for granted, as a birthright. The children see themselves as Lao-American or as American of Lao descent. As with ethnic groups before them, each generation is more firmly rooted in the American way of life, yet there remains the possibility of reconfirming a unique Lao ethnic identity and maintaining distinctive Lao values and traditions.

NOTES

1. Unless noted otherwise, the case material for this chapter is based on ethnographic data gathered in the St. Louis refugee community and from local employers, service providers, and school personnel. The author gathered this information from a variety of sources from 1981 to the present.

2. The St. Louis community differs from some other areas with respect to Lao refugees in that there is no Lao *wat* in the metropolitan area.

3. *Phii* as used here refers to spirits outside of oneself. Although the *phii* may possess a medium's body (as during a divination ceremony), they are not one's own spirits. The spirits belonging to each individual person are referred to as *kwan*.

4. Another factor influencing their depression may be the particular and traumatic experiences that women suffer during flight and during internment in refugee camps (see Agger 1995; Cha and Small 1994; Ramirez 1995).

REFERENCES

Agger, Inger. 1995. Abused Refugee Women: Trauma and Testimony. *Refuge: Canada's Periodical on Refugees* 14(7):19–22.

Bach, Robert L., Linda W. Gordon, David W. Haines, and David R. Howell. 1983. The Economic Adjustment of Southeast Asian Refugees in the U.S. In *World Refugee Survey 1983*. Edited by Rosemary E. Tripp. Washington, D.C.: U.S. Committee for Refugees (USCR) of the American Council for Nationalities Service (ACNS). Pp. 51–59.

———. 1984. Geographic Variations in the Economic Adjustment of Southeast Asian Refugees in the U.S. In *World Refugee Survey 1984*. Edited by Rosemary E. Tripp. Washington, D.C.: U.S. Committee for Refugees (USCR) of the American Council for Nationalities Service (ACNS). Pp. 7–9.

Bell, Robert A. 1991. Gender, Friendship Network Density, and Loneliness. *Journal of Social Behavior and Personality* 6(1):45–56.

Blanchard, Kendall, and John C. Harding. 1984. Economic Change and Adaptation among the Lowland Lao in Murfreesboro, Tennessee: The Viability of Network Exchange (1). Paper presented at the American Anthropological Association Annual Meeting, Denver, November.

Boserup, Ester. 1970. *Women's Role in Economic Development*. London: George Allen and Unwin.

Brown, MacAlister. 1982. The Communist Seizure of Power in Laos. In *Contemporary Laos*. Edited by Martin Stuart-Fox. New York: St. Martin's Press. Pp. 17–38.

Camus-Jacques, Genevieve. 1989. Refugee Women: The Forgotten Majority. In *Refugees and International Relations*. Edited by Gil Loescher and Laila Monahan. Oxford: Oxford University Press. Pp. 141–157.

Cha, Dia, and Cathy A. Small. 1994. Policy Lessons from Lao and Hmong Women in Thai Refugee Camps. *World Development* 22(7):1045–1059.

Chan Kwok Bun. 1990. Introduction. In *Indochinese Refugees 15 Years Later*. Edited by Chan Kwok Bun. [special issue of *Southeast Asian Journal of Social Science* 18 (1)]. Singapore: Department of Sociology, National University of Singapore.

Chotisukharat, Sanguan. 1971. Supernatural Beliefs and Practices in Chiengmai. *Journal of Siam Society* 59, pt. 1(January):211–231.

Crisp, Jeff. 1987. Refugees in Thailand. *Refugees* 45:18–34.

Denton, R. K. 1976. Ethnics and Ethics in Southeast Asia. In *Changing Identities in Modern Southeast Asia*. Edited by David J. Banks. The Hague: Mouton Publishers. Pp. 71–81.

DeVoe, Pamela A. 1982. Employers' Perceptions of Southeast Asian Refugee Employees in Metropolitan St. Louis: A report. St. Louis: Missouri Institute of Psychiatry, School of Medicine, University of Missouri at Columbia.

———. 1991. Refugee Children in School: Understanding Cultural Diversity in the Classroom. *Anthro Notes* (National Museum of Natural History Bulletin for Teachers) 13(2):1–4, 10–11.

———. 1993a. The Silent Majority: Women as Refugees. In *The Women and International Development Annual*, Vol. 3. Edited by Rita S. Gallin, Anne Ferguson, and Janice Harper. Boulder, Colorado: Westview Press. Pp. 19–51.

———. 1993b. Southeast Asian Refugee Employees and Their Employers in the American Mid-West: Proponents, Picadors, or Pawns? In *Refugee Empowerment and Organizational Change: A Systems Perspective*. Edited by Peter Van Arsdale. Arlington, Virginia: American Anthropological Association. Pp. 50–62.

———. 1994. Refugees in an Educational Setting: A Cross-Cultural Model of Success. In *Reconstructing Lives, Recapturing Meaning: Refugee Identity, Gender, and Culture Change*. Edited by Linda A. Camino and Ruth M. Krulfeld. Basel, Switzerland: Gordon and Breach Publishers. Pp. 235–249.

DeVoe, Pamela A. and Ann Manry Rynearson. 1983. *Social Relations in a Refugee Neighborhood: Indochinese in St. Louis, MO*. Report for the Office of Refugee Resettlement. Washington, D.C.: Division of Health and Human Services.

Dommen, Arthur J. 1985. *Laos: Keystone of Indochina*. Boulder, Colorado: Westview Press.

Epstein, T. Scarlett, and Rosemary A. Watts. 1981. *The Endless Day: Some Case Material on Asian Rural Women*. New York: Pergamon Press.

Gandour, M. J., and J. T. Gandour. 1976. A Glance at Shamanism in Southern Thailand. *Journal of Siam Society* 64, pt. 1 (January):97–103.

Haarhoff, J. P. 1973. People of Laos. In *Peoples of the Earth: South East Asia*. Edited by Andrew Turton. Danbury, Connecticut: Danbury Press.

Hackett, Beatrice Nied. 1988. Relative and Relational Power for Ethnic Chinese Cambodian Refugees: Economics with a Twist. Paper presented at the American Anthropological Association (AAA) Annual Meeting, Phoenix, Arizona, November.

Haines, David W. 1985. Initial Adjustment. In *Refugees in the United States: A Reference Handbook*. Edited by David W. Haines. Westport, Connecticut: Greenwood Press. Pp. 17–35.

———. 1987. Patterns in Southeast Asian Refugee Employment: A Reappraisal of the Existing Research. *Ethnic Groups 7* (March): 39–63.

———. 1989. Introduction. In *Refugees as Immigrants: Cambodians, Laotians, and Vietnamese in America*. Edited by David W. Haines. Totowa, New Jersey: Rowman and Littlefield. Pp. 1–23.

Hamilton, Virginia, Managing Editor. 1986. Little-Known Ethnic Lao Refugees Resettle in Larger Numbers. In *Refugee Reports*. Nashville, Tennessee: A Project of the American Council for Nationalities Service. Pp. 1–6.

Hanks, Jane Richardson. 1965. A Rural Thai Village's View of Human Character. In *Felicitation Volumes of Southeast Asian Studies*. Bangkok: The Siam Society.

Indra, Doreen. 1987. Gender: A Key Dimension of the Refugee Experience. *Refugees* 6: 3–4.

Kaufman, Howard Keva. 1960. Concepts of *bun* and *bab*. In *Bangkhuad: A Community Study in Thailand*. New York: J. J. Augustin Incorporated Publisher. Pp. 196–209.

Keyes, Charles F. 1983. Economic Action and Buddhist Morality in a Thai Village. *Journal of Asian Studies* 42(4):851–868.

Kirsch, Thomas. 1982. Buddhism, Sex-Roles and the Thai Economy. In *Women of Southeast Asia*. Edited by Penny Van Esterik. Occasional Paper No. 9. Dekalb, Illinois: Northern Illinois University. Pp. 16–41.

Klausner, William J. 1964. Popular Buddhism in Northeast Thailand. In *Cross-Cultural Understanding*. Edited by F. S. C. Northrop and Helen H. Livingston. New York: Harper and Row. Pp. 87–92.

Knudsen, John Chr. 1991. Therapeutic Strategies and Strategies for Refugee Coping. *Journal of Refugee Studies* 4(1):21–33.

Krulfeld, Ruth M. 1992. Cognitive Mapping and Ethnic Identity: The Changing Concepts of Community and Nationalism in the Laotian Diaspora. In *Selected Papers on Refugee Issues 1992*. Edited by Pamela A. DeVoe. Arlington, Virginia: American Anthropological Association. Pp. 4–26.

———. 1994. Buddhism, Maintenance, and Change: Reinterpreting Gender in a Lao Refugee Community. In *Reconstructing Lives, Recapturing Meaning: Refugee Identity, Gender, and Culture Change*. Edited by Linda A. Camino and Ruth M. Krulfeld. Basel, Switzerland: Gordon and Breach Publishers. Pp. 97–127.

LeBar, Frank M., and Adrienne Suddard, Editors. 1960. *Laos: Its People, Its Society, Its Culture*. New Haven: HRAF Press. Pp. 44–46.

Loescher, Gil. 1989. Introduction. In *Refugees in International Relations*. Edited by Gil Loescher and Laila Monahan. New York: Oxford University Press. Pp. 1–33.

Manich, M. L. 1967. *History of Laos: Including the History of Lannathai, Chiengmai*. Bangkok: Chalermnit.

Montgomery, R. 1991. Predicting Vietnamese Refugee Adjustment to Western Canada. *International Migration* 29(1):89–113.

Peachey, Linda, and Titus Peachey. 1983. Religion in Socialist Laos. *Southeast Asia Chronicle* 91(October):16–19.

Potter, Sulamith Heins. 1977. *Family Life in a Northern Thai Village*. Berkeley: University of California Press.

Rajah, Ananda. 1990. Orientalism, Commensurability, and the Construction of Identity: A Comment on the Notion of Lao Identity. *Sojourn: Social Issues in Southeast Asia* 5(2):308–333.

Ramirez, Judith. 1995. The Canadian Guidelines on Women Refugee Claimants Fearing Gender-Related Persecution. *Refuge: Canada's Periodical on Refugees* 14(7):3–7.

Ranard, Donald W. 1990. A Buddhist Temple in Rural Virginia. *Refugees* 79(October): 32–33.

Rumbaut, Rubén G. 1989. Portraits, Patterns, and Predictors of the Refugee Adaptation Process: Results and Reflections from the IHARP Panel Study. In *Refugees as Immigrants: Cambodians, Laotians, and Vietnamese in America*. Edited by David W. Haines. Totowa, New Jersey: Rowman & Littlefield. Pp. 138–198.

Rutledge, Paul. 1990. Boon Vongsurith. *Journal of Refugee Studies* 3(4):365–369.

Rynearson, Ann Manry, and Pamela A. DeVoe. 1984. Refugee Women in a Vertical Village: Lowland Laotians in St. Louis. *Social Thought* 10(3):33–48.

Silk Sarongs and City Streets. 1986. Video produced by the International Institute of Metropolitan St. Louis, St. Louis, Missouri (28 minutes).

Southeast Asian Refugee Studies Newsletter. A publication of the Southeast Asian Refugee Studies Project, Center for Urban and Regional Affairs, University of Minnesota. Minneapolis, Minnesota.

Spero, Abby. 1985. *In America and in Need: Immigrant, Refugee, and Entrant Women.* Washington, D.C.: American Association of Community and Junior Colleges.

Stier, Haya. 1991. Immigrant Women Go to Work: Analysis of Immigrant Wives' Labor Supply for Six Asian Groups. *Social Science Quarterly* 72(1):67–82.

Tambiah, S. J. 1970. *Buddhism and the Spirit Cults in North-east Thailand.* Cambridge: Cambridge University Press.

Thee, Marek. 1973. *Notes of a Witness: Laos and the Second Indochinese War.* New York: Random House.

Toye, Hugh. 1968. *Laos: Buffer State or Battleground.* London: Oxford University Press.

Turton, Andrew. 1972. Matrilineal Descent Groups and Spirit Cults of the Thai-Yuan in Northern Thailand. *Journal of Siam Society* 217–256.

U.S. Committee for Refugees (USCR). 1990. 1989 World Refugee Statistics. In *World Refugee Survey 1989 in Review.* Edited by Virginia Hamilton. Washington, D.C.: U.S. Committee for Refugees of the American Council for Nationalities Service.

Van-es-Beeck, Bernard J. 1982. Refugees from Laos, 1975–1979. In *Contemporary Laos.* Edited by Martin Stuart-Fox. New York: St. Martin's Press. Pp. 324–334.

Van Esterik, Penny. 1980. Cultural Factors Affecting the Adjustment of Southeast Asian Refugees. In *Southeast Asian Exodus: From Tradition to Resettlement, Understanding Refugees from Laos, Kampuchea and Vietnam in Canada.* Edited by Elliot L. Tepper. Ottawa: The Canadian Asian Studies Association. Pp. 151–171.

———. 1982. Introduction. In *Women of Southeast Asia.* Edited by Penny Van Esterik. Occasional Paper No. 9. Dekalb, Illinois: Northern Illinois University. Pp. 1–15.

Zaharlick, Amy, Steward Jobrack, and Theresa Calip-Dubois. 1993. Economic and Sociocultural Influences on the Fertility Transition of Lao Refugees. In *Selected Papers on Refugee Issues:II 1993.* Edited by MaryCarol Hopkins and Nancy D. Donnelly. Arlington, Virginia: American Anthropological Association. Pp. 177–194.

Chapter 7

Afghans

JULIENE G. LIPSON AND PATRICIA A. OMIDIAN

Through the centuries, the area that is now Afghanistan has been fought over by Greeks, Kushans, Indians, Huns, Persians, Arabs, Turks, Mongols, British, and Russians. Most recently, it has been torn by more than 15 years of political strife and war. Afghan citizens began leaving their country in 1979 after a coup that preceded the invasion of Afghanistan by the former USSR. Prior to the withdrawal of Soviet troops in 1989, Afghan refugees comprised the largest refugee population in the world, some 6.5 million people living in refugee camps and cities in Pakistan and Iran, with smaller numbers in India, Europe, and North America; it remains the largest despite repatriation of some 3 million people. Although many Afghans want to return to their country, ongoing civil war between political parties has discouraged most Afghans living in Europe and the United States from returning.

This chapter introduces the Afghan refugee population in the United States, based mostly on our research with those in the San Francisco Bay Area. We attempt to depict both the heterogeneity of Afghans in the United States and their common cultural characteristics and dilemmas. Readers should keep in mind that for every common theme, there are variations and exceptions. The Afghan community is like a mosaic in which the tiles can be viewed up close to reveal their different colors and shapes or from afar to reveal an overall recognizable pattern.

Afghans began coming to the United States under refugee status in 1980, with 2,000 to 4,000 arriving yearly until fiscal year 1989 after the withdrawal of former USSR troops from Afghanistan (U.S. Committee for Refugees 1994a). This withdrawal spurred a politically influenced decision that Afghans were no longer legitimate refugees; most were thereafter denied priority-one category for visas (in danger of immediate loss of life).

No one knows exactly how many Afghans live in the United States. Estimates range from 45,000 to 75,000 (Rahmany 1993), with 55 to 67 percent in the San Francisco Bay Area. Other large communities are in Los Angeles, New York, the Washington, D.C., area, and Portland. Of these, 27,050 Afghans were admitted under refugee status between 1982 and 1994 (U.S. Committee for Refugees 1994a). The 1990 census underestimates the Afghan refugee population because many Afghans misunderstood its purpose and were afraid to cooperate. In fiscal year 1994, only 21 Afghans were admitted to the United States as refugees; many others came through family reunification channels.

The Afghan population in the San Francisco Bay Area continues to grow through secondary migration. This area is attractive because of the size of the existing Afghan population, the presence of extended family members, the weather, and, before the 1994 elections, a relatively generous welfare system. We attempted to more accurately enumerate the size of the San Francisco Bay Area Afghan community through querying a variety of county and private social service agencies, local mosques, and school districts. However, complete data could not be obtained from any one source, and we estimate that there are 15,000 to 20,000 Afghans in the area (Lipson and Omidian 1993).

The Afghan population in the United States is heterogeneous in social class origin, ethnic group and religion, political stance, degree of acculturation, and financial stability. The cosmopolitan, urban, formerly wealthy, and highly educated elite began arriving in the early 1980s. Family reunification in the mid- to late 1980s brought their middle-class relatives who are less educated, some illiterate even in their own languages. Although few refugees of rural origin could afford to leave Pakistan or Iran, there is a small but significant group who maintain their very traditional lifestyle. As Muslims, Afghans generally are quite religious but vary from strictly observing all practices to being more informal (for example, praying by oneself rather than ritually). They also range from very cosmopolitan to very traditional, with more well educated people from Kabul tending to be more cosmopolitan, depending on family background, strength of religious adherence, and political stance. Families from other cities and rural areas tend to be more traditional, with women uneducated, wearing traditional dress, and secluded from contact with unrelated men.

AFGHANISTAN

Afghanistan is a land-locked, mountainous country with an agriculture-based economy located in southwest Asia between Iran, Pakistan, Tajikistan, and Uzbekistan.[1] No systematic nationwide census has been conducted since 1978, and as of 1994, population estimates ranged from 11 to 17 million. With an area only 6 percent smaller than Texas, Afghanistan was, and still is, one of the world's poorest countries. Its vital statistics reflect this poverty; for example, life expectancy at birth was 46 years for males and 44 years for females (*World Almanac* 1993).

It has only been in the past 30 years that Afghanistan has become more urbanized and modernized, including development of educational and transportation systems. Major cities were finally connected by highways and railway systems in the mid-1970s, yet 85 percent of the population still relied on donkey and foot travel (Canfield 1986). Before the 1979 invasion and subsequent war, educational opportunities for village children allowed them to obtain government jobs and settle in urban centers, although merchants have been urban for generations. However, 88 percent of the population is illiterate (*World Almanac* 1993).

Afghanistan is a mosaic of social groups that differ by social class, urban and rural origin, ethnic group and language, tribe, region of the country, and religion. What is common to Afghans, however, is Islam and several strong cultural values, such as the importance of the family.

In prewar Afghanistan, there was a small but growing middle class that included many people trained in the West or former USSR. They differed in education and experience from their rural relatives and in wealth from the elite. Yet middle-class people were connected to both the rural and the elite population by extensive kinship systems. The relatively few university-educated middle-class people became part of a new network made up of classmates.

Afghanistan has many ethnic groups, the most populous of which are Pashtuns (38 percent), Tajiks (25 percent), and Hazaras (19 percent) (*World Almanac* 1994). The official languages are Pashtu (spoken in the south and east primarily by Pashtuns) and Dari (spoken in the west, central region, and the north by Tajiks and Hazaras); Uzbeks and Turkoman peoples speak Turkic dialects. These ethnic groups sometimes have more in common with their neighbors outside Afghanistan than with other Afghans.

Afghanistan's social organization reflects its origin as a tribal society based on nomadic pastoralism, although agriculture and village life have become more prominent. The prewar rural population was about 87 percent of the total Afghan population (Canfield 1986). Ethnic diversity and regional and village loyalties characterize the country as a whole, and intergroup conflicts are part of its social fabric. This pattern is reflected in Afghan communities in the United States and elsewhere.

Nearly all Afghans are Muslims, although a small number of Sikhs, Hindus, Christians, and Jews live there as well. The strong Islamic identity creates a mask of homogeneity that does not really reflect Afghan society. Two thirds of the population are Sunni Muslim, and the remaining 5 million are Shi'a of the Imami and Ismaili sects (Nyrop and Seekins 1986). Afghanistan's history reflects the importance of religion, with riots and killings between sects within regions and discrimination by the majority of the minority (Dupree 1980). However, since 1979, when Afghanistan's Communist leaders, aided by the Soviet army, tried to impose secular laws at the local level, these schisms were put aside, and Islamic symbols motivated the population against the government (Canfield 1986; Nyrop and Seekins 1986). Islam symbolizes how Afghans, in

Afghanistan and elsewhere, define themselves and explain the world around them.

EXODUS AND TRANSIT

Modernization of Afghanistan ceased in 1978. In the years following the 1978 coup and 1979 Soviet invasion, Afghanistan has been devastated by three wars: against the Soviet army and the Afghan government it was trying to support (1979–1989); against Communist government forces after the departure of the Russian army (1989–1992); and among warlords and factions vying for power in a bloody civil war (1992–1995). Over 40 percent of the population has been killed or forced to leave the country. Much of the remaining rural population was forced out of the countryside and into urban centers. The United Nations estimates that over 1 million have died. There are still approximately 1 million internal refugees and 3.5 million waiting in Pakistan, Iran, India, Europe, and the United States. Soviet and Afghan government forces systematically devastated the countryside, destroying whole villages in order to clear the rural areas of havens for the resistance forces.

When Soviet troops withdrew in 1989, an even bloodier battle ensued as government troops battled the resistance for control of Afghanistan. In 1992, the Communist president Muhammad Najibullah resigned when competing factions began taking the capital, Kabul. Since the fall of the Communist government, Kabul has been subject to more bombings than during ten years of war against the Soviet army. The battle continues to rage as control of the capital shifts from one faction commander to another, and it appears likely that it will wax and wane into the next century. After a new wave of shelling in Kabul and the north occurred in 1994, Pakistan closed its borders to prevent entrance of a new flood of Afghan refugees. Some 600,000 Afghans fleeing the fighting in and around Kabul and Kunduz became internally displaced in the first quarter of the year (U.S. Committee for Refugees 1994b). Along with the violence, food and energy shortages have made life in some parts of Afghanistan nearly intolerable.

During this whole period, Afghan citizens have observed or experienced atrocities and traumas. Some were imprisoned in Kabul by the Communist regime, and a number of the imprisoned were also tortured (Psychiatry Centre for Afghan Refugees 1988). Many of these Afghans still suffer from posttraumatic stress syndrome years later. The story of Modeer Saheb,[2] a well-educated, older man who had worked for an international agency in Kabul, is typical but by no means the worst:

Communist soldiers knocked on the door of Modeer Saheb's home in the middle of the night, trying to catch him hiding Mojahed (resistance fighters). When he heard the first knock, he awakened his wife and adult daughter, Fatima, so they could dress and be ready for a search. By the time he got to the door, the soldiers fired a bullet through it, taking off the end of his finger. After searching the house and finding only the family, a guard picked up a family diary from Modeer's desk which included who traveled where, who married whom, who was born, and who died. All family members had contributed to writing about the events and their feelings. The guard read about the "martyrdom" of Fatima's friend, Naheed, who was killed by soldiers firing into a crowd of school children protesting the communists, and her anger describing the communists using very "bad" language. Using this "evidence," the soldiers arrested and imprisoned Modeer and Fatima. In prison, when the guards attempted to separate Modeer and Fatima, he protested that his daughter should not be alone with soldiers, so one kicked him so hard in the groin that he fainted. After eight hours, the soldiers returned to release them because of the intervention of a colleague's son in the civil police. The guard demanded a written apology for the words in the diary, then hooded both father and daughter and drove them home. Since this incident Modeer has continuously had lower back trouble. (Omidian 1992, also see Omidian 1996)

The political climate for middle- and upper-class Afghans was one of uncertainty and even fear. Family members could disappear in the night, never to be heard from again; young men would be conscripted into the army from the streets as they went to school or the market, and office workers distrusted everyone—the person at the next desk might be a spy. Those who had worked with Americans before the coup were particularly vulnerable.

Afghans escaped Afghanistan any way they could, usually with little notice, and many had traumatic experiences getting out and finding safety. Many walked over the 10,000- to 15,000-foot mountain passes at night because of the constant threat of Communist helicopters. They experienced freezing weather, shelling and destruction, injuries, and death of family members along the way. A 70-year-old widow described this: "When the Communists came, we escaped. We walked through back roads of high mountains of Afghanistan. I was on a donkey, I fell, my head break. They just did home remedies, but with mercy of God, it cured itself" (Lipson 1993). Many never made it over the border to safety as planes strafed the refugee caravans, killing and wounding women and children; thieves and thugs ambushed families to rob them of gold or jewels or to kidnap the young women. Others were captured near the border and sent back or, more often, imprisoned. Afghan refugees experienced multiple losses; relatives were killed or left behind; they lost their status, language, and vocational competencies. Loss of home is mentioned repeatedly: "I am depressed for my country, my home, my relatives . . . my heart breaks."

Life was difficult in the country of first asylum, especially for women. In Pakistan, for example, women in the 344 refugee camps were confined to the family tent or mud hut, and even those in the cities could go out only completely veiled. Those who worked with foreign relief agencies were often harassed or had their lives threatened by conservative Afghans for working with men. Many suffered from the intense heat that was so different from the climate of Afghanistan. Hypertension, depression, and other health problems were common, but the women had little access to care because there were few female health providers, and they were usually not allowed to be seen by a male doctor.

Moving On: Leaving the Region for Other Places

Life in the first country of asylum was difficult and often transitory. Refugees living in Pakistan experienced numerous problems, although they lived in the more familiar atmosphere of a country with a Muslim majority, and Afghan and Pakistani Pushtuns have ethnicity in common. But Pakistan is also a country of limited resources, intense poverty, and different climate. The Afghan educated and elite found life in Pakistan hard and uncompromising. Many men could not find work, and women were restricted in ways that they had not previously experienced in Afghanistan. Many families were fearful because of rumors of daughters being kidnapped for houses of prostitution in other countries. Because of these rumors and intermittent violence toward Afghans by Pakistanis, many families restricted their wives and daughters to home, which also limited their opportunities for education.

In Iran, Afghans faced other problems. Unlike Pakistan, Iran was at war with Iraq and needed laborers to replace Iranian men who went to war. Although this allowed many Afghans to find work, religious differences made these advantages tenuous. The majority of Afghans are of the Sunni sect, a minority in Iran. Some changed their surnames in order to avoid harassment. In addition, Afghans began to be blamed for many of the growing social problems in Iran, including violence, theft, and other social ills.

Educated and elite families often decided, prior to leaving Afghanistan, to resettle in the United States or Europe. Others found life too difficult in Pakistan or Iran and chose to apply for asylum and refugee resettlement while in their first country of asylum. Choice of country rested on two primary factors: (1) previous work and/or friendship with people from a particular country, which opened the door for sponsorship; and (2) the desire to join family members already resettled abroad. Family connections are very important in Afghan culture, and families could be counted on to assist the newcomers. Of those interviewed by Omidian (1992, 1996), few expressed a desire to live in the United States. Most said that had it not been for the war that pushed them, they would never have come to the United States. Several said that they knew what the United States was like from having obtained their U.S. college degrees in the 1970s. They thought that America was no place to raise a family. Once the war began, however, they had to risk losing their culture in order to save their children and to give them the best chance in life. Yet for still others, America was the first choice, a land of opportunity, a gathering place for Afghans living outside the region, and the country with the greatest amount of religious freedom, an important consideration.

INITIAL RESETTLEMENT

Most Afghans entered the United States as refugees, but since 1989, most have come under family reunification criteria, with a visa contingent on having family members or an organization guarantee their support for a period of time. Once a visa is obtained, Afghans are processed through one of several private or nonprofit resettlement agencies.

Family members usually meet new arrivals at the airport and transport them home, where they stay until they locate separate housing, preferably in close proximity; in some cases, a parent or unmarried children will move in permanently. Welcoming parties and social gatherings for the new arrival(s) are often held for weeks by family and friends. Family connections and close physical proximity are very important to Afghans, as noted by one student who was asked to define the concept of "health": "Health and illness are difficult to define because everyone has his or her own cultural definition for it. For instance, for an Afghan immigrant, being healthy is having family members all here and together; it does not matter too much if physically they aren't doing too well." Thus, being reunited with family members is an event that goes beyond the social realm into the individual's notion of well-being.

After the welcoming and excitement of reuniting family members, however, Afghan refugees' initial adjustment is far from easy. For most people, there are four crucial problem areas: inadequate finances, limited job opportunities, educational discrepancies, and neighborhood problems.

Finances

Afghans experience immediate problems with money, jobs, and school. New arrivals are financially supported by family members until they can obtain work or other monetary support. If they enter as refugees, they receive several months of special support with the stipulation that they take English as a Second Language (ESL) classes and obtain vocational counseling. When this funding runs out, California Afghans are often encouraged by other Afghans to apply for welfare as soon as possible.

Money is a chronic problem for many Afghans. Even formerly wealthy new arrivals experience financial difficulties. For example, families with three houses and many servants in Afghanistan now live in small and crowded apartments (e.g., nine family members in two bedrooms). It was possible to live a sumptuous lifestyle in Afghanistan on what in the United States is very little money, but many of the wealthy sold their possessions or had to leave precipitously without having done so. With Immigration and Naturalization Service (INS) quota changes by the mid-1990s, there is a small but growing number of Afghans who spent their entire assets in Afghanistan or a transit country on false documents so that they could request asylum once they were on U.S. soil. This did not work for one woman, who was apprehended and imprisoned for two years and now attributes being "mentally ill" to this experience.

Job Opportunities

One of the most significant resettlement challenges faced by refugees is earning a livelihood. Home country skills and status are not usually transferable to the United States. Men, in particular, experience stress and depression related to loss of status brought on by unemployment and loss of their traditional breadwinner role. Those from middle-class backgrounds are more willing to accept entry-level jobs than are well-educated or upper-class refugees, who are too proud to accept menial jobs. An example involves the many physicians unable to pass the licensure exam because of finances, English problems, or outdated medical training (Lipson and Omidian 1992a). Vocational counselors may inadvertently insult their Afghan clients by not recognizing the importance of former social status.

A newly arrived man described the problems he faces as he and his young family adjust to life here. Neither he nor his wife had extended family or social networks in the area, and connections and social interactions are critical to an Afghan's emotional well-being. With no family members to guide him, he had to obtain advice from strangers, who "cannot be trusted":

It is very difficult to be comfortable outside of your own country. I worked for six years in Pakistan for the United Nations vocational training program. I had deceived myself; I thought I could be busy here and happy, but I have been here nine months now and nine months with no job. This is the first time I have ever eaten for free. Welfare is not good; it makes people lazy. Welfare is deceptive—it is not enough money to live on. If you work, you have to report it, but if you do not work you cannot live. Every time you get a job you lose. There are some people here that like to stay on welfare. Their life in Afghanistan was very hard and they were poor. Here, being on welfare makes them feel better as they do not struggle.

A former director in Afghanistan's Ministry of Agriculture said:

I thought I could get a good job because I was American-educated. I applied for every job I thought was appropriate. The welfare department sent me letters saying I am capable of working and I should take any job. Honestly, taking a job in a fast food restaurant is very humiliating for me, but being on welfare is even more humiliating. (Lipson and Omidian 1992b)

In the opinion of some Afghan community members, 90 percent of the San Francisco Bay Area Afghan families are supported by Aid to Families with Dependent Children (AFDC). Afghans themselves have strong and mixed feelings about the issue of public assistance. Most families think that they do not really have a choice, considering what jobs are available to them. An Afghan social worker noted that "Afghans are not lazy; they want to work hard, but they cannot live on what they get paid. With the job or without the job, there is not enough money either way."

Educational Discrepancies

School and learning English are also sources of potential difficulty for newcomers. The education of many children was interrupted for several years by war and/or no education available in transit locations. Depending on the school, they may be placed in ESL classes until they are able to speak enough English to function at a minimal level. When they enter regular classes, they may be placed with children two or three years younger. Children are sometimes teased by their classmates for being different. In general, however, younger children learn English quickly and adapt far better than do their elders.

Adult newcomers who entered as refugees were provided special financial support originally for up to three years, but that period has declined sharply over the last decade. Funding cutbacks have decreased the number of ESL classes; even those available are inappropriate for many Afghans, such as women illiterate in their own language, who cannot manage public transportation, or are responsible for young children.

Neighborhood Issues

Finally, Afghans vary in where they settle. Most prefer to move into neighborhoods where other Afghans live, and they sometimes encounter hostility from non-Afghan neighbors, particularly when they wear traditional dress. Public anti-immigrant sentiment of the past few years, especially during California's economic crisis of the early 1990s, has made life difficult for all immigrant groups, particularly those who stand out in appearance and speak accented or little English. For example, a traditional older man complained about the following incident:

When I walk to the grocery store, people honk or yell at me from their cars. I don't know what they are saying, but it is embarrassing. I am proud to wear my own clothes and my hat that I wore in the JIHAD. My father and grandfather never wore pants! I wish I was martyred in Afghanistan! (Lipson and Omidian 1992b)

When they first arrive, Afghans tend to settle in neighborhoods with cheaper rents. Such neighborhoods tend to be more dangerous as well, causing some older people, women, and children to sequester themselves indoors all day until a man or someone with a car can come to take them out. Isolation and loneliness are quite common among newcomers who know little English or who cannot drive. This loneliness is magnified by the difference in social customs that they knew in Afghanistan, where doors were always open and visitors are welcomed;

women and older people, in particular, spend time each day visiting and being visited.

But transportation is still a problem for those who have been in the United States longer, especially when it is complicated by not knowing English, as an older man described:

It's again the question of transport. I have a lot of friends and want to go and meet them, [but] I have not a private car. I have not the money to buy it. Then I have to ask my children to give me a lift, they are busy. My friends, they go to the grocery store and want to buy something but do not know the name and are not able to ask somebody. Then they have to ask their children to go with them; [the children] have their own appointment with their doctors and [must] go to their work. Also, when they go to the doctor, it is very difficult for them to express their needs. Therefore, they feel that they are more dependent here while in [our] country they have not this problem. They are home-locked, they cannot go to their relatives.

INTEGRATION

While the Afghan community perceives great variation in adaptational success of different families in the United States, outsiders view the majority of families as having difficulty since many remain on welfare or on disability.

For Afghan refugees, integration into U.S. society means being able to earn a living, functioning at a sufficient level at work or in school, meeting minimal everyday needs, and experiencing some level of satisfaction and stability. For the great majority of Afghans, integration does not mean assimilation. There are considerable differences in acculturation between Afghans who have been in the United States for 14 years and new arrivals but very little assimilation in general, except among children and teens. However, such "assimilation" is really more surface appearance and behavior, and most young people attempt to maintain their Afghan identity.

Integration occurs at different rates, depending on a number of factors, such as education, the person's expectations, occupation in Afghanistan, time and age of arrival in the United States, English proficiency, and familiarity with Western ways. Gender and generation are especially critical in influencing how much and how quickly Afghans integrate, so the following sections separately address the issues experienced by men, women, and youth.

Men's Issues

Employment issues are most problematic for Afghan men[3] because relatively few women in Afghanistan worked or financially supported the family. Had they remained in Afghanistan, older men would have retired and turned their family affairs over to a son. In the United States, although not perceived as "retired" by social service agencies, cultural norms and expected roles and status prevent most older Afghans from starting over. Those who arrived at a younger age have been somewhat more successful in gaining employment, but most remain on public assistance if they have families to support. The major employment for this generation is buying and selling goods at local flea markets, an activity that brings in cash while allowing families to keep Medi-Cal (California's Medicaid program for low-income families) and other benefits to which they have become accustomed.

Men who arrived in the United States early in the refugee process, between 1979 and 1984, face a similar problem. Resettled throughout the United States and Canada, they rapidly learned the language and found jobs with the help of American friends. After working a few years, they began to miss the Afghan community and, on the advice of family and Afghan friends, moved to the San Francisco Bay Area. Most now regret having moved because they had to start over, for the second or third time, at the bottom. Most have not regained even the small advances they had made.

Men over 35 fall into two groups: (1) the educated elite, who are older and skilled and want to practice their professions but cannot because of the slow economy and licensing requirements (e.g., doctors) or of being technologically outdated (e.g., engineers); and (2) the unskilled, who have no transferable job skills. Men in both groups are unable to find "meaningful" employment. Only entry-level jobs may be available, on which they cannot support families and which usually do not provide health insurance, an important consideration for a family with five to nine children. Many are thus inclined to remain at home on public assistance for fear of losing status and benefits like Medi-Cal.

Some Afghans came to California believing themselves entitled to compensation because of having lost everything in Afghanistan. One resettlement counselor observed, "They have the impression that welfare is a must for making it in this country. They are misinformed from the first day they arrive by people already here, and even before they arrive by family members who told them what to ask for" (Lipson and Omidian 1992b). However, this is rarely the case in other states with fewer Afghans and more restrictive welfare policies.

During informal discussions on community problems, men described the work/welfare dilemma in two ways. Those struggling by on public assistance alone, such as this highly educated and very frustrated man, tended to say such things as:

There are three kinds of Afghans in the U.S. First the very rich that escaped with their money. The second are people who were in power to save their life, the communists; here they live the good life as they get more money than most of the people. They can go to any school and are not stopped by GAIN [a retraining program available to refugees but restrictive]. Then there are the rest of us who were not high up in the government and who only came looking for better opportunities.

The other view is expressed by men who work full-time and struggle to meet family and social obligations; they focus more on time than money and express anger at "wealthy" Afghans who do not work and parents who do not get "real work" to get off welfare:

The wealthy are those who have lots of red rugs and live on AFDC, SSI, and the flea market. Yet, they go where they want and can see friends and relatives when they want. They can observe the holy days without worry of the job. They do not see a reason now to work hard when they can socialize and travel all they want. Those who work are jealous and angry about those who do not.

Most men, whether employed or unemployed, find life difficult at best and feel that they have lost more than they have gained by living in California. Their worldview, including their ability to practice Islam, is under siege; if they work, there is no time for family; if they are unemployed, they have failed to provide for their families. It is a wound that does not heal. Time only makes the problem more acute.

A small proportion of families has gained financial security through all adult and adolescent members working, even though none of the jobs pay well (e.g., gas station attendant, hotel maid, fast-food clerk). This kind of family cooperation is comparable to the excellent economic adjustment of Cuban immigrants in the United States; their relatively high family income level is due to proportionately more workers per family than the U.S. population (Perez 1986). Among Afghans, this method of increasing family income is not without its costs, as expressed by one woman who worried that

[y]oung people need after-school sports like volleyball or baseball. Unfortunately, our children go after school to work, hard work, physical work. This kind of job makes them very exhausted. They are not able to do their homework like American students, and at school they are sleepy. (Lipson and Omidian 1992b)

Women's and Family Issues

Traditional customs related to women[4] in Afghanistan include arranged marriages and polygyny, when affordable. In this strongly patriarchal culture, women are generally less educated, marry young, have many babies (preferably boys), do not work outside the home, and are restricted to socializing mainly with women relatives. This pattern varied for urban-educated women in the 1970s. Many worked outside the home and may have even indicated their interest in a specific potential husband. However, even professional women had less freedom than women in the United States—"only going to the office and home."

Afghan women's lives in the United States have changed, and they puzzle about their proper roles. Women seem to acculturate more quickly than men do; they become caught between the Afghan community's expectations that they behave traditionally and their desire for American-style freedom and independence. One man claimed that typical Afghan women in California prefer to stay home and cook for the family, take care of the children, clean house, and socialize with Afghan female friends, especially by telephone. In contrast, a woman stated: "Ladies adjusted well to this society; they drive, they work, they speak English. It is easy to cook here; they have more time for visiting and shopping, going to the park; they are more active than the men." However, many work hard to support their families.

Obtaining a job is often easier for women and teens, and they are less upset by taking jobs beneath their ability or background. However, family conflict may result from the husband not working and the wife taking a menial job (e.g., hotel maid); disturbing the traditional patriarchal role can cause marital problems. But even when the wife works full-time, she is still expected to cook, clean the house, and care for the children.

Many women experience intergeneration and intergender conflicts over women's freedom, the conflict between maintaining traditional values and becoming Americanized, role overload from adding new American roles to their preexisting or expected Afghan roles, lack of role models and suitable spouses for single women, and parenting difficulties. Women's experiences vary with their age, background, and individual personalities. Elderly women appear the most stressed and unhappy of any Afghans in the United States. Often widows, they live with sons' or daughters' families; however, they are socially isolated and lonely because the adults are working and the children are at school. As they rarely speak English, they are essentially homebound, afraid of going out because they will get lost. Unable to take public transportation to visit friends or other family members (Omidian and Lipson 1992), they miss the constant visiting that is characteristic of social life in Afghanistan. They feel trapped, like a 75-year-old woman who said, "At this age, for me America is nothing. I want to be in my country, die in my country, but because my kids are here and they need me, I have to be here, not go."

Single Afghan women refugees face different challenges than do their married counterparts. Most single women live with parents or siblings; they continue to be called girls, no matter what their age. Because marriage and children are central to Afghan women's identity, remaining single is viewed as unnatural. However, finding an appropriate husband is difficult. Afghan women who have been in the United States longer than a few months may be perceived as contaminated by American ideas and not properly naive or submissive by Afghan men, who frequently marry women still living in Afghanistan or Pakistan. When they want to complete a college education, they despair of being an "old maid" whom no one will marry (Omidian 1992, 1996). Although divorce among Afghans is increasing, stigma and family pressure keep most women in bad marriages from divorcing; divorcees may be shunned by their families and they may be unable to marry again. Those who move back in with their parents find that their status has changed. It is only when parents recognize that the daughter was in an abusive relationship that they give her moral support.

Other family role changes are related to children acting in the role of family spokesperson for parents who speak little or no English, acting as interpreters with schools and social or health care services. As children are expected to respect and obey their parents, especially their fathers and anyone older, children's power to interpret the outside world creates considerable family stress.

Youth's Issues

Young people are the most torn between Afghan and American culture. Respect for their elders is still a strong part of Afghan culture for many young people. But they view the concept of respect in the context of new choices that they would not have had to make in Afghanistan. At the same time, they feel obligated to maintain as much Afghan identity as they can, being respectful and meeting family expectations whenever possible. Many young women attending college see themselves as having to struggle on two fronts: first, with family members who are suspicious of their interactions with young men on campus and their desire for a degree; and second, with the American public that stereotypes Muslims as radical fanatics.

Because of their increased contact with other American subcultures and their quicker adaptation to school and work, young people face more situational dissonance than do their elders. They struggle daily with the fit between the "ideal" and the "real" and thus are constantly redefining and evaluating their social identity. Young people complain that America forces people to ignore the needs of their extended family:

We fool ourselves that our life will be better. For the old, they came here for the young people. Their life will not get better. This puts pressure on the young to do well, and this is very difficult. As young, we got everything, but now we cannot help them [parents], so we feel bad. We cannot return the help. In this country you have to support yourself first, and that is hard. Sometimes the old people ask us to help and we cannot, so we feel real sorry. (Omidian 1992:195)

Young people understand their parents' views and also understand their own dilemma—how to stay socially interconnected and Afghan while in America: "The biggest worries that the parents have right now is that their kids would change, and the biggest worry that kids have is they don't want to change, but they change" (Omidian 1992, 1996).

But while parents are troubled by the rapidity with which their children adjust to American life, they are proud of the children who do well. High academic achievement is seen by others as a sign of successful parenting. They also hope that the children will have more opportunities in the United States. Highly educated parents expect their children to follow in their footsteps, but parents with little or no education do not understand the educational system and cannot assist their children with their educational goals. Whether or not they are educated, parents struggle to understand an educational system that, in their minds, undercuts their authority over their children. "Back home" the schools support parents' and families' full control over the children. As one high school girl said:

The boys, they stay out late and stuff. That's OK, I mean the parents can't do anything about it. But when they come home, the father goes, "Well, if you were back home you wouldn't do this. Our relatives, what would they say?" So, as much as he enjoys outside he'll pay when he comes home and I'm sure they would get in a fight. My family went through that, my brother and my dad.

Afghan youth often discuss freedom of expression in America, but most young people and their parents feel that the advantages of personal freedom are wasted on issues that are harmful to people, like taking drugs. They think that no one needs this much freedom because people should rely on others and be part of a social network to live a happy life. Both young people and their parents think that Americans live without enough guidance and discipline.

On a broader level, some Afghan refugee youth have experienced war stress similar to that experienced by young Americans who live in urban war zones and witness drive-by shootings. An Afghan man in his early twenties, who lived in Kabul until two years ago, connects living in war with growing up quickly. He described seeing a boy, late for school, run across the street between a jeep and a tank. The jeep hit him and threw his body under a tank that rolled over him:

Then another tank and another. The tanks never stopped. There was no meaning to them in this death. In the end, there was no way to see the body as a person and yet someone had to tell the family. For months after this I could not sleep as I kept seeing this boy and this body. It is still fresh in my mind and I see it clearly still. I could never forget it. I also decided that what happened to Afghanistan was from God. We were drinking and leaving the way of God and this is how we are punished. This was what we deserved. After this life, I am older than the old men who tell me to respect them. What do they know? (Omidian 1994b)

In Kabul, this young man was motivated to make high grades to be admitted to the university; as long as he was a good student, he would not have to die as a soldier. In the wake of this pressure, he is looking forward to university classes in the United States for their own sake. Many Afghan youth who arrived in the late 1980s and the early 1990s faced an existence that most Americans see only at the movies.

A significant unifying factor is added to this mosaic of variation based on age, gender, ethnicity, education, and time in the United States. All Afghans living outside of the region maintain close ties with family members left behind. With the war likely to continue well into the latter half of the 1990s, trauma to, and displacement of, loved ones is still a reality to be faced. Many who survived the war against the Communist government are fleeing their homes as the political factions vie for power and bomb previously untouched civilian targets. Most families send money to help newly displaced relatives because few organizations are currently helping new refugees.

At the same time, people living in the United States are traveling to Pakistan and Afghanistan to visit and choose spouses for unmarried children and siblings. These marriages strengthen ties that might otherwise be lost. Also, by marrying a son or daughter to someone living in Pakistan or Afghanistan, families ensure the continuity of Afghan culture. Many feel that children raised in the United States cannot learn to be proper Afghans, and such marriages reinforce cultural identity.

CONCLUSIONS AND PROSPECTS

The first Afghans arrived in the United States less than a century ago; as late as 1977, the few who came to study returned home (Angary 1991). The past 15 years have seen many changes in the new Afghan population in the United States; its short history reveals both problems and successes. As civil unrest and war continue, fewer Afghans think that they can return to their country, and more are now becoming U.S. citizens. In addition to the danger in Afghanistan, parents are concerned that their children, raised in the United States, are too Americanized to function in Afghanistan; they also want to continue to take advantage of the educational and economic opportunities of America's industrialized society.

The Afghan community is heterogeneous in background, problems, and successes. As of 1995, problems for some Afghan families are the same as those experienced by other families in the early and mid-1980s—culture conflict, isolation, financial and occupational problems, mental health and other health problems primarily based on stress and posttraumatic stress disorder, poor access to health care and lack of culturally appropriate services, and family stress based on changing roles in the context of American culture. These are likely to worsen in the mid-1990s antiimmigrant climate and amid federal plans to disassemble the welfare system in California.

Other families, however, are relatively satisfied with their lives in the United States and appreciate the country's opportunities and technological time savers. Many of these families have been in the United States longer, know English, and have relatively stable jobs. However, they are now facing the dilemma of maintaining Afghan culture with their acculturated children and coping with stressful role changes within the family. Many men, for example, are threatened by the increasing assertiveness of women who function responsibly in the public sphere and help to support the family financially.

In the nine years that we have known the Afghan population in northern California, we have seen a number of changes. One of these changes is increased economic stability; for example, some families have been able to purchase homes and their own businesses. Some children have changed from being respectful young Afghans to Afghan gang members who vie for power with other ethnic gangs; others excel in school, many going on to college and university. These students are looking toward professional education, which should remedy one of the major problems faced by Afghans in the area, a lack of Afghan health, mental health, and social service providers.

The community has not yet become cohesive, but there are signs of change in this arena as well, particularly among young people and women, who are not involved in the men's politics and who are eager to work together for the good of the community. There are thriving Afghan clubs at local high schools, colleges, and universities where people socialize and support Afghan culture and community events. For example, the San Jose State University and Chabot College Afghan Clubs helped to put on an Afghan Community Health Fair in 1993. The Afghan Women's Association International, based in Hayward, accomplished what no other Afghan organization had been heretofore able to do— mobilize people and resources throughout the whole Bay Area to collect and donate clothing, blankets, and food to ship 100,000 pounds to Jalalabad, Afghanistan, to help the 600,000 new refugees who fled from Kabul beginning in early 1994.

It is difficult to predict the future prospects of the Afghan refugee community. There are many positive signs of integration and success in American society along with maintenance of Afghan ethnic identity and increased community cooperation, particularly among the young people. But along with those who are doing well are pockets of Afghans who may take many years to heal, if they heal at all. The lives of some remain miserable because of posttraumatic stress disorder, isolation, and loneliness; others appear to be becoming a passive ''welfare subculture,'' working the system for what they can get and raising the ire of their fellow Afghans. Overall, the varying courses of adjustment to American society reflect the heterogeneity of Afghans as a refugee subculture. Like a mosaic of tiles, we must view this subculture from various distances and angles to appreciate its complexity and overall patterns.

NOTES

This chapter is based on nine years of research with Afghans in the San Francisco Bay Area. Large sections based on publications and presentations are identified by superscripts rather than citation.

1. The sections on Afghanistan and youth issues are based on Omidian's (1992) Ph.D. dissertation.

2. Names used in this chapter are fictional.

3. Description and quotes on men and jobs are based on Omidian (1994a, 1994b).

4. The section on women relies heavily on Lipson and Miller (1994).

REFERENCES

Angary, Mir Tamim. 1991. *Afghanistan: Fighting for Freedom.* New York: Dillon Press.

Canfield, Robert. 1986. Ethnic, Regional, and Sectarian Alignments in Afghanistan. In *The State, Religion, and Ethnic Politics: Afghanistan, Iran and Pakistan.* Edited by A. Banuazizi and M. Weiner. Syracuse: Syracuse University Press. Pp. 75–103.

Dupree, Louis. 1980. *Afghanistan.* Princeton: Princeton University Press.

Lipson, Juliene. 1991. Afghan Refugee Health: Some Findings and Suggestions. *Qualitative Health Research* 1(3):349–369.

———. 1993. Afghan Refugees in California: Mental Health Issues. *Issues in Mental Health Nursing* 14(4):411–423.

Lipson, Juliene, and Suellen Miller. 1994. Changing Roles of Afghan Refugee Women in the U.S. *Health Care for Women International* 15(3):171–180.

Lipson, Juliene, and Patricia Omidian. 1992a. Afghan Refugees: Health Issues in the United States. *Western Journal of Medicine* 157(3):271–275.

———. 1992b. We Don't Know the Rules: Afghan Refugees' Health and Interactions with the U.S. Social Environment. Presented at the American Anthropological Asociation annual meeting, San Francisco, December.

———. 1993. Health among San Francisco Bay Area Afghans: A Community Assessment. *Afghanistan Studies Journal* 4:71–86.

Lipson, Juliene, Patricia Omidian, and Steven Paul. 1995. Afghan Health Education Project: A Community Survey. *Public Health Nursing* 12(3):143–150.

Nyrop, Richard, and Donald Seekins. 1986. *Afghanistan: A Country Study.* Washington, D.C.: U.S. Government Printing Office.

Omidian, Patricia. 1992. Aging and Intergenerational Conflict: Afghan Refugee Families in Transition. Unpublished Ph.D. dissertation, University of California, San Francisco.

———. 1994a. Afghan Refugee Males: Betwixt and Between. In *Endangered Minority Male: Volume I.* Edited by J. Nieto and P. Rainey. Bakersfield, California: Heritage of Aztlan. Pp. 107–116.

———. 1994b. "I'm Doing the Best I Can!": Conflicting Cultures/Conflicting Realities for Children of Middle Eastern Parents. In *Endangered Minority Male: Volume II.* Edited by J. Nieto and P. Rainey. Bakersfield, California: Heritage of Aztlan. Pp. 53–59.

———. 1996. *Transitions and Transformations: Aging and Family in an Afghan Refugee Community.* New York: Garland Publishers, Inc.

Omidian, Patricia, and Juliene Lipson. 1992. Elderly Afghan Refugees: Tradition and Transition in Northern California. In *Refugee Issues Papers.* Edited by Pamela DeVoe. Washington, D.C.: American Anthropological Association. Pp. 27–39.

Perez, Lisandra. 1986. Immigrant Economic Adjustment and Family Organization: The Cuban Success Story Reexamined. *International Migration Review* 20:4–20.

Psychiatry Centre for Afghan Refugees. 1988. *The Impaired Mind.* Peshawar, Pakistan.

Rahmany, Khalil. 1993. *A Long Journey: The Psychological Adjustment of the Afghan Refugees in the United States.* Unpublished Ph.D. dissertation, The Rosebridge Graduate School of Integrative Psychology, Concord, California, 1992.

U.S. Committee for Refugees. 1994a. Refugee Reports 15(3).

———. 1994b. *Refugee Reports.* 15(12).

World Almanac and Book of Facts 1994. 1993. Rahway, New Jersey: Funk and Wagnalls Corporation.

Chapter 8

Hmong

Timothy Dunnigan, Douglas P. Olney, Miles A. McNall, and Marline A. Spring

The Hmong were relatively unknown to the American public when they began arriving in the United States from Thailand refugee camps during the spring of 1976. This Laotian ethnic minority had been mentioned in news reports about "tribal" conflicts in Laos during the Vietnam War, but they were called the Meo, which is a derogatory Vietnamese term unacceptable to the Hmong. As the Meo, they were described as a primitive hill tribe who fought fiercely and effectively on the side of the democratically elected government of Laos against Communist insurgents called the Pathet Lao. The tragic results of Hmong involvement with the U.S. Central Intelligence Agency (CIA), a connection dating back to the early 1960s, did not fully come to light until after the Pathet Lao and North Vietnamese took over the country in 1975. Descriptions of the plight of these former allies in the news media fostered a sense of indebtedness toward the Hmong and stimulated concern for those languishing in Thailand refugee camps. Unfortunately, media exposure also created some misleading images of Hmong society.

Two decades have produced a generation of Hmong who have been through the entire kindergarten-through-college school system in the United States. The Hmong community in general has matured to the point where the 6,000 Hmong who continue to enter the country each year no longer have to deal with the same problems of physical survival as their predecessors. While finding good jobs remains difficult for many Hmong particularly for older persons, the young are now much better prepared to move into skilled and professional jobs. As a result, Hmong unemployment rates are falling. The early crisis of resettlement has abated, but new problems, as well as opportunities, have emerged.

Widely divergent views have developed in the Hmong community with respect to a number of issues that should be familiar to most Americans. Not surprisingly, there is much debate about how the Hmong should involve themselves in politics as a way of influencing domestic and international policies. They are concerned about the quality and content of educational programs that will shape the values of their children. They are struggling with the meaning of gender and age-based differences in a society that seems to set no boundaries. And, of course, the Hmong are concerned about maintaining a unique cultural heritage while establishing, or continually creating, an American identity.

LAOS

The population of Laos is ethnically diverse. The politically dominant Lao, who speak a language closely related to Thai, are concentrated primarily in the alluvial plains of the Mekong River. Linguistically similar groups inhabit the mountain valleys of central and northern Laos. Living on the mountain slopes are populations of Mon-Khmer speakers. The Hmong and Mien, whose languages have been classified as Sino-Tibetan, occupy the highest elevations. As LeBar and Suddard (1960:2) point out, "To the elite—virtually all Lao—the history of Laos is the story of the Lao." This is true despite estimates (Hickey 1955) that the nondominant minorities total half the population. The lowland bias is reflected in most historical and cultural surveys of Laos. Relatively little coverage is given the ethnic minorities, and their importance in recent history is only now being assessed.

Hmong are relative newcomers to Laos, having migrated from China and Vietnam beginning in the first part of the nineteenth century. The area of greatest settlement was the province of Xieng Khouang. Significant numbers also moved into adjacent provinces of Sam Neua, Luang Prabang, and Phong Saly. This concentrated the Hmong in northeastern Laos near the border with Vietnam, an area that became strategically important during the Vietnam War. Adequate documentation of early Hmong history is lacking (see Savina 1924; Dreyer 1976; Weins 1967; Larteguy 1979). Fortunately, additional information based on historical documents and oral traditions is being systematically recorded by a new generation of Hmong and non-Hmong scholars.

Observers writing in the 1950s and 1960s describe Hmong political organization as being generally limited to the village (Hickey 1955; Halpern 1964; LeBar and Suddard 1960; LeBar, Hickey, and Musgrave 1964). Mention is made of Hmong "kings" in China and Vietnam who, for fairly brief periods, controlled large areas and dominated neighboring groups, situations that are called "unusual" by Hickey (1955:310; see also Tapp 1985). Although periods of Hmong hegemony were probably infrequent, they have managed on a number of occasions to unify into supralocal organizations against outside political threats, as at the time of the Vietnam War.

In the course of their long history, the Hmong have accommodated to a variety of political systems in China and Southeast Asia. When political solidarity did not ensure their independence from some dominant nationality, they often enjoyed considerable autonomy because of the way they were integrated into state structures. For instance, LeBar and colleagues (1964:70) describe the following situation in sixteenth-century Kweichow, China: "Tribal chieftains, including Miao [Hmong] chieftains, were appointed to hereditary administrative positions, adopting Chinese surnames and entering into a kind of feudatory arrangement with the imperial government on behalf of tribesmen within their jurisdiction."

The Hmong in Laos sought similar arrangements with French colonial administrators and various Lao political leaders. Hmong strategy was to maximize their autonomy by supporting established authorities or emerging powers. The rewards consisted of increased control over their own affairs at the local level and a sharing in the benefits of national development. In areas where they were numerically and politically weak, they were subjected to discrimination and exploitation by other ethnic groups (Gunn 1990). The struggle for a measure of self-governance in Laos before 1975 has been interpreted by some critics of the U.S. involvement with the Laotian Hmong as a secessionist movement (see Adams and McCoy 1970). By 1975, however, Hmong integration into the political, military, economic, and educational institutions of Laos had progressed to a point where ethnic separatism would have been extremely unlikely, had the royalist government prevailed.

It must be acknowledged that the Hmong have long been perceived in Vietnam, Thailand, and Laos as politically suspect because of their cultural distinctiveness, independence, and ethnic loyalty. On a number of occasions the Hmong have rebelled against the exactions of hostile governments (Jenks 1985). An uprising lasting from 1918 to 1922 spread through parts of northeast Laos and northwest Tonkin (North Vietnam). Because one of the main leaders was Pa Chai, a native curer who prophesied the destruction of the Lao and French oppressors by supernatural means, French historians have denigrated the rebellion as "the crazy man's war" (Larteguy 1979:91–95; Smalley, Vang, and Yang 1990). It was after this rebellion was suppressed that other Hmong leaders were allowed greater political authority by the French in populous Hmong regions of Laos.

Another nativistic movement arose during the mid-1960s in Laos when intensified fighting between government troops and Communist insurgents began destroying many Hmong villages. The movement's prophet was Shong Lue Yang, who promoted Hmong unity and devised a special script for writing the Hmong language. Shong Lue was killed in 1971 by political rivals, but his followers continue to maintain active organizations in Laos, Thailand, and the United States. Some of its adherents, a small but undefined portion of the Laotian Hmong who are implacable enemies of the Pathet Lao and Vietnamese, have conducted resistance activities in Laos intermittently since 1975 (Smalley, Vang, and Yang 1990).

Notwithstanding these episodic revolts, the Hmong assiduously cultivated alliances with other groups and outside political leaders. The choosing of certain allies by Hmong leaders caused deep internal divisions. Two powerful lineages belonging to different clans began in the 1930s to compete for official French recognition in the Nong Het area of Xieng Khouang. The rivalry led to the formation of pro- and anti-French factions and eventually drew many Hmong into the Indochinese wars as combatants on both sides (Lee 1982). The Hmong who achieved political ascendancy during the late colonial period transferred their allegiance to the French-supported constitutional monarchy established in 1949. These same Hmong became allies of the United States as the latter replaced the French as the military backers of rightist elements in the Royal Laotian government. A much smaller Hmong faction joined with Lao Issara in agitating for an independent Laos, free from French influence. After independence, the disaffected Hmong became part of the Pathet Lao movement.

Lee (1982:203) describes the situation of the Hmong as the war was drawing to a close:

By 1973, the Hmong formed 32 percent of the 370,000 refugees on government support in Laos, and 70 percent of 155, 474 in Xieng Khouang—the biggest ethnic group affected by the war. About 12,000 are believed to have died fighting against the Pathet Lao from 1962 to 1975. This heavy toll was partly the result of the military draft introduced by the RLG [Royal Laotian government] in its offensive against the PL [Pathet Lao] and North Vietnamese forces. . . . An American refugee worker established that 20 percent of Hmong civilians died in the early 1960s as a result of sickness or enemy attacks during their flight to refugee camps.

The Hmong had become refugees in their own country long before it became necessary for many of them to seek sanctuary in Thailand.

The present status of the Hmong in Laos is difficult to ascertain. Hmong resistance movements continued throughout the 1980s, possibly with the covert help of China, Thailand, and the United States. The Chao Fa established a stronghold in the mountainous and forested region of Phu Bia, near the important strategic area known as the Plain of Jars. Although rumors of guerrilla actions still emanate from Laos, the government claims to have instituted programs and reconciliation and development for the Hmong and is now cooperating with the United Nations High Commissioner for Refugees (UNHCR) in the repatriation of Hmong refugees still left in Thailand camps.

For a time after 1976, refugees accused the Pathet Lao and their Vietnamese allies of carrying out lethal "gas" attacks against both resistance fighters and noncombatant Hmong in Laos. A Canadian research team conducted a small-scale epidemiological study of Laotian Hmong and Khmer from Kampuchea and concluded that chemical/biological warfare was being waged in Southeast Asia. The lethal agents, the researchers surmised, were mycotoxins (Humphreys and Dow 1982; Schiefer 1982). The U.S. State Department also took this position (Haig 1982; Schultz 1982). Strong denials were issued by the governments of Laos, Vietnam, and the Soviet Union. Evans (1983) dismissed the claims of chemical/biological warfare as fabrications, but his arguments were more ideo-logical and empirical. Whether Hmong were deliberately exposed to unusually large amounts of mycotoxins by their political enemies has never been conclusively determined.

The controversy concerning the possible use of various kinds of poisons by newly established governments in Laos and Kampuchea in order to eliminate pockets of resistance became much more narrowly focused when journalists began reporting that Hmong "tribesmen" had experienced chemical attacks in the form of "yellow rain" (Whiteside 1991a, 1991b). The metaphor was mistakenly attributed to the Hmong, and subsequent investigations centered on small yellow droplets that had appeared on vegetation in areas where chemical attacks were said to have occurred. When some scientific analyses indicated the presence of deadly fungus-produced poisons, the U.S. State Department believed that they had conclusive evidence of chemical warfare (Seiders 1986). Other scientists made a considerably more mundane and convincing case for the deposition of feces excreted from swarming bees (Seeley et al. 1985; Marshall 1986a, 1986b).

Because early investigations were so limited, and the issue reduced to arguments about a single putative vector for a certain type of poison, outside observers still do not know what happened to convince many Hmong that they had been targeted for "kemi" attacks. Extremely ethnocentric speculations about Hmong "primitive" perceptions under conditions of extreme stress (e.g., Evans 1983; Whiteside 1991b) offer no answers. Accusations of chemical warfare during the early postwar period in Southeast Asia continue to be made (Hamilton-Merritt 1993), but the issue may never be resolved.

THE EXODUS FROM LAOS TO THAILAND

When the Pathet Lao came to power in 1975, the United States abruptly ceased aiding its Laotian allies. Most Hmong who had sided with the Royalists believed that their position was untenable. General Vang Pao, who commanded most of the Hmong troops and contingents from other ethnic groups, departed by air from Laos for asylum in Thailand on May 14. He was accompanied by his family and members of his support staff. Soon afterward, a great many Hmong began fleeing overland to Thailand. By the end of the year, UNHCR (1983) counted 44,659 "Lao hill people," most of them Hmong, living in the refugee camps of Thailand. The flow of Hmong refugees out of Laos lessened considerably during 1976 and 1977 but again increased to rather high levels in 1979–1980. There has since been a sharp decline in the rate at which Hmong refugees have crossed from Laos into Thailand. According to the U.S. Committee for Refugees (1994b), only 1,155 Highland Lao entered Thailand in 1994.

Thailand camps were established at Nong Khai and Nam Phong to receive the first waves of Hmong refugees. The Thai government began in 1979 to concentrate ethnic and nationality groups at particular locations, the main

Hmong camp being Ban Vinai, which opened in December 1975. Smaller groups of Hmong were interned at Chiang Khong, Ban Nam Yao, Sop Thuang, and Chiang Kham. While waiting to be resettled in a third country, Hmong families spent some time at transit centers like Phanat Nikhom.

The Thai Ministry of the Interior assumed responsibility for setting up the refugee services and managing basic services, such as food, shelter, and sanitation. The UNHCR funds camp operations, and a number of voluntary agencies, or VOLAGs, provide additional services in Thailand, ranging from medical care to educational programs. Hmong residents of Ban Vinai were eligible to participate in more than 17 such services (CCSDPT 1982:3; Long 1993).

Several levels of organization, official and unofficial, evolved within the camps. A Thai served as commander of Ban Vinai and was assisted by a Hmong subcommander. The camp was divided into 7 residential areas, each having its own leader. A residential area was further divided into three subsections consisting of a number of ten-room dwellings encircled by smaller units. A leader was designated for every subsection and large dwelling. Persons were elected to these leadership positions by the residents and were expected to assign labor tasks, oversee the fair distribution of food, and ensure that information was disseminated properly (Smalley n.d.; CCSDPT 1982; Long 1993). In contrast to Ban Vinai, Sop Thuang was divided into 12 areas according to ethnic group distinctions, and the houses were arranged as they had been in the refugees' home villages.

The unofficial camp organization at Ban Vinai is nicely summarized by Smalley (n.d.:19).

The deeper cultural and emotional life of the Hmong refugees was not lived only within these loosely superimposed hierarchies. It was lived also within traditional families, lineages, subclans and other social relationships which people brought with them as they migrated. Some families had been shredded, with members lost in war and escape, others still back in Laos. But the intricate and extensive ways which Hmong have of relating people to people were brought with them. A lineage head might be in another section of the camp, but even so that was closer than a half day's walk or more distance than he might have been in Laos. The members of a village might be scattered all over Ban Vinai, but those who were there still looked to their village headman from Laos or some other leader they had known. . . . Decisions were made within the traditional frameworks, marriages were made within the traditional patterns, ceremonies were performed within traditional groupings. All this was constrained by the camp situations of course. Adaptations had to be made. But these fundamental parts of Hmong life went on in camp, and on that level the Thai, international, and even the Hmong camp hierarchy was relatively irrelevant.

For the first seven years, more Laotian Hmong entered Thailand than left for other countries. The Hmong refugee population in Thailand reached a peak of 55,000 in 1982 (DeVecchi 1982:23) and then slowly came down. The UNHCR has had a voluntary repatriation program in place since the early 1980s, but only about 5,000 Hmong have accepted the organization's help in returning to Laos (U.S. Committee for Refugees 1994a:4). The situation for the Hmong changed dramatically in the early 1990s when the Thai government decided to try speeding up both the resettlement and repatriation of refugees by closing camps and making the situation more uncomfortable for those who remained. Ban Vinai was closed late in 1992, as was Chiang Kham the following year. At the end of 1993, 23,220 Highland Lao were interned at two camps, Ban Na Pho and Phanat Nikhom, and this number was reduced to 10,044 by September 1994 (U.S. Committee for Refugees 1994b). With the closing of camps in Thailand, up to 12,000 Laotian Hmong left United Nations jurisdiction without authorization and settled around a monastery north of Bangkok.

It should be noted that the Thai government's recent push for repatriation has created considerable tension between competing political segments of the U.S. Hmong community. Some groups are cautiously supporting voluntary repatriation because they would like to see a rapprochement between the People's Democratic Republic of Laos and the United States that would lead to a substantial investment of American money in Laotian economic development. Opposing groups want Western countries to withhold their support in the hope that the present Communist regime in Laos will either collapse or at least undergo major democratic reform. They claim that Hmong who are repatriated from Thailand will face new persecutions and, therefore, should stay put for the time being.

RESETTLEMENT IN THE UNITED STATES

The magnitude of the refugee problem and the threat it posed to political stability throughout Southeast Asia was not immediately appreciated by the international community after the Vietnam War. Only 12,300 Laotians classified as belonging to "hill tribes" were resettled in third countries from 1976 through 1978. International concern for the refugees increased markedly with the fall of the Pol Pot regime in Kampuchea and the advent of the Vietnamese boat people crisis. As a result, more Hmong and refugees belonging to other ethnic groups were received by third countries. Resettlement figures for Laotian hill tribes for 1979 and 1980 were 13,000 and 29,000, respectively. After 1980, the Hmong showed less interest in permanent resettlement. Only 8,000 moved to third countries between January 1981 and May 1983 (UNHCR 1983).

By May 1983, the United States had accepted about 50,000 Hmong; France, 7,000; French Guiana, 1,200; Canada, 800; Australia, 300; Argentina, 200; and various other nations, including China and Japan, 300 or so (UNHCR 1983). Resettlement continued for the next decade, with another 66,000 going to the United States and only a few thousand going elsewhere.

The resettlement experience has been different for the Hmong in each country, ranging from participation in an extensive agricultural experiment in French Guiana (involving the creation of two self-sufficient Hmong villages in the jungle) to a bewildering variety of programs offered in the context of urban Amer-

Table 8.1
Hill Tribe Resettlement in the United States

Year	Number	% of Total
1975	301	0.3%
1976	3,058	2.7%
1977	1,655	1.4%
1978	3,873	3.4%
1979	11,301	9.8%
1980	27,242	23.7%
1981	3,704	3.2%
1982	2,511	2.2%
1983	738	0.6%
1984	2,753	2.4%
1985	1,944	1.7%
1986	3,668	3.2%
1987	8,307	7.2%
1988	4,168	3.6%
1989	8,476	7.4%
1990	5,207	4.5%
1991	6,369	5.5%
1992	6,833	5.9%
1993	6,741	5.9%
1994	6,253	5.4%
Total	115,102	100.0%

Source: U.S. Committee for Refugees 1994a.

ica. (See Table 8.1 for numerical data on Hmong resettlement in the United States.) The U.S. quota for accepting additional Laotian Hmong from Thailand continues to be 6,000 per year, a figure that has been met for the past seven years. The Hmong who remain in Thailand appear to be biding their time until some more acceptable option becomes available.

Approximately 90,000 Hmong were counted in the 1990 U.S. census. About 80,000 Hmong had been admitted to the United States by 1990, and considering their relatively high birthrate, the census estimate is undoubtedly much too low. Unfortunately, there have been no other official surveys that provide more reliable figures. In 1990, Hmong were found living in all but seven states, but just three states accounted for 90 percent of the Hmong population—California (46,892), Minnesota (16,833), and Wisconsin (16,373) (Schlader, Schwartz, and Detzner 1995). The largest concentrations of Hmong were located in the Central

Valley of California, the Minneapolis–St. Paul area of Minnesota, and the Wisconsin cities of Milwaukee, Appleton, and Wausau. This distribution is more a reflection of secondary migration than of initial resettlement. A majority of families have moved from locations where they were originally sponsored to areas where they could live close to relatives and have access to better employment, education, and social services.

HMONG KINSHIP

Barney (1967:275–276) describes the essential characteristics of Hmong (Meo) kinship categories and groups, which are formed primarily on the basis of descent through the male line.

The patrilineal clan system of the Meo dominates their social organization, serving as a primary focus for their culture as a whole by tying together social, political, economic and religious aspects of behavior. The basic unit of the Meo social structure is the "household" or patrilineal extended family, meaning not only those who live under one roof, but also including all those under the authority of one household head. Thus a single household could include a man's unmarried daughters, his sons and their wives and children, and possibly his sons' sons' children and might also include a few other feeble or otherwise dependent relatives. All members of the household carry the clan name of the household head in addition to their given name. The clan name refers to descent from a mythical ancestor, and common membership in a clan serves as a bond of kinship and friendship between people who would otherwise be strangers. Members of the same lineage, who can trace their common descent from a known ancestor, refer to lineage mates by a common term meaning "my olders and youngers" [*kwv tij*].

As an enclaved minority in Laos practicing swidden agriculture, the Hmong developed patterns of kin group formation that have helped them survive as refugees in Thailand and other countries of asylum. Members of the extended family were sometimes forced to separate in order to find sufficient agricultural land in the Laotian highlands. Nonetheless, they remained in contact with one another and made every effort to reunify in an area that would support the entire group. When families became fragmented during the flight from Laos to Thailand, and again in the course of permanent resettlement, the Hmong placed greater reliance on lineage and even clan ties as a basis for close cooperation. Solidarity among one's patrilineal relatives still provides the greatest security for the Hmong, even in urban America (Dunnigan 1982).

In the 1960s and early 1970s, some Hmong extended families and lineage groups were able to prepare for the future through occupational diversification. In addition to farmers, their membership included soldiers, traders, students, various kinds of technicians attached to the military and international development missions, and other people with special knowledge who served their respective kinship groups as circumstances changed. The expectation of mutual assistance among family and lineage members remains strong. Status and wealth differences do exist between nuclear families that make up the patrilineal group, but the general goal is to advance the socioeconomic position of all members.

Linkage through marriage entails additional reciprocity. Upon marrying, Hmong women customarily leave their "patrikin" and become fully integrated into the families of their husbands. This establishes an alliance of lineages belonging to different clans. Should there be marital discord, the wife's consanguineal relatives try to help arrange a reconciliation. A divorced woman returns to her natal group until she remarries. The children ordinarily remain with their father's group, but a variety of arrangements are becoming more common in the United States.

Married couples sometimes choose to live with the wife's patrikin. This is most likely to happen when the wife's relatives are better able to help the new couple. The couple's offspring will try to maintain understandings of mutual obligation with both the affiliated lineage and their own patrikin. The option of emphasizing relations of descent or marriage at different times, depending upon circumstances, further enhances the security of individuals and small family units.

ASPECTS OF HMONG RELIGION

Before being exposed to the missionizing efforts of Westerners in Laos, most Hmong believed in the existence of what they called *dab* or spirits. Various kinds of dangerous spirits inhabited the "wild" domain of the forests. Some had the power to possess people or capture souls and cause illness. Other "domestic" spirits of the home and garden protected families as long as family members acted properly. Deceased ancestors could also aid or punish their living relatives and had to be honored in prescribed ways. To these beliefs were added the philosophies and practices of Taoism, Confucianism, Buddhism, and beginning in the 1950s, Christianity. A relatively small number of Laotian Hmong were converted to Catholicism and Protestant fundamentalism, but about half the Hmong who resettled in the United States claimed adherence to a form of Christianity. Hmong Protestant congregations usually elect their own lay leaders and tend to separate themselves from non-Hmong for worship and socializing. Religiously trained Hmong have little difficulty gaining a following from among their own people.

The Hmong desire religious consensus within the kin group, or at least among its core members. The conversion of key leaders provides strong incentive for other members to follow the same course. Lineage organizations have sometimes directly addressed the problem of achieving religious unity by choosing as a group to accept a particular form of Christianity or to return to an earlier set of beliefs and practices. In part, the continued attraction of the pre-Christian religion can be attributed to the fact that sacred rituals help to define the boundaries of the kinship group. Shared funerary practices and ways of honoring the ancestors can be used to establish and reinforce lineage ties even when genealogical connections are unclear. Moreover, many Hmong continue to use native curers, a practice that strict Hmong Christians condemn. For the most part, religious differences have not prevented interlineage cooperation. Tensions that occasionally exist between non-Christian and Christian groups related by marriage are usually managed without overt conflict.

ECONOMIC ADAPTATIONS

The main occupation of the Hmong in Laos was swidden agriculture. Forest growth had to be cut and burned on the land that was cultivated. A variety of crops were planted for three or four years on average until soil exhaustion required the development of new plots. Old fields were sometimes replanted after a long period of fallow. Hmong strategies of field rotation, crop sequencing, soil selection, fertilization, and so on, were quite sophisticated and productive, although the long-term environmental effects of such slash-and-burn methods have been criticized and possibly exaggerated (see Geddes 1976). Hmong who had access to fertile areas with permanent sources of irrigation water practiced intensive agriculture. The Hmong also raised horses, pigs, cattle, carabaos, and chickens.

Besides planting varieties of rice, corn, and many types of vegetables, the Hmong cultivated opium poppies as an important cash crop. They were one of many ethnic groups producing raw opium for a market that had de facto legitimacy in Laos. A relatively small number of Hmong were itinerant traders who brought a variety of commodities to isolated settlements and collected opium from the producers for resale to higher-level distributors. Because the Hmong used opium as a broadly useful medicine (Westermeyer 1982), it has been difficult to convince some of the older, infirm Hmong living in the United States to cease using opium entirely.

As hostilities escalated after 1961 in northeastern Laos, more and more Hmong were prevented from supporting themselves by farming. Families that congregated in large refugee settlements in north central Laos at least tried to maintain gardens. Later, in Thailand, some of the Hmong were initially allowed to plant on land close to the refugee camps. Unfortunately, their harvests were eventually hijacked by armed local Thai, and afterward the Hmong only planted on scarce small plots within the camps.

Middle-aged and older Hmong would like to practice farming in the United States. Family groups have leased acreage in order to produce vegetables for home consumption and commercial sale through farmers' markets. Young Hmong men and women are also working family plots as a way of earning income. During the early 1980s there was considerable interest in publicly and privately funded farming projects that had the objective of training the Hmong to farm according to the production and marketing techniques generally practiced in the United States. As a result of participating in these experiments, many Hmong discovered that, like other American small farmers, they could not make a living solely from agriculture. The attraction of farming for the Hmong was apparent in the large migration to the central valley of California in 1982–1983 (Bays 1994). Although it is extremely difficult to become an established grower, some families were able to buy or lease land in the vicinity of Fresno and Merced where they raised labor-intensive commercial crops such as pea pods and tomatoes. For the vast majority of the migrants to the Central Valley, the dream of farming never materialized. A minority of Hmong families living in other states have been able to acquire rural land and raise some crops to supplement their income.

The economic history of the Laotian Hmong during the Vietnam War and postwar internment in Thailand has not been sufficiently researched. Yang (1976) describes some of the Hmong responses to economic opportunities that came with the political destabilization of Laos between 1961 and 1975. What has not been precisely documented is the extent to which Hmong increased their participation in sectors of the Laotian economy outside of agriculture. Data collected by researchers associated with the Life Course Center at the University of Minnesota show that a number of refugees living in Minneapolis–St. Paul, including women, had operated as small-scale entrepreneurs in Laos and Thailand (see also Bays 1994). These experiences may have provided a basis for undertaking business ventures in the United States such as butcher shops, grocery stores, restaurants, commercial sewing businesses, craft sale outlets, and automotive sales and repair shops. Middle-aged and older Hmong refugees often express a desire to own and operate small businesses, but only a small percentage ever achieve what could be called long-term success.

The fact that so few Hmong who resettled in the United States between 1975 and 1985 possessed the specific vocational skills and knowledge of English demanded by potential employers seemed to be reflected in the general psychological adjustment of the refugees (Westermeyer, Vang, and Lyfong 1983; Westermeyer, Vang, and Neider 1983a, 1983b, 1983c; Williams and Westermeyer 1983). Westermeyer, Vang, and Neider (1984) reported a high rate of depression among Hmong refugee subjects, with 40 percent achieving "depressive" scores on the Zung Depression Scale. They found some improvement over time, but the lack of employment opportunities seemed to contribute to the high rates of depression.

From the beginning of refugee resettlement in the United States, Hmong leaders have stressed the need for vocational training, and a great many Hmong have attended vocational/technical institutes. Young graduates are now finding employment in areas ranging from legal and medical services to domestic help. There are Hmong travel agencies that specialize in tours to Laos, Hmong real estate firms, and a growing variety of Hmong-owned retail businesses. Hmong with advanced education are providing some professional services to their own people, but, judging from 1988–1991 data (McNall, Dunnigan, and Mortimer 1994), most working Hmong still hold low-paying service, clerical, or light manufacturing jobs that require few skills and no more than a functional knowledge of English. One third of the employed Hmong engage in "bench work" as sewing machine operators or assemblers, and the most frequently reported service-type job is that of janitor.

Many Hmong continue to reside in public housing or substandard units located within the deteriorating inner city. The tendency for Hmong to cluster in certain areas appears to be determined not only by the availability of inexpensive housing but also by a strong desire on the part of the Hmong to reside near relatives. By being persistent and filling vacancies as they come available, Hmong have slowly taken over whole apartment buildings.

Disadvantaged minorities who had already established themselves in neighborhoods with relatively cheap housing stock initially resented the influx of Hmong refugees. The resentment was sometimes expressed in vandalism and physical violence. In some cases, local leaders representing the different groups were able to get together and work out strategies for reducing tensions. Attacks directed specifically at the Hmong have lessened, and much of the earlier concern has shifted toward the common problem of youth gang activity.

Owing a home is highly valued by the Hmong. If they have limited means, families will not hesitate to purchase a home close to relatives who rent in the inner city, but more affluent families have shown a pattern of outward movement similar to that followed by the general population. Hmong families tend to initially relocate to a first-tier suburb and, if their fortunes continue to improve, eventually seek housing in a relatively affluent outer-ring community. What is different about the Hmong compared with the general population is that the former show a tendency to migrate as a group. If a prominent family of an important Hmong leader settles in a new neighborhood or community, this encourages other family members and Hmong friends to investigate the possibility of moving into the same area.

EDUCATION

Despite current economic hardships and an historically limited experience with formal education, the Hmong community has had reason to be pleased with the educational accomplishments of its youth. Data gathered in St. Paul, Minnesota (McNall, Dunnigan, and Mortimer 1994) show the Hmong doing very well in high schools and pursuing postsecondary education at rates comparable to the general population. Hmong students in St. Paul spend more hours per week on homework and earn higher grade-point averages than their peers in all four years of high school. In addition, they less often get into trouble at school or drop out than non-Hmong. After high school, Hmong youth spend roughly the same amount of time in school as the non-Hmong (see Table 8.2). In addition, there are no differences between Hmong and non-Hmong in the type of schooling pursued, at least during the first year after high school. In other words, the two groups are enrolled in community, vocational, and four-year colleges at

Table 8.2
Percentage in School after High School: Hmong and Non-Hmong Compared

Year	Hmong	(N)	Non-Hmong	(N)	Chi-square	p
1	81%	64	77%	616	0.63	0.43
2	61%	53	60%	411	0.01	0.91
3	51%	43	58%	405	1.29	0.26

Note: None of the indicated differences are statistically significant.
Source: Youth Development Study (NIMH grant #42843).

nearly the same rates (see Table 8.3). For both, four-year colleges represent the schooling of choice.

While Hmong are generally doing well in school, graduating from high school, and finding work or matriculating at postsecondary institutions, there is a minority who are being drawn into the kinds of youth gang activities that have become a national concern. The extent to which Hmong youth actually join gangs and commit crimes has not been adequately researched, but public apprehension over "Asian gangs" has been fueled by alarmist stories in the mass media. Hmong parents living in high crime areas do fear that their children will be lost to the streets and the criminal justice system even though such tragedies are still uncommon. Moreover, Hmong secular and religious leaders strongly promote organized activities that give youth an opportunity to experience legitimate successes.

MARRIAGE AND FERTILITY

Hmong experience near-universal marriage and regard having children both as a natural process and as a necessary step in attaining a mature social status. Although marriage negotiations occur between the families of the engaged couple, our surveys indicate that a majority of Hmong who married in Laos chose their own partners with the approval of parents. Donnelly (1994) indicates that young Hmong persons often based their choice on the advice of others. Less than a quarter of Hmong in a 1992 Minnesota community survey (Spring n.d.) characterized their marriages as being arranged by parents. Another 10 percent reported having been married as the result of *zij pojniam*, which literally translates as "seizing a wife." While it can refer to the deviant and risky practice of taking a woman by force and trying later to mollify her family into accepting the marriage, it also applies to instances where males claim the right to propose to a woman by taking hold of her arm outside of her house and not relinquishing

Table 8.3
Postsecondary Schooling: Hmong and Non-Hmong Compared

Type	Hmong	(N)	Non-Hmong	(N)	Chi-square	p
Community College	9%	6	16%	99	2.51	0.11
Vocational College	16%	11	18%	106	0.05	0.82
Four-Year College	55%	37	47%	282	1.79	0.18

Note: None of the indicated differences are statistically significant.
Source: Youth Development Study (NIMH grant #42843).

it until senior members from both families arrive for purposes of marriage negotiation. The fascination among Westerners with Hmong customs of arranged marriage and so-called marriage by capture has distorted the perceived prevalence of such practices.

Based on interviews with Hmong women in the United States, Donnelly (1994) and Bays (1994) concluded that most women married in Laos between the ages of 14 and 22. A 1992 Minnesota study (Spring n.d.) tallied a number of marriages that fell outside this range. The lowest age was 10 years, and the highest was 27 years. Hmong males indicated that they were somewhat older when they first married, between 16 and 36 years of age. A couple's first child usually arrived within the first 2 years and served to strengthen the marriage. Hmong desire many children because they perpetuate the family and increase its prospects for success (see "An Adaptation Model" below).

An issue of concern for social policymakers in the United States has been the relatively early age at which Hmong, especially women, get married and have children. Judging from several reports (Spring n.d.; Bays 1994), most Hmong women marry in the United States between the ages of 11 and 23. One range reported for Hmong males is 16 to 35 (Spring n.d.). Most Hmong women give birth within the first year of marriage (Spring n.d.; Symonds 1984). Early marriages followed fairly quickly by childbirth are known to result in increased fertility levels, and it is not surprising that researchers report high birthrates for Hmong throughout the United States (Hahn and Muecke 1987; Hopkins and Clarke 1983; Rumbaut and Weeks 1986; Weeks et al. 1989).

Of the approximately 30,000 Minnesota Hmong who were counted in the 1990 census, one third were born in the United States, and three fifths were below the age of 18 (Yang and Murphy 1993). While Hmong compose at least

6 percent of the population of St. Paul, Minnesota, 25 percent of students entering first grade in 1992–1993 were Hmong. Nearly a third of a Hmong female cohort studied in St. Paul (Hutchison and McNall 1994) were married and gave birth by the end of their junior year of high school, and about half were married and had at least one child before the end of their senior year. It seems that not only do the Hmong marry and have children relatively early; they also appear to have more children.

Early marriage, early childbearing, and high fertility are all thought to have particularly damaging consequences for the educational and occupational achievement of young Hmong adults (Downing et al. 1984; Vangay 1989). Yet, as we have seen, Hmong females as well as males have attained educational success to a degree that is, in some respects, superior to that of the general population. Hmong marriage and fertility patterns do not produce lower grades, more high school dropouts, or lower levels of enrollment in postsecondary educational institutions. In general, early marriage and childbearing do not appear to serve as an impediment to young Hmong adults' pursuit of education. The reasons for this are not clear, but it seems reasonable to assume that, by virtue of the extended kin networks in the Hmong community, young Hmong women are able to take advantage of the child care services of older female relatives.

High fertility levels in the Hmong population are distinguished by short intervals between births. This pattern of childbearing is known to increase the risks of illness and death for both mother and child in other groups. Even though Hmong women appear to underutilize Western prenatal health care services, studies reveal that their birth outcomes are better than the national average (Spring et al. 1995; Helsel, Petitti, and Kunstadter 1992; Rumbaut and Weeks 1989; Erickson et al. 1987; Richman and Dixon 1985; Hopkins and Clarke 1983; National Center for Health Statistics 1989). Because they view pregnancy as a natural rather than a medical condition, are generally pleased with birth outcomes, and realize that mother and child survival rates have risen in the United States, Hmong have few incentives to fully utilize the reproductive services offered at medical clinics.

COMMUNITY POLITICS

Almost 15 years ago in St. Paul, Minnesota, the Hmong organized a national conference on resettlement issues. One of the best-attended sessions focused on the development of effective community leadership. Participants expressed the opinion that key leaders who had held the Hmong together in Laos and Thailand were being ignored by American authorities. If this continued, they reasoned, the Hmong would become fractionalized and incapable of exerting any political influence. The speakers recalled that they had advanced materially in Laos only after Hmong began serving as district officials, judges, military officers, legislative representatives, and even department ministers. In these positions, they were able to mobilize support for national goals while securing for the Hmong some of the economic and educational advantages enjoyed by the lowland Lao.

Early in the resettlement process, Hmong refugees began exerting pressure on the various service agencies to hire certain bilinguals. Some agency directors may have seen this as an attempt on the part of formerly powerful people or emerging leaders to selfishly promote themselves and their supporters, but many agencies understood the advantages of recruiting respected members of the client community to help solve difficult problems.

Not wanting to be entirely dependent on the established resettlement agencies, the Hmong formed mutual assistance associations in many parts of the country. Very quickly their efforts resulted in the formation of a national organization with regional branches for the purpose of providing a wide range of services directly to the refugees. These groups sought federal and local funds to support their new programs. The resulting competition for government dollars created some tensions between the Hmong and established agencies (Olney 1993).

So long as all the kin groups were struggling to survive in the United States, the appeal of a national mutual assistance association was strong. Divisions based on kinship, regional loyalty, dialect, and political alliance could be bridged by a coalition of leaders headed by General Vang Pao. As the situation improved for some groups, the perceived need for a single national organization became less general. Some Hmong wanted to concentrate exclusively on local and lineage-level concerns. Rather than being merely symptomatic of a kind of ethnic community breakup, these changes are indicative of a recurring cycle of alliance building in the face of a common threat, followed by segmentation when the need for general cooperation subsides (Dunnigan 1982; Olney 1993). As the needs of various groups and communities have changed, a variety of new forms of associations have developed to serve special segments of the population, such as women, youth, and elders. Still other associations have arisen in response to new political issues both within the United States and internationally.

AN ADAPTATION MODEL

As indicated above in the discussion of kinship and economics, Hmong in the United States have access to social resources often not available to members of the general population. The Hmong participate in rather extensive helping networks based primarily on kinship that afford individuals and nuclear families considerable security, economic as well as social and psychological. Reliance on kin group support is hardly unique to the Hmong. Kibria (1994) describes a similar system of reciprocity for Vietnamese refugees living in Philadelphia. Both her methods of study and conceptualization of Vietnamese adaptation suggest a way of understanding the coping strategies of the Hmong.

Using such standard ethnographic practices as in-depth interviewing, participant observation, and case study analysis, Kibria (1994:81) was able to determine that multifamily Vietnamese households tend to employ a "patchwork" strategy involving "gathering together a wide variety of resources from diverse social and economic arenas," which have the effect of mitigating "the instability and scarcity of resources." One factor reinforcing the gathering and sharing of essential goods within the Vietnamese household, according to Kibria, is an "ideology of family collectivism."

The Hmong household, which constitutes an important arena of resource sharing, often consists of three generations and may include several nuclear families of siblings. These siblings are usually, but not always, brothers. There are also larger kin groups upon which the Hmong often depend for certain kinds of assistance. The Hmong expression *tsev neeg* refers to all people under one roof, most specifically a resident family or household. Like the English word *family,* the meaning of *tsev neeg* can be extended to include all cooperating descendants of certain parents or grandparents. A number of nuclear and extended households may regard themselves as belonging to one *tsev neeg* and, as a result, feel strongly obliged to assist one another. Member households could be localized in a particular city or scattered across many countries. Although it is tempting to call such groups patrilineages, it must be recognized that the intimate involvement of affines, that is, relatives by marriage, in these reciprocal relationships tends to blur group boundaries, at least to some extent.

The pooling of resources within and between *tsev neeg,* particularly at the local level, has benefited the Hmong immensely. For instance, family associations consisting of linked patrikin and close affines (see Dunnigan 1982) have formed semicorporate organizations that offer loan and life insurance benefits to members. Of course, not all shared resources can be quantified in terms of cash values. Those who belong to large, highly diverse kin groups are also more likely to have direct access to persons with specialized knowledge and skills in areas of ritual performance, curing, marriage negotiation, adjudication of social conflicts, and so on. It is through the different contributions of many individuals that kin-based groups become more self-sufficient and prestigious.

Kibria's (1994) study of Philadelphia Vietnamese provides a good model for researching Hmong refugee adaptations. We would, however, suggest two modifications. Because the Hmong household is so thoroughly embedded in the larger kin network, at least in most instances, it would be a mistake to focus solely on the residence group as the unit of study. Behavior within the household often cannot be fully understood without an extensive examination of more encompassing kinship structures. We also have some doubt about the validity of the Western collectivism versus individualism dichotomy mentioned so often in cross-cultural research. Like the Vietnamese, the Hmong certainly do appear to have a distinctive ideology consisting of beliefs and values that facilitate cooperation among kin group members. However, the benefits of mutuality redound to each individual, and the strategy of supporting common interests in order to ensure one's own claim to group support can be viewed as a matter of practical self-interest. It is a strategy that cannot be reduced to the single premise that "the kin group is far more significant than the individual" (Kibria 1994:

90). Hmong youth, as they approach adulthood and face the prospects of marrying and establishing themselves in careers, usually discover significant personal advantages in staying closely allied with their extended families. What Kibria (1994) says about the Vietnamese of Philadelphia also applies to the Hmong. Only immediate relatives can be counted upon to help individuals survive the difficult problems that lie ahead.

REFERENCES

Adams, Nina S., and Alfred W. McCoy. 1970. *Laos: War and Revolution.* New York: Harper & Row.

Barney, Linwood. 1967. The Meo of Xieng Khouang Province, Laos. In *Southeast Asian Tribes, Minorities, and Nations.* Edited by Peter Kunstadter. Princeton: Princeton University Press. Pp. 271–294.

Bays, Sharon. 1994. Cultural Politics and Identity Formation in a San Joaquin Valley Hmong Community. Unpublished Ph.D. dissertation, University of California, Los Angeles.

Committee for the Coordination of Services to Displaced Persons in Thailand (CCSDPT). 1982. *CCSDPT Handbook: Refugee Services in Thailand.* Bangkok: Du Maurier Associates for the Committee for the Coordination of Services to Displaced Persons in Thailand.

DeVecchi, Robert. 1982. Politics and Policies of "First Asylum" in Thailand. In *World Refugee Survey, 1982.* Edited by Rosemary Tripp. New York: American Council for Nationalities Service. Pp. 20–24.

Donnelly, Nancy D. 1994. *Changing Lives of Refugee Hmong Women.* Seattle: University of Washington Press.

Downing, Bruce T., Douglas P. Olney, Sara R. Mason, and Glenn L. Hendricks. 1984. *The Hmong Resettlement Site Report: Minneapolis–St. Paul.* Submitted by the Northwest Regional Educational Laboratory, Portland, to the Office of Refugee Resettlement, Washington, D.C.

Dreyer, June. 1976. *China's Forty Millions: Minority Nationalities and National Integration in the People's Republic of China.* Cambridge: Harvard University Press.

Dunnigan, Timothy. 1982. Segmentary Kinship in an Urban Society: The Hmong of St. Paul–Minneapolis. *Anthropological Quarterly* 55(3):126–136.

Erickson, Deanne, Ingrid Swenson, Edward Ehlinger, Sheldon Swaney, Gertrude Carlson, and Karen Gleiter. 1987. Maternal and Infant Outcomes among Caucasians and Hmong Refugees in Minneapolis, Minnesota. *Human Biology* 59(5):799–808.

Evans, Grant. 1983. *The Yellow Rainmakers: Are the Soviets Using Chemical Weapons in Southeast Asia?* London: Verse Editions and NLB.

Geddes, William R. 1976. *Migrants of the Mountains.* Oxford: Clarendon Press.

Gunn, Geoffrey C. 1990. *Rebellion in Laos: Peasant Politics in a Colonial Backwater.* Boulder, Colorado: Westview Press.

Hahn, Robert A., and Marjorie A. Muecke. 1987. The Anthropology of Birth in Five U.S. Ethnic Populations: Implications for Obstetrical Practice. *Current Problems in Obstetrics, Gynecology and Fertility* 4:133–171.

Haig, Alexander M., Jr. 1982. *Chemical Warfare in Southeast Asia and Afghanistan.* Special Report 98. Washington, D.C.: U.S. Department of State.

Halpern, Joel. 1964. *Economy and Society of Laos: A Brief Survey.* Southeast Asia Studies Monograph Series, No. 5. New Haven: Yale University Southeast Asia Studies.

Hamilton-Merritt, Jane. 1993. *Tragic Mountains.* Bloomington: Indiana University Press.

Helsel, Deborah, Diana B. Petitti, and Peter Kunstadter. 1992. Pregnancy among the Hmong: Birthweight, Age, and Parity. *American Journal of Public Health* 82(10): 1361–1369.

Hickey, Gerald C. 1955. The Ethnic Minorities of Laos. In *Area Handbook on Laos.* Edited by Gerald C. Hickey. Chicago: University of Chicago Press.

Hopkins, David D., and Nancy G. Clarke. 1983. Indochinese Refugee Fertility Rates and Pregnancy Risk Factors, Oregon. *American Journal of Public Health* 73(11): 1307–1309.

Humphreys, G. R., and J. Dow. 1982. *Report of the Medical Team's Epidemiological Investigation of Alleged CW/BW Incidents in Laos and Cambodia.* Ottawa: Canada.

Hutchison, Ray, and Miles McNall. 1994. Early Marriage in a Hmong Cohort. *Journal of Marriage and the Family* 56:579–590.

Jenks, Robert D. 1985. The Miao Rebellion, 1854–1872: Insurgency and Social Disorder in Kweichow during the Taiping Era. Unpublished Ph.D. dissertation, Harvard University.

Kibria, Nazli. 1994. Household Structure and Family Ideologies: The Dynamics of Immigrant Economic Adaptation among Vietnamese Refugees. *Social Problems* 41(1):81–96.

Larteguy, Jean. 1979. *La fabuleuse aventure du peuple de l'opium.* Paris: Presses de la Cite.

LeBar, Frank M., Gerald Hickey, and John Musgrave, Editors. 1964. *Ethnic Groups of Mainland Southeast Asia.* New Haven: Human Relations Area Files Press.

LeBar, Frank M., and Adrienne Suddard. 1960. *Laos: Its People, Its Society, Its Culture.* New Haven: Human Relations Area Files Press.

Lee, Gary Yia. 1982. National Minority Policies and the Hmong. In *Contemporary Laos.* Edited by Martin Stuart-Fox. New York: St. Martin's Press. Pp. 199–219.

Long, Lynellyn D. 1993. *Ban Vinai: The Refugee Camp.* New York: Columbia University Press.

Marshall, Eliot. 1986a. Response to Seiders' Letter to the Editor. *Science* 234:528–529.

———. 1986b. Yellow Rain Evidence Slowly Whittled Away. *Science* 233:18–19.

McNall, Miles, Timothy Dunnigan, and Jeylan T. Mortimer. 1994. The Educational Achievement of the St. Paul Hmong. *Anthropology and Education Quarterly* 25(1):44–65.

Meier, Peg. 1983. Hmong, Opium: A Culture Clash. *Minneapolis Star/Tribune,* October 1.

National Center for Health Statistics. 1989. *Advance Report of Final Mortality Statistics, 1987.* Monthly Vital Statistics Report 38, No. 5 supp. Hyattsville: Public Health Service.

Northwest Regional Educational Laboratory (NWREL). 1984. The Hmong Resettlement Study. Northwest Regional Educational Laboratory. (Unpublished)

Olney, Douglas P. 1983. Hmong Community Survey, Minneapolis–St. Paul. (Unpublished)

————. 1993. We Must Be Organized: Dual Organization in an American Hmong Community. Unpublished Ph.D. dissertation, University of Minnesota.

Richman, Debra, and Suzanne Dixon. 1985. Comparative Study of Cambodian, Hmong and Caucasian Infant and Maternal Perinatal Profiles. *Journal of Nurse Midwifery* 30(6):313–319.

Rumbaut, Rubén G., and John R. Weeks. 1986. Fertility and Adaptation: Indochinese Refugees in the United States. *International Migration Review* 20(2):428–466.

————. 1989. Infant Health among Indochinese Refugees: Patterns of Infant Mortality, Birthweight, and Prenatal Care in Comparative Perspective. *Research Sociology of Health Care* 8:137–196.

Savina, F. M. 1924. *Histoire des Miao*. Hong Kong: Imprimerie de la Societe des Missions-Etrangeres.

Schiefer, H. B. 1982. *Study of the Possible Use of Chemical Warfare Agents in Southeast Asia*. A Report to the Department of External Affairs. Ottawa, Canada.

Schlader, Jill, Michell Schwartz, and Daniel Detzner. 1995. *Southeast Asian Refugees: Statistics*. Southeast Asian Refugee Studies Project, Occasional Paper No. 12. Minneapolis: Center for Urban and Regional Affairs.

Schultz, George P. 1982. *Chemical Warfare in Southeast Asia and Afghanistan: An Update*. Special Report No. 104. Washington, D.C.: U.S. Department of State, Bureau of Public Affairs.

Seeley, Thomas D., Joan W. Nowicke, Matthew Meselson, Jeanne Guillemin, and Pongthep Akratanakul. 1985. Yellow Rain. *Scientific American* 253(3):128–137.

Seiders, Barbara A. B. 1986. Letter to the Editor. *Science* 234:528.

Smalley, William A. n.d. From Laos to the United States. (Unpublished)

Smalley, William A., Chia Koua Vang, and Gnia Yee Yang. 1990. *Mother of Writing*. Chicago: University of Chicago Press.

Spring, Marline A. n.d. Hmong Community Survey, Minneapolis–St. Paul. (Unpublished)

Spring, Marline A., Paul J. Ross, Nina L. Etkin, and Amos S. Deinard. 1995. Sociocultural Factors in the Use of Prenatal Care by Hmong Women, Minneapolis. *American Journal of Public Health* 85(7):1015–1017.

Symonds, Patricia V. 1984. A Flower Ready for the Bee: Hmong Perceptions of Adolescent Pregnancy. M.A. thesis, Brown University.

————. 1991. Cosmology and the Cycle of Life: Hmong Views of Birth, Death and Gender in a Mountain Village in Northern Thailand. Unpublished Ph.D. dissertation, Brown University.

Tapp, Nicholas. 1985. Categories of Change and Continuity among the White Hmong (Hmoob Dawb) of Northern Thailand. Unpublished Ph.D. dissertation, School of Oriental and African Studies, University of London.

United Nations High Commission for Refugees (UNHCR). 1983. *Monthly Statistics*. Bangkok, Thailand.

U.S. Committee for Refugees. 1994a. *Refugee Reports*. December 31. Washington, D.C.

————. 1994b. *World Refugee Survey*. Washington, D.C.

Vangay, Jonas Vang Na. 1989. *Hmong Parents' Cultural Attitudes and the Sex-Ratio Imbalance of Hmong Merced High School Graduates*. Merced: Mong Pheng Community Incorporated.

Weeks, John R., Rubén G. Rumbaut, C. Brindis, C. C. Korenbrot, and D. Minkler. 1989. High Fertility among Indochinese Refugees. *Public Health Reports* 104(2):143–150.

Weins, Harold J. 1967. *Han Chinese Expansion in South China.* Hamden, Connecticut: Shoe String Press.

Westermeyer, Joseph. 1982. *Poppies, Pipes and People: Opium and Its Use in Laos.* Berkeley: University of California Press.

Westermeyer, Joseph, Ton Fu Vang, and Gaohli Lyfong. 1983. Hmong Refugees in Minnesota: Characteristics and Self Perceptions. *Minnesota Medicine* 66:431–439.

Westermeyer, Joseph, Ton Fu Vang, and John Neider. 1983a. A Comparison of Refugees Using and Not Using a Psychiatric Service: An Analysis of DSM-III Criteria and Self Rating Scales in a Cross Cultural Context. *Journal of Operational Psychiatry* 14(1):36–40.

———. 1983b. Migration and Mental Health among Hmong Refugees: Association of Pre- and Post-migration Factors with Self Rating Scales. *Journal of Nervous and Mental Disease* 171(2):92–96.

———. 1983c. Refugees Who Do and Do Not Seek Psychiatric Care: An Analysis of Premigratory and Postmigratory Characteristics. *Journal of Nervous and Mental Disease* 171(2):92–96.

———. 1984. Acculturation and Mental Health: A Study of Hmong Refugees at 1.5 and 3.5 Years Post-migration. *Social Science and Medicine* 18(1):87–93.

Whiteside, Thomas. 1991a. Annals of the Cold War: The Yellow-Rain Complex—1. *The New Yorker,* February 11: 38–67.

———. 1991b. Annals of the Cold War: The Yellow-Rain Complex—2. *The New Yorker,* February 18: 44–68.

Williams, Caroline, and Joseph Westermeyer. 1983. Psychiatric Problems among Adolescent Southeast Asian Refugees: A Descriptive Study. *Journal of Nervous and Mental Disease* 171(2):79–83.

Yang, Dao. 1976. *The Hmong of Laos in the Vanguard of Development.* Translation of *Les Hmong du Laos face au developpment.* Vientiane, Laos: Siasavath Publishers. National Technical Information Service, order No. JPRS L/5562.

Yang, Pai, and Nora Murphy. 1993. *Hmong in the '90s: Stepping Towards the Future.* St. Paul: Hmong American Partnership.

Chapter 9

Khmer

CAROL A. MORTLAND

Khmer refers to the dominant group of inhabitants of Cambodia, a small country in Southeast Asia. Cambodia first came to American attention during the Vietnam War, spawning controversy and division within the United States that continues. In the late spring of 1970, President Richard Nixon announced that America and South Vietnamese troops had invaded Cambodia in pursuit of Vietnamese Communists who had for years been using the country as a staging area in their fight against South Vietnam. Four students were killed at Kent State University by the United States National Guard while protesting the invasion of Cambodia in what was only the most dramatic of thousands of protests that occurred throughout the United States.

Although the American government's stated aims in Cambodia were to help preserve peace and independence for Cambodians, much of America's attention resulted primarily from her own concerns, stated as maintaining American honor and withdrawing American soldiers as quickly as possible from Southeast Asia. And despite their claims, many opposing Americans were concerned less with the welfare of the Khmer people than they were with national concerns, for example, the safety of American soldiers and the effects of the war on the domestic economy.

This pattern in American-Cambodian relationships has continued to the mid-1990s, with the United States concerned primarily with easing the impact of resettled Cambodians on Americans rather than easing the impact of resettlement on Cambodians. Overlooked in Americans' concerns with their own realities are Khmer realities. This is especially relevant when looking at Cambodian migration to the United States.

Cambodians and their homeland, Cambodia, have experienced enormous change in the past quarter century. The country has been led by six governments since World War II: French colonizers, King Sihanouk monarchy, Lon Nol republic, Khmer Communists, Vietnamese-established socialism, and the coalition government. The Khmer themselves have been displaced. All have experienced change in their occupations, residence patterns, schooling, religious practice, and family and neighbor relationships. In the 1990s, Cambodians reside in numerous countries throughout the world, in circumstances unimaginable for most when they lived in Cambodia. Almost 150,000 Khmer live in the United States.

This chapter briefly reviews the history of Cambodians in the United States, focusing especially on the most important events of their lives: flight from their homeland, life in refugee camps and processing centers, and movement to America. The chapter also addresses the various strategies Cambodians have used to resettle in the United States: efforts to preserve their culture in the face of American pressure to change, the struggle to live near one another, and the reestablishment of patron-client ties and proper behavior. Cambodians go through predictable patterns of migration and resettlement, just as other migrants do. These patterns can be seen not only in the circumstances they face but in the ways they react to situations and the tactics they choose to deal with their new environment.

THE HOME COUNTRY

Cambodia before 1975

Although the archaeological record indicates that Cambodia was occupied by hunters and gatherers by 9,000 years ago (Mourer 1977; Higham 1989), Cambodians themselves anchor their roots in the majesty of Angkor. The Angkorean civilization, centered in northwest Cambodia, flourished from the beginning of the 800s A.D. to the mid-1400s. The center of Angkor was the court, occupied by the king. Angkorean rulers were absolute and semidivine. They used the labor of their subjects to grow rice that supported the kingdom and to construct the reservoirs and canals that aided intensive rice cultivation. Angkorean laborers also built the stone temple tombs and palaces, statues and relief sculptures, and roadways and bridges that demonstrated the power of Angkorean kings. Angkorean society consisted of sharply defined classes, including an elite composed of royalty and priests and a mass of commoners, many of whom were slaves. The elite were surrounded by luxury and servants—even a special vocabulary was used for them—while commoners served, labored, and obeyed.

From the mid-1200s, kingdoms both to the east and the west of Angkor began threatening Angkorean dominance, and by the mid-1400s, the city of Angkor was abandoned. Attacked repeatedly on both sides, areas of Cambodia for various periods of time came under the control of either Thai or Vietnamese rulers, sometimes both at the same time. In 1863, France pushed Cambodia's neighbors back and established a protectorate over Cambodia, thus preserving Cambodia as a modern entity (Chandler 1983). France governed Cambodia for 90 years. While protecting Cambodia from conquest by her neighbors, France allowed the Cambodian monarchy to continue, its officials now assisting the French in governing and collecting taxes. To assist in the civil service and on newly established rubber plantations and industries, the French brought in large numbers of Vietnamese; Cambodians consequently received little education as a result of colonization. They received few other benefits from the French, whose exploitation of Cambodia primarily benefited France.

Norodom Sihanouk, a young prince chosen to succeed his grandfather because of his apparent compliance with French interests, surprised France with his determination to secure independence for his country. Ninety years after France created the colony, he succeeded, and Cambodia became independent. In the period following, Sihanouk was just as determined to serve as predominant, sole ruler, and again he succeeded, dominating Cambodian life from 1955 to 1970 (Chandler 1991a). Like Cambodian leaders before him, Sihanouk found models for behavior for a modern world in an ancient, often mythical, past, believing himself an infallible leader ruling by divine right over childish subjects with no rights but those he granted them. He likened himself to the kings of Angkor, and his relationship to his people the same as that between Angkorean rulers and their people.

During the second half of the 1950s and the 1960s, Cambodia's neighbors again threatened Cambodia: Vietnam's war and both Vietnam's and Thailand's ties to the United States jeopardized Cambodia's neutrality, and Sihanouk's major accomplishment was the degree to which he was able to keep Cambodians free of the international tempest surrounding them.

The Sihanouk years are now seen as years of peace and prosperity by both Cambodians and observers. Despite the war to the east in Vietnam, most Cambodians continued to live as they had before: residing in rural villages where their parents had lived before them, supporting their families by rice cultivation, observing traditional Khmer Buddhism, and seeking protection and resources through a system of patronage (Ebihara 1968; Martel 1975). Public schools began to replace monastery schools, an occasional relative traveled to town to work, and Western technology and bureaucracy began a local appearance. Despite these changes, Cambodia remained by and large agricultural, traditional, Buddhist, and isolated.

But growing discontent from an increasingly educated population, effects from Vietnam's war, and a poorly managed economy began to affect Sihanouk's dominance and Cambodia's stability. A coup d'état in 1970 replaced Sihanouk with his prime minister, Lon Nol. After the coup, Cambodia's involvement in the Vietnam War increased enormously. American money, corruption, and incursions from soldiers from the various Vietnamese and allied armies who carried their war into Cambodia all contributed to the destruction of Cambodian society and agriculture and the growth of the Cambodian Communist rebellion. The United States, which had secretly begun bombing North Vietnamese border sanctuaries in Cambodia in March 1969 even before the coup, dropped as many bombs on Cambodia between 1969 and 1973 as were dropped in Japan during World War II (Shawcross 1979).

Cambodia rapidly fell to chaos in the early 1970s, and by 1975, even massive financial and military assistance from the United States could no longer bolster a corrupt and inept government and substitute for a collapsed economy. It has been estimated that between 600,000 and 800,000 Cambodians were killed during this period (Ea 1987; CIA 1980; Foreign Broadcast Information Service 1976). During the same period, the Cambodian Communists or Khmer Rouge grew from a meager few thousand in 1970 to a force large enough to occupy the country in 1975.

Democratic Kampuchea, 1975 to 1978

The Khmer Rouge marched into Phnom Penh, the capital of Cambodia, on April 17, 1975, and within hours began to evacuate the city. Khmer Rouge cadre turned the residents and war refugees of Cambodia's cities and towns into the countryside and set them to work farming. Cambodia became a labor camp. Over the next four years, the Khmer Rouge controlled the daily lives of everyone: telling people what work to do and how to do it, where to live and move, when to eat, whom to live with, even what to wear and say.

Describing events in Cambodia during the Khmer Rouge regime is an exercise in extremes; the enormity of change and the extent of horror endured by Cambodians are difficult to overstate, almost impossible to comprehend. The leaders of Democratic Kampuchea were a small group, most of whom had studied Marxism in Paris as students in the 1940s and 1950s. First among them was Pol Pot, whose name is used now by Cambodians to refer to the Khmer Rouge years. Pol Pot and his colleagues wished to create a new society in which the poor were free from exploitation by the rich, and all Cambodians were free from foreign powers. In Democratic Kampuchea, Cambodians would abandon their Western aspirations and return themselves to the days of Angkor, remembered as a time when Cambodians were independent, strong, and self-sufficient. But the ambitions of the Khmer Rouge leaders led them to disregard the realities of Cambodia's people and land. Weakened by years of war, Cambodian transportation, markets, and animals and resources for agriculture were disorganized or lacking, and townspeople were inexperienced at rural labor.

Ebihara (1985) notes the more dramatic transformations effected by the new rulers. First, the Khmer Rouge collectivized the economy by organizing families into work cooperatives and older children and youth into mobile work teams. These cooperatives and teams, often joined into larger groups, provided the labor for rice cultivation and building irrigation systems. Cambodians remember working from sunrise to sometimes long after sunset every day of the week, often walking long distances to work sites, usually eating little more than rice soup. Cambodians also remember vividly Khmer Rouge efforts to disrupt traditional family life. Work teams replaced the family as the basic economic unit. Children over eight or nine were placed in separate teams and occasionally sent away from their parents, smaller children were encouraged to spy on their parents, husbands and wives were often separated, and marriage was permitted only when and to whom the Khmer Rouge dictated. At weekly political meetings, Cambodians were reminded that their families were now replaced by Angka, the unseen but all-pervasive organization said to be running Democratic Kampuchea. A last change of enormous consequence to the Khmer was Democratic Kampuchea's efforts to erase religion. Cambodian Buddhism has long been a fundamental part of Khmer culture; Cambodians say, "To be Cambodian is to be Buddhist." But during the "Pol Pot" years, temples were destroyed, monks defrocked or killed, and rituals forbidden.

In the Cambodian revolutionaries' attempts to remake society into Democratic Kampuchea, one in five or seven or eight of all Cambodians died from execution, starvation, and illness (Vickery 1988; Chandler 1991a; Kiernan 1993). Estimates of how many Cambodians died as a result of Khmer Rouge activities from 1975 through 1978 have been a topic of disagreement, ranging from more than 2 million dead (Ea 1987) to far fewer than that (Vickery 1988). Vickery (1990) claims that between 700,000 and 1 million people above a normal peacetime death rate perished during the 1975–1978 period—about half from illness, hunger, overwork; the other half possibly executed—while the total population declined by 400,000. Banister and Johnson (1993) suggest a figure of 1.05 million dead. Kiernan's (1990, 1993) estimates are higher: concluding after extensive research that 1.5 million of Cambodia's 8 million people died during the Khmer Rouge regime.

Most writers agree with Chandler (1991a) that 1 million perished under the Khmer Rouge. One especially disastrous result of the above-normal death rate in Cambodia during the 1970s has been an imbalance in the sex ratio of Cambodians, both in Cambodia and in resettlement countries. It is estimated that a higher-than-usual number of widows head Cambodian households, both in Cambodia and in the United States (see, for example, Boua 1982; Ebihara 1985; United Nations Development Programme 1989; UNICEF 1990).

Government, education, religion, finance, markets, agriculture, transportation, communication, family, festivals—every aspect of special and everyday life was affected; virtually all was destroyed or changed. Most Cambodians had to move, most lost everything they owned, and virtually everyone had relatives and neighbors killed. Cambodians lost their past and their country; many feared they had lost their culture. By the end of the Khmer Rouge regime, they had only their memories and rumors of hope and food on the Western border.

After the Khmer Rouge

Although Vietnamese and Cambodian Communists had initially cooperated in founding their revolutionary movements, success brought hostility between the two groups, both of which in 1975 became seated governments (Chanda 1986; Evans and Rowley 1983). In late 1978, after a number of skirmishes between the Vietnamese and the Khmer Rouge along the Cambodian-Vietnamese border, Vietnam invaded Cambodia. By January 1979, Vietnamese troops occupied Phnom Penh, and the Khmer Rouge retreated to the west, toward Thailand.

Vietnam installed a new regime, called the People's Republic of Kampuchea. The Khmer population immediately went on the move, returning to home villages, looking for relatives, seeking food. The fighting and population movement hindered harvesting the rice crop in late 1978, and starvation was averted for many only with international assistance.

For the next decade, Cambodia, now called Kampuchea, slowly rebuilt herself under Vietnamese occupation. Cambodian Buddhism, family life, farming, and marketplaces were reestablished. This was done in the face of enormous obstacles, such as shortages of men to do male agricultural chores, poor health as a result of malnutrition and illness during the Khmer Rouge years, and an international aid blockade that denied Western developmental aid to the country. Another major obstacle was the growth of resistance armies in the West. First, there were the Khmer Rouge. Camped along the Cambodian-Thai border and supported by foreigners, including China and Thailand, the Khmer Rouge resumed the resistance fighting in which they had been engaged before 1975. They were joined by three other resistance armies, different in ideology and strategy but united in trying to replace the Vietnamese-backed government of Kampuchea with their own rule.

Disagreement over the nature of Vietnamese occupation existed both among Western observers and resettled Cambodians, ranging from accusations that Kampuchea was being Vietnamized at the expense of Cambodian culture to portrayals of Vietnamese as kindly protectors of a Cambodian-run country. What is evident is that Cambodians' initial relief at the relatively benign rule of the Vietnamese was replaced over time with increasing hostility toward their occupiers (Chandler 1991a). Although the Vietnamese appeared to many to have no intention of leaving Kampuchea, Vietnam withdrew its troops in the late 1980s.

In July 1991, the four Cambodian resistance groups agreed to a United Nations–brokered peace plan for Kampuchea, whose name had been changed to the State of Cambodia in 1989. The United Nations' peacekeeping mission to Cambodia lasted 18 months, cost nearly $2 billion, and involved 22,000 civilians and soldiers. The mission included organizing and managing a national election through which Cambodians elected a government and national assembly and drafted a constitution (U.S. Committee for Refugees 1994). National elections were held in May 1993, and in September the constitution was ratified. Sihanouk became head of state of a constitutional monarchy, now the "Kingdom of Cambodia," and Buddhism was restored as the state religion. Power was shared by the two leading parties, represented by First Prime Minister Prince Norodom

Ranariddh, Sihanouk's son, and Second Prime Minister Hun Sen, who was Cambodia's prime minister through the later 1980s. The Khmer Rouge signed the initial peace agreement but reneged and later attacked the peace process; although a reduced force, they continue to wage a brutal war in the northwest of the country.

In a sense, "Cambodia" includes approximately 250,000 Cambodians who have been resettled around the world (Chandler 1991a) in no less than 19 countries. Close to 150,000 Cambodians have been resettled in the United States. How they reached America is the next issue to be addressed.

EXODUS AND TRANSIT

Flight from Cambodia

For Cambodians in the United States, the flight from Cambodia to Thailand has become a major story in their repertoire, the focus of many of their memories (cf., for example, Ledgerwood 1990a; Marcucci 1986). Most Cambodian refugees are in the United States inadvertently, not because they wanted to live in America but because they wanted to escape Khmer Rouge rule. Their stories of flight reflect this reality, revealing a hiatus between a remembered Cambodia, both as it was in the horror days of the Khmer Rouge and in the relatively peaceful years before, and America.

The first wave of Cambodians to flee the Cambodian Communists did so in 1975 before the Khmer Rouge gained power, when approximately 35,000 Khmer fled west to Thailand and another 150,000 escaped east to Vietnam. Virtually all those in the first wave were resettled in Western countries, primarily France, the United States, Canada, and Australia. Cambodians initially escaping the Khmer Rouge included officials, professionals, and those of the moneyed or aristocratic classes who feared oppression or reprisals from the new Communist rulers and who had the means and connections to leave their homeland. Other early escapees were farmers and townspeople from western Cambodia who were able to slip across the border into Thailand (Ebihara 1985). Few Cambodians were able to escape their homeland during the Khmer Rouge years, although they report having fervently wished to do so; the severity of Khmer Rouge rule and their own weakened physical state made escape virtually impossible. Only with the fall of Democratic Kampuchea was flight again possible.

The second exodus of Cambodians from their country began with the invasion of Cambodia by Vietnamese in December 1978 and continued through the first months of 1979. As Khmer Rouge control broke down, 100,000 Khmer fled to Thailand, most fleeing the Khmer Rouge, others escaping the advancing Vietnamese soldiers, some eluding both. Khmer Rouge cadres also fled toward guerrilla bases in the northwest of Cambodia ahead of the invading Vietnamese troops, forcing many Cambodians to flee with them, using them as a shield, either before or behind them (Reynell 1989). These escapees came from a cross section of Cambodian life: urban professionals and businessmen, middle-class townspeople, and farmers, even Khmer Rouge cadres. Most began their flight to escape the horrors of the Khmer Rouge years, and many fled because they were hungry and had been hungry for four years.

A third major Cambodian exodus occurred from late spring of 1979 to the early months of 1980. During this period of worsening food shortages inside Cambodia, the number of fleeing Khmer increased drastically when rumors spread that food was available on the Thai-Cambodian border. In response to international dismay at the plight of Cambodians and the Thais' hostile reception, Thailand allowed international assistance, primarily in the form of food and basic medical supplies, to be given to Cambodians on the border in late 1979. Fighting between the Vietnamese army occupying Cambodia and Khmer insurgents in western Cambodia caused further flight toward Thailand. This wave of escapees also included a cross section of the Cambodian population: urbanites, townspeople, and peasants.

The United Nations and the International Committee of the Red Cross also established a "land bridge" on the Cambodian-Thai border to provide food, tools, and seed rice to Khmer inside Cambodia. The land bridge program brought as many as 1 million Cambodians to the border, many of whom traveled there to get rice and other assistance, carried it back to their families or to sell, returned to the border for additional assistance, and again hauled it home (Mason and Brown 1983). While intended to encourage Cambodians to stay within their country, the land bridge program did continue to draw Cambodians' attention, and their presence, to the border.

When Cambodians in these first three waves fled their country, they were not thinking of migration. They were thinking of temporary refuge, then of eventually returning home, of finding their children and parents, of finding food. They feared the Khmer Rouge, they feared the Vietnamese, they feared everything Cambodia had become. They fled "yet another army, yet another war" (cf. Ledgerwood 1990a:196; Smith 1989). They were thinking they would die if they stayed in Cambodia, and going was the only alternative they saw. This was especially true of those who fled to Thailand immediately after the fall of the Khmer Rouge.

Only later did Cambodians begin traveling to the border in order to gain admittance to a Thai refugee camp and, ultimately, resettlement in the United States. As the months passed, an increasing number of Cambodians began to see resettlement to a Western country as a possibility, even a goal. American embassy officials, for example, suspected that a number of middle-class Cambodians made the decision to leave Cambodia for Thailand refugee camps so they could be resettled in the United States. But they, and the majority of rice farmers who made up the refugee flow, never realized the extent of the process they had entered: its length, complexity, irreversibility, and short- and long-term consequences. Cambodians did not realize that they had commenced a new phase in their lives, that they were now setting out on their "refugee career" (Reynell 1989).

Those Cambodians who fled Cambodia during the 1980s comprise a fourth, much smaller wave of Cambodian escapees, most of whom were unsuccessful in their attempt to resettle in a third country. During the 1980s, some Cambodians returned to Cambodia voluntarily. Several hundred thousand additional Khmer remained in Thai refugee camps, and another several hundred thousand lived in a series of makeshift encampments along the Thai-Cambodian border. These camp Khmer were supported to varying degrees by assistance channeled through the United Nations.

Between March 1992 and May 1993, 362,200 Cambodians were trucked to Cambodia from Thailand as part of the United Nations' brokered peace plan for Cambodia. By that time, most of the camp residents had been there for years; Lynch (1989) found in 1989 that 89 percent of the adult population of Site II had been on the border by 1983 and thus in camps since that time. Over half of those repatriated had never seen Cambodia before, having been born in the refugee and border camps (cf. French 1994 for a vivid description of camp life). Another 5,300 Cambodians returned home on their own, and 576 were forcibly repatriated by Thailand (U.S. Committee for Refugees 1994).

Movement to America

The first wave of Cambodians to be resettled in the United States consisted of 6,000 people[1] resettled from 1975 to 1977 (Gordon 1984), most from the educated and urbanized Cambodian middle class and most connected to Americans or the American war effort in Southeast Asia. An additional 1,300 arrived in 1978 (*Refugee Reports* 1988).

A second wave came in 1979, when increased international concern over the refugee situation in Southeast Asia prompted the United States to enlarge relevant admission quotas and ease selection criteria. This allowed some 10,000 primarily rural Khmer who had fled Cambodia before the Khmer Rouge takeover but lacked sufficient ties to Americans or the American war effort to also enter the United States (Ebihara 1985). This second wave consisted of farmers, fishermen, and artisans who had more difficulty finding employment and housing and other necessities of life than did the first group of middle-class Cambodians due to differences in education, urban living, and English-language experience. While both groups struggled with life in a vastly different environment, neither had lived through the Khmer Rouge regime.

The third wave of Cambodians to come to America was by far the largest and longest. The number of Khmer arriving in 1980 was nearly triple that in 1979, and Cambodians continued coming in similar numbers each year through 1985. The number dropped in half in 1986, and to less than a sixth in 1987. The total number of Cambodians to arrive between 1980 and 1986 was 125,186 (*Refugee Reports* 1988, 1993). These Cambodians had endured nearly four years of Democratic Kampuchea; most fled Cambodia at the earliest opportunity.

The fourth wave consists of Cambodians who arrived from 1987 to 1993, when selection criteria for Cambodians entering the country stiffened considerably (Robinson and Wallenstein 1988). This wave totaled 8,627 and included primarily family reunification cases: Cambodians coming to join relatives. Many of these Khmer came as immigrants rather than refugees.

Resettlement to the United States for Cambodians in Thailand meant the end of powerlessness, the beginning of a life with economic promise and hope. Before resettlement or repatriation, however, most Cambodians spent years in refugee camps. A comparison of resettled Cambodians' flight and refugee camp stories reveals much about camp life. Like any transition experience, flight is remembered as a specific, separating event: dangerous, harrowing, frightening. But Cambodians remember themselves as active and capable in their flight from Cambodia, as people who made decisions, were at least somewhat in control of their destiny, and were daring, even heroic. Refugee camp stories, in contrast, are condensed: Years are told in a sentence or two. Camp life is remembered as a blur, a lengthy span of relative nonevents. Life in the camps—its beginning, endurance, and ending—was controlled by others, and the passivity of the Khmer made them anything but heroic in their own eyes. To remember that time is to recall their powerlessness.

RESETTLEMENT AMERICAN STYLE

Although resettlement in the United States brought Cambodians escape from the powerlessness of the refugee camps, they were in some sense moving into yet another structured setting controlled by other people's perceptions and goals. They found themselves part of a larger Southeast Asian population, including Lao and a much greater number of Vietnamese. Many refugee programs and Americans treated these refugees as a homogenous group, with similar experiences and expectations. The Khmer were categorized with people whose language they did not understand, often surrounded by those they had always thought of as traditional enemies; in addition, social services often encompassed refugee and immigrant clients from elsewhere in the world. This caused confusion and hardship for both Americans and refugees but led also to unique personal and working contacts for some Cambodians, as their world was enlarged to include both Americans and other newcomers.

Americans were unaware of key social distinctions within Khmer society: Villagers were lumped with Phnom Penh elite, farmers with bureaucrats, soldiers with schoolteachers. They were now recognized as "Cambodians" and "refugees" by those around them, and distinctions among them that they considered important were ignored, for example, factors such as: class, level of education, and residence, that existed when they were in Cambodia; factors such as: type of employment, English-speaking ability, utilization of social services, education, and residence in America.

When Americans recognized Cambodians as a distinct group, they noted the differences between Cambodians and other immigrant groups: less education, English, and familiarity with Westernization; more mental and physical problems. Virtually every popular and scholarly article on Cambodians emphasizes their problems, underscoring first the enormity of change Cambodians experience after resettlement. Observers note that most Cambodian refugees resettled in the United States went no further than the primary grades in Cambodia, there was virtually no exposure to English in the countryside, and most lived in rural settings without benefit of modern technology (e.g., Rumbaut and Ima 1988). In addition, Cambodians brought with them the scars of malnutrition, overwork, and anguish from the Khmer Rouge years. So Cambodians arrived, in Americans' views, wounded in body and mind and lacking language, work skills, or appropriate attitudes. Many American agencies and individuals concluded that Cambodians needed to be taught how to live in America.

Americans envision the United States as a refuge for immigrants and as a country built by immigrants who have contributed the best of themselves and their cultures. Hostility or ambivalence toward a group of migrants is usually expressed by reluctance to admit them or fund programs to serve them, even in verbal or physical attacks on people or their possessions. It was only after extensive lobbying of Congress by the Citizens' Commission on Indochinese Refugees in 1978, for example, that Cambodians were added to the list of Indochinese eligible for admission to the United States under presidential parole authority (Loescher and Scanlan 1986).

But for at least a century, the United States has treated immigrants as people whose difference is less an advantage than a handicap to their integration into American society. The American reception of Cambodians has mirrored that given to immigrants before; reflecting ideas first expressed toward immigrants in the Americanization movement of the late 1880s and early 1900s, most American immigrant education programs in the United States have been designed to teach immigrants to abandon their inferior traditions, seen to encompass notions of hierarchy and privilege, laziness, lack of self-reliance, and dependency. Instead, immigrants are taught American attitudes, values, and behaviors in the hope that they will become free, democratic, rational, hard working, and self-sufficient and thus better able to assimilate to American life (Tollefson 1989).

Americans' ambivalent welcome to Cambodians after their arrival in the United States can be seen among those closest to the immigrant situation: policymakers, resettlement workers, and volunteers. Some Americans have gone to extraordinary degrees to help Cambodians in their resettlement; American sponsors and volunteers have devoted literally millions of unpaid hours assisting Cambodians in a myriad of tasks (e.g., Criddle 1992). The American government, through resettlement and social service agencies, has spent hundreds of millions of dollars on the resettlement of Cambodians alone. The purpose of most of this money and effort has been to change Cambodians, teaching them not only English and employment skills but also American values and behavior.

Even before arrival in the United States, Americans began the attempt to transform Cambodian refugees into American citizens. From late 1980, Cambodians accepted for resettlement in the United States were sent to processing centers in Southeast Asia for up to six months of language, cultural orientation, and vocational training. But some observers questioned the value of such instruction in helping refugees adjust to America after they were resettled (Tollefson 1989; Mortland 1987), and most Cambodian refugees did not think they needed transformation at the hands of Americans.

The primary concern of the American refugee program has been that refugees become economically self-sufficient as quickly as possible after arrival (Refugee Act of 1980; ORR 1994). Americans state, and Cambodians agree, that English-language ability and job skills appropriate to the American workplace are the most important factors influencing Cambodians' employability. In addition, the level of education received in Cambodia, familiarity with Western culture, an urban background, literacy, and youth contribute to employability in America (ORR 1994). In the effort to create self-sufficient Cambodians as quickly as possible, educational programs for Cambodians continued after their arrival in the United States in the form of English-language, cultural orientation, and vocational training classes.

The quality and duration of programs and eligibility requirements for students varied greatly across the United States. In some locales, Cambodians were encouraged to study for as long as two years at government expense, then to continue their education at mainstream institutions if at all possible. Only after extensive training were they expected to seek full-time employment. In other locations, Cambodians were required to obtain employment as quickly as possible, studying English in their free hours. Sponsor expectations and connections, local job opportunities, and the national economic situation at the time of arrival also affected the rate and type of employment accessed by Cambodians. As the 1980s passed and increasing numbers of Cambodians arrived in the country, the refugee resettlement program shifted toward early employment above all else.

The federal government and resettlement programs continue this emphasis on early employment for refugee and immigrant arrivals, including the handful of Cambodians who have arrived annually in the 1990s (ORR 1994). Federally funded English-language, vocational training, and employment skills classes previously attended by Cambodians have been drastically reduced, and those that remain are usually local creations, often maintained by volunteers. Younger Cambodians now learn English in the public schools, where they are learning or have learned to speak without accent and often at the expense of Cambodian-language acquisition. Few older Cambodians any longer devote much time to learning English, although some continue to learn English on the job or from their children.

When Cambodian refugees were initally resettled in the United States, Americans were concerned with lessening the impact of Cambodians, and other refugees, on the United States (Refugee Act of 1980). In addition to attempts to change Cambodians in the processing centers and subsequently through language, vocational, and cultural orientation courses in the United States, efforts were made to place Khmer in areas where they would "blend" into surrounding communities. Khmer were thus "scattered" throughout the United States and initially placed with American sponsors because of the scarcity of Cambodians living in America. Through scatter placement and American sponsorship, policymakers tried to prevent Cambodians from settling into ethnic enclaves, hoping thus to reduce refugee visibility, increase their economic prospects, and decrease refugee costs to American taxpayers (Skinner and Hendricks 1979).

Cambodians, however, did not remain dispersed. They moved for a variety of reasons, most obviously to be with one another, and the immediate result of their movement was the rapid creation of Cambodian enclaves in several cities (Mortland and Ledgerwood 1987). An increasing number of resettled Cambodians became sponsors to their own relatives, adding to Cambodian clustering. In an effort to prevent secondary migration by new arrivals to areas of high Khmer concentration (for example, Long Beach, Seattle, and Philadelphia), the federal government clustered Khmer arrivals in 12 cities: Atlanta, Boston, Chicago, Cincinnati, Columbus, Dallas, Houston, Jacksonville, New York City, Phoenix, Richmond, and Rochester (Refugee Resource Center 1982). The program had mixed results (Bruno 1984, for example): Some Cambodians received little assistance, others moved to new locales despite pressure not to do so, and many felt coerced into particular options by program requirements and staff.

Efforts by the federal government to influence Cambodian residence in the United States continued into the late 1980s, although efforts in the early 1990s reflected an increased awareness by service providers and policymakers that Cambodians would move to join one another. The Office of Refugee Resettlement in the Department of Health and Human Services funded the research and publication of a report entitled *Profiles of Some Good Places for Cambodians to Live in the United States* (North and Nim Sok 1989). The report describes 22 communities where there were available jobs, generally self-sufficient Cambodian residents, a moderate-sized Khmer community, and minimum crime problems.[2] The report details job opportunities, size of Cambodian community, and town characteristics. The key for Americans is size of the Cambodian community: Five of the cluster cities[3] were dropped from this list, no longer considered desirable because "too many" Cambodians now lived there. Ironically, the presence of a Cambodian enclave with uniquely Khmer services, such as Buddhist temples, is one of the attractions of these "good places for Cambodians to live"; American program officials saw some value in ethnic community resources but not too concentrated or too many.

Americans also see Cambodian families as exhibiting numerous problems (Rumbaut 1995). Cambodian parents are learning what immigrant parents in the United States have learned before them: that immigrant children are concerned with the new land and ways, not the old (Steinberg 1989). While their parents struggle to retain their traditions, their children struggle to learn the new country. Since language learning ability is inversely related to age, children often need not even struggle in their efforts to learn English and American culture. Cambodian-American children (those who came to America as relatively young children or who were born in America), like the children of immigrants before them, are characterized by the experience of living in two worlds and, despite their wishes to fit in, not fully belonging to either.

American concerns about the Khmer, however, are sometimes shared by the Khmer themselves. Issues of family tensions and health problems provide examples. A gulf has grown up between Khmer who came to the United States as adults and will never be "Americans" by culture and their children who are trying desperately to be American. This loss of their children is an additional blow to Cambodians in the United States who now worry, among other things, that their children will not take care of them in their old age. Both Americans and Cambodians worry that Khmer children will follow less desirable models for American youth: dropping out of school, joining gangs, using drugs. American social service programs concentrate on helping Cambodian youth stay in school, providing counseling for families suffering from generational conflict, and facilitating after-school tutoring and recreational programs. Cambodian parents concentrate instead on trying to instill Cambodian values in their children: teaching them proper Cambodian behavior, encouraging their attendance at Cambodian Buddhist events, and cautioning them constantly about the dangers of American ways (for example, Ledgerwood 1990a; Kulig 1991).

Cambodians' health has been a major concern for both Cambodians and Americans since Khmer arrival in the United States (cf. Nguyen-Hong-Nhiem and Halpern 1989 and Welaratna 1993 for Khmer descriptions of life in America). The physical and mental consequences of the Khmer Rouge years are enormous, especially for first-generation immigrants, and include premature death, illness, and depression (Frye 1991; Kulig 1991; Rasbridge 1991; Pickwell 1990; Mitchell 1987; Marcucci 1986). Many Cambodians came to America with serious medical conditions, for example, tuberculosis, extended malnutrition, and injury. Older women, especially, exhibit multiple problems: headaches, dizziness, confusion, even blindness. Cambodians are also seen as a population at risk emotionally (Bowlan and Bruno 1985; Kinzie 1987; Kinzie et al. 1984; Mollica 1988; Mollica, Wyshack, and Lavelle 1987; Eisenbruch 1991; Owan 1985; Williams and Westermeyer 1986). Similar physical and mental problems are experienced by the Khmer in Cambodia (Ebihara 1993).

Cambodian resettlement concerns have not always coincided with Americans' concerns for them; Khmer often comment, however, on the enormous efforts undertaken on their behalf by American organizations and individuals. But as government funding and programs for Cambodians have lessened, Cambodians have been left increasingly to their own devices.

RESETTLEMENT CAMBODIAN STYLE

When resettlement is viewed in terms of assimilation to American behavior and ideas, as most Americans view it, resettlement can be judged in terms of success and failure. But Cambodians view resettlement differently. For most Khmer, resettlement in America was initially a dream come true; for most, the dream changed as awareness of the permanency of their losses and the strangeness of America gradually settled over them. The ability to support themselves in America brings satisfaction, as it did before in Cambodia; yet their inability to regain what they have lost leaves them dissatisfied. All are occupied with the daily necessities of living with strangeness.

Although Cambodians find it extremely difficult to describe their experiences and losses, despite their interest and need to do so, their resettlement strategies in the United States are ways they express themselves in their new environment. By looking at their strategies for survival and renewal in America, we can "hear" through their actions what they find difficult to express: who they were, who they are.

Much of what Americans want to change about Cambodians is what Cambodians value most. Even when Cambodians themselves want the change, they often want it differently than do Americans. Language is a case in point. Cambodians know they must learn English and have made valiant efforts to do so. Their problem lies in the extreme differences between English and Cambodian, absence or scarcity of language training facilities, and competing obligations of work and school. But they also want to retain their language. Cambodians have major concerns that their children learn their own language. Some of their earliest efforts were to set up language classes for children. And a major disappointment has been that their children will not learn to write and speak Cambodian, although most understand it. Many parents have given up the effort, especially as it becomes obvious that children themselves are not interested.

The greatest concerns of the Khmer in the United States are finding means of successfully surviving in America, preserving their culture, and ensuring the future of their children. Cambodians say if they lose their culture, they will lose their identity as Cambodians (Ngor Haing 1987; May Someth 1986; Szymusiak 1986; Criddle and Mam 1987; Yathay Pin 1987). We see the same concern over loss in American writings about Cambodians (Coleman 1987; Crystal 1988; Florentine Films 1991; Marcucci 1986; Ebihara, Mortland, and Ledgerwood 1994; Mortland 1994a). Preserving their culture becomes the primary means Khmer use to secure their other aims. The strategies they use to achieve these goals follow methods that have worked for them in the past. These include, first, utilizing all available resources; second, reestablishing traditional relationships; third, reinstituting proper behavior; and fourth, reconstructing religion. Each of these is discussed in more detail below.

First, Cambodians have been active participants in utilizing all the resources of their environment, just as villagers in rural Cambodia had long drawn their income from a mix of farming and fishing and townspeople supplemented their primary incomes with part-time businesses or jobs, and they continue to do so. Realizing that employment is the swiftest and more respectable way in America to obtain resources, Khmer have sought employment at the highest levels of income and prestige (in traditional Khmer terms) available to them. Many study at night to enhance language and job skills. Since many Khmer are limited to entry-level positions by rudimentary English and American job skills, they increase income by pooling their resources, working more than one job, having multiple job holders in a household, and utilizing a family member's eligibility for social services. Often the adults in a family work outside the home, leaving child care, cooking, and household chores to a less employable member (for example, because of age or physical or mental difficulties). I have not found data to collaborate Welaratna's (1993; see also Rumbaut and Ima 1988) conclusion that many Cambodians seek human service employment in the United States, such as nursing. Rather, my data suggest that Cambodians with educational opportunities, thus able to escape entry-level positions, seek training in areas they feel are most likely to result in jobs, such as business, computer-related technologies, and electronics. The dream of many is to begin their own business, and some have done so: for example, donut shops, laundries, grocery stores, and restaurants. Over time, like immigrants before them, an increasing number of resettled Cambodians obtain employment and become economically self-sufficient (Gallagher 1988; ORR 1994).

Cambodian employment in the United States is an interesting phenomenon: Many of the educated and urbanized Cambodians resettled in the United States have experienced a decline in socioeconomic status; most never regain the status and wealth they enjoyed in Cambodia. For former peasants, however, American jobs have brought knowledge, possessions, and independence inconceivable for them in Cambodia. Women, too, have benefited from expanded opportunities in education and employment; in fact, women have sometimes been more successful than their menfolk in obtaining employment (Ui 1991). Cambodian women are more eager to seize these opportunities than men are to see them do so, for such employment can shift the traditional balance of power away from men. Because of the high percentage of widows, thus female-headed households, in the United States, employment is often a necessity rather than an option.

Cambodians utilize American services as provided and instructed by Americans (cf. Rasbridge and Marcucci 1992, for an interesting example). They have also taken advantage of other resources wherever available, often advising startled American neighbors on the best places to find little-known sales, overstocks, giveaways, and fishing sites. Some have utilized public services in unorthodox ways, usually by receiving benefits for which they are not eligible or working for cash (so that neither employer or employee has to pay taxes), always with an eye to maximizing resources and future opportunities. Some Khmer justify their actions by saying they are just doing what Americans do; others assert that what they are doing seems less criminal than what Americans are doing: drugs, crime, stealing, and stealing from other poor people; and some claim that Americans owe them for a variety of reasons: because of the tragedies they have endured, because of America's previous involvement in Cambodia.

Cambodians use the resources they obtain in America, such as money, jobs, and technology, to retain and reestablish Cambodian culture (e.g., Hopkins 1992). They use cars and telephones, for example, to communicate with family and friends within their own town and to keep in contact with the nearest temple, Cambodian stores, and relatives. They use cassettes and videotapes to correspond with relatives in Cambodia and other resettlement countries and to listen to the music, plays, and films of their homeland made in Hong Kong and California. They use whatever resources are at hand, including funding from Americans, to re-form dance troops and musical orchestras (Sam 1994; Ung 1988). College students have formed discussion groups to discuss, foremost among other topics, their own experiences and Cambodian politics.

An additional strategy Cambodians use to survive in America, invest in their children, and preserve their culture is to reestablish traditional social relationships among themselves and establish them with Americans, and they expend considerable effort on this from the time of their initial arrival in the United States. First, they seek to reassemble their families, often out of the fragments left by Khmer Rouge atrocities and resettlement procedures that separated nuclear from extended families. Cambodians often moved from their initial placement site in the United States to rejoin these extended family members, for example, aunts and uncles, married siblings, in-laws, and adopted kin, a relationship for which Cambodians use kinship terminology (Ebihara 1968).

Second, Cambodians attempt to contact, then often join, other relatives, fellow villagers, and friends, both from Cambodia and the refugee camps, as soon as possible after arriving in the United States. Living near one another in tenements or apartment complexes, or driving several hours on weekends to join countrymen, allows Cambodians to share information and resources. Smith (1989) gives an example of one migration: 400 Khmer who moved from Chicago to Madison because of its lower crime rate and more rural aspect. Their fishing and gardening activities in Madison, combined with specific economic strategies and cultural practices, has allowed the Khmer to reproduce many aspects of traditional Cambodian life. Over time, many Cambodian adults have in effect retired into their ethnic communities, restricting their contacts primarily to other Cambodians, having little to do with the larger surrounding community. Even if such residence patterns involve conflict with other Cambodians, conflict among one's own people is preferable for many Khmer than being alone among strangers. Cambodians continue to redistribute themselves in the United States (e.g., Smith-Hefner 1990) to join family or friends; to seek employment opportunities, lower living costs, or more generous assistance programs; and to join or escape particular Khmer enclaves.

Third, Cambodians reestablish patron-client ties in the United States (Mortland and Ledgerwood 1988; Ledgerwood 1990b). For Cambodians in America, a patron can be one of the best hedges against a repeat of past experiences. Thus, in traditional Khmer fashion, they have cultivated patrons both among more powerful and resourceful Cambodians and among Americans. These patrons provide resources, services, and information desired by Cambodians in exchange for loyalty and service. Cambodian patrons have gained additional access to resources by acquiring offical recognition as leaders of their community, forming organizations to receive additional benefits that are then funneled to both patron and followers (Mortland 1993); the federal government continues to fund these Cambodian self-help organizations (ORR 1994). These organizations have been engaged in a number of different activities, including providing social services, such as counseling, substance abuse treatment, job placement, and vocational training; and cultural preservation, such as teaching the Khmer language, forming dance troops or orchestras, and encouraging traditional crafts.

Sometimes, however, Cambodians have endeavored to escape their traditional ties to patrons in order to control areas of their own and their children's lives in the light of new options and constraints existing in America. For example, they seek social mobility through education and occupation, and escape from the control of local or religious leaders. As time goes on, an increasing number of Cambodians, especially the younger generation, are escaping or never experiencing the control of traditional patrons.

The tendency of the Cambodian people toward extravagant deference to superiors is backed by a religious tradition that relates position to meritorious behavior, with individuals deserving their place in life, and to a social structure that overwhelmingly favors those at the top with wealth and strength. Ordinary Cambodians have little choice but to defer. This tendency has contributed to what Chandler has called "Cambodia's tragedy" (Chandler 1991b). The best most Cambodians could do was to align themselves with a particular superior, seeking protection in exchange for their loyalty and labor. These ideas—of leaders' rights, followers' obligations, and patronage—continue to shape the attitudes and activity of many Cambodians in the United States and to vie for attention with their attempts to reestablish aspects of their lives over which they have traditionally prevailed: for example, family, food, and home life.

An important resettlement strategy Khmer use in the United States is to renew proper behavior and order among themselves. Cambodians have suffered a tremendous loss of order, even before the Khmer Rouge period, certainly during it, and following their escape to camps in Thailand. Their sense of lost order continues after resettlement in the United States, replaced by American concepts of what is proper and right. While Americans attempt to convert Khmer to an American sense of order, Cambodians have eagerly sought to re-create proper Cambodian order as quickly as possible in their new lives. They have done so by reestablishing proper etiquette toward one another, based on traditional Khmer hierarchical relationships. The sharp definition in class and behavior has continued throughout Cambodian history and remains evident among the Cambodians in America. Cambodians emphasize that inferiors must obey superiors:

thus, children must obey their parents; wives, their husbands; youth, their elders; and students, their teachers. Cambodians struggle especially to keep their women virtuous and their daughters pure, even to the extent of marrying them at even younger ages than in Cambodia (Ledgerwood 1990a). In this way, the Khmer regain a sense of security. What Chandler (1982) says of the nineteenth century is true for the twentieth: When Cambodians live in their proper places, they experience more balance, safety, and Cambodian identity than when they do not.

Lastly, Cambodians in America place tremendous importance on reestablishing their religion; they consider the practice of Khmer Buddhism vital to the preservation of their culture, even their identity. Almost immediately after arrival in the United States, the Khmer sought ways to practice their religious rituals, one of their first desires being to conduct rituals for their dead, which they had previously been unable to do, either for lack of means or permission. Cambodians soon set up temples in apartments, then houses, and after some years, some communities began constructing temple buildings. Khmer served as sponsors for monks to come to America from the Thai refugee camps, borrowed or purchased religious paraphernalia from other Buddhist countries, and held their rituals with whatever leadership was available.

Khmer religion consists of Buddhist practices along with beliefs in spirits. Cambodians in America devote considerable effort to propitiating a variety of spirits, from territorial spirits to ancestor spirits and including a sizable number of additional categories. Cambodians call on the spirits to prevent misfortune, especially illness, from striking them and to assist in bringing them fortune and happiness. These rituals may be conducted privately in one's own home or at a public gathering.

While many Cambodians have reduced their participation in Buddhist temple activities and spirit rites in the United States, primarily because of time and work constraints, most continue to hold to the traditional Buddhist and folk beliefs they were taught as children. Some conceal these beliefs by attendance at Christian churches or expressions of disbelief, but the majority of resettled Cambodians do not abandon their traditional ideas. Despite considerable obstacles—hostile American neighbors, lack of men wishing to go into the monkhood, fading memories of liturgy, prayers, and ritual detail—and competing American religions, schedules, and interests, most Cambodians continue to practice their religion at home and at over 50 temples across the country.

A resettlement problem unique to Cambodians in its severity results from the years they spent under the Khmer Rouge regime, during the years from 1975 to 1978 (Mortland 1994b). Cambodians find it difficult to explain what has happened to them and their country in the past several decades. Most Cambodians have struggled to find answers in their traditional religion; some have looked at alternate explanations, such as that provided by Christianity. For most, however, the enormity of the tragedies they experienced and the migration they have endured brings questions that continue to plague them: How could this have happened? Did they do something to cause what happened to them?

Additionally, successful survival in America and the preservation of Khmer culture are not inherently opposites. Cambodian notions of being "refugees" change with time. Some begin to find refugee status offensive, a way for Americans to pity Cambodians without listening to them, to decide what is best for Cambodians without consulting them. Some Khmer have become permanent residents, American citizens, or self-proclaimed "people without a country." Others have moved reluctantly or proudly on through immigrant status to citizenship.[4] Some Cambodians say they will always be refugees because the Khmer Rouge forced them from their land. Others continue their dependency as refugees, relying on social services and defining themselves (and being defined) primarily as victims. Children of Cambodians who were born in the United States may deal less with being Cambodian-Americans than with being a minority; for many who live in low-income urban areas, daily reality resembles that of other youth around them, with Cambodian concerns relevant primarily at home.

Similarly, Cambodian notions of "Americanness" and "Khmerness" vary. Cambodians go back and forth between what they perceive to be American and what they perceive to be Cambodian, using whichever fits their need of the moment. They thereby create Cambodian responses to American realities and reinvent their Cambodian past. They are aided in their recreation of identity by contrasting themselves and a "mythic" Cambodian past to Americans and America. As their leaders in Cambodia did before them (Chandler 1990, 1991b), Khmer Americans hark back to the splendors of Angkor in establishing and reestablishing their identity as Cambodians. Thus, they can speak of life as it was, as it should be, stating indirectly what is difficult to state directly, for example, that a life without Cambodianness is not life, that life in America is only bearable for Cambodians if they remain faithful to their cultural traditions.

CONCLUSIONS AND PROSPECTS

Americans cite a multitude of reasons to explain why Cambodians are unsuccessful in adjusting to America: their rural backgrounds, unfamiliarity with Western ways, lack of education or literacy in their own language, lack of English, lack of employable skills, and the physical and mental scars of the Khmer Rouge years. An alternate view is that Cambodians are successfully adjusting to life in the United States. As Welaratna (1993) notes, Cambodians are seeking to ensure the economic and emotional welfare of their families in ways that differ from Americans, placing family and social interaction above individual advancement. Many Cambodians conclude that they have been successful in their adjustment to America. Those who conclude otherwise judge Khmer success by American, rather than Cambodian, goals.

Because of their horrendous experiences under the Khmer Rouge and traumatic resettlement, Cambodians have been forced to examine themselves and their culture, to reflect on ultimate questions, on what is of highest priority to them (Mortland 1994b; Welaratna 1993). Their conclusions can be read in their strategies for living in America. These have included vigorously seizing opportunities for employment and education, utilizing traditional relationships such as family and patronage to obtain resources and services, redefining proper behavior for Cambodians who must live in such different circumstances, reestablishing places of worship, and reasserting the value of Cambodian culture and themselves as Cambodians. Finally and sometimes despairingly, Cambodians place their hopes on their children.

First-generation Cambodian immigrants continue to view reality in America through a traditional prism, through the meanings and relationships of their homeland. As American immigrants before them, they will always do so. Their children, however, have shifted perspective and now utilize an American prism to view their new homeland. Although Cambodia and Cambodian ways continue to affect the lives of these second-generation Cambodian-Americans, their sights are already and primarily trained on American culture.

ACKNOWLEDGMENTS

My gratitude to May M. Ebihara, Judy Ledgerwood, and David W. Haines for their comments on this chapter.

NOTES

1. Published numbers vary, depending on which government sources are used. In addition, both calendar and fiscal years have been used by the federal government in publishing statistics. Sources for resettlement figures used in this chapter are as follows: for 1975 through 1978, from Gordon (1984); from 1979 through 1981, from the Office of Refugee Resettlement, U.S. Department of Health and Human Services, as cited in *Refugee Reports* (1988); and for FY 1982 through FY 1993, from the Bureau for Refugee Programs, U.S. Department of State, compiled by the U.S. Committee for Refugees, cited in *Refugee Reports* (1993). Resettlement by year of Cambodians to the United States is thus:

1975	4,600
1976	1,100
1977	300
1978	1,300
1979	6,000
1980	16,000
1981	27,100
1982	20,234
1983	13,115

1984	19,851
1985	19,097
1986	9,789
1987	1,539
1988	2,805
1989	1,916
1990	2,166
1991	38
1992	141
1993	22
Total	**147,113**

2. The 22 cities are Mobile Bay, Alabama; Phoenix, Arizona; Denver, Colorado; Danbury/Hartford, Connecticut; Jacksonville and St. Petersburg in Florida; Atlanta, Georgia; Chicago and Joliet in Illinois; Des Moines, Iowa; Portland, Maine; Lincoln, Nebraska; Rochester, New York; Charlotte and Greensboro in North Carolina; Columbus, Ohio; Portland, Oregon; Providence, Rhode Island; Memphis and Nashville, Tennessee; Dallas, Texas; and Salt Lake City, Utah.

3. Boston, Cincinnati, Houston, New York City, and Richmond.

4. On average, Cambodians who become naturalized citizens do so in their tenth year after resettlement (ORR 1994).

REFERENCES

Banister, Judith, and E. Paige Johnson. 1993. After the Nightmare: The Population of Cambodia. In *Genocide and Democracy in Cambodia. The Khmer Rouge, the United Nations and the International Community.* Edited by Ben Kiernan. New Haven: Yale University Southeast Asian Studies. Pp. 65–139.

Boua, Chanthou. 1982. Women in Today's Cambodia. *New Left Review* 131: 45–61.

Bowlan, Jeanne, and Ellen Bruno, Editors. 1985. *Cambodian Mental Health. The Cambodian Women's Project Conference Proceedings.* New York: The American Friends Service Committee.

Bruno, Ellen. 1984. *Acculturation Difficulties of the Khmer in New York City.* New York: The Cambodian Women's Program, American Friends Service Committee.

Central Intelligence Agency (CIA). 1980. *Kampuchea: A Demographic Catastrophe.* Washington, D.C.: Central Intelligence Agency.

Chanda, Nayan. 1986. *Brother Enemy: The War after the War.* New York: Harcourt, Brace, Jovanovich.

Chandler, David P. 1982. Songs at the Edge of the Forest: Perceptions of Order in Three Cambodian Texts. In *Moral Order and the Question of Change: Essays on Southeast Asian Thought.* Edited by D. K. Wyatt and A. Woodside. New Haven: Yale University Southeast Asian Studies Monograph Series 24. Pp. 53–77.

———. 1983. *A History of Cambodia.* Boulder: Westview Press.

———. 1990. Reflections on Cambodian History. Cambodia 1990. *Cultural Survival Quarterly* 14(3):16–19.

———. 1991a. *The Land and People of Cambodia.* New York: HarperCollins.

—————. 1991b. *The Tragedy of Cambodian History. Politics, War, and Revolution since 1945.* New Haven: Yale University Press.

Coleman, C. M. 1987. Cambodians in the United States. In *The Cambodian Agony.* Edited by David A. Ablin and Marlowe Hoods. Armonk: M. E. Sharpe. Pp. 354–374.

Criddle, Joan D. 1992. *Bamboo & Butterflies. From Refugee to Citizen.* Dixon, California: East/West Bridge Publishing House.

Criddle, Joan D., and Teeda Butt Mam. 1987. *To Destroy You Is No Loss: The Odyssey of a Cambodian Family.* New York: The Atlantic Monthly Press.

Crystal, Eric. 1988. Fragments of a Civilization. In *First International Scholars Conference on Cambodia. Selected Papers.* Edited by A. Judkins. Geneseo: Department of Anthropology and the Geneseo Foundation. Pp. 13–22.

Ea, Meng-Try. 1987. Recent Population Trends in Kampuchea. In *The Cambodian Agony.* Edited by David A. Ablin and Marlowe Hoods. Armonk: M. E. Sharpe. Pp. 3–15.

Ebihara, May M. 1968. *Svay. A Khmer Village in Cambodia.* Ph.D. dissertation, Columbia University. Ann Arbor: University Microfilms.

—————. 1985. Khmer. In *Refugees in the United States. A Reference Handbook.* Edited by David W. Haines. Westport: Greenwood Press. Pp. 127–147.

—————. 1993. A Cambodian Village under the Khmer Rouge, 1975–1979. In *Genocide and Democracy in Cambodia. The Khmer Rouge, the United Nations and the International Community.* Edited by Ben Kiernan. New Haven: Yale University Southeast Asian Studies. Pp. 51–63.

Ebihara, May M., Carol A. Mortland, and Judy Ledgerwood, Editors. 1994. *Cambodian Culture since 1975: Homeland and Exile.* Ithaca, New York: Cornell University Press.

Eisenbruch, Maurice. 1991. From Post-traumatic Stress Disorder to Cultural Bereavement: Diagnosis of Southeast Asian Refugees. *Social Science and Medicine* 33(6): 673–680.

Evans, Grant, and Kelvin Rowley. 1983. *Red Brotherhood at War.* London: Verso.

Florentine Films. 1991. *Rebuilding the Temple. Cambodians in America.* Haydenville: Florentine Films.

Foreign Broadcast Information Service. 1976. Asia and Pacific Daily Report. *Foreign Broadcast Information Service* 4:63.

French, Lindsay. 1994. Enduring Holocaust, Surviving History: Displaced Cambodians on the Thai-Cambodian Border, 1989–1991. Unpublished Ph.D. dissertation. Harvard University.

Frye, R. 1991. Cultural Themes in Health-Care Decision Making among Cambodian Refugee Women. *Journal of Community Health Nursing* 8(1):33–44.

Gallagher, Dennis. 1988. United States and the Indochinese Refugees. In *Indochinese Refugees: Asylum and Resettlement.* Edited by Supang Chantavanich and E. Bruce Reynolds. Bangkok: Institute of Asian Studies, Chulalongkorn University. Pp. 230–248.

Gordon, Linda. 1984. *Southeast Asian Refugee Migration to the United States.* Washington, D.C.: Office of Refugee Resettlement, U.S. Department of Health and Human Services, September.

Higham, Charles. 1989. *The Archaeology of Mainland Southeast Asia. From 10,000 B.C. to the Fall of Angkor.* Cambridge: Cambridge University Press.

Hopkins, MaryCarol. 1992. Becoming Bicultural: Preserving Culture through Adaptation. In *Selected Papers on Refugee Issues.* Edited by Pamela A. DeVoe. Washington, D.C.: American Anthropological Association. Pp. 71–80.

Kiernan, Ben. 1990. The Genocide in Cambodia, 1975–1979. *Bulletin of Concerned Asian Scholars* 20(2): 35–40.

———. 1993. Introduction. In *Genocide and Democracy in Cambodia. The Khmer Rouge, the United Nations and the International Community.* Edited by Ben Kiernan. New Haven: Yale University Southeast Asian Studies. Pp. 1–32.

Kinzie, J. D. 1987. The "Concentration Camp Syndrome" among Cambodian Refugees. In *The Cambodian Agony.* Edited by D. Ablin and M. Hood. New York: M. E. Sharpe. Pp. 33–352.

Kinzie, J. D., R. H. Fredrickson, Roth Ben, Jenelle Fleck, and William Karls. 1984. Posttraumatic Stress Disorder among Survivors of Cambodian Concentration Camps. *American Journal of Psychiatry* 141(5):645–650.

Kulig, Judith. 1991. Role, Status Changes and Family Planning Use among Cambodian Refugee Women. Doctor of Nursing Science, University of California at San Francisco.

Ledgerwood, Judy. 1990a. *Changing Khmer Conceptions of Gender: Women, Stories, and the Social Order.* Ph.D. dissertation, Cornell University. Ann Arbor: University Microfilms.

———. 1990b. Portrait of a Conflict: Exploring Changing Khmer-American Social and Political Relationships. *Journal of Refugee Studies* 3(2):135–154.

Loescher, Gil, and John A. Scanlan. 1986. *Calculated Kindness: Refugees and America's Half-Open Door, 1945 to the Present.* New York: The Free Press.

Lynch, James F. 1989. *Border Khmer: A Demographic Study of the Residents of Site II, Site B, and Site 8.* Bangkok: The Ford Foundation.

Marcucci, John. 1986. *Khmer Refugees in Dallas: Medical Decisions in the Context of Pluralism.* Ph.D. dissertation, Southern Methodist University. Ann Arbor: University Microfilms.

Martel, Gabrielle. 1975. *Lovea. Village des environs d'Angkor,* Vol. 98. Paris: Publications d'École Française d'Extrême-Orient.

Mason, Linda, and Roger Brown. 1983. *Rice, Rivalry and Politics: Managing Cambodian Relief.* Notre Dame: University of Notre Dame Press.

May Someth. 1986. *Cambodian Witness: The Autobiography of Someth May.* London: Faber and Faber.

Mitchell, F. 1987. *From Refugee to Rebuilder: Cambodian Women in America.* Ph.D. dissertation. Ann Arbor: University Microfilms International.

Mollica, Richard F. 1988. The Trauma Story: The Psychiatric Care of Refugee Survivors of Violence and Torture. In *Post-Traumatic Therapy and Victims of Violence.* Edited by Frank M. Ochberg. New York: Brunner/Mazel. Pp. 295–314.

Mollica, Richard F., Grace Wyshack, and James Lavelle. 1987. The Psychosocial Impact of War Trauma and Torture on Southeast Asian Refugees. *American Journal of Psychiatry* 144(22):1567–1572.

Mortland, Carol A. 1987. Transforming Refugees in Refugee Camps. *Urban Anthropology* 16(3–4):375–404.

———. 1993. Patron-Client Relations and the Evolution of Mutual Assistance Associations. In *Refugee Empowerment and Organizational Change. A Systems Per-*

spective. Edited by Peter W. Van Arsdale. Arlington: American Anthropological Association. Pp. 15–36.

———. 1994a. Cambodian Refugees and Identity in the United States. In *Reconstructing Lives, Recapturing Meaning. Refugee Identity, Gender, and Culture Change.* Edited by Linda A. Camino and Ruth M. Krulfeld. Basel, Switzerland: Gordon and Breach Publishers. Pp. 5–7.

———. 1994b. Khmer Buddhists in the United States: Ultimate Questions. In *Cambodian Culture since 1975. Homeland and Exile.* Edited by May M. Ebihara, C. A. Mortland, and J. Ledgerwood. Ithaca: Cornell University Press. Pp. 72–90.

Mortland, Carol A., and Judy Ledgerwood. 1987. Secondary Migration among Southeast Asian Refugees in the United States. *Urban Anthropology* 16(3–4):291–326.

———. 1988. Refugee Resource Acquisition, the Invisible Communication System. In *Cross-Cultural Adaptation: Current Approaches.* Edited by Young Yun Kim and William B. Gudykunst. Newbury Park, California: Sage Publications. Pp. 286–306.

Mourer, Roland. 1977. Laang Spean and the Prehistory of Cambodia. *Modern Quaternary Research in Southeast Asia* 3:29–56.

Ngor Haing. 1987. *A Cambodian Odyssey.* New York: Macmillan.

Nguyen-Hong-Nhiem, Lucy, and Joel Martin Halpern, Editors. 1989. *The Far East Comes Near: Autobiographical Accounts of Southeast Asian Students in America.* Amherst: University of Massachusetts Press.

North, David, and Nim Sok. 1989. *Profiles of Some Good Places for Cambodians to Live in the United States.* Washington, D.C.: Office of Refugee Resettlement, U.S. Department of Health and Human Services.

Office of Refugee Resettlement (ORR). 1994. *Refugee Resettlement Program. Report to the Congress. FY 1993.* Washington, D.C.: Office of Refugee Resettlement, U.S. Department of Health and Human Services.

Owan, Tom Choken, Editor. 1985. *Southeast Asian Mental Health: Treatment, Prevention, Services, Training, and Research.* Washington, D.C.: U.S. Department of Health and Human Services.

Pickwell, S. 1990. *Journey to the Promised Land: The Health Consequences of Refugee Status for Cambodians in San Diego.* Ph.D. dissertation. Ann Arbor: University Microfilms International.

Rasbridge, Lance A. 1991. Infant/Child Feeding among Resettled Cambodians in Dallas: Intracultural Variation in Reference to Iron Nutrition. Unpublished Ph.D. dissertation, Southern Methodist University.

Rasbridge, Lance A., and John L. Marcucci. 1992. Reactions to Coupon Coercion. Dallas Cambodian Women's Autonomy in the Acculturative Process. In *Selected Papers on Refugee Issues.* Edited by Pamela A. DeVoe. Washington, D.C.: American Anthropological Association. Pp. 81–88.

Refugee Act of 1980. 1980. *Public Law 96-212,* March 17, 1980, 96th Congress. Washington, D.C.

Refugee Reports. 1988. Statistical Issue. *Refugee Reports* 9(12):10.

———. 1993. Refugees Admitted to the United States by Nationality. *Refugee Reports,* December: 10–11.

Refugee Resource Center. 1982. *Cambodian Cluster Project. October, 1981–March, 1982. Final Report.* New York: Refugee Resource Center, Committee on Migra-

tion and Refugee Affairs, American Council of Voluntary Agencies in Foreign
Service.

Reynell, Josephine. 1989. *Political Pawns. Refugees on the Thai-Kampuchean Border.*
Oxford: Refugee Studies Programme.

Robinson, Court, and Arthur Wallenstein. 1988. *Unfulfilled Hopes: The Humanitarian
Parole/Immigrant Visa Program for Border Cambodians.* Washington, D.C.: U.S.
Committee for Refugees.

Rumbaut, Rubén G. 1995. Vietnamese, Laotian, and Cambodian Americans. In *Asian
Americans. Contemporary Trends and Issues.* Edited by Pyong Gap Min. Thousand Oaks, California: Sage Publications. Pp. 232–270.

Rumbaut, Rubén G., and Kenji Ima. 1988. *The Adaptation of Southeast Asian Refugee
Youth: A Comparative Study.* Washington, D.C.: U.S. Government Printing Office.

Sam, Sam-Ang. 1994. Khmer Traditional Music Today. In *Cambodian Culture since
1975. Homeland and Exile.* Edited by May M. Ebihara, C. A. Mortland, and J.
Ledgerwood. Ithaca: Cornell University Press. Pp. 39–47.

Shawcross, William. 1979. *Sideshow. Kissinger, Nixon and the Destruction of Cambodia.*
London: André Deutsch.

Skinner, Kenneth A., and Glenn L. Hendricks. 1979. The Shaping of Ethnic Self-Identity
among Indochinese Refugees. *Journal of Ethnic Studies* 7(3):25–41.

Smith, Frank. 1989. *Interpretive Accounts of the Khmer Rouge Years: Personal Experience in Cambodian Peasant World View.* Madison: Center for Southeast Asian
Studies, University of Wisconsin.

Smith-Hefner, Nancy J. 1990. Language and Identity in the Education of Boston-Area
Khmer. *Anthropology and Education Quarterly* 21(3):250–268.

Steinberg, Stephen. 1989. *The Ethnic Myth. Race, Ethnicity, and Class in America.* Boston: Beacon Press.

Szymusiak, Molyda. 1986. *The Stones Cry Out.* Translated by L. Coverdale. New York:
Hill and Wang.

Tollefson, James W. 1989. *Alien Winds: The Reeducation of America's Indochinese
Refugees.* New York: Praeger.

Ui, Shiori. 1991. "Unlikely Heroes": The Evolution of Female Leadership in a Cam-
bodian Ethnic Enclave. In *Ethnography Unbound. Power and Resistance in the
Modern Metropolis.* Edited by M. Buraway. Berkeley: University of California
Press. Pp. 161–177.

Ung, Chinary. 1988. The Regeneration of Khmer Music and the Performing Arts in the
United States. In *First International Scholars Conference on Cambodia. Selected
Papers.* Edited by Russell A. Judkins. Geneseo: State University of New York at
Geneseo, Department of Anthropology and the Geneseo Foundation. Pp. 37–45.

United Nations Children's Fund (UNICEF). 1990. *Cambodia: The Situation of Children
and Women.* Phnom Penh: UNICEF, Office of the Special Representative.

United Nations Development Programme. 1989. *Report of the Kampuchea Needs Assessment Study.* United Nations Development Programme. August 1989.

U.S. Committee for Refugees. 1994. *World Refugee Survey.* Washington, D.C.

Vickery, Michael. 1988. How Many Died in Pol Pot's Kampuchea? *Bulletin of Concerned Asian Scholars* 20(1):70–73.

———. 1990. Cambodian Political Economy, 1975–1990. *Cambodia 1990, Cultural
Survival Quarterly* 14(3):23–27.

Welaratna, Usha. 1993. *Beyond the Killing Fields: Voices of Nine Cambodian Survivors in America.* Stanford: Stanford University Press.

Williams, Carolyn L., and Joseph Westermeyer, Editors. 1986. *Refugee Mental Health in Resettlement Countries.* Washington, D.C.: Hemisphere Publishing.

Yathay Pin. 1987. *Stay Alive My Son.* New York: The Free Press.

Part IV

Historical Approaches

Chapter 10

Eastern Europeans

ELZBIETA M. GOZDZIAK

As long as there have been Germany and Russia, there have been refugees from Eastern Europe seeking refuge or temporary safe haven in other countries. The royalty and peasants, intelligentsia and rural shopkeepers: They had little in common except their experiences of persecution, war, and famine. In New York, Chicago, Detroit, Cleveland, Pittsburgh, and Los Angeles, they built their churches, spoke their native languages, and published magazines filled with nostalgic poetry and angry prose. They might speak wistfully of going back, but totalitarian regimes refused them visas. They were forced to leave their countries in waves, beginning in the nineteenth century, when Russia and the Austro-Hungarian empire posed a threat for smaller nations. Each subsequent upheaval, from the Russian revolution of 1917 through the Hungarian Uprising of 1956 to the Prague Spring of 1968 and Polish martial law in 1981, sent more people packing.

The east of the West or the west of the East? What is Eastern Europe? The answer changes from country to country, affording interesting insights into the motives involved in the perception of one's neighbors. Some scholars and indeed many inhabitants of the region reject the term entirely, preferring *Central Europe;* others argue about the boundaries. Hungarians and Czechs tend to consider the territory of the old Austro-Hungarian empire to be the historical core of the region. For Poles, the "other Europe" covers the whole area between Germany and the former Soviet Union.

Recognizing that Eastern Europe is far more of a political expression than a geographical one and acknowledging its considerable ethnic diversity, I will focus my attention in this chapter on three different countries—Poland, Hungary, and Romania—as refugees from these countries represent the largest groups of Eastern Europeans resettled in the United States. This chapter provides a synthesis of available research on resettlement experiences of different waves of immigrants and refugees from Eastern Europe in order to elucidate commonalities and differences in their resettlement experiences and to shed light on the processes of uprooting and adaptation.

POLES

The Country

Poland's borders have shifted countless times in the course of the country's turbulent history. At its peak, the union of Poland and the Grand Duchy of Lithuania expanded almost to Moscow at the end of the fifteenth century. Poland ceased to exist as an independent state after its neighbors—Prussia, Austria, and Russia—partitioned the country in 1795. Most recently, Poland's borders were significantly shifted westward after World War II. Poland lost such cities as Vilnius, Pinsk, Brest, and Lvov in the east but gained Wroclaw and Szczecin in the west. Modern Poland shares borders with Russia, Lithuania, Ukraine, the Czech Republic in the east, and Germany in the west. The Tatra Mountains form its border with Slovakia in the south, and the Baltic Sea constitutes a natural frontier in the north.

With a population of 38 million and an area of 120,725 square miles, Poland is the largest and most populous nation in the region. According to official Polish sources, ethnic Poles constitute 99 percent of the country's population. Of the approximately 500,000 reported as ethnic minorities, the Ukrainians and Byelorussians form the largest groups, with much smaller groups of Slovaks, Czechs, Lithuanians, Germans, Russians, Roma (Gypsies), and Jews.

History and Politics

The name of *Polska* (Poland) does not emerge until the tenth century—and then only as a domain of one small Slavonic tribe, the Polanie ("the people of the open fields") who settled on the banks of the Warta river in the vicinity of modern Poznan. The first Polish state was formed in 966 when Prince Mieszko I married Czech Princess Dabrowka from Prague and accepted Catholicism. The nation was frequently at war, against the Tartars in the east and the Teutonic Knights in the west. But in the fourteenth century, Poland thrived as an advanced European state, founding the Jagiellonian University in Krakow and establishing a strong monarchy that defeated the Teutons at Grunwald in 1410. The Jagiellonian period following the defeat of the Teutonic Order was Poland's golden age. The size of the combined Polish-Lithuanian empire grew to impressive proportions. In 1492 it stretched from the Baltic to the Black Sea and was twice the size of modern France. Literature and science were blooming; its achievements were crowned by the famous discovery by Mikolaj Kopernik (Copernicus) of the earth's movement around the sun.

However, in the following centuries, Poland fell behind the rest of Europe. Its famously independent nobles insisted on autonomy and the power of veto— excellent for liberty but bad for national strength. Poland's elected monarchs were no match for the surrounding absolute sovereigns, and between 1772 and 1795, Prussia, Austria, and Russia divided the country among them, erasing the Polish state from the political map of Europe for the next 150 years. The Poles, however, hung on to their national identity tenaciously while there was no Poland per se and in 1830, 1848, and 1863 rebelled against the foreign rule.

At the outset of World War I, both sides sought Polish support by promising Poland independence, which finally came about at the end of the war on November 11, 1918. The new nation's frontiers were determined partially by negotiations and partially on the battlefield. Despite a long history of constitutional government, Poland could not long sustain a democracy and by 1926 fell under the quasi-dictatorial rule of Marshal Jozef Pilsudski.

World War II began with the German attack on the Polish garrison outside Gdansk on September 1, 1939. Only a week earlier, the Nazis and Soviets had concluded the infamous secret pact that proposed a new partition of Poland. Accordingly, on November 1, Russia appropriated eastern Poland, and Germany occupied the rest. Although Polish units fought on the Allied side throughout the war, the territory of Poland was at the mercy of the occupiers. Over the next six years, 6 million Poles were killed, half of them Jews. In 1944 and 1945 the Red Army "liberated" Poland, using its presence to impose a socialist regime and to annex the eastern third of the country. Between the Holocaust and the annexation, Poland went from being a multiethnic state with large Jewish, Ukrainian, Lithuanian, Byelorussian, and German populations to one of the most ethnically homogeneous countries in the world.

In the decades after the war, Poles frequently agitated against communism, a form of government they bitterly resented. In 1956, 1968, 1970, 1976, 1980– 1981, and 1988–1989, large-scale unrest broke out in Poland. The months of domestic strikes and protests in 1980–1981 spawned the creation of the Solidarity trade union under the leadership of Lech Walesa. In August 1980, the government signed an agreement with Solidarity allowing the independent trade union the right to strike and to print free publications. In December 1981, the government, with General Wojciech Jaruzelski at the helm, rescinded the agreement and banned Solidarity under the rule of martial law.

The government lifted martial law in 1983 but did not permit Solidarity to function officially until April 1989 when it agreed to Eastern Europe's first free parliamentary elections in 50 years. Solidarity overwhelmed the Communists in the June 1989 election, and by August, Solidarity journalist Tadeusz Mazowiecki took over as Poland's first non-Communist prime minister since World War II. The silver lining of freedom was soon to be tinged by dark economic thunder clouds. In 1990, the government embarked on a crash program to dismantle the Communist economy and introduce a free market–oriented capitalist system. While virtually all retail business was soon in private hands in Poland,

and a cornucopia of Western goods appeared in shops, prices rose dramatically, and as a result, the quality of life decreased substantially. Since economic change is slower than political restructuring, it was not possible to overcome rapidly the legacy of economic mismanagement and moribund bureaucracy so characteristic of the Communist economy. In December 1990, Poles elected former electrician Lech Walesa president. But three years later, in 1993, voters elected legislators who claimed that slowing the pace of reform, both economic and social, would soften the blows of transition.

The Exodus

Of all the Eastern European diasporas, the Polish is the biggest and one of the oldest. The first political exiles left after Poland was carved up by its neighbors in 1795. Most of them, however, went to Paris, not to America. In 1854, the first band of Poles who migrated "for bread" left Upper Silesia and struck out for east Texas, where they founded America's first Polish colony, Panna Maria, located 60 miles southwest of San Antonio. Farming colonies grew also in Missouri, Ohio, Indiana, Illinois, Arkansas, Oklahoma, and Minnesota. Rural Michigan drew seasonal agricultural workers from Detroit throughout the nineteenth century. By the end of the century, Polish immigrants began to take over abandoned and worn-out farmlands in the East. Poles worked as agricultural laborers in Connecticut, and Polish enclaves were established in the villages of Northampton, Greenfield, Hatfield, South Deerfield, and Sunderland, Massachusetts. In New Jersey and on Long Island, Poles took up truck farming, supplying the nearby urban market (Bukowczyk 1987).

The great period of Polish immigration to the United States began in the 1880s and lasted until the change in the American immigration law in 1924. The precise number of Poles who arrived in America during that interval is difficult to establish primarily because Poland was under foreign political domination during most of that time, and arriving immigrants were registered by country of residence, not by ethnicity. Thus, Polish immigrants were listed as Austrian, Austro-Hungarian, Russian, or German subjects.

The turn-of-the-century cohort consisted largely of labor migration predominantly from the peasant classes (Thomas and Znaniecki 1927; Radzialowski 1974; Golab 1977; Kleeman 1985). The group was characterized not only as being 90 percent peasant but also as being about one third illiterate, including people who looked to the church, and the parish priest in particular, for community leadership, guidance in their lives, and support in social, family and spiritual matters. The immigrants were mostly young men who imported their families, or went back to get them, after becoming established in a job and a community in the United States (Znaniecki Lopata 1976). Most settled in urban centers, near other Polish immigrants (Lieberson 1963). They tended to find work in industry. Hamtramck, Michigan, for example, attracted Poles from other settlements as the automobile industry expanded its needs for unskilled workers (Wood 1955).

The next wave of Poles arrived after World War II and the installation of Communist government in Poland. Between 1945 and 1969, approximately 162,000 Polish refugees came to the United States (U.S. Department of Justice 1969). These refugees were very different from their predecessors. The 1949 influx of 27,000 Poles (Znaniecki Lopata 1976), facilitated by the Displaced Persons Act, included primarily servicemen and others who refused to repatriate to Poland after the war, mainly for political reasons (Mostwin 1980). Poles who escaped Poland in the early 1950s were predominantly middle-class professionals. Many of them held university degrees or were highly skilled artisans (Goode and Schneider 1994). Because of their different backgrounds and experiences, these groups did not slip easily into the life of the Old Polonia as the Polish-Americans are called (Znaniecki Lopata 1976; Goode and Schneider 1994).

The 1968 wave included refugees expelled from Poland in that year after a series of student unrests and strikes as well as a number of people who came to the United States under the relaxed travel restrictions of the late 1960s and 1970s as Poland opened up to the West under the regime of Edward Gierek. Some of the latter émigrés intended to work in the United States to earn hard currency to be spent or invested in Poland. These ''visitors'' on temporary visas found employment within the working-class Polish ethnic communities of Chicago, Philadelphia, and New York. Some extended or overstayed their visas and remained illegally, while others were allowed to stay in the United States and work legally under the Extended Voluntary Departure (EVD) program.

The last wave were the post-Solidarity refugees (Goode and Schneider 1994). Polish refugees admitted under the Refugee Act of 1980 number more than 38,000, with the largest numbers having arrived in 1982 and 1983 (ORR 1993). This wave brought a fresh Polish presence to the United States. The newcomers included a number of young single men with skilled-craft backgrounds and young families in which the parents often came from the intelligentsia (Cichon, Gozdziak, and Grover 1986; Goode and Schneider 1994).

Arrival and Adaptation

The earliest arrivals from Poland might not have known a soul in this strange New World. Those who followed, on the other hand, might have received railroad tickets sent to them by their kin, been met by friends or relatives, or joined up with recruiters who would hasten them to their final destinations.

Polish immigrant farmers faced the challenge of life in a new land with the inevitable culture shock and adjustment to exotic and often difficult surroundings. The immigrants from Silesia who landed in Texas encountered foreign-looking Mexicans, and unfamiliar hot climate, and a wide diversity of new fauna and vegetation. They quickly learned, however, to rely upon wild game and corn, known to them as ''Turkish wheat,'' and discovered new crops such as sweet potatoes. Few Polish newcomers grew cotton until after the Civil War, but Polish farm products did include corn, vegetables, cattle, oxen, pigs, and chickens. Incidentally, none of these Polish immigrants owned slaves (Bukowczyk 1987).

The Polish immigrants who arrived between the 1850s and 1880s took up farming because land in the West was still cheap. They considered themselves permanent settlers, and they wanted to put down roots in America. The Poles who came between the 1880s and World War I, on the other hand, confronted inflated land prices, high capital requirements, and low market prices for farm commodities (Bukowczyk 1987). They also viewed themselves as temporary sojourners and therefore eschewed farming and its inherent long-term commitment. Instead, they joined the ranks of unskilled laborers and went to work in the mines and factories of America's Second Industrial Revolution.

The first temporary sojourners were slow to adapt to America. They showed little upward mobility and lived in insular ethnic enclaves, trying to preserve their folk customs and peasant values oriented toward stability and family, security and steady work. Catholic to the core—their religion was a distinctive blend of magic and mysticism, rural superstition, and orthodox belief—they hoped for a better afterlife and venerated Matka Boska, the Blessed Virgin, Poland's patroness. Subsequent groups of Polish immigrants, although still mostly of rural background, represented a variety of types of peasants, differentiated by subclass, degree of urban influence, and region. They had "progressed from the first generation of largely uneducated former peasants living in poor, urban ethnic neighborhoods, to the financially well-off second generation that did not use higher education as a means of upward mobility and thus stayed in blue-collar jobs and life styles, to the increasingly educated third and fourth generations who can be expected to move up the socioeconomic ladder" (Znaniecki Lopata 1976: 116–117).

The post–World War II refugees present a distinctly different picture of adjustment and adaptation. The war did not exile only the elite of scholars, artists, and scientists. It uprooted thousands of Polish refugees—some fled Nazi oppression, others the Soviet "Iron Curtain" that fell over postwar Eastern Europe. Between the end of World War II and 1968, some 40,000 Polish ex-servicemen and underground insurgents came to the United States (Bukowczyk 1987). Unlike the Hungarian political refugees, most Polish displaced persons, whether they were veterans or not, did not come to America to continue political or ideological battles but to rebuild their own disrupted lives. They migrated as families and intended to stay here. Most of them were adults in their early middle age; about one third were infants, children, and adolescents, some of whom were orphans. They were resettled with sponsor families—not all Polish—throughout America but concentrated primarily in industrial states with large Polish-American communities: New York, New Jersey, Illinois, Connecticut, and Michigan.

Displaced children who came to the United States from Poland adjusted well, although traumatized orphans were often described by social workers as "undisciplined, unstable, primitive, even bestial, but longing for affection . . . precocious and hardened" (Korewa 1957: 58–59). In many cases, adults faced larger problems of transition and adjustment. Wrenching wartime experiences in labor and concentration camps, and later in refugee camps, had made them, according to one report, "sensitive, suspicious, and generally alert against real or imaginary threats to their dignity, security and welfare" (Heberle and Hall 1951: 3).

With scant information about the United States, gleaned mostly from literature, newspapers, movies, and American GIs, Polish refugees did not fit easily into American society. Because refugee policy favored persons with an agricultural background, many displaced Poles—most with urban backgrounds—lied in order to get into the country (Bukowczyk 1987). They soon found themselves placed in unsatisfying farm occupations for which they had no skills. Many left rural areas as soon as they could to search for higher wages (Heberle and Hall 1951). Middle-class refugees who made it into better-paying factory jobs, the only employment they were suited for, as they lacked English, felt declassé. Working-class people, artisans, and farmers fared better and integrated easily into blue-collar Polish America (Bukowczyk 1987; Znaniecki Lopata 1976).

Most Polish refugees of that era, however, fitted no better into Polonia than they did into mainstream America. Many shunned the older Polish-American working-class urban enclaves and gravitated toward suburbs. The intelligentsia rejected the lifestyle of working-class Polish-Americans, while older Polonia came to resent the displaced persons (or DPs as they were often called); felt jealous of their superior education, higher social status, and greater chances for upward mobility; and mockingly called them "princes," "barons," or "masters" because of their middle-class dress, educated speech, and predilection for Polish military titles. When the refugees attempted to speak for Polish America, older Polonians took offense because they expected to be followed, not to be led, by the newcomers (Bukowczyk 1987). The DPs, on the other hand, expected to assume the traditional class role that persons of their position had held in prewar Poland. They were dismayed by the "lack of respect for educated people" and shocked by the poor Polish spoken by the Polonians who retained peasant linguistic characteristics (Blejwas 1981).

More recent post-Solidarity refugees fit into Polish America no better than the displaced persons, perhaps even worse. However, their ambitions and good education fostered swift assimilation into the mainstream American society. They faced resentment from the Old Polonia, because their aspirations and lifestyles were different—European and more middle-class (Goode and Schneider 1994; Cichon, Gozdziak, and Grover 1986; Bukowczyk 1987). On their part, the newcomers criticized Americans and Polish-Americans for their "shallow view of freedom" (*Detroit Free Press* 1985). Exiled Solidarity activists were disheartened by the priorities of Polish-American ethnic leaders who found it

more important to fight the proverbial Polish joke than to lend support to the
new Polish cause (*New York Times* 1984).

While not very successful in getting along with the Old Polonia, the newcomers adjusted very well to mainstream America. They made a relatively rapid
rise in occupational and socioeconomic status. They generally came to this country with a level of education comparable to or higher than that of an American
secondary school. Usually, they had studied at least one foreign language and
possessed a trade or professional skill. They either knew some English or learned
it quickly, entered a trade related to their own, and advanced to a higher wage
level and even supervisory positions within a few years. They were very ambitious and economically oriented and therefore highly motivated to work and
move up the economic ladder. Among the Eastern Europeans surveyed by the
Center for Applied Linguistics (CAL), Poles were the only ones who had more
than one job at a time (Short 1988).

Almost all of the Polish refugees surveyed for the study of economic and
social adjustment of Eastern Europeans, Afghans, and Ethiopians conducted in
1986 by the Research Management Corporation (RMC) for the federal Office
of Refugee Resettlement (ORR) exhibited a substantial improvement over time
in earnings and job status. They quickly moved into technical, administrative,
sales, and skilled trade positions, often in the construction and manufacturing
industries (Cichon, Gozdziak, and Grover 1986). All Polish refugees studied by
RMC participated in the labor force and had equally high employment rates: 81
to 100 percent (Cichon, Gozdziak, and Grover 1986). Baker (1989) found that
Poles settled in Boise, Idaho, were motivated, willing to work hard to get ahead,
and committed to economic success. Even those who were not doing well economically were optimistic about their future economic position. Polish refugees
in Philadelphia, especially those who secured employment in their fields, spent
less time looking for their first job (anywhere from a couple of months to a
year) than, for instance, Soviet Jews (anywhere from five months to five years)
(Schneider 1988). Poles resettled in Dallas initially were working in service
areas, such as housekeeping, dishwashing, and landscaping. In Chicago most
initial positions held by Polish men were in building maintenance, construction,
and factories, while women tended to have clerical jobs. Poles in New York
City also obtained initial jobs in the service industry, but many also entered
skilled and semiskilled trade positions in factories, sales, and administrative
work (Cichon, Gozdziak, and Grover 1986). Goode and Schneider (1994) found
that the newcomers from Poland who settled in Philadelphia worked as skilled
craftspeople, in construction, in a variety of semiskilled service sector jobs, and
sometimes in professional firms in the primary and secondary sectors. Poles
studied by Baker in Boise, Idaho (1988, 1989) secured employment in a variety
of low-income positions. The single largest employer was a producer of computer chips. Others worked as salesmen, janitors, auto mechanics, nurse's aides,
and waiters. Some continued their crafts such as cabinet maker and barber. Five
particularly successful males secured employment as computer programmers,

but most professionals found their training to be nontransferable and exhibited less enthusiasm about their immigration experience than other types of workers. Seventy-five percent of the employed Polish refugees surveyed by RMC reported finding their jobs through informal referrals among acquaintances, 21 percent answered ads in newspapers or professional journals, and only one individual reported getting his job directly through a voluntary agency (Cichon, Gozdziak, and Grover 1986).

There was little variation in labor force participation by gender among the Polish refugees studied by RMC. The majority of both men and women worked. The exceptions were mothers of children under the age of six who had child care responsibilities (Cichon, Gozdziak, and Grover 1986). Baker's analysis (1988, 1989) demonstrates that the Polish refugee women in Boise were more likely to have lower economic status and lower-paying jobs. Fifty percent of the women in his study did not work outside the home. Most of the younger married females were seeking additional training. The most popular vocational goal of the refugee women was nursing.

Two years after the completion of the RMC study, I interviewed a number of the surveyed refugees by telephone (Gozdziak 1989) and found that the prospects for long-term self-sufficiency had increased even further. Many respondents had received promotions, found better jobs, completed recertification processes, or obtained additional skills (e.g., word processing, computer programming). The one subgroup that had more difficulty with rapid entry into the American labor force were the highly skilled professionals, doctors, and lawyers. In contrast, their less-educated countrymen, who had easily transferable skills (carpenters, masons, electronic technicians, etc.), were making the transition into the U.S. labor market far more rapidly (Gozdziak 1989).

In the mid-1980s, refugees from Poland had the lowest use of public assistance of all refugees resettled in the United States, at roughly 14 percent (ORR 1986). Use of public assistance among Poles was relatively low in the three sites visited by the RMC research team. In Dallas, no member of the sample had ever used welfare, partly because Texas provisions were inadequate for support. RMC reported that almost all Polish refugees were self-sufficient and attained that status within a fairly short period of time: between two weeks and 3 months. In Chicago and New York City, however, this positive picture of self-sufficiency was disrupted in some cases. After a year or two of being self-supporting, many Poles decided to go on public assistance. Data on refugee cash and medical assistance in Cook County indicate that Poles used assistance very little in the early months after arrival but used it considerably more in the 7 to 12 and 13 to 18 months after arrival. The explanation of the 7–12 months surge may be that the alternative resettlement project in Chicago prevented its clients, which included Polish refugees, from utilizing welfare during the first 6 months after arrival. However, the second surge, at 13 to 18 months, appeared to be a result of disillusionment with unsatisfactory jobs, layoffs, and adjustment difficulties after the initial novelty wore off (Cichon, Gozdziak, and Grover 1986).

There was controversy among service providers regarding the Polish refugees' attitudes toward adjustment. Some staff, usually representatives of the Old Polonia, claimed that the newcomers from Poland had unrealistic expectations of the lifestyles they should lead in the United States, that they wanted welfare and schooling provided for them until they could get the high-status jobs they held in Poland, and that they would accept nothing that came from thrift stores. Other service providers saw the same characteristics as sources of pride and motivation that prompted the Poles to pursue professional recertification and strive for economic and social self-sufficiency (Cichon, Gozdziak, and Grover 1986).

Overall, most recent newcomers from Poland experienced an initial period of disillusionment, followed by gradual adjustment to life in America. Initial adjustment problems included loneliness, sadness at separation from family, and depression. Coming from an extremely homogeneous society, many Poles experienced anxiety about the ethnic and racial diversity of American cities. Their initial insecurities were also exacerbated by the instability of employment in the United States and the lack of free health care, social welfare, and retirement benefits. Despite the initial adjustment problems, most Poles adapted well to their new lives in the United States, moving over time into middle-class neighborhoods and working and socializing in the broader American society.

HUNGARIANS

The Country

Hungary is a mostly flat country located in the Carpathian Basin, surrounded by mountainous neighboring countries. The two major rivers cutting through Hungary are the Danube and the Tisza. Bordered by the Czech and Slovak Republics, Austria, Romania, Serbia, Slovenia, Croatia, and Ukraine, Hungary is enveloped largely by Slavs. A small country of 35,000 square miles, the size of Indiana, Hungary is inhabited by about 11 million people. Hungary is relatively ethnically homogeneous. Some 93 percent of the population call themselves Magyars, descendants of nomadic plains people, and speak a Finno-Ugric language, most closely related to Finnish and Turkish. Gypsies make up the largest minority group. Other minorities include Germans, Slovaks, Croats, and Romanians. Along with Poland, Hungary is an eastern outpost of Roman Catholicism, a faith adopted by King Stephen in A.D. 1000. Today some 67 percent of the population remains Roman Catholic, with 20 percent Calvinist and 5 percent Lutheran (Heinrich 1986).

History and Politics

The Hungarians were the last of the major peoples of Eastern Europe to appear in the region. When the Magyar tribes, originally from the Asian side of the Ural Mountains, numbering around 250,000 people, took possession of the

Carpathian Basin at the end of the ninth century, they already had a sophisticated tribal organization and a distinct linguistic and cultural identity. Skilled horsemen who depended on pastures and spoils of war for survival, they quickly broke the resistance of the Slavic plowmen and, under the leadership of their chief, Arpad, easily subjugated the established Slavic tribes. This historical process is reflected in the vocabulary of modern Hungarians, whose agricultural terms are mostly of Slavic origin.

The successful conquest of the Danube Valley generated confidence, and the Magyars began to raid westward. By A.D. 924 they plundered as far as Champagne in what is now France. However, the Germans stopped their westward expansion in 955, and that forced the Magyars to settle permanently in Pannonia. In 1000 Arpad's great-great-grandson accepted Christianity and was crowned as King Stephen I. From the very beginning, the Hungarian state was inhabited by non-Magyars as the so-called crownlands of St. Stephen included Slovakia, Croatia, and Transylvania.

In 1241, Odgai, the son of Genghis Khan, and his "Golden Horde" (i.e., the Mongols) charged through and rampaged Hungary for two years. In the wake of the invasion, King Bela IV began serious fortification of Buda Hills, a project that continued until the middle of the nineteenth century. During the reign of Bela IV, Hungary became increasingly powerful and expanded into neighboring lands. When the last king of the Arpad dynasty died without an heir in 1301, a series of foreign-born kings held sway over Hungary as enemies slowly whittled down the empire. The threat of Ottoman invasion in the middle of the fifteenth century, however, galvanized the stagnant country. A Hungarian nobleman, Janos Hunyadi, led the Christian forces to a monumental victory over the Ottoman Turks in 1456 near modern-day Belgrade. His son, Matthias Corvinus, was crowned king in 1458. Under his rule, Hungary experienced a golden age of artistic and intellectual development. After his death, scheming nobles and an unsuccessful peasant revolt in 1514 considerably weakened Hungary. The Ottoman armies again swept north up the Danube and in 1526 defeated the Hungarians in the Battle of Mohacs. The Ottoman forces captured the fortified city of Buda in 1541, and an Ottoman pasha reined in Buda until Habsburg-led troops crushed the Turks in 1686, put down a rebellion led by Ferenc Rakoczi, and ruled Hungary from Vienna. The Habsburg emperor was the new master.

The early 1800s saw renewed attempts to regain independence from Habsburg Austria. These efforts culminated in the revolution of 1848, which proclaimed a separate Hungarian state, and was only put down after the Austrian government received help from Russian troops in 1849. A more stable settlement came with the Compromise of 1867, masterminded by Ferenc Deak, which recognized Hungary's independent status within the Habsburg Austro-Hungarian empire. Under the Compromise of 1867, Hungary, and especially its major city, Budapest, experienced rapid economic and cultural growth. The prosperity ended with the outbreak of World War I, the resulting defeat of the Habsburgs, and the division of the empire. Under the Treaty of Trianon, two thirds of Hungarian territory were distributed among Serbia, Croatia, Slovakia, Ukraine, and particularly Romania, which gained Transylvania. While the Treaty of Trianon accorded independence to some 10 million non-Magyars, it also severed 3 million ethnic Hungarians from their homeland, dooming many to oppression, discrimination, and violation of human rights under regimes committed to ethnic homogeneity, especially the ethnic cleansing policies of Ceauşescu's Romania. Hungary's misery was exacerbated by a bloody power struggle between Communist and rightist forces at the end of World War I, followed by the Great Depression that engulfed the whole continent. Power fell to the conservative forces led by Admiral Miklos Horthy, whose principal policy became the recovery of the territories lost at Trianon. This led to an alliance with Germany during World War II.

The country's occupation by Soviet forces after World War II resulted in the formation of a Communist government. In 1956, reformist currents appearing throughout Eastern Europe encouraged increased Hungarian opposition to the stifling presence of the Communist regime. On October 23, 1956, a mass meeting in front of the Budapest radio station was dispersed with gunfire. The result was a 13-day "Hungarian Uprising," which, in the early morning of November 4, was met by the armed forces of the Warsaw Pact and Soviet tanks. About 2,000 people died in the uprising, and approximately 200,000 Hungarians fled the country, seeking refuge in the West.

After order was brutally restored, Janos Kadar, the new Soviet-backed leader, slowly introduced economic reform. As a result, Hungary became one of the most prosperous and liberal of all Eastern European countries. The most significant of the reforms was the New Economic Mechanism (NEM) introduced in 1968. NEM decentralized many aspects of the economy and fostered limited forms of private enterprise. Political reform followed in the 1980s. In May 1989, six months before the fall of the Berlin Wall, Hungary began dismantling portions of the barbed-wire frontier with Austria, thus becoming the first country to create a gap in the Iron Curtain. A few days later, Janos Kadar was ousted after 33 years in power. In September, the government decided to let thousands of East Germans flee to the West through Hungary. The decision prompted an exodus of some 57,000 East Germans and eventually forced a desperate East German government to open the Berlin Wall.

The first free elections since World War II were held in April 1990 and resulted in a total defeat of the Communists. Unfortunately, like its neighbors, Hungary found life after communism difficult. By the mid-1990s, shops were full and new businesses booming, but unemployment was on the rise. Hungary's relationship with Slovakia was tainted by the aborted dam project at Nagyamaros, and relations with Romania were strained by unresolved minority issues.

The Exodus

Until very recently, Hungary was an emigration rather than an immigration country. Four distinct periods of Hungarian immigration to the United States can be identified. Within each of these periods, different waves can be distinguished. The first and the largest Hungarian immigration to America commenced in the mid-1800s and lasted until the end of World War I (Dovenyi and Vukovich 1994; Huseby-Darvas 1995). While the early wave was characterized as labor migration (Dovenyi and Vukovich 1994; Huseby-Darvas 1995), the importance of political, social, and cultural factors cannot be omitted, given the ethnic composition of the early cohort. Ethnic minorities were more likely to emigrate than ethnic Hungarians; there is evidence that entire ethnic rural communities sought refuge in the United States (Dovenyi and Vukovich 1994).

The second, interwar influx of Hungarian immigrants began a movement of political expatriates (Benkart 1980). It was numerically much smaller, as the flows of all Eastern Europeans were greatly reduced both by restrictive immigration policies and by the Great Depression. Despite these limitations, in the five-year period between 1922 and 1927, an estimated 70,000 ethnic Hungarians arrived in the United States: 40,000 from Hungary and 30,000 from neighboring territories (Dovenyi and Vukovich 1994).

The third, post–World War II period included four distinct waves of political refugees. The first wave consisted of some 16,000 displaced persons, including former concentration camp inmates and members of the retreating Hungarian army, who did not want to return to Hungary after the end of the war (Vardy 1985). The 45-ers, as they were also called, constitute the core of the postwar trans-Atlantic migration. The DPs were followed by a second wave of the so-called 47-ers, most of whom actually fled Hungary between 1947 and 1949. The elite among them were those political emigrants who participated in the various postwar coalition governments of Hungary but were eventually pushed out by the Communists. This wave included leaders and members of the Smallholder Party, the National Peasant Party, and the Social Democratic Party. The political elite among the 47-ers was followed by thousands of politically less exposed Hungarians who left their homeland between 1947 and the mid-1950s largely because of their growing disenchantment with the oppressive regime. Altogether, between the end of World War II and the Hungarian Revolution of 1956, 26,532 Hungarian refugees entered the United States (Vardy 1985).

In 1957, some 38,000 Hungarians, the vast majority of whom were young students, professionals, intellectuals, and scientists, were admitted to the United States under the Hungarian Parole Program. The period between the early 1960s and late 1980s saw another wave of Hungarian refugees in America, the so-called orphans of Kadar and Ceauşescu. The latter were ethnic Hungarians from Transylvania fleeing Romanian ethnic cleansing and villagization programs. These cohorts were not as numerous as their predecessors; according to the

Office of Refugee Resettlement, approximately 6,000 refugees from Hungary were resettled under the Refugee Act of 1980 (ORR 1993).

Arrival and Adaptation

All of the different waves of Hungarian immigration to the United States occurred in various political and social contexts and were characterized by diverse push-and-full factors, varied scope and destination, and distinct educational levels and social backgrounds impacting both people's desire and ability to adapt to the ways of the host society (Huseby-Darvas 1995).

Like other Eastern Europeans who arrived in the United States at the turn of the century, the Hungarian immigrants were, for the most part, unskilled agrarian laborers who came to America with the intention of saving money and returning to Hungary to improve their economic and social standing there. Broken families, with men outnumbering women, poor living conditions in overcrowded boarding houses, and hard work characterized the life of most Hungarian immigrants around the turn of the century.

At the outbreak of World War I, most Hungarians abandoned the idea of returning home; the "sojourners" became permanent immigrants. They settled mostly near the mines and steel furnaces of Ohio, Pennsylvania, New York, and New Jersey. However, large groups also settled in Illinois, Indiana, Michigan, and West Virginia (Szeplaki 1975; Huseby-Darvas 1995). Some cities and towns developed large Hungarian-American colonies that were much more noticeable than those in scattered mining camps. New York, Cleveland, Pittsburgh, and Chicago, in particular, counted many thousands of Hungarians among their vast immigrant populations. Smaller Hungarian settlements developed in Bridgeport, Connecticut, New Brunswick and Passaic, New Jersey, South Bend, Indiana, and Youngstown, Ohio (Benkart 1980).

While most of the early-immigrants came as unskilled workers, some gradually worked their way into skilled factory positions, after becoming familiar with industrial routines in the American mines and mills. The few women in the early Hungarian settlements went into partnership with their husbands as boardinghouse keepers. In 1910, for example, half of the Hungarian couples in the United States were taking in boarders (Benkart 1980). Opening small businesses in America required capital the sojourners did not have or did not want to invest. However, as their repatriation plans were abandoned, some opened meat markets and spice shops; others began to take interest in union organization to improve working conditions and to protect job security.

As permanent immigrants, Hungarians in the 1920s were willing to invest in building an American ethnic community. Separated from their homeland, they could no longer take their religious, linguistic, and cultural heritage for granted. Their concern for their homeland as expressed in fund-raising efforts to support Hungarian prisoners of war and maintenance of religious and cultural legacies (symbolized by their patronage of Hungarian churches) was combined with a greater interest in American politics. Although in 1920 fewer than a third of Hungarian immigrants were citizens of the United States, by the end of that decade, a majority of them were naturalized (Benkart 1980).

The interwar and post–World War II cohorts were quite unlike the older generation of immigrants both in their urban background and in the nature and intensity of their political convictions. The interwar immigrants included mostly middle-class business and professional people. Among them were four internationally acclaimed scientists—John von Neuman, Leo Szilard, Edward Teller, and Nobel laureate Eugene Wigner—as well as four future conductors of American symphony orchestras—Antal Dorati, Eugene Ormandy, Fritz Reiner, and George Szell. Composer Bela Bartok and novelist Ferenc Molnar both arrived in 1940 (Benkart 1980). Initially, some experienced downward mobility, but eventually most succeeded economically. In Cleveland during the 1920s, Hungarians began moving into better residential areas, a trend that the depression stalled only temporarily.

Although the DPs and the 47-ers were divided from each other only by a few years, they represented two different worlds that could hardly be expected to get along. Many of the DPs experienced downward social mobility. Classical training, unmarketable in America, diplomas from military academies, doctorates in Hungarian law, and an inability to speak English forced many of them to accept menial jobs in shops and factories. Former high-ranking judges, for instance, became unskilled workers in Detroit's automobile industry (Huseby-Darvas 1995). The artisans and shopkeepers fared much better and became skilled workers or shop owners.

The 47-ers, particularly the prominent personalities among them, were in a much better position. Not only were they not tainted as being pro-Nazi, they were held up as representatives of the Western-type democracy in Hungary and thus enjoyed the political and financial support of the American government. Upon arrival, many of them were given important positions in America's cold war institutions such as the Free Europe Committee and Radio Free Europe (Vardy 1985).

The 56-ers were possibly the most successful in their economic and social adaptation in the United States. They were a product of a powerful social transformation that had taken place before the revolution. The majority of the refugees were single men in their late teens, early twenties, or thirties. They were either students or at the outset of their professional careers. Their education was very practical and progressive; there were many engineers and medical doctors among them. Their practical training opened good prospects for them in American industrial establishments or in technical colleges and universities, and their lack of strong national sentiments fostered swift assimilation. They were the first to marry non-Hungarians in large numbers, and they consciously severed ties to Hungarian-American communities and organizations, perhaps with the exception of the church.

However, their achievements not only resulted from their demographic and personal characteristics but were also nurtured by the reception of the host society. The publicity about the Hungarian Uprising encouraged American society to think about those who were affected by the dramatic events as worthy of assistance; the result was an outpouring of public support and generosity and a very remarkable resettlement program. In November 1956, the National Academy of Sciences formally resolved to accord assistance to its Hungarian colleagues who might come to the United States, recognizing that as the minimum assistance due to those who risked their lives on behalf of the fundamental principles of freedom (Forbes 1988). As the newcomers arrived, the academy's staff matched the individual aspirations and capabilities of the refugees with positions in the academic or industrial world of the United States that would enable them to contribute their particular talents to American society. The rationale for the special program was not to give advantage to the newly arrived scientists or engineers but to eliminate some of the obstacles confronting the refugees who arrived without resources, friends, or contacts, and who often had no knowledge of English and lacked familiarity with the procedures for finding a position in their professions in America. The objective of the academy's program was to enable the newcomers to become integrated into their local and professional communities as quickly as possible. It is a pity that this approach was not incorporated into the resettlement programs developed for other Eastern European refugees under the Refugee Act of 1980.

ROMANIANS

The Country

Located on the Balkan Peninsula, Romania borders the newly independent state of Moldova to the east, Ukraine to the north, Hungary and Serbia to the west, and Bulgaria to the south. Much of Romania is mountainous or hilly, with the Carpathian Mountains and Transylvanian Alps stretching across about a third of the country from the north to the southwest. Victim of successive waves of invaders, Romania has seen its borders change countless times over the course of history. In modern times, as a result of the Treaty of Trianon signed after World War I, Romania received the much-disputed Transylvania, home for some 3 million ethnic Hungarians. After World War II, Romania lost Bessarabia to the Soviet Union. The country, about the size of Great Britain, has a population of 23 million, of whom 90 percent are Romanians. The 10 percent who constitute Romania's ethnic minorities are Hungarian, German, Serbian, Turkish, Ukrainian, Jewish, and Roma (Gypsies).

Romanians vociferously distance themselves from their Slavic, Magyar, and Balkan neighbors, emphasizing instead the connection with imperial Rome. They speak a language that sounds a bit like Italian, if not vernacular Latin, and use the Latin alphabet—where one might expect Cyrillic script, since Orthodoxy is a predominant religion. They claim to be Roman by descent and place much emphasis on this pedigree.

History and Politics

The Thracians, the ancestors of modern Romanians, inhabited ancient Romania as early as the sixth century B.C. The Romans came to conquer and colonize the newly consolidated Dacian empire in A.D. 106. Intense Romanization of the area over the next 200 years had a strong impact on its language and other aspects of Dacian culture. The Romans withdrew in A.D. 271 under the onslaught of invading barbarian tribes, but the Dacians retained Roman culture and the Latin language. From the third to the tenth century, successive waves of Goths, Slavs, Huns, Bulgars, and Magyars continued to invade the Dacians. Orthodox Christianity was brought in by the Bulgars in 846. By the early Middle Ages, the three states comprising present-day Romania—Transylvania, Wallachia, and Moldavia—formed separate feudal kingdoms. Continual Turkish occupation separated and dominated them for hundreds of years.

In 1600 the three Romanian states were briefly united, but it was not until 1862 that Alexandru Ion Cuza created a nation-state by joining Wallachia and Moldavia. In 1866, Alexandru abdicated and was replaced by Prussian Prince Charles Hohenzollern Siegmaringen. Prince Charles became King Carol I by a unanimous vote in 1881 and was crowned in the Bucharest Cathedral. After World War I, when the Austro-Hungarian empire was defeated, Transylvania was returned to Romania and joined Wallachia and Moldavia to form a new state. During World War II, the fascist Romanian Iron Guard ousted King Carol II, and Romania entered the war alongside the Axis.

On December 30, 1947, King Michael flew into exile, and Romania became a socialist state under the rule of Gheorghe Gheorghiu-Dej. Gheorghiu-Dej supported the Soviet suppression of the 1956 uprisings in Poland and Hungary, although soon afterwards he started edging toward an isolationist tack that took Romania out of Moscow's direct sphere of influence but was not less loyal to the precepts of Stalinism. In 1962, Romania stopped participating in Warsaw Pact military maneuvers. Gheorghiu-Dej died suddenly in March 1965 and was replaced by a seemingly gray little man who had worked his way up the Communist Party ladder by never rocking the boat. This was Nicolae Ceauşescu. Ceauşescu continued Romania's maverick foreign policy, condemning the Soviet invasion of Czechoslovakia in 1968. In 1984, Romania sent athletes to the Los Angeles Olympics, even though the rest of the Soviet bloc boycotted the games.

Despite the relative flexibility of its foreign policy, Communist Romania maintained one of Eastern Europe's most rigid and repressive societies. The realities of life for ordinary citizens have been compared to George Orwell's *Nineteen Eighty-four*. A vast police state grew to monitor its citizens, all forms of birth control were illegal, conversations with foreigners were suspect, and the

Ceauşescu personality cult was indescribable. Ceauşescu's economic policies, especially his obsessive attempt to rid the country of foreign debt, caused immeasurable hardship. He exported absolutely everything that could fetch hard currency, including food and oil, and correspondingly slashed imports. Once the "breadbasket of the Balkans," Romania emerged as the "basket case of the region." When Mikhail Gorbachev's reforms offered new economic hope for Eastern Europe in the mid-1980s, Ceauşescu remained the region's staunchest opponent of change, declaring perestroika to be in total contradiction to socialist principles.

Scattered public protests began to surface in 1987, and in the city of Brasov that year, they amounted to a riot. The anger of the Romanian people finally boiled over when security forces killed hundreds of pro-democracy demonstrators in the western city of Timisoara in December 1989. Protests spread across the country, and the army revolted against Ceauşescu. The bitter fighting that erupted in Bucharest and other Romanian cities was some of the worst seen in Europe since World War II. On Christmas Day, 1989, Ceauşescu and his wife, Elena, were executed.

In the first free postwar elections in May 1990, Romanians gave an overwhelming 89 percent support to the National Salvation Front and Ion Iliescu— a former Communist and Ceauşescu ally who helped lead the revolution. Despite the seemingly fair election, protests against the government continued through 1990, including a 53-day-long spring occupation of University Square in Bucharest. In June 1990, the Interior Ministry forces cleared away these protesters, killing several demonstrators and wounding hundreds. The following day, with the approval of the government, 7,000 miners swept through the streets to beat antigovernment protesters. In October 1990, the government accelerated its plans to introduce a free market economy by removing price subsidies and devaluing its currency. Protests and calls for the government to resign continued after these announcements.

Unlike elsewhere in Eastern Europe, political and economic reform proceeded very slowly in Romania. As indicated by the fall 1992 election, many of Ceauşescu's legacies, attitudes, and institutions remained intact. Romania continues to have the lowest standard of living in the region after Albania. An unemployment rate of 30 percent, inflation of over 300 percent, and frozen salaries cause much suffering and economic dislocation. It may take decades to recover from the consequences of Ceauşescu's regime that left the economy destroyed, the country polluted, and the people destitute from exploitation and numb from years of repression.

The Exodus

There were virtually no Romanians in America before 1870. Romanian immigration to the United States mounted between 1870 and 1900 when, according to one source, some 18,000 Romanian citizens entered the United States (Bobango 1980). Another source estimated the number at 22,000 (Wertsman 1975). In the next decade the number of Romanians increased to 62,153 and continued at the rate of 27,000 per annum for the next four years, dropping to approximately 4,500 during World War I (Bobango 1980). However, until 1895 almost all of them were Jews from Moldavia, Bessarabia, and Bukovina. Ethnic Romanians started arriving after 1895. They were mostly peasants from Transylvania, and a few Macedonian Romanians from the European parts of Turkey, northern Greece, and Albania.

By 1920 an estimated 85,000 Romanians had come to the United States (Bobango 1980). These statistics, however, are tenuous at best. The majority of Romanians, approximately 85 percent, were from Transylvania, Bukovina, or the Banat. These territories were not a part of the Romanian kingdom until 1918. Therefore, many arrivals, although ethnically Romanian, were counted as Hungarians, Austrians, or Russians. As late as 1923, the ''country of origin'' designation used by the Immigration and Naturalization Service (INS) was based on pre–World War I boundaries, which further confuses the figures.

The years 1920–1924 saw another influx of Romanians who hurried to reach America before immigration restrictions closed the door. The Immigration Act of 1924 set a Romanian quota of approximately 1,000 persons per year. Worldwide economic depression contributed to a further decline in immigration rates. At the end of 1940, there were 115,940 Romanians living in the United States, 61,596 male and 54,344 female (Anagnastosache 1944). Approximately 10,000 Romanians entered the United States under the Displaced Persons Act of 1949. A 30-year hiatus followed. The most recent wave of Romanian refugees came to the United States in the early and mid-1980s, when about 40,200 Romanians were resettled under the provisions of the Refugee Act of 1980 (ORR 1993).

Romanians were driven from their homeland by political, economic, and social conditions. Motivations for leaving home were many, including seeking refuge from forced Magyarization and conversion to Catholicism in Transylvania, evading military service in the Austro-Hungarian army, escaping agricultural exploitation, and more recently, fleeing the Communist regime of Nicolae Ceauşescu.

Arrival and Settlement

Unlike the pre-1895 Romanian immigrants who arrived in America with their families, most of those who came afterward were single men between the ages of 18 and 45. The vast majority were unskilled and only semiliterate laborers. Not all Romanians came to the United States to stay. Some, particularly those who arrived before 1920, intended to return home after saving enough money to buy land and improve their economic and social standing in their native villages. Approximately two thirds of the early arrivals returned home. Repatriation was especially high after World War I when many saw their native lands incorporated into the Romanian kingdom (Bobango 1980).

Romanians settled in the industrial heartland of the mid-Atlantic and Great Lakes, establishing ethnic enclaves in New York, Philadelphia, Pittsburgh, Chicago, Detroit, and Cleveland. Few Romanians settled in the West or South before the 1960s, when many retired to California and some to Florida. On the other hand, Los Angeles and Orange County, California, proved to be a magnet for the largest group of Romanian refugees fleeing Ceauşescu's Romania.

There was a considerable secondary migration among the early Romanian immigrants. Single industrial workers would often remain in one city for a year or two, moving on to a different urban center in search of better-paying jobs. The second location sometimes became permanent, but a third or fourth move was not uncommon. This transitory lifestyle was abandoned once families arrived. The villages that produced the earliest and most numerous migrations were ethnically mixed. Romanians were thus used to living in diversified neighborhoods, and it was not unusual to find Romanians in America residing alongside Poles, Slovaks, and Russians.

The political refugees who arrived in the United States in the 1980s present a very different picture than their compatriots from the early part of the century. The older settlers call the newcomers *Noi-veniti* (newly arrived) and find that they have very little in common with them (Bobango 1980). The recent refugees tend to be better educated and far more politically aware than the earlier immigrants, who remain largely ignorant of current Romanian issues. The newcomers resettled primarily in New York City, Chicago, and Los Angeles. The majority were married adults in their twenties and thirties. The most common households were nuclear families with one to three children, although in Chicago the number of children was generally quite high, as the Windy City received quite a few Pentecostal families (Cichon, Gozdziak, and Grover 1986).

The educational levels of this cohort were fairly high. College graduates among those surveyed by RMC included some 45 percent in Los Angeles, 53 percent in New York City, and 11 percent in Chicago. Consistent with their educational backgrounds, the work experience of Romanians in Los Angeles and New York City was largely professional, including architecture, engineering, accounting, education, and medicine. While Chicago had its share of professionals, the majority were skilled tradesmen (Cichon, Gozdziak, and Grover 1986). Romanians' knowledge of English upon arrival followed the pattern of their educational backgrounds. Those in Chicago had little knowledge of English, with fewer than 5 percent claiming to know it reasonably well, while 30 and 24 percent of those in Los Angeles and New York City, respectively, reported knowing English well upon arrival (Cichon, Gozdziak, and Grover 1986).

Economic and Social Adaptation

Economic assimilation and ensuing upward social mobility were rapid among the early immigrant arrivals from Romania. By 1914 they accumulated enough capital to become small entrepreneurs, owners of restaurants, boardinghouses, saloons, pool halls, and immigrant banks. By the early 1920s traditional large families were disappearing. Fewer children, the acquisition of property, and willingness to finance their children's education may partially account for the early prosperity of this group.

There were three distinct groups among the early Romanian immigrants: (1) Those who lived in ethnic neighborhoods and whose lives centered around the factory, beneficial society, and the church; (2) those, mostly second generation, who moved away from the urban colonies into suburbs and detached themselves from Romanian culture; and (3) those who spent their workday in the old neighborhood and their leisure hours and Sundays at Romanian clubs and churches but chose to live elsewhere (Bobango 1980). The early Romanian immigrants quickly realized the need to assimilate into the larger American society. They sent their children to public schools to increase their exposure to mainstream America, reserving the role of parish schools to assist in the retention of Romanian language and culture. They also married outside the group, even crossing religious boundaries.

Two institutions, the boardinghouse and the mutual benefit society, have been credited with easing the transition between the Old and the New World. The boardinghouse provided camaraderie and helped perpetuate old ways: ethnic foods, musical traditions, and folkways. Because of the reluctance to use American banks, the boardinghouse boss served as custodian to the lodgers' savings, acted as agent for sending money home, and purchased their steamship tickets. The boardinghouse was a forerunner of the later widespread and colorful combination of saloon, pool hall, steamship agency, and money-lending and savings establishment known as the immigrant bank. The boardinghouse as an institution lasted well into the 1930s (Bobango 1980).

In 1902, Romanians in Cleveland organized a mutual benefit society called Carpatina (The Carpathian), and the following year the Vulturaul (Eagle) Romanian Society of Assistance and Culture was established in Homestead, Pennsylvania. The next decade saw the rapid proliferation of similar societies. They were organized along the lines of small insurance companies and were directly controlled by the policyholders' representatives (Wertsman 1975; Bobango 1980).

Economic adaptation of the most recent wave of Romanian refugees was as rapid as that of the earlier arrivals. Seventy-five to 95 percent of the newcomers participated in the labor force, and they had equally high (75 percent) employment rates. The survey of Romanian refugees conducted by CAL indicated that most of the refugees started working within 6 months of their arrival in the United States. The percentage rose from 69 percent in months 1 to 6 to 74 percent in months 7 to 18. Of those refugees who worked at the time of the survey, almost 70 percent found their first jobs within 3 months of arrival in this country (Short 1988). The majority of Romanians secured employment in building maintenance, factories, merchandise delivery or warehousing, and construction, with only slight variation in pattern across sites. In New York City some professionals obtained initial jobs in fields related to their own but at a lower skill level than they had practiced in Romania. For example, civil engineers worked as draftsmen and designers (Cichon, Gozdziak, and Grover 1986).

Most initial jobs paid between $3.35 and $8.00 per hour. However, Romanians with trade skills and reasonable ability in the English language earned markedly better wages. They sometimes landed jobs for $6.00 to $10.00 per hour soon after arrival in the United States (Cichon, Gozdziak, and Grover 1986; Short 1988). The RMC study indicates that Romanians who had initial wages of $5.00 per hour increased their earnings to approximately $6.50 per hour to $12.00 per hour within their first two years in the United States. Romanians made a relatively rapid rise in occupational and socioeconomic status. Those who advanced rapidly generally had smaller families; those who did not progress so swiftly had larger families and less education and were generally members of the Fundamentalist religious sects (Gozdziak 1989).

Concomitant with the high levels of labor force participation was a rather high but fairly short use of welfare among Romanians studied by RMC. Those in Los Angeles showed the highest usage level, with approximately 70 percent of the sample using it at some point in the three years studied. However, the majority used public assistance from 6 to 18 months. In Chicago, about 60 percent of Romanians reported using public assistance, but their use averaged under 7 months. Those who did stay on for longer periods of time were the elderly or those with larger families and only one employable adult. The New York City levels were much the same as in Chicago, but the reasons given for the longer-term use of public assistance focused more on needing support while refugees went to school to study English or pursued advanced degrees and professional recertification (Cichon, Gozdziak, and Grover 1986).

Approximately three fourths of the Romanians surveyed by RMC became self-sufficient within their first three years in the United States. This proportion was consistent across the sites studied. However, the length of time it took to become self-supporting varied across cities. In Chicago and New York City, it took the Romanians on average 2 to 6 months to become self-sufficient, while in Los Angeles it was 12 months, with a considerable number of families remaining on welfare for 18 to 24 months. As was the case with labor force participation, those with no trade skills, large families with young children, and poor English skills depended on public assistance the longest (Gozdziak 1989).

Social interactions of Romanian refugees, both among themselves and with the larger American society, defy easy characterization. It appeared that about half of the sample examined by RMC socialized very little, even within their own community. This lack of social ties was most often attributed to the fact that they were working so hard that they had little leisure time, and to rumors of spies sent by Bucharest to the United States to disrupt the refugee community and report on individuals. The latter perception was a unique barrier to the formation of any sense of trust among the newcomers. However, despite the fact that the larger Romanian community was divided, the bonds between family members and fellow church members were strong. The strength of those bonds contributed to the economic success of many Romanian families.

The newness of post–World War II Romanian immigration to the United States and the lack of commonalities between the Romanian-Americans and newcomers from Romania mean that there are few established Romanian institutions to which recent refugees can turn for community support. The activities of the Iuliu Maniu Foundation in New York, the orthodox Brotherhood, Romanian Welfare, Inc., and the Cultural Association for Romanians and Americans of Romanian Descent are very modest (Bobango 1980) and not always sensitive to the needs of the newcomers. Romanians surveyed by RMC reported difficulties finding help in upgrading their skills and identifying recertification and professional training programs. Staff in service agencies were unable to refer them or provide information about résumé banks, professional associations, or other mainstream services (Cichon, Gozdziak, and Grover 1986). Employment services were also of little help to large Romanian Pentecostal families, particularly those with small children and without easily transferable skills. Employment programs were set up to serve the breadwinner, rather than an entire household. Planning for household self-sufficiency, employment counselors did not apply multiple-wage-earner strategies and failed to realize that employment of a single family member was not sufficient to take large households out of poverty.

PROSPECTS

For the most part, the research provides good news—most Eastern European refugees and immigrants attain jobs within the first six months to a year in the United States, with many of them going to work even earlier. The prospects for long-term self-sufficiency are also good. With few exceptions, the majority of Eastern European households are moving out of poverty within the first two years. As their English-language proficiency increases with time in the country, many are able to obtain jobs in fields related to their professional background. The research indicates also that Eastern European refugees have been a tremendous resource for the local communities in which they resettled. Interviews with employers who had a long history of hiring Eastern Europeans yielded very positive comments about refugees as employees and their contribution to the local labor markets. Employers had to stretch to find enough adjectives of praise for their refugee employees—"hard working," "reliable," "honest," and "the best workers we have" were commonplace (Gozdziak 1989).

Although the majority are becoming economically self-reliant, the road to long-term self-sufficiency is considerably more difficult for Eastern Europeans with large families and young children and without easily transferable skills. Eastern Europeans who are advancing rapidly are "making it" not because of, but rather despite, a resettlement system that, on the whole, has not responded to the needs of this population. Service systems, as well as state and federal policies, tend to continue to focus—sometimes almost exclusively—on Southeast Asian refugees, even though the last decade saw an increased proportion of new arrivals from other parts of the world.

It would be impossible to write about Eastern European refugees in the 1990s without mentioning two very important phenomena: first, the possibility for some refugees to return to their homeland and, second, the fact that Eastern Europe has changed from a refugee-producing region into a region of refuge.

The possibility of return hinges on the policies of the home country. Different regimes developed different attitudes to their exiles. Hungarian and Polish Communists, always on the lookout for hard currency, realized the potential of their diasporas as early as the 1970s and tried to lure them back with publications, congresses, and encouragement to invest. But exiles were unwelcome in Romania, Czechoslovakia, and Russia, where hard-liners feared they might infect others with bourgeois ideas ("The Homecoming" 1993). Now the situation of displaced Eastern Europeans has changed, and many are returning home, at least for a visit, if not to stay. While they bring with them good things—capitalist skills, money to invest, knowledge of how democracy and civil society work—the reactions to the returnees vary. Some countries such as Hungary, Poland, Slovakia, and the Czech Republic have been welcoming; others, such as Romania, Albania, and Bulgaria, remain suspicious.

The other important change is that after being for centuries a refugee-producing region, Eastern Europe has recently become a safe haven for many people fleeing persecution. Of all the countries in Eastern Europe, Hungary, because of its proximity to the West and to the civil conflict between the Serbs and the Croats, and because of the large number of ethnic Hungarians living in neighboring states, has become a magnet not only for Hungarians from Transylvania but also for ethnic Romanians and, before the reunification of Germany, for East Germans. The influx began in 1987. By early 1991, over 50,000 refugees had arrived, of whom 85 percent were from Romania, and of those, 80 percent were ethnic Hungarians (Joly and Poulton 1992). Poland suffers greater economic problems than Hungary, and it has not attracted as many asylum seekers or refugees. It remains, however, a transit country for many Romanian Roma who want to get to the West (Gozdziak 1994).

REFERENCES

Anagnastosache, George. 1944. Romanians in America. *The New Pioneer* 2(3): 57–61.
Baker, Richard P. 1988. Eastern European Refugees: Implications for Social Work. *Journal of Sociology and Social Welfare* 16(3): 81–94.
———. 1989. Refugee Assimilation: A Study of Polish and Czech Refugees. *Humboldt Journal of Social Relations* 15(2): 157–183.
Benkart, Paula. 1980. Hungarians. In *Harvard Encyclopedia of American Ethnic Groups.* Edited by Stephan Thernstrom. Cambridge, Massachusetts: The Belknap Press of Harvard University Press. Pp. 462–471.

Blejwas, Stanislaus. 1981. Old and New Polonias: Tensions within an Ethnic Community. *Polish American Studies* 38(2): 55–83.

Bobango, Gerald. 1980. Romanians. In *Harvard Encyclopedia of American Ethnic Groups.* Edited by Stephan Thernstrom. Cambridge, Massachusetts: The Belknap Press of Harvard University Press. Pp. 879–885.

Bukowczyk, John J. 1987. *And My Children Did Not Know Me.* Bloomington: Indiana University Press.

Cichon, Donald J., Elzbieta M. Gozdziak, and Jane G. Grover. 1986. *The Economic and Social Adjustment of Non–Southeast Asian Refugees,* Vol. 1. Dover, NH: Research Management Corporation.

Detroit Free Press. 1985. August 19.

Dovenyi, Zoltan, and Gabriella Vukovich. 1994. Hungary and International Migration. In *European Migration in the Late Twentieth Century. Historical Patterns, Actual Trends, and Social Implications.* Laxenburg, Austria: International Institute for Applied Systems Analysis. Pp. 187–205.

Forbes, Susan S. 1988. Historical Overview of the Flows of Intellectual Refugees. In *Scientists in Exile. Issues and Perspectives on the Refugee Experience.* Edited by Kathie McClesky and Susan S. Forbes. Washington, D.C.: Refugee Policy Group and American Association for the Advancement of Science. Pp. 1–7.

Golab, Caroline. 1977. *Immigrant Destinations.* Philadelphia: Temple University Press.

Goode, Judith, and Jo Anne Schneider. 1994. *Reshaping Ethnic and Racial Relations in Philadelphia. Immigrants in a Divided City.* Philadelphia: Temple University Press.

Gozdziak, Elzbieta M. 1989. *New Americans: The Economic Adaptation of Eastern European, Afghan and Ethiopian Refugees.* Washington, D.C.: Refugee Policy Group.

————. 1994. Cyganed (Gypped) Out of Refuge: Romanian Roma in Poland. In *Selected Papers on Refugee Issues: III.* Edited by Geoffrey MacDonald and Amy Zaharlick. Washington, D.C.: American Anthropological Association. Pp. 46–59.

Heberle, Rudolph, and Dudley S. Hall. 1951. *New Americans: A Study of Displaced Persons in Louisiana and Mississippi.* Baton Rouge, Louisiana: Displaced Persons Commission.

Heinrich, Hans-Georg. 1986. *Hungary. Politics, Economics and Society.* London: Frances Pinter Publishers.

"The Homecoming." 1993. *The Economist,* December 26, 1992–January 8, 1993: 73–76.

Huseby-Darvas, Eva. 1995. Long Distance Nationalism among American-Hungarians in Southeast Michigan. Unpublished manuscript.

Joly, Danielle, and R. Poulton. 1992. *Refugees: Asylum in Europe?* London: Minority Rights Group.

Kleeman, Janice. 1985. Polish American Assimilation: The Interaction of Opportunity and Attitude. *Polish American Studies* 42(1): 11–26.

Korewa, Maria Barbara. 1957. Casework Treatment of Refugees: A Survey of Selected Professional Periodicals for the Period from January 1, 1939 to January 1, 1956. Master's thesis, Wayne State University.

Lieberson, Stanley. 1963. *Ethnic Patterns in American Cities.* New York: Free Press.

Mostwin, Danuta. 1980. *The Transplanted Family: A Study of Social Adjustment of the*

Polish Immigrant Family to the United States after the Second World War. New York: Arno Press.

New York Times. 1984. June 22.

Office of Refugee Resettlement (ORR). 1986. *Report to the Congress: Refugee Resettlement Program.* Washington, D.C.: U.S. Department of Health and Human Services.

———. 1993. *Report to the Congress: Refugee Resettlement Program.* Washington, D.C.: U.S. Department of Health and Human Services.

Radzialowski, Thadeus. 1974. The View from a Polish Ghetto: Some Observations on the First Hundred Years in Detroit. *Ethnicity* 1: 125–150.

Schneider, Jo Anne. 1988. In the Big Village: Economic Adjustment and Identity Formation for Eastern European Refugees in Philadelphia, Pa. Unpublished Ph.D. dissertation, Temple University.

Short, Deborah. 1988. *Eastern European Refugee Survey.* Washington, D.C.: Center for Applied Linguistics.

Szeplaki, Joseph. 1975. *The Hungarians in America 1583–1974. A Chronology and Fact Book.* Dobbs Ferry, New York: Oceana Publications.

Thomas, William I., and Florian Znaniecki. 1927. *The Polish Peasant in Europe and America.* New York: Knopf.

U.S. Department of Justice. 1969. *Annual Report to the Commissioner of Immigration and Naturalization Service.* Washington, D.C.: Government Printing Office.

Vardy, Steven Bela. 1985. *The Hungarian Americans.* Boston, Massachusetts: Twayne Publishers.

Walters, E. Garrison. 1988. *The Other Europe. Eastern Europe to 1945.* Syracuse, New York: Syracuse University Press.

Wertsman, Vladimir. 1975. *The Romanians in America 1748–1974. A Chronology and Fact Book.* Dobbs Ferry, New York: Oceana Publications.

Wood, Arthur Evans. 1955. *Hamtramck: Then and Now.* New York: Bookman Associates.

Znaniecki Lopata, Helena. 1976. *Polish Americans. Status Competition in an Ethnic Community.* Englewood Cliffs, New Jersey: Prentice-Hall.

Chapter 11

Chinese from Southeast Asia

JOHN K. WHITMORE

The years 1978 to 1980 were major in the movement of Chinese out of Vietnam and Cambodia. These people found themselves at the mercy of both political and economic change within Southeast Asia and international rivalries outside. Given the pressures, they decided that they wanted out—not just out in general but out to the United States. They came not as a separate and distinct group but mixed with ethnic Vietnamese and Khmer from Vietnam and Cambodia at the same time that Lao, Hmong, and other groups were also entering the United States. Once here, there is the question of their relations with the Chinese-Americans already in residence.

Generally, less is known of the Chinese refugees from Southeast Asia than of any other major group from that region. Many studies exist of the Chinese people themselves, as well as a good number on the Chinese in Southeast Asia. Yet little attention has been paid to the Chinese communities in Saigon/Cholon and Phnom Penh, not to mention the smaller ones in Haiphong and Hanoi. Tsai (1968) examined his own community in southern Vietnam in great detail, and Willmott (1967, 1970) studied the Chinese in Cambodia, particularly Phnom Penh. I have used these major studies as well as a number of other sources to describe these Chinese communities, with special attention to their historical background. Recent work (e.g., Amer 1991; Tran 1993) helps to fill out this discussion.

This chapter brings together the information available on the Chinese communities of Indochina (especially Vietnam but also Cambodia; the Chinese community in Laos does not concern us here) and joins it with data from surveys of Chinese refugee groups in the United States. The result is a description of these refugees, their lives, and their prospects in the United States through the 1990s.

BACKGROUND

Although Chinese have had contact with, and lived on, the eastern mainland of Southeast Asia for more than two millennia, the important growth of Chinese communities in Vietnam, Cambodia, and elsewhere in Southeast Asia has only come about in the past 400 years. The rise of regional and international trade in the sixteenth and seventeenth centuries, including the increasing involvement of the Europeans, brought Chinese into the ports of Vietnam, Cambodia, Thailand, the Philippines, and Indonesia (Whitmore 1983; Willmott 1967). Difficulties of trade with the Japanese and the Europeans in China led Chinese traders to Southeast Asia for easier contacts, and the fall of the Ming dynasty in China to the Manchu power, in 1644, resulted in a flood of loyalists onto the coasts of the southern seas.

The early Chinese communities formed close to the contemporary centers of power and contributed much to the growth of the capitals, as at Phnom Penh. On occasion, the Chinese (or people of Chinese ancestry) became involved in the wielding of local political power. In Vietnam the Chinese had a choice of becoming Vietnamese (being known as *Minh-huong*) or remaining Chinese. If they chose the former, they adopted Vietnamese ways and came under Vietnamese law; if the latter, they stayed in the Chinese communities and were treated as foreigners. Interestingly, the diplomatic corps of nineteenth-century Vietnam was made up largely of *Minh-huong,* including the great Phan Thanh Gian, who dealt with the French in the 1860s (Woodside 1971; Nguyen Hoi Chan; 1971).

Another important development involving the settlement of Chinese in Vietnam took place during the seventeenth century in the south (generally known as Cochin China). Vietnamese had begun settling in this area only in the previous century, and the Saigon area became Vietnamese only in the 1690s. When 3,000 Chinese arrived off the coast of central Vietnam in flight from the Manchu conquerors in the 1670s, the local Vietnamese lord took it on himself to suggest that they keep going to inhabit open land around what is now Bien-hoa, north of Saigon. This land had been in the Cambodian domain, but the Chinese settlements there and elsewhere helped, ultimately, to bring it into the Vietnamese realm (Nguyen Hoi Chan 1971; Tsai 1968).

Trade and Chinese settlement did not flourish to nearly the same degree around the cities of the north, the capital Thang-long (now Hanoi) and the provincial centers, during the seventeenth and eighteenth centuries. It was mainly in the mountains, near the Chinese border and in the mining areas, or along the coast, that the Chinese population could be found. In the south the final quarter of the eighteenth century brought war and destruction to the Chinese communities. Out of the dynastic conflagration of the times emerged the settlement called Saigon by the Vietnamese and T'ai-ngon by the Chinese as the major trading center of the Mekong Delta area. By 1801 the Vietnamese were calling the Chinese community there "Cho-lon," or "Large Market" (Nguyen Hoi Chan 1971; Tsai 1968; de Poncins 1957).

With the establishment of the Nguyen dynasty in the first years of the nineteenth century, the new rulers drew a sharp line between the *Minh-huong* and the Chinese sojourners. The latter were officially recognized through their *bang*. Such organizations were natural to the overseas Chinese, being based on dialect and home province. Hence, the *bang* served as fairly autonomous and self-governing administrative units for the Vietnamese government, and their chiefs acted as the links between the Vietnamese bureaucracy and the Chinese population. The various chiefs accepted the responsibility for collecting taxes and controlling the flow of Chinese immigrants for the capital in Hue (Nguyen Hoi Chan 1971; Nguyen The Anh 1971; Tsai 1968).

Substantial though the Chinese population was in Vietnam by the middle of the nineteenth century, the major growth in the Chinese community came during the 90 years of the French colonial period. The European powers of the late nineteenth century, including the French, were drawing coolie labor out of China by the thousands. Encouraged by the French, the Chinese also took the opportunity to move south into better economic conditions, and from the 1860s, boatloads of Chinese immigrants arrived in Vietnam (hence, the Vietnamese term *nguoi tau,* "boat people," for them). The French had conquered the far south of Vietnam, called by them Cochin China, in the 1860s and removed it from the control of Hue. Saigon and the Mekong Delta would officially remain a separate colony under French law into the 1940s, whereas from the 1880s the north and center (called by the French Tonkin and Annam) were ostensibly under Vietnamese administration. The Chinese tended to gather in the French-controlled areas, the south and the urban centers, particularly the ports. Hence, Cholon, adjacent to Saigon, Haiphong, the French port of the north, and Hanoi, the French administrative center for Indochina, became the major places of Chinese settlement. Phnom Penh in Cambodia and, to a much lesser degree, Vientiane in Laos were also French administrative centers and locations of Chinese communities. Other Chinese lived in lesser population centers scattered across Vietnam and Cambodia. The main point to be made here is that the Chinese formed almost entirely an urban population, pursued economic advancement in urban occupations, and had access to all parts of the colony (Tsai 1968; Ky 1963; Marsot 1993).

The number of Chinese in the south of Vietnam grew rapidly. By 1889, almost 60,000 (according to official French count) lived scattered about the south alone. Seventeen years later the figure had doubled. Through the colonial period and into the 1950s the Chinese population of southern Vietnam greatly outstripped that of the north and center. In the early 1930s the French counted more than 200,000 Chinese immigrants in the south (with more than 70,000 *Minh-huong*), more than 50,000 in the north, but only 10,000 in the center. The Chinese community in Cambodia expanded rapidly in the 1920s as well, to more than 200,000. Twenty years later, at the end of the colonial period, the number of Chinese in southern Vietnam may have quadrupled to more than 800,000 and that in Cambodia almost doubled to more than 400,000, whereas the numbers in the north and center of Vietnam had only grown slightly. (Some 40,000 of Chinese descent are supposed to have come south in 1954–1955.) The Saigon/ Cholon metropolitan area seems to have had more than 575,000 Chinese and other urban areas in the south more than 90,000; another 130,000-plus appeared to be scattered among villages of the south. Thus, about 84 percent of the Chinese in southern Vietnam were urban, and 16 percent, rural. Some 35,000 were in Haiphong in the north, and another 15,000 were in Hanoi. The urban/ rural ratio in Cambodia was much closer, being 59 percent to 41 percent. These figures tend not to include those of Chinese descent whose families had lived in Vietnam before the French, that is, for Vietnam, the *Minh-huong* (Tsai 1968; Ky 1963; Willmott 1967; Tran 1993; Marsot 1993).

The Chinese tendency to organize themselves by dialect group and region of birth in the homeland was accepted and reinforced by the French administration. In this way the French refrained from direct interference into Chinese affairs, unless necessary, and placed responsibility for the activities of the Chinese community in the hands of the organizational leaders, whom they could replace. These organizations, the *bang,* took care of taxation, immigration, and police matters for the French within their own groups. In Vietnam the largest group of Chinese—perhaps half—were the Cantonese from Kwangtung province in China, with the Teochiu from the northeast coast of Kwangtung almost a third. In Cambodia (as in Thailand) the situation was reversed (Teochiu more than three quarters and Cantonese a tenth). Other major dialect groups of some size (2 to 10 percent) in Vietnam and Cambodia were Hakka, Hokkien (from Fukien province), and Hainanese (Tsai 1968; Willmott 1967; Skinner 1951; Marsot 1993). The dominant language for the entire Chinese community in Vietnam (unlike elsewhere in Southeast Asia) was Cantonese, and a large proportion of those in Cholon knew neither Vietnamese nor French (nor, later on, English) (Tsai 1968; de Poncins 1957). From the 1880s the French colonial system recognized these five dialect groups as the official congregations (*bang*), with Chinese not belonging to any of them included with the Hakka. These five remained the basic organization of the Chinese community through the colonial period. They had their own temples, schools, hospitals, and cemeteries. As Willmott (1967:84) noted for Cambodia, "[A] speech group was the constituency for business relationships, marriage partners, associations, and relations with the administration." Local branches of the *bang* officially served the Chinese population scattered among the towns of the countryside. Saigon, Cholon, Tra Vinh, and Long Xuyen in Vietnam and Phnom Penh and Kompong Cham in Cambodia had branches of all five *bang;* other towns of any size had two, three, or four *bang.* Smaller towns only had one, encompassing all the local Chinese of whatever group (Tsai 1968; Willmott 1970; Skinner 1951; Marsot 1993).

The importance of the Chinese community in twentieth-century Indochina lay in its economic function. The French facilitated the Chinese participation in the colonial economy, thus greatly advancing the French extractive powers. The Chinese had greater liberties than the Vietnamese, Khmer, and Lao. They could move among the five *pays* of French Indochina (Tonkin, Annam, Cochin China, Cambodia, and Laos), and they had access to the countryside and its peasants. They handled goods and accumulated large commercial fortunes. The Chinese profited greatly from the alcohol, salt, and opium monopolies imposed by the French on Vietnamese and Cambodian societies. Not only did the Chinese merchant community help underwrite the French administration by way of the monopolies, but it was also most important in supplying the colonial structure and instrumental in the major export from the colony, rice. With French encouragement, their contacts in the rural towns and villages, their ownership of the rice-hauling junks and the rice mills, and their monetary loans to the peasants, the Chinese merchants controlled the movement of rice within Vietnam and Cambodia and facilitated its export abroad from Saigon/Cholon (amounting to two thirds of French Indochina's total export value). Pepper was another agricultural product controlled by the Chinese. Through the international network of Chinese firms, such exports moved from the Chinese communities of Vietnam and Cambodia to Chinese firms in the major port cities of Southeast Asia and China. It was the Chinese who kept the flow of commercial goods going into and through the colony, profiting greatly thereby. With such advantages, the bulk of the Chinese community within Vietnam and Cambodia was involved in business of one sort or another (Ky 1963; Ngo 1971; Murray 1980; Tsai 1968; Willmott 1967; Marsot 1993; Brocheux 1995).

To quote Tsai Maw-kuey (1968:135), a Chinese from southern Vietnam, "All observers, whatever their nationality, are in accord that in South Vietnam the Chinese held and still hold all the levers of commerce, of industry, and of handicrafts and that they continue to play the most important role in the economic life of the country." Compared with other countries of Southeast Asia, the Chinese communities in Indochina were much more involved in business than in laboring occupations (a majority in commerce and another third in industry and artisanry). Saigon/Cholon was the hub of the Chinese economic network, and Phnom Penh was the center of its Cambodian hinterland during the colonial period.

As noted earlier, the major activity of the Chinese was the rice trade. Besides the control of the rice market, Chinese merchants strongly dominated the handling of foodstuffs in general, both wholesale and retail. Their enterprises supplied the major cities and extended deep into the villages of the countryside. The Chinese businessmen were also heavily involved in buying and selling numerous other items in Vietnam and Cambodia, and diversity was one of their economic strengths. Hundreds of Chinese firms controlled the production and trade of textiles and wood and metal goods. (See the Appendix to this chapter for detail on the economic activities of the different dialect groups.) Fundamental to such Chinese economic success were two elements: (1) commercial organization and networks (within the colony and without) and (2) the extension of credit (within their own community and to others).

The strength of the Chinese community lay, according to Tsai (1968:116), in its "perfect internal organization . . . whose power and efficacy are often underestimated or ignored." *Hui* (as opposed to the official *bang*) were groups formed to achieve any one of a number of specific goals. They were interlinked to create an informal network or series of networks that stretched throughout the colony and abroad. Any Chinese could belong to one such grouping or several, depending on personal interests. Three general types of *hui* existed: (1) by common family name or locality of origin; (2) by professional association; and (3) by shared interest (temples, schools, sports, etc.). Organized similarly, these groupings drew many people (and their families) into their workings and thus tied together the diverse Chinese community. Through such contacts were social ties and commercial links achieved, bringing trust to the relationships and providing access, in Lim's (1984) terms, "to labour, credit, information, market outlets, and security." Under the overarching structure of the five *bang,* such ties and links reached from the big cities into the countryside and to other big cities, at home and abroad. The urban connections and greater efficiency in operation led the Chinese to be preferred intermediaries (Tsai 1968; Willmott 1967; Ky 1963; Barton 1984).

The economic links that followed these social ties included better terms of credit and loans and went beyond the Chinese community to link members of the local population to the resulting economic structure. Based on the "confidence and spirit of cooperation" built up through the commercial and social networks, as Tsai (1968) described it, the Chinese system of credit, a "system both ingenious and original," further tied the Chinese networks together and stretched into the countryside. Among themselves, the Chinese merchants would often pool funds and take turns sharing the proceeds. In the process of handling commerce in the countryside (particularly in rice), these merchants would advance credit to their customers, mainly in the dry season, before the monsoon. As buyer from and seller to the peasant farmers, the Chinese village shopkeeper kept the flow of goods going in both directions, using loans of cash and other items to maintain this flow. The village shopkeeper in turn dealt with the town merchant, also receiving credit to facilitate local commerce. The provincial merchant himself operated on credit extended by the major merchants in the large cities (Saigon/Cholon, Phnom Penh). Ultimately, credit came from the Chinese banks in these cities (Tsai 1968; Ky 1963; Willmott 1967; Barton 1984; Menkhoff 1993).

A major interest for all Chinese groups was education. The five *bang* had public schools for their own members (that still required some tuition), and there were many expensive private schools. By the end of the colonial era, there were well over 200 schools with a total of more than 50,000 students, male and female, mainly at the primary level and spread across southern Vietnam. Cambodia had about half as many schools and students. Chinese families were prepared to make sacrifices for their children to attend these schools, but inevitably, attendance rose and fell with commerce. The schools were enmeshed in the local Chinese social structures. Mandarin, the official language of China, served as the language of instruction among almost all groups, some Cantonese being the exception, and problems existed in the quality of both teaching and texts. The desire for education was so great that it led to overcrowding in the classrooms. A variety of approaches (traditional, modern, nationalist, etc.) complicated the situation further. A French-Chinese high school supplied many of the intermediaries between the colonial regime and the Chinese commercial sector. The educational goal was mainly to provide a basic literacy and competence with numbers as well as to make contacts within the Chinese community, thus aiding the business sector. In general, Chinese education in Indochina lagged behind that found elsewhere in Southeast Asia (Tsai 1968; Willmott 1967, 1970; Skinner 1951).

The situation of the Chinese in Vietnam and Cambodia changed considerably with independence in the mid-1950s. The next 20 years saw major restrictions placed on the Chinese community in its economic and professional pursuits. Both the Saigon and Phnom Penh regimes put important limits on the economic activities open to nonnationals (mainly the Chinese). In Vietnam, such activities included many of those dominated by the Chinese (shopkeeping, the rice trade, fish, tea, soy, transportation, scrap iron, textiles, and general dealing, among other fields). This situation affected more than 40 percent of the Chinese enterprises in Saigon/Cholon and more than 60 percent of all firms in the forbidden activities. The purpose was to convert the Chinese into Vietnamese citizens. The result was that some Chinese became Vietnamese, others officially turned their businesses over to their Vietnamese wives or children, others (illegally) found a Vietnamese to front for them, and quite a few (almost a thousand) simply closed up shop. Even though about a half million Chinese apparently accepted Vietnamese citizenship during 1956 and 1957, the economic system slowed drastically as many middlemen ceased operations. Other restrictions included immigration, travel, the practice of Western medicine, books, and schools. Cambodia, on independence, did not restrict the Chinese quite so widely as did the Vietnamese but tried to keep them out of rice, salt, shipping, general trade, secondhand dealing, and loans. It also removed the restrictions of the *bang* system, the result being a loosened boundary between the Chinese and the Khmer communities and a greater opening for Cambodian citizenship. Tighter controls did exist for Chinese schools (Tsai 1968; Willmott 1967, 1970; Fall 1959; Tran 1993).

The disappearance of the official *bang* in both countries left the way open for the growth in variety and importance of the voluntary organizations (*hui*). At the same time, with the great decline in rice exports and the rise of American aid, both linked to the war, the economic role of the Chinese shifted somewhat from the commercial to the industrial and service sectors. Urbanization and commerce boomed. Many of the older economic pursuits thrived and grew with the flood of foreign wealth, mainly into southern Vietnamese society but also into Cambodia (Tsai 1968; Willmott 1970). Clifton Barton (1984:49) felt ''that a figure of seventy to eighty percent was a fairly accurate representation of the

portion of the total volume of commercial and industrial activity that was controlled by overseas Chinese businessmen during the decade 1965–1975,'' and
Tsai Maw-kuey (1968:76) could say in that year, "Incontestably, Cholon is,
after Singapore, the greatest Chinese city outside China."

The Chinese in northern Vietnam benefited from rapprochement between Hanoi and Peking and were allowed to remain Chinese citizens at the same time
as they held the same rights as Vietnamese (Amer 1991). A well-to-do Chinese
from Hanoi noted that the Chinese had the privileges, but not the disadvantages
(as military duty), of their Vietnamese compatriots. The Chinese continued their
urban and intermediary occupations within the context of the developing socialist system through the two decades of war. This included the privilege of
visiting China and carrying on clandestine trade between the two countries. As
Charles Benoit (1981:146) has noted, "[T]heir stellar success at running what
amounted to an alternative economic system" meant the continuation of the
Chinese community serving the Vietnamese economic system.

THE REFUGEE MOVEMENT

The mid-1970s saw little change in the situations of the Chinese communities
in southern Vietnam, northern Vietnam, and Cambodia. The war in all three
zones restricted the Chinese activities, as it did everybody's, but the role of the
Chinese remained the same. They continued to operate in the urban sector, keep
the economy going, and act as the intermediaries. With the end of the fighting,
in 1975, the situation for the Chinese in northern Vietnam changed little,
whereas that in the south underwent the strains of the transition from Saigon to
Ho Chi Minh City (Amer 1991; Tran 1993). Some Chinese were in the first
wave of refugees (an unpublished Michigan survey in 1980 showed that about
15 percent of Chinese respondents came before 1978). Nevertheless, the Vietnamese government policy toward the cities and the Chinese was initially moderate, particularly in comparison with that of the new Cambodian government.
The fall of Phnom Penh to the Khmer Rouge in mid-April 1975 marked an
immediate effort to clear from the cities not only the accumulated mass of
refugees from the countryside but the urban population as a whole. The Chinese
were thus removed from the towns and pushed into the countryside (with no
protest from Peking). Many of the Chinese left, going either east into southern
Vietnam, particularly Saigon/Cholon, or west into Thailand.

The major flood of Chinese refugees came in the midst of international power
struggle and Vietnamese policy change. Increasing tensions with China led initially to security measures concerning those of Chinese descent on the northern
border, in late 1977 and early 1978. Then the Vietnamese government both
began to speak of forcing Vietnamese citizenship (and thus military duty) on
the Chinese and decided that a change in economic policy was needed. That
spring the government moved directly to control the urban economic sector, one
that they had largely left alone in prior years. This move took place not only in

the recently reunified south but also in the north, in Haiphong and Hanoi. Since, even in the north, it was the Chinese who were heavily involved in urban commerce, this effort to bring central control into the cities meant that the Chinese community was greatly affected. At the same time, relations between Vietnam and Cambodia worsened, and the friction along their common border became bloody. The Chinese regime was strongly behind that of Pol Pot against the Vietnamese. In addition, the autumn of 1978 saw the breakdown in the talks between the Vietnamese and the United States, with the Americans formally recognizing the People's Republic of China in December. In November the Socialist Republic of Vietnam joined the Council for Mutual Economic Assistance, the eastern European economic bloc, and moved much closer to the Soviet Union.

Thus, the Chinese in Vietnam were caught two ways. Official Vietnamese economic policy acted against their interests at the same time that China was beginning to lean heavily on the Vietnamese. Peking took the occasion both to make an example of the Vietnamese regarding the handling of overseas Chinese in Southeast Asia and to lean on the Vietnamese as being pro-Soviet. The Vietnamese in turn saw China on all sides of them, to the south and west (in Cambodia) as well as to the north and east. The Chinese in Vietnam, and eventually even those of longtime Chinese descent, were caught in both an economic squeeze and a security fear. They were being forced to leave the cities and any areas, particularly in the northern mountains and coasts, in which the Vietnamese thought they were a risk, a potential fifth column. They were to go to designated areas in the countryside or up into the highlands. The Chinese did not like the choices being offered them within Vietnam, and many took the opportunity to leave. The Vietnamese initially tried to calm their fears, but ethnic tensions continued to rise through 1978, and with the heavy fighting on the border in early 1979, the Vietnamese became active in getting the Chinese out (Grant et al. 1979; Benoit 1981; Amer 1991).

By the middle of 1978, the atmosphere of impending war and tales of good reception in China led more Chinese refugees to leave Vietnam. Rumor, panic, and propaganda sent over 150,000 across the border from northern Vietnam into China, where they were stuck away in the hills of Kwangsi province. Thereafter, most left by sea as China closed its border, those in the north going to Hong Kong and those in the south going to Malaysia, Indonesia, or the Philippines. These were the "boat people." Technically, this was illegal emigration, but testimony indicates that it evolved into a semilegal system as Vietnamese officials took payments to allow the flow of Chinese out of the country to continue. The organization of the departure was handled through the old commercial channels, and the boats lying offshore were arranged by the local and international networks of Chinese contacts. Thus, the blame for the poor conditions of the refugees must lie with both the government that allowed it to occur and the community that organized it, under however trying conditions (Grant et al. 1979; Benoit 1981; Amer 1991).

The flow of Chinese refugees continued from 1978 through 1979. Vietnam invaded Cambodia in late December 1978, hoping to end the dirty border war with Pol Pot. Deng Xiaoping then visited the United States and, on leaving, declared that China would "punish" Vietnam. The United States did not demur. The subsequent invasion led to three weeks of fighting that were bloodier than any three weeks in the first or second Indochina wars. Tensions rose steeply, and the Vietnamese began to make it clear to the Chinese that they should leave. Other Chinese refugees came out of Cambodia to the Thai border after the Vietnamese destruction of the Pol Pot regime and the subsequent fighting and famine. By 1980, over 200,000 Chinese had left Indochina and were seeking refuge in countries beyond Asia, particularly in the United States.

The sea voyages were horrendous for the overloaded craft, and many of the refugees were lost at sea or ravaged by pirates in the Gulf of Siam. Estimates of the losses range up to 50 percent of all those who left Vietnam. Problems still remained for the survivors on their arrival at foreign shores. The countries of first asylum, particularly Malaysia, but also Indonesia, the Philippines, and Hong Kong, were nervous about taking so many illegal Chinese into their populations. The first camps for the refugees were hastily improvised in deserted locations, the island Pulau Bidong off the east coast of the Malay Peninsula being the prime example. Here the refugees were kept alive through international efforts until they could be screened and admitted into a third country for permanent settlement. Later, transitional camps were set up at Bataan (in the Philippines), on Galang (an island in Indonesia), and in Hong Kong for those being admitted to the United States. There the refugees received orientation to American life, English training, and instruction in some vocational skills. The procedures whereby the Chinese refugees entered the United States were the same as those for the Vietnamese, Lao, Hmong, and others—once screened by the Immigration and Naturalization Service, they had to have personal sponsors, generally found by one of the voluntary agencies (VOLAGs) that had signed a contract with the State Department to take responsibility for the refugees. In this way the Chinese refugees were placed as single nuclear families (parents and children) in scattered localities across the country. One problem in examining the Chinese as a separate refugee group is that official records were usually kept on country of origin rather than ethnicity (Peters et al. 1983), and sorting them out from the Vietnamese and Khmer refugee populations, especially the former, is often difficult.

SOCIAL AND ECONOMIC STATUS IN THE
UNITED STATES

The Chinese refugees were, on the average, the earliest of the ethnic groups coming to the United States in the second wave of Indochina emigration (1978 on). The Lao and Hmong, although they were in the Southeast Asian camps longer than the Chinese, tended to arrive here only after the boat people. The

Vietnamese of the second wave mainly came later still. A study of Vietnamese, Chinese from Vietnam, and Lao refugees who arrived in the years from 1978 to 1982 conducted by the Institute for Social Research (ISR) of the University of Michigan for the Office of Refugee Resettlement, U.S. Department of Health and Human Services [HHS] (Caplan, Whitmore, and Bui 1984; Caplan, 1989) shows the Chinese to have been here an average of 28.5 months; the Lao, 25 months; and the Vietnamese, only 23 months.

The ISR study surveyed the three refugee groups in five sites around the country (Boston, Chicago, Houston, Seattle, and Orange County, California). The resulting data provide a profile of the Chinese refugees from Vietnam and enable preliminary comparisons between this group and the Vietnamese and Lao (see also Haines 1989). Of the total adult population of 4,160 in the survey, 836 were Chinese from Vietnam (20 percent, compared with 50 percent Vietnamese and 30 percent Lao). Fifty-five percent of these adults were male and 45 percent female. The Chinese refugee population tended to be older than the Lao and the Vietnamese, with an average age among adults of 33. Eighteen percent were 16 to 19 years of age, 36 percent in their twenties, 18 percent in their thirties, 13 percent in their forties, 8 percent in their fifties, and 7 percent 60 and over, a much flatter distribution than for the other two groups, which had a higher percentage of younger adults. The highest percentage of Chinese among the local survey populations lived in Seattle (39 percent), with Chinese making up 29 percent of the Chicago survey, 18 percent in Orange County, and only 9 percent and 8 percent, respectively, in Houston and Boston. Seventeen percent of the Chinese in the survey had moved, a percentage slightly higher than for the Vietnamese and the Lao.[1]

As would be expected from a historical view of the Chinese in Vietnam, the refugees were predominantly urban (87 percent), and their occupations there reflect this—31 percent of all the adults had held such urban jobs as proprietors, clerks, assistants, construction workers, auto mechanics, machine operators, and factory workers. Another 33 percent had been students. Their educational background was not high—more than half the adults had had no more than a primary education in Vietnam, another 40 percent had had some secondary education but no more, and only 4 percent had ever studied at a university.

Half the Chinese households (50 percent) were single nuclear families, and another 29 percent were extended families. The remaining fifth of the households contained at least one single, unrelated adult (whether living alone, with other singles, or with one or another type of family unit). Compared with the Vietnamese and the Lao in this survey, the Sino-Vietnamese tended to have both a higher percentage of single-person households and a higher percentage of extended family households. Yet these Chinese households were on the average the smallest (5.2 persons) and had the fewest children (1.6), the fewest children under age six (0.44), and the highest percentage of adults (75 percent). The average age of the youngest child was over six years old, the highest of the three groups, and thus this average child was in school. Overall, the Chinese refugees from Vietnam had households that were smaller, with more adults and older children, and possessed moderate levels of education and occupation in Southeast Asia compared with the Vietnamese and Lao refugees.

The question of English proficiency was a major one for the refugees. Because knowledge of English was strongly correlated with education, the Sino-Vietnamese were likely to be only moderately proficient in English, and this proved to be the case. Not quite half the Chinese households (478) had anyone who knew any English when they arrived in the United States, and in less than a tenth (8 percent) of the households did anyone know English even fairly well. In less than a fifth of the households (17 percent) did half the adults know some English. These figures are slightly higher than the Lao figures but are much lower than the Vietnamese. The relative pattern for current English among the three ethnic groups generally follows that for English on arrival, as all three groups showed consistent gains. Although fewer Chinese in the survey had taken English classes in the Asian camps (14 percent as compared with the overall mean of 23 percent), there was little difference among the three groups in taking English classes in the United States (40 percent were currently taking classes, and more than three quarters had had such classes at one time or another). The major reasons for Chinese respondents not taking current English classes were that the respondents were too old or too busy.

The Chinese from Vietnam, seeking contacts, were more involved in general employment services (40 percent) than were either the Vietnamese or the Lao (28 percent each), whereas vocational training, which requires more education and better English, had fewer Chinese (6 percent) than Vietnamese (9 percent) but more than Lao (4 percent). The unemployment rate for the Chinese from Vietnam (46 percent) was slightly worse than that for the Vietnamese (43 percent) and the Lao (40 percent) in the sample, despite the Chinese having been in the country longer. A partial explanation for this difference might be that the smallest numbers of Chinese in the sample came from the two areas with the best economic conditions, Houston and Boston. Moreover, such aggregate figures are misleading and need to be examined in terms of the length of time the refugees have been in the country. Thus, the Chinese unemployment rate dropped steadily, from more than 90 percent for those here a year or less to about 30 percent for those here between three and four years.

Another aspect of employment for the Chinese from Vietnam also reflects that for the Vietnamese and the Lao. When they were able to find work, the jobs were most often lower in status and poorer paying and had less of a future than the ones they held in Southeast Asia. If lucky, the refugee found a similar job; more often, it would be less than what he or she had had. For example, although operating a machine is a relatively common job for the refugees here, those (like many Chinese) who used to operate machines in Vietnam have had difficulty getting jobs here, undoubtedly because of poor English. The jobs obtained by the refugees tended to be in less stable sectors of the economy, where the work is part-time, seasonal, and irregular, with low wages. The Chinese held jobs that were less likely than those held by either the Vietnamese or the Lao to have employment benefits in general (55 percent) or health benefits (49 percent), paid vacations (45 percent), or retirement pensions (18 percent) in particular; they were, however, about equal in dental plans (27 percent). Even though the Chinese had a higher unemployment rate than the Lao, they had been employed for a slightly longer average time (14 months to 13 months) and had a slightly higher average hourly wage ($4.89 to $4.76). In general, the Chinese from Vietnam tended to fall between the Vietnamese and the Lao in job status, being lower than the former and higher than the latter (11 percent with high-status jobs, 9 percent being professionals or managers).

The Sino-Vietnamese who were not in the labor force included current students (working and nonworking), housewives, the disabled, retirees, and those who were simply not looking for work at the time. They again fell between the Vietnamese and the Lao in the percentage of adults fitting these categories (56 percent), and the same is true for the percentage of students (17 percent).

An important aspect of the ISR study was its focus on the household rather than on the individual. In the short time that the refugees had been here at the time of the survey (fall 1982), few of them, as individuals, had been able to get jobs good enough to lift them out of poverty. What is important, then, is the combination of resources the household was able to bring together in order to support all its individuals. Those on public assistance, for example, tended to have a mix of available resources. The Chinese from Vietnam had 67 percent of their households receiving some sort of public cash assistance, and almost all of them also received food stamps. This was higher than for the Lao and slightly lower than for the Vietnamese. As with unemployment, the percentages of those on cash assistance declined steadily from the first year of residence to the fourth. Another important instance of the mix of resources for the household is the number of jobs held by individuals in the household. For the Chinese, as for the refugees as a whole, there was a steady and significant progression upward in the number of households having more than one job.

On this basis of mixed resources in the household, the key question is not whether any one individual (or, for that matter, household) receives any kind of public assistance; rather, it is whether the household has any earned income. Fifty-nine percent of the Chinese households had some form of earned income, slightly lower than for the Lao but higher than for the Vietnamese. The next question is the source of the refugee household's total income (public assistance, earned, or a combination of the two). The Chinese households were high on combined incomes, slightly low on public assistance alone, and fairly low on earned income alone. This is understandable, considering the tendency of the Chinese to live in more complex extended families. The adults of these households were pooling their resources, both earned income and assistance, to further their mutual aim. Over time the number of households on only cash assistance dropped sharply from the first to the fourth year of residence, the number with combined incomes peaked in the third year and then fell off, and the number on earned income alone rose from the first through the fourth year. An important point to be made here is that the search for work continued through time, irrespective of eligibility for assistance or its cutoff.

One important reason for this, besides the desire for work itself, is that earnings are needed for households to rise significantly above the federal poverty level. In general, the households in the survey averaged 79 percent of the poverty level if they received only cash assistance, 146 percent if they combined income sources, and 218 percent if they had earned income alone. Approximately the same percentages held true if the households had no jobs, one job, or more than one job. The Chinese from Vietnam fit this pattern. Although half the Chinese households were living below the poverty level (essentially the same as the Vietnamese and the Lao), there was a steady rise in the percentage of the poverty level met from those in the country only a few months to those who had been here longer than three years.

Overall, Caplan and others (Caplan, Whitmore, and Bui 1984; Caplan, Whitmore, and Choy 1989) suggested that among the Vietnamese, Chinese from Vietnam, and Lao in the sample, ethnicity was a less important factor than a number of others—length of time in the United States, Southeast Asian education and occupation, arrival English proficiency, site, and household composition. Arrival English, which has a certain correlation with education in Southeast Asia, was a strong predictor of economic self-sufficiency. Household composition, in terms of the number of employable adults, was also of significance. The single nuclear family had the worst economic standing, particularly if it was large, except in cases in which some of the members had a decent level of English.

Dunning (1982) examined Sino-Vietnamese refugees in southern California and Texas within a year or two of their arrival. He found them falling short of the ethnic Vietnamese refugees (many of whom had been here since 1975) in economic performance. Actually, when compared with other 1979 arrivals, the Chinese were doing fairly well. One area Dunning examined that the ISR survey did not was sociocultural adjustment. Dunning's data showed the Chinese to have been more adaptive culturally to the surrounding environment than were the Vietnamese, considering the longer time spent here by the Vietnamese. Yet Peters and others (1983) showed in their study of Sino-Vietnamese from West Philadelphia that the Chinese from Vietnam had not integrated appreciably with any surrounding groups. The area in which they lived was quite mixed (blacks, whites, Asians, and native Americans), and a Chinatown existed in downtown Philadelphia. There were Korean establishments, and—to quote the study (1)— "in the past two years there has been an explosive expansion of Southeast Asian refugee fruit and vegetable vendors as well as small food stores, many of which are owned by Sino-Vietnamese." Nevertheless, tensions pervaded the neighborhood and existed between the Vietnamese and Chinese; the different Chinese groups from Southeast Asia (mainly Vietnam and Cambodia) had not mixed appreciably (partly owing to language differences—Cantonese versus Teochiu), and, to quote from the report again (6), "in general, very little interaction or integration has occurred between the Sino-Vietnamese refugees and the local Chinatown community." First of all, few of the refugees could afford to live there, but, more basically, a line existed between the "Hong Kong-and-Taiwan-connected" community and the Southeast Asian Chinese.

Little information has come to hand concerning Chinese refugees from Cambodia. Their experiences were quite different from their compatriots in Vietnam (unless they passed through Vietnam on their way out). Many of them would have settled in the Khmer cluster projects, and indications are that they left those sites to settle elsewhere. Their educational and occupational backgrounds are undoubtedly quite similar to those from Vietnam, and we need to know more about their ability to establish themselves in this country. One major point to consider is that they would have arrived here about two years later, on the average, than the Chinese refugees from Vietnam, in mid-1981 compared to 1979. The work of Hackett (1989) on such refugees in and around the Washington, D.C., area during the mid-1980s showed a situation similar to that in Philadelphia. They, too, tended to stay out of the Chinatown in the city and to operate in the Indochinese community on the outskirts. In both these cases, the Chinese refugees were, for the time being, left to develop both their Chineseness and their Americanness largely on their own.

Educational Achievement

The interest of the Chinese community in education has always been strong. Its schools had provided both competence in reading and numbers as well as broader social contacts within the community for the students and their families. Yet the ISR study showed a majority of the Chinese adults with no more than primary schooling, 40 percent with some secondary schooling but no more, and less than a twentieth having any contact with higher education. This illustrated the needs of the community—its heavy commercial involvement and little opportunity for government or professional roles.

Arriving in the United States, the Chinese refugees joined the other ethnic groups from Southeast Asia in taking advantage of the American public school system. The broad desire for education that was hemmed in by so many social, economic, and political forces in Indochina found an outlet here. The second ISR study drew 200 households from the original 1,384 to examine the efforts of the refugee children in American schools (Caplan, Whitmore, and Choy 1989; Caplan, Choy, and Whitmore 1991, 1992). The finding was a consistent level of quality among the students (kindergarten to twelfth grade) both at the local level (as seen in grades) and on the national level (standardized tests). While the study looked predominantly at urban dwellers whose children attended inner-city schools, the focus on education of the refugee families allowed the schools to teach and the students to absorb the preferred information.

The Chinese students consistently placed between the Vietnamese and the

Lao in grade-point average (GPA). On a 4.0 scale, the overall GPA for the Chinese was 2.99. As might be expected, they did better in mathematics (3.23) than in fields requiring more English usage. In science, for example, it was 2.87, and lower for the social sciences and the humanities. Interestingly, there was a strong correlation of proclaimed religious belief with GPA; the children of Vietnamese and Chinese families claiming Confucian belief had 3.37, while Mahayana Buddhists had 3.13. Yet no correlation existed between either ethnicity or religion and performances on the standardized tests. All ethnic groups and religious beliefs did equally well. Overall, 60 percent of the refugee children placed in the top half of the national total. In mathematics, the figure was 85 percent, with 49 percent in the top quartile, almost double the national average, while the reading and language test had only 45 percent in the top half. Interestingly, 70 percent of the refugee students placed in the top half of the spelling test.

None of the standard variables provided a strong correlation with these results. Neither prior socioeconomic status nor educational background of the refugee families explained anything. The range of GPA and test results was generally narrow, and scholastic success ranged through all elements of the refugee community. What was equal among these elements was, first, desire for and focus on education and, second, accessibility to the public school system.

The study's approach, then, was to look to the refugee family and its values for an explanation of the children's success. One interesting detail, unlike almost every other known population, was that as the number of children per family increased from two up, the GPA tended to hold steady or even rise. Our explanation is that the family, like the household economically, joined forces here to encourage and support the students. A very strong consensus existed for education, cooperation, harmony, and responsibility. This was opposed to the values those families believed to be held by their nonrefugee neighbors: material goods and fun/excitement, which the refugees themselves put last. The Chinese refugees actively employed the value system brought with them from Southeast Asia within their new environment. Rather than simply assimilating and blending into the surrounding community, they maintained their own counsel and urged their children on in the classroom. Family involvement and hard work fit well into the American opportunity structure and provided the basis for the student's success.

The Importance of Contacts

The strength of the Chinese communities in Vietnam and Cambodia, as described earlier, lay in the strongly interlocked nature of their social and economic networks, sources of both information and funds. Barton (1984) has shown how strongly personal integrity meshed within these networks, such that individual and family success depended on maintaining contacts across the community and beyond. In this vein, one can see the significance of the many groups and associations, organized for a great number of social purposes, in setting the scene for such contacts to take place. Involved here were both informality and a strong sense of propriety in carrying out one's economic dealings.

What does this mean for the Chinese refugees from Southeast Asia in the United States? To succeed as they succeeded in Vietnam and Cambodia, they have to re-form the type of networks and the access to capital that were available to them there. This has already occurred to a limited degree in some places. The *New York Times* reported on the success of some Sino-Vietnamese refugees who had arrived in 1975 and linked up with contacts in New York City's Chinatown. To quote Seth Mydans (1984), "As a Chinese, Mr. Chao benefits from a worldwide network of more than 21 million overseas Chinese whose family and clan connections link them across national boundaries as a powerful economic force." According to this report, "many" of the New York Chinese refugees moved into Chinatown, where links reached out to California, Houston, Louisiana, and Washington, not to mention Singapore, Malaysia, Thailand, and Taiwan. The specific links mentioned here were Teochiu.

Such linkages had not yet appeared among the Chinese refugees in locations like Philadelphia and Washington, D.C. Both Peters and others (1983) and Hackett (1989) showed developments that may have been only in a nascent stage. Certainly, the "Food Cart Network" around the University of Pennsylvania would seem to have been a classic case of such economic organization. But the Philadelphia area had not shown any strong tendency to establish the multitude of associations that flourished so successfully in Southeast Asia. As a consequence, both information and capital would have been difficult to obtain. Nevertheless, the potential for developing contacts and building trust still existed.

Moving from the small numbers of Chinese refugees on the East Coast in the early and mid-1980s to the large community in California through the entire decade, one can see what the overseas Chinese pattern can accomplish. Gold (1994) has described the impact of the refugee Chinese on the local economy. Utilizing both their Southeast Asian background and experience and their broad contacts with other overseas Chinese here and abroad, a number of these refugees have established major enterprises, including, to quote Gold (198), "almost complete dominance" in areas such as "wholesale, import/export, real estate development, and manufacturing concerns." How have they achieved this dominance?

Essentially, they applied the strategy and tactics that had gained them such a strong position in Indochina to the situation at hand in the United States. Within the context of the American urban economy, these Chinese refugees made contact with and brought together ("integrated") a number of local elements, Asian and otherwise, to take advantage of opportunities offered. As in Southeast Asia, where they gained trust and access through their contacts, here again they have made their connections, both within and outside their own community. Operating within the context of local, national, and international patterns, the Chinese refugees have, through these multiple contacts, gained a place within the south-

ern California economy and, in the process, have played a major role in re-
forming it.

Gold describes how, through the use of overseas capital, cheap immigrant
labor, and government benefits, these refugees "catalyze the economic transformation of southern California" (202). By being aware of available opportunities, of the variety of resources at hand, and of the contacts needed to take
advantage of these, many Chinese refugees have set themselves up in thriving
businesses. These businesses, ranging from tiny family operations to large commercial enterprises, tie together the variety of different elements from their own
kin group, their own dialect group, overseas Chinese here and abroad, other
ethnic groups, refugees and nonrefugees, and local, state, and federal governments. These elements include capital, advice, trust, imported goods, cheap labor, markets, benefits, and local dynamics. While difficulties and high risk
continue to hamper the economic development of Chinese refugees (such as a
need for skilled workers and managers and the tendency to jump into uncertain
situations), the gains have often been great.

One specific result has been a large, positive impact on urban areas. By providing jobs, low-cost goods and services, and stable neighborhoods, the Chinese
refugees have helped to renovate the inner cities and integrate the local economy. On the one hand, stepping into low-paying jobs while simultaneously
creating other low-paying jobs for other ethnic groups and, on the other, bringing
this economy in contact with international supply and demand, these refugees
have tied all these elements together through their own expansive contacts and
connections.

Thus, the characteristics of the Chinese refugee community in this country—
urban, small and medium business backgrounds, and moderate levels of education—mean that economic success and social integration (into Chinese-
American society) depend on the opportunity and ability to reach out and make
contact. Developing networks is a key to this success. Chinese refugees who
remain isolated, however hardworking, stay at the mercy of their poor English,
undeveloped educations, and lack of capital. For them, success will depend on
their children and the American school system.

APPENDIX

The Chinese wholesale commerce in foodstuffs included fish products, pepper, tea, livestock, market gardening, and raising fowl (ducks in Vietnam, chickens in Cambodia). Beyond the wholesale stage lay the retail groceries, butcher
shops, street vendors, soup stalls, cafes, restaurants, and so on. Overall, the
Chinese handled 85 percent of the commerce in foodstuffs and 90 percent of
the preservation and sale of meat and fish. More than 1,400 firms in Saigon/
Cholon alone handled textiles and their products; almost 900 firms dealt with
metal products, including jewelry; and more than 200 firms were involved with
wood products, including paper. The Chinese in South Vietnam handled all the

textile production, almost half (48 percent) the commerce in textiles, almost all (98 percent) the commerce in metals, and 40 percent of forestry exploitation (Tsai 1968; see also Ky 1963; Tsung 1959). Willmott (1967) demonstrates a similar pattern for Cambodia.

Tsai Maw-kuey (1968), a member of the Hokkien *bang,* has broken down these economic activities in terms of the five dialect groups. Although the Cantonese and Teochiu were dominant numerically (this being the only place in Southeast Asia where the Cantonese were the largest group), the Hokkien were dominant in commercial circles. The other two groups (Hakka and Hainanese) had their own limited specialties. The Cantonese concentrated on urban general stores, restaurants, groceries, butcher shops, and other aspects of the food trade; the clothing and cloth business; construction and wood products; Chinese hotels and theaters; beauty salons; and mechanics. The Teochiu worked mainly in the tea business, wholesale and retail, but also in fish (from both the Mekong Delta and Cambodia) and their products, Chinese medicinal herbs, metalworking, and trucking. The Teochiu also had the most extensive international contacts and hence foreign trade and banking. The Hokkien, for their part, had a role far greater than their numbers. This group controlled the rice trade, with its shipping and milling, as well as the secondhand, hardware, and junkyard businesses. Living and intermarrying in the countryside, the Hokkien shopkeepers provided the key economic link between the mass of the Vietnamese population and the urban Chinese merchants. Through this link came rice and scrap iron, the products of agriculture and war, to the international market. The last two groups, Hakka and Hainanese, restricted themselves to limited and well-defined specialties: medicinal herbs, baked goods, leather products, textiles, plastics, ceramics, and rubber goods for the Hakka, who were much more involved in artisanry and industry than the other groups; European-style cooking—with its restaurant and cafe trade—Western films, and pepper growing for the Hainanese.

In Cambodia, Willmott (1970) shows the Teochiu, rather than the Cantonese and the Hokkien, to be dominant in number and through the countryside as the shopkeepers who handled local commerce and the rice trade. As in Vietnam, the Teochiu handled import-export but here were more widely involved in dry goods and groceries as well as pharmacies, vegetable farming, and street peddling. The Cantonese lived mainly in Phnom Penh, Battambang, and Kampong Cham and, with their great diversity of businesses, served as extensions of the commercial interests of Cholon. Occupations of specialization were construction, transportation, carpentry, mechanics, and wine. The Hokkien focused on banking, import-export, foodstuffs, and as in Vietnam, hardware. The Hakka and Hainanese were like their fellows in Vietnam. The former worked in bakeries, medicinal herbs, and leather, and the latter concentrated on restaurants and hotels. Here the Hainanese also included textile products, however.

Gold (1994) has pointed out that in southern California the Teochiu (Chao Zhou) were restauranteurs, Hainanese owned grocery stores, and the Hakka were herbalists. The majority of Cantonese were presumably involved in the major enterprises he described.

NOTE

1. I wish to thank Mr. Bui Long Quang for his aid in providing me with these figures.

REFERENCES

Amer, Ramses. 1991. *The Ethnic Chinese in Vietnam and Sino-Vietnamese Relations.* Kuala Lumpur: Forum.

Barton, Clifton A. 1984. Trust and Credit: Some Observations regarding Business Strategies of Overseas Chinese Traders in South Vietnam. In *The Chinese in Southeast Asia, Vol. 1, Ethnicity and Economic Activity.* Edited by L. Y. C. Lim and L. A. P. Gosling. Singapore: Maruzen Asia.

Benoit, Charles. 1981. Vietnam's "Boat People." In *The Third Indochina Conflict.* Edited by D. W. P. Elliot. Boulder, Colorado: Westview Press. Pp. 139–162.

Brocheux, Pierre. 1995. *The Mekong Delta: Ecology, Economy, and Revolution, 1860–1960.* Madison, Wisconsin: Center for Southeast Asian Studies, University of Wisconsin.

Caplan, Nathan, Marcella H. Choy, and John K. Whitmore. 1991. *Children of the Boat People: A Study of Educational Success.* Ann Arbor: University of Michigan Press.

———. 1992. Indochinese Refugee Families and Academic Achievement. *Scientific American* 266(2):36–42.

Caplan, Nathan, John K. Whitmore, and Quang L. Bui. 1984. *Economic Self-sufficiency among Southeast Asian Refugees.* Report to the Office of Refugee Resettlement. Ann Arbor, Michigan: Institute for Social Research.

Caplan, Nathan, John K. Whitmore, and Marcella H. Choy. 1989. *The Boat People and Achievement in America: A Study of Family Life, Hard Work, and Cultural Values.* Ann Arbor: University of Michigan Press.

de Poncins, Gontran. 1957. *From a Chinese City.* Garden City, New York: Doubleday.

Dunning, Bruce B. 1982. *A Systematic Survey of the Social, Psychological and Economic Adaptation of Vietnamese Refugees Representing Five Entry Cohorts, 1975–1979.* Washington, D.C.: Bureau of Social Science Research.

Fall, Bernard B. 1959. Commentary. In *Vietnam, the First Five Years.* Edited by R. W. Lindholm. East Lansing: Michigan State University Press. Pp. 111–117.

Gold, Steven J. 1994. Chinese-Vietnamese Entrepreneurs in California. In *The New Asian Immigration in Los Angeles and Global Restructuring.* Edited by Paul Ong, Edna Bonacich, and Lucie Cheng. Philadelphia: Temple University Press. Pp. 196–226.

Grant, Bruce, et al. 1979. *The Boat People: An "Age" Investigation.* New York: Penguin Books.

Hackett, Beatrice Nied. 1989. Overlapping Self- and Other-Defined Ethnic Identities: Adjustment and Chinese Cambodian Refugees in the Washington Metropolitan Area. Unpublished paper.

Haines, David W., Editor. 1989. *Refugees as Immigrants: Cambodians, Laotians, and Vietnamese in America.* Totowa, New Jersey: Rowman and Littlefield.

Ky Luong Nhi. 1963. The Chinese in Vietnam. Unplublished Ph.D. dissertation, University of Michigan, Ann Arbor.

Lim, L. Y. C. 1984. Chinese Activity in Southeast Asia: An Introductory Review. In *The Chinese in Southeast Asia.* Edited by L. Y. C. Lim and L. A. P. Gosling. Singapore: Maruzen Asia. Pp. 1–29.

Marsot, Alain G. 1993. *The Chinese Community in Vietnam under the French.* San Francisco: EMText.

Menkhoff, Thomas. 1993. *Trade Routes, Trust and Trading Networks: Chinese Small Enterprises in Singapore.* Fort Lauderdale, Florida: Breitenbach.

Murray, Martin J. 1980. *The Development of Capitalism in Colonial Indochina, 1870–1940.* Berkeley: University of California Press.

Mydans, Seth. 1984. Chinese Refugees from Vietnam Thrive in Chinatown. *New York Times,* February 11:29, 32.

Ngo Vinh Long. 1971. Use of the Chinese by the French in Cochinchina, 1886–1910. Harvard University *Papers on China* 24:125–145.

Nguyen Hoi Chan. 1971. Some Aspects of the Chinese Community in Vietnam, 1650–1850. Harvard University *Papers on China* 24:104–124.

Nguyen The Anh. 1971. *Kin-te va Xa-hoi Viet-nam duoi cac vua trieu Nguyen* (The economy and society of Vietnam under the Nguyen kings). (2nd Edition). Saigon: Lua-thieng.

Peters, H., B. Schieffelin, L. Sexton, and D. A. Feingold. 1983. *Who Are the Sino-Vietnamese? Culture, Ethnicity, and Social Categories.* Philadelphia, Pennsylvania: Institute for the Study of Human Issues.

Skinner, G. William. 1951. *Report on the Chinese in Southeast Asia.* Ithaca, New York: Cornell University, Southeast Asia Program.

Tran Khanh. 1993. *The Ethnic Chinese and Economic Development in Vietnam.* Singapore: Institute of Southeast Asian Studies.

Tsai Maw-kuey. 1968. *Les Chinois au Sud Vietnam.* Paris: Bibliotheque Nationale.

Tsung To Way. 1959. A Survey of Chinese Occupations. In *Vietnam, the First Five Years.* Edited by R. W. Lindholm. East Lansing: Michigan State University Press. Pp. 118–125.

Whitmore, John K. 1983. Vietnam and the Monetary Flow of Eastern Asia, Thirteenth to Eighteenth Centuries. In *Precious Metals in the Later Medieval and Early Modern Worlds.* Edited by J. F. Richards. Durham, North Carolina: Carolina Academic Press. Pp. 363–393.

Willmott, William E. 1967. *The Chinese in Cambodia.* Vancouver: University of British Columbia.

———. 1970. *The Political Structure of the Chinese Community in Cambodia.* New York: Humanities Press.

Woodside, Alexander B. 1971. *Vietnam and the Chinese Model.* Cambridge, Massachusetts: Harvard University Press.

Chapter 12

Haitians

FREDERICK J. CONWAY AND
SUSAN BUCHANAN STAFFORD

Haitians have a rich cultural and historical heritage, even though they come from one of the poorest countries in the Western Hemisphere. Haiti is the second oldest republic in the Americas, the product of an eighteenth-century revolution grounded in the "rights of man." Yet the struggle for the extension of human rights has been the most poignant theme of Haitian life in the 1990s.

Haiti is a mountainous country located on the island of Hispaniola, the second largest island in the Caribbean. Lying between Spanish-speaking Cuba and the Dominican Republic (with which it shares Hispaniola), Haiti retains its distinct linguistic and cultural identity. It is the largest country where French Creole and French are the major languages. Haiti is both the most densely populated and the most rural nation in the Caribbean region. Peasant agriculture is the basis of the economy, but the agricultural sector has been neglected for more than a century.

Although Haiti seems remote to many Americans, it has had a long and intimate relationship with the United States. The United States has been Haiti's most important trading partner since the nineteenth century and has played an important role in shaping Haiti's politics. The United States invaded Haiti twice in the twentieth century, most recently in 1994. In spite of the intimacy, Haitians remain exotic and in many ways invisible to many Americans.

The refugee status of Haitians in the United States is complex. Successive U.S. administrations have resisted giving refugee status to Haitians, even during times of fierce political repression in Haiti. Very few Haitians have been granted political asylum, and only a political and legal crisis in Florida in the early 1980s led to a quasi-refugee status of "Cuban/Haitian entrant." Nevertheless, many Haitian immigrants in the United States consider themselves to be in exile from their country. Others consider themselves to be nonpolitical immigrants.

This chapter will distinguish between the specific category of "Haitian entrant" and the more general categories of Haitian exile and immigrant.

An important theme in legal battles about Haitians' refugee status has been a comparison of their treatment with that of neighboring Cubans, who were almost always given refugee status until 1995. Thus, a chapter on Haitians as refugees must include some discussion of Cuban immigration, especially during the "Mariel crisis" of 1980. It is also necessary to consider U.S. policies that have resulted in the forced repatriation of thousands of Haitians desiring entry into the United States. These "refused refugees" are an important part of the Haitian story.

Proverbs are used frequently in Haitian conversations. The most famous Haitian proverb is "*Deye mon gen mon,*" which means "Behind mountains there are mountains." This is not only a physical image of Haiti's rugged landscape but a testament to the struggles of Haitians to establish a satisfying life and to their determination to overcome seemingly endless obstacles. These obstacles have been encountered both in Haiti and in the United States. The 1990s have been a period of significant political and cultural openings in Haiti and consequently of some of the fiercest political repression there in this century. The 1990s have also raised significant questions for Americans about their relationships with Haitians.

THE HOME COUNTRY

Early History

Haiti is the second oldest republic in the Americas, established on January 1, 1804, when an army of former slaves defeated Napoleon's forces. The Haitian Revolution ended more than three centuries of colonial rule by Spain and France. That rule began during Columbus's first voyage in 1492. By the 1550s, the indigenous Tainos had been almost exterminated, and the importation of African slaves by the Spanish was well under way. The French took possession of Saint-Domingue, as colonial Haiti was known, at the end of the seventeenth century. The French greatly increased the importation of slaves to work plantations of sugar cane, coffee, cotton, and indigo. By the middle of the eighteenth century, Saint-Domingue had become the most profitable colony in the world. It was far more valuable to the French than were the 13 North American colonies to Britain.

The wealth of Saint-Domingue was produced by slaves who worked in one of the most brutal plantation systems in the history of the Americas. In the decades before the start of the Haitian Revolution, the life expectancy of Africans, once they arrived in Saint-Domingue, was less than ten years. In the 1790 census, the 452,000 slaves constituted 87 percent of the population (Leyburn 1966:18).

Thirteen years of intermittent warfare during the revolution destroyed most of the infrastructure of the hated plantations. Early Haitian governments sought to reestablish the plantation system to restore export-oriented agriculture. The former slaves, however, had no interest in providing income to their rulers at the expense of their freedom. They left the plantations, taking up land granted by the government or simply removing themselves to the uninhabited mountains.

These new peasants developed an agriculture oriented toward subsistence and the local market, which required neither the capital nor the harsh labor exacted by exports such as sugar. Land was owned by individuals, worked by extended families, and passed on to their children. In the first 50 years after independence, Haitian land was transformed into a system of small holdings owned by individual peasants and large holdings owned by the state and leased out. Increases in population have resulted in smaller parcels being inherited by more individuals. Data from 1970 indicate that 85 percent of agricultural holdings were less than one hectare (Wilkie and Haber 1983:56). Haiti is a country in which the peasantry is desperately poor but tends to own land. Ties to the land are thus far more than sentimental, and Haitian peasants leave their land only under dire circumstances. In contrast to other Latin American countries, there is not a mass of landless peons working for an elite that owns most of the cultivated land. Conflicting class interests in Haiti have historically been more disguised.

Aside from temporary work groups, the extended family was the largest social group in rural areas. Attempts at establishing peasant organizations were suppressed. The relationship of the central state to a local area was channeled through the local *chef de section,* a military appointee. The direction of control and communication was entirely from the top down. With some embellishments, the same system operated through the end of the Duvalier regimes in the mid-1980s.

The ruling group consisted of two elements: an educated elite and the military leadership. From the beginning, the elite was largely mulatto, a group that had been partially free and often owners of slaves during the colonial period. The early military leadership consisted predominantly of former black slaves. Haitian law never recognized these color distinctions, but they remained important socially.

With the abandonment of the plantations, the elite group lost its chance to maintain dominance through control of land and agriculture. Some land remained in the hands of the elite, but their principal economic opportunities lay in the fields of commerce, the professions, and control of the political process. Politics soon became a struggle to gain control of government finances and patronage, removed from the agricultural base on which all depended. In spite of a number of uprisings, the peasant majority became irrelevant to Haitian politics—at least until the late 1980s—and no government in the past 150 years has made a significant investment in the rural sector.

Culture and Language

The ruling group, especially the educated elite, was oriented toward French cultural models. They sought to contrast themselves as sharply as possible with the peasantry, who were oriented toward their own cultural models forged from Haitian and African experiences. Thus, Haiti developed two cultures, a national peasant-based culture and an elite culture that was ambiguous in its identification, but that served to "delegitimize" the peasantry.

The use of language in Haiti is a good example of this, since language even more than color has been a class marker in Haiti. Creole is the language shared by all Haitians. Its vocabulary is largely derived from French, but its grammar is distinct, making the two languages mutually unintelligible. Historically, 5 to 10 percent of the population has also spoken French. Until the late 1980s, French was the only official language, the medium of law, oration, and literature, of all proper formality. Creole is viewed as the language of intimacy, humor, and through its proverbs, the wisdom of the lower classes.

With attitudes that pertain to all Haitian culture, both the monolingual Creole speaker and the bilingual Creole/French speaker are ambivalent toward the two languages. The elite are both sentimental toward Creole and disdainful of it. At the same time, there is a somewhat stilted quality to Haitian French; it is a language without slang. French symbolizes social dominance, but French utterances often lack substance, for example, in political oratory. The monolingual Creole speaker shares many of these attitudes. Creole is seen both as the truly Haitian form of expression and as a kind of baby talk without a grammar. Creole marks a person as "stupid." On the other hand, the Creole phrase *pale fwanse* ("to speak French") means "to be a hypocrite."

French does more than symbolize social dominance; it helps to reproduce it. Creole speakers who wish to become educated have until recently needed to do so in French. Literacy had to be acquired through a second language. The government official or the lawyer who insists on speaking French to a peasant even though both could use Creole continues the linguistic exploitation. Giving Creole legal equality with French was an important component of the political struggles of the 1980s.

Creole is not the only aspect of Haitian peasant culture that is denied legitimacy. The folk religion, vodoun, is perceived by the elite as powerful, even a necessary resort at times, but a threat to their status in Western civilization. Common-law marriage (*plasaj*), however long-standing, must be ratified in an expensive church ceremony to receive respectability. The physical features of the masses are despised and feared by many of their lighter-skinned compatriots. These characteristics of Haitian culture are the heritage of the colonial period, which ended formally almost two centuries ago.

From Independence to the Midtwentieth Century

After independence in 1804, neither France nor the United States gave Haiti diplomatic recognition, though trade links, especially with the United States, were very active. France waited 25 years before recognizing Haitian sovereignty—and then only at the crippling price of 60 million francs in "indemnities." The United States did not recognize Haiti until the U.S. Civil War. Even the Vatican considered Haiti "schismatic" until 1860.

Beginning with the need to pay the French indemnity, Haitian governments began to borrow heavily from French, American, and German sources. The late nineteenth and early twentieth centuries were marked by increased political and financial instability, as one group after another grabbed the presidency.

This period climaxed in 1915, when the U.S. Marines invaded Haiti, ostensibly because of the political crisis but principally to gain control of Haiti's finances at a time when German influence in Haiti was ascendant. The gold in the national treasury was removed to a bank in New York, and the Haitian currency, the gourde, was tied to the U.S. dollar by treaty. More than 3,000 Haitian guerrillas were killed by the U.S. Marines in the aftermath of the Occupation.

The U.S. Marines remained in control of Haiti until 1934. American financial control did not end until 1946. The U.S. Marines established temporary stability by forming the Haitian Army and through elections that gave the presidency to a series of elite politicians. During the Occupation the road system was improved, and attempts were made to reorient the classical French education system. None of these actions permanently changed Haiti's political or economic structure, however.

The lasting legacy of the Occupation was rather the intellectual and ideological ferment caused by the shock to Haitian sovereignty and pride. The Occupation confirmed that the United States, and not France, was to be the metropolitan center for Haiti in the twentieth century.

The Duvalier Era

The midtwentieth century saw the beginning of an unprecedented period of personal rule by the Duvalier family, which remained in power for almost three decades. The orientation of the François Duvalier government (1957–1971) was in part a reaction against the dominance of the mulatto elite. Duvalier's main program, however, came to be the establishment of absolute personal power. A period of terror in the early 1960s resulted in the departure of many professionals and businesspeople, as well as in the alienation of foreign governments and a sharp reduction in foreign aid and investments. The road system deteriorated, and many economic ventures halted. In 1964, François Duvalier had himself declared president for life. He maintained power through a reshuffled army and his own militia, commonly known as the Tonton Macoutes, as well as through the tacit support of the U.S. government. Duvalier did what no other Haitian president had done before him: he died a natural death in the National Palace and passed on the reins of power to his son.

The Duvalier period generated the first important wave of Haitian exiles to the United States. Most of these exiles were upper- and middle-class Haitians; they entered the United States legally, though generally as immigrants rather than refugees. They established vibrant, though class-divided, communities, especially in New York. Many intended to return to Haiti but had to wait as long as two decades before they felt safe to do so.

The 15 years (1971–1986) of the Jean-Claude Duvalier regime were a period of change for Haiti. Since most of the government's opponents were subdued, there was a reduction in political terror. The regime established a modus vivendi with the business elite. Foreign aid soared, resulting notably in the reconstruction of the road system and some infrastructure in the capital, Port-au-Prince. Investments created an important light-industry sector, with mostly American companies taking advantage of Haiti's low wages. These industries included the assembly of clothes, softballs and electronic equipment and even the sorting of grocery coupons. Remittances from Haitians abroad became an increasingly important element in the economy. Decades of government neglect unraveled the Haitian environment to the point that agriculture was in serious decline. Pressure for arable land forced people to cultivate steeper mountain slopes; stories were told of people "falling off their gardens." Deforestation has continued apace. With the tree cover gone, tropical rains that once nourished crops became a *lavalas,* a torrent that carried away the soil.

The influence of the United States on Haitian affairs, which was obscured under François Duvalier, again became apparent during his son's regime. The Carter administration pressured the Haitian government to relax controls on the radio and press in the late 1970s. Tight political control was resumed a few days after the Reagan victory in the American presidential election in 1980 and remained until the last weeks of the Duvalier regime. Jean-Claude Duvalier was supported by the Reagan administration until public unrest made his rule untenable early in 1986.

It was during the Jean-Claude Duvalier regime that the major flow of Haitians leaving for the United States occurred, beginning in the late 1970s and culminating in 1980. Most of the thousands who fled Haiti at this time left in boats without visas or other documentation. After a series of battles in American courts, most of these Haitians were given the status of "Cuban/Haitian entrant." This status did not certify them as refugees, but it did grant them an ambiguous legal position in the United States. During the last five years of the Duvalier period, however, Haitian "boat people" were intercepted by the U.S. Coast Guard. The great majority were forcibly repatriated to Haiti, with the cooperation of the Haitian government.

After the Duvaliers

In the hours after the Duvalier family was escorted from Haiti on a U.S. government airplane in February 1986, a new government announced itself to the nation. All of its members, except for a few who resigned in the following months, had been figures in the Duvalier regime. The politics of this and succeeding Haitian governments was widely called "Duvalierism without Duvalier."

The departure of Jean-Claude Duvalier opened a national dialogue on a level never previously experienced in Haiti. Peasant groups, labor unions, and political parties formed. The greatest achievement of this period was the adoption of a new constitution in 1987, the first drafted with widespread public participation. The constitution restricted the power of the executive, recognized Creole as the official language, and removed restrictions on practicing the vodoun religion.

The key political term of the late 1980s was *dechoukaj,* the "uprooting" of the Duvalierist past. An important focus of "uprooting" was the Tonton Macoutes, who sought refuge as attachés in the Haitian Army, remaining an important force for political repression. With the exception of the first months of the Aristide administration, the post-Duvalier period was marked by human rights abuses that surpassed even those of the François Duvalier regime. The repression was unusually broad in its scope. Because large numbers of urban and rural poor insisted on being part of the political process, they became the victims of political persecution in unprecedented numbers. During most of this period, the United States maintained its policy of intercepting and returning Haitians who attempted to enter the United States without visas.

The constitution provided for presidential elections in 1987 and the establishment of an independent electoral council. The election never took place. It was stopped by a massacre of people in Port-au-Prince as they waited to vote. After a series of coups, elections were again scheduled for December 1990. This time the elections were held successfully and were regarded by international observers as fair.

The Aristide Presidency

Father Jean-Bertrand Aristide won the presidential election of 1990 with 67 percent of the votes. He was swept into power by the *lavalas,* a torrential flood of popularity, especially among the poor. Aristide was a Catholic priest who served at the church of Saint Jean Bosco in a poor neighborhood of Port-au-Prince, where he began preaching for social justice in the last months of the Duvalier regime. A series of assassination attempts brought Aristide to national and international attention.

Aristide took an active role in the anti-Duvalier movement that was fostered by the Catholic Church. The Church hierarchy, however, was opposed to Aristide's activism, and he was expelled from his religious order. Later, the Vatican was the only state to recognize the military government that overthrew him.

The eight months of the Aristide administration were marked by decreases in human rights abuses (though anti-Aristide elements in the army remained active) and in numbers of Haitians attempting to leave the country. Aristide began to reform the civil service and the justice system. He spoke of economic as well as social justice, even though his economic policies were vague. Most important, the election of Aristide marked a symbolic shift: The man of the people had been elected. These changes were intolerable to many in the business sector, the military, and the old Duvalierists. In September 1991, the Haitian Army staged a coup against Aristide, who barely escaped to exile in Venezuela and the United States. Haiti was plunged into three years of political and economic turmoil.

In response to the coup, the Organization of American States (OAS) imposed an embargo on Haiti. The U.S. government refused to recognize the de facto military government but joined the embargo with considerable ambivalence. The coup leaders had close ties to the United States: They had previously received military training in the United States and funds from the Central Intelligence Agency (CIA) (Farmer 1994:219).

In June 1993, under pressure from the United Nations and the United States, the coup leader, General Raoul Cedras, and President Aristide signed the Governor's Island Accord, which provided for Aristide's return to Haiti in October 1993, supported by a multinational force to "professionalize" the Haitian Army. The military government had no real intention of permitting Aristide to return, however, and repression of his followers increased steadily. The stalemate ended in September 1994, when U.S. military forces occupied Haiti for the second time this century.

The U.S. invasion of Haiti, conducted peacefully because of last-minute negotiations, restored Aristide to the Haitian presidency but circumscribed his ability to implement his policies. The National Treasury was truly emptied after three years of corrupt military rule. Thousands of deaths had more than decimated the *lavalas*. American troops maintained order in the capital but did little to "uproot" the Duvalierist resistance. Political security in the countryside remained fragile at best. In March 1995, the unilateral American force was converted to a multinational United Nations force commanded by an American officer. The future of Haitian society, of the environment upon which it was based, and of the politics that directed it was as uncertain as ever.

EXODUS AND TRANSIT

Leaving Haiti

Given the conditions described above, it is not surprising that 1 million Haitians have emigrated since the 1950s (Allman 1981). An estimated 400,000 to

500,000 Haitians have settled in the United States, with major communities in the metropolitan areas of New York, Miami, Boston, Chicago, and Philadelphia.

Haitians have emigrated to the United States since prerevolutionary times and have come from all sectors of Haitian society. They started to arrive in great numbers when the elite and middle class fled the Duvalier regime in the late 1950s and resettled in the northeastern United States. They were joined by a steady stream from the urban working class seeking relief from declining political and economic conditions throughout the 1960s and 1970s. Joining those who legally immigrated and many who overstayed their tourist visas, a small but steady stream of Haitians entered the United States clandestinely by boat beginning in 1972. As conditions in Haiti declined precipitously, the number of Haitians risking their lives at sea increased dramatically in the late 1970s, culminating in an influx of 25,000 in 1980, at the same time as 125,000 Cubans flooded into south Florida. With its proximity to Haiti, south Florida, especially Miami, was the intended destination for thousands of "boat people" fleeing Haiti in the 1980s and 1990s.

For a number of years, the Bahamas had served as a focus of emigration for Haitian peasants. (Considerable migration to the Dominican Republic still takes place, especially during the cane-cutting season; the same was true of Cuba until 1959.) By the mid-1970s, however, the Bahamians showed less tolerance for Haitian workers as tourism waned and the economy declined. In 1978, when the Bahamian government threatened to deport illegal Haitians, many of them chose to continue their search for a better life in Miami rather than return to Haiti. The movement to Miami had begun.

As the Bahamas became less attractive and as smuggling operations from Haiti became more sophisticated (and commercialized), the outflow of people from Haiti to Florida increased. In addition, requirements for obtaining entry visas from the U.S. consulate in Haiti stiffened, making it more difficult than ever to travel to the United States legally. A series of favorable court rulings (see below) for Haitians seeking asylum in the United States, which included work authorization on release from detention, added impetus to the movement. Many Haitians who were determined to leave Haiti, but who could not afford documents or an airplane ticket, sold their meager assets to pay for the trip by sea or joined with others to build boats for the 700-mile voyage. Unknown numbers of Haitians have died in their attempt to reach the United States, as craft designed for coastal traffic foundered or dishonorable captains abandoned their human cargo to their fate.

Most Haitians were unable to make the voyage in a single crossing. They had to stop at Cuba or islands in the Bahamas to replenish supplies or make repairs. The Cubans generally provided the Haitians assistance and towed them back into the Gulf Stream to continue their voyage. The Bahamian reception was less than congenial and sometimes inhumane, as witnessed by the Cayo Lobos incident in early 1981, when the Bahamian government refused to rescue shipwrecked Haitians from a deserted, waterless island. The Haitian government also declined to intervene. Haitians who did make the voyage directly from Haiti to Florida often spent 10 to 14 days at sea and staggered ashore dehydrated, famished, and ill.

Although the majority of Haitians arrived in Florida by boat during this period, commercial airlines also brought undocumented Haitians directly from Port-au-Prince to Miami. The "Boeing people," as they were called, were more often from the more-educated working and middle classes than were the arrivals by sea. Well-organized commercial ventures that routed Haitians through the Dominican Republic, Jamaica, and Curacao often ended with sadly disappointed Haitians who discovered that their costly visas were not valid for the United States.

Prior to 1977, approximately 7,000 boat people were recorded by the U.S. Immigration and Naturalization Service (INS). In 1978–1979 alone, more than 8,300 entries were recorded. The influx jumped to 40,000 Haitian entries in 1980 and the first six months of 1981 (Cuban-Haitian Task Force 1981). The INS estimated that between 40 and 50 percent of the arrivals during this period may have escaped detection, so the figures may record only half of the actual arrivals.

Unlike Haitians arriving in south Florida in the 1970s, most of those who arrived during the 1980–1981 influx had embarked from Haiti (and not the Bahamas), pouring out from all areas of the country. The main areas of departure were from the northern and northwestern coasts of Haiti. The Department of the North was most frequently listed as the place of origin by arriving Haitians. The Department of the West, including Port-au-Prince, was the second largest sending area. (Many of the Haitians arriving from this region entered by airplane and were stopped at Miami International Airport.) The third major area of outflow was the Artibonite Valley, where large-scale thefts of peasant land have been alleged. The number of recorded arrivals listing southern regions as their origin was the smallest.

U.S. Policy towards Haitians Seeking to Leave Haiti

Haitians arriving in the United States have faced a public perception of themselves as illiterate, impoverished individuals who would drain public resources. Haitians were further stigmatized as health risks. In the 1970s they were identified with tuberculosis. In the early 1980s, they were declared to be a population at risk for the human immunodeficiency virus (HIV) by the federal Centers for Disease Control (CDC) and the New York City Health Department. In the 1990s, the HIV issue surfaced again in the Food and Drug Administration's ban on blood donations by Haitians.

The most consistent aspect of the U.S. federal government's response to the Haitian boat people is the view that they are not collectively entitled to be designated as refugees, as individuals who fear returning to their own countries because they fear persecution on the basis of race, color, national origin, religion, social group, or political opinion. In the view of the U.S. Department of State and the INS, Haitians are "economic" rather than "political" refugees; that is, their motivation to enter the United States stems from the desire for employment rather than from actual persecution or fear of persecution. Thus, since the 1970s, Haitians' claims for asylum as refugees have been almost uniformly rejected, despite evidence that human and civil rights have been regularly violated in Haiti and that persecution for political opinions occurs there. Opposition to this stance has taken two directions: first, that Haitians should be considered legal refugees and second, that their claims should be accorded due process in any case.

Haitians and their advocates have fought an unparalleled series of legal battles to ensure that claimants receive due process of law: fair treatment, including access to Creole interpreters and attorneys at INS hearings; and work authorizations on release from INS detention. In 1978, a flagrant violation of Haitians' rights occurred when the INS attempted to clear a backload of Haitian asylum cases by processing 150 per day and by revoking work authorizations. Advocates for the Haitians took the INS to court. In June 1980, a federal court, ruling in *Haitian Refugee Center v. Civiletti,* ordered new INS asylum hearings for approximately 5,000 Haitians and rebuked the federal government for intentional discrimination and racism.

Haitians and the Mariel Crisis

The Cuban Mariel exodus of April 1980 greatly complicated matters. Faced with the prospect of providing refugee status to 125,000 Cubans and pressured by the Haitian dilemma, the Carter administration equivocated, creating the ambiguous legal category of "Cuban/Haitian entrant (status pending)." The category included undocumented Haitians and Cubans who arrived in the United States before October 10, 1980. Cubans and Haitians entering the United States without documentation after that date were subject to exclusion and deportation by the INS, although they were eligible for the same social service benefits as entrants while they were in the United States.

Faced with the Mariel crisis, the Carter administration directed the Federal Emergency Management Agency to handle the immediate problems of shelter, food, and other necessities for the arriving Cubans and later for the Haitians. In June 1980, the Cuban-Haitian Task Force, a special interagency unit, attempted to institute a method for processing and resettling the entrants. Expecting to begin a new life in Miami, arriving Haitians who were encountered by the INS found themselves transported to the Krome South camp and later to the Krome North camp, parts of a former Nike missile base in the Everglades swamp. The camp was initially plagued with numerous problems: inadequate staff, especially Creole interpreters; lack of running water, sanitation, and supplies; lack of telephones and other means of communication for the Haitians; and lack of shelter other than tents and hangars. By the end of 1980, the government had begun to build permanent structures, including dormitories.

Anxiety, confusion, and pain marked the faces of Haitians who did not understand the chaotic resettlement process, were unsure of their fate, and tried their best to wait out the boredom of each day. Concertina wire atop the camp fence grimly reinforced the notion that the United States might not be the friendly haven the Haitians had sought.

In cooperation with voluntary agencies, such as the U.S. Catholic Conference, the Lutheran Immigration and Refugee Service, Church World Service, World Relief, and HIAS (Hebrew Immigrant Aid Society), the Cuban-Haitian Task Force developed a more systematic, responsible settlement approach requiring verified sponsors and reducing time spent in the camp. The Fascell-Stone Amendment to the Refugee Assistance Act of 1980 provided Haitians and Cubans with a limited range of federal benefits and made states eligible for 100 percent reimbursement for cash and medical assistance to them. Thus, funds became available to assist Haitians with their immediate needs and with longer-term social service needs.

Growing numbers of Haitian minors posed special problems during this period, as they often entered in the company of siblings, unrelated adults, or kin whose relationship could not be verified immediately, rather than with their parents. Many of these minors were declared to be "unaccompanied," in some cases according to a narrow American definition of kinship rather than the more extensive Haitian system. Thus, some minors were unnecessarily separated from bona fide relatives or adoptive parents. Unaccompanied minors were placed in a separate facility at Krome South until care and sponsorship were developed by the Office of Refugee Resettlement (ORR), which was responsible for them. The Haitian minors were gradually transferred to Greer Woodycrest, a facility in Millbrook, New York, where they received care and educational opportunities until appropriate placements were made. Krome South closed in July 1981, and all the minors were resettled out of Greer Woodycrest by January 1982.

The 1980s: Interdiction and the IRCA

The new Reagan administration, seeing the flow of Haitians unabated, addressed Haitian emigration in two ways: by halting the resettlement of undocumented Haitians and by preventing their arrival in the United States in the first place through a policy of "interdiction."

Beginning in May 1981, undocumented Haitians were detained rather than released. Krome North was turned into a permanent detention camp. Five federal prisons, the INS processing center in Brooklyn, and a former military base at Fort Allen, Puerto Rico, were also pressed into service. Except for those released on humanitarian parole, nearly 1,800 Haitians spent 15 months in bleak despair until they were released by federal court order. The court rebuked INS for failing to follow proper administrative procedures. A federal appeals court further rebuked the federal agencies involved for racism and discrimination.

The interdiction policy began in September 1981, when the U.S. Coast Guard began patrolling the Haitian coasts for the purpose of intercepting Haitian vessels on the high seas. Passengers were interviewed to determine whether they had a legitimate claim to political asylum in the United States, and the great majority were forcibly brought to Port-au-Prince. The Haitian government concurred in this policy, although its legality under international law has been questioned. The U.S. Supreme Court, however, ruled in 1993 that the U.S. government was not barred from returning aliens found outside U.S. borders (Mitchell 1994:76). The interdiction policy remained in effect for ten years. Only 28 of the 25,000 Haitians interviewed were granted political asylum (Mitchell 1994:73).

The interdiction policy greatly reduced the outflow from Haiti, with an occasional boat landing in full view of sunbathers basking on south Florida beaches. Although the newly arrived Haitians were no longer singled out for incarceration—Krome North now resembled a small United Nations with aliens of many nationalities confined there—this fact did not make their detention easier to bear as their claims for asylum were decided.

On a more positive front for some of the Haitian exiles, the Immigration Reform and Control Act (IRCA) of 1986 helped to resolve the legal status of Cuban-Haitian entrants and some illegal immigrants who arrived before 1982. Through the IRCA, Haitians could regularize their status through the Cuban-Haitian Entrant Adjustment and Special Agricultural Worker provisions. By doing so, they became eligible for permanent residency, and their documentation for employment became less confusing. In Florida, implementation of the IRCA proceeded well, with 20,000 Haitians processing applications.

The 1990s: The Aftermath of the Coup against President Aristide

At least 1,500 Haitians were killed during the first six weeks after the coup against President Aristide in September 1991. The first response of the Bush administration was to stop interviewing passengers on intercepted Haitian boats: They were simply all repatriated. Soon the spectacle of Haitians being forced to disembark at Port-au-Prince led to a shift in American immigration policy toward Haitians. Undocumented Haitians were now sent to the U.S. military base at Guantánamo, Cuba. The U.S. administration maintained that neither U.S. nor international law regarding the treatment of refugees applied to the Haitians at Guantánamo. In the seven months between September 1991 and March 1992, some 34,000 Haitians were detained, more than during the entire previous decade (Farmer 1994:269).

A third of the Haitians interviewed at Guantánamo were given permission to apply for political asylum in the United States, in sharp contrast to the figures for Haitians who had been interviewed aboard U.S. Coast Guard vessels (Mitchell 1994:74). The growing numbers of Haitians at the Guantánamo base led the Bush administration to revert to its policy of interdiction and forcible return. The executive order for this change in policy authorized the INS to interview Haitian passengers to determine their refugee status, but interviews were not conducted.

In the meantime, the Haitians who had been taken to Guantánamo were tested for the presence of HIV, in contrast to other groups, notably Cubans who entered the United States by boat or airplane. Two hundred sixty-eight of the Haitians at Guantánamo were found to be HIV positive. They were isolated at Camp Bulkley on the Guantánamo base and were reported to be mistreated and forced to receive injections of medications and long-term contraceptives. In early 1993, a federal court found conditions at Camp Bulkley to constitute "cruel and unusual punishment" under the U.S. Constitution, and the HIV-positive Haitians were brought to the United States (Farmer 1994:277).

The Bush administration treatment of Haitians leaving their country became an issue during the 1992 U.S. presidential campaign. As the Democratic candidate, Bill Clinton denounced forced repatriation and delay in restoring Aristide to power. Shortly before his inauguration, however, Clinton reversed his campaign positions. Concerned with American political pressure against a new influx of Haitians, the Clinton administration continued the policy of forcible repatriation until just before the U.S. invasion of Haiti in October 1994. A few weeks after the invasion, the Clinton administration forcibly repatriated most of the remaining Haitians at Guantánamo in spite of continued insecurity and human rights abuses by members of the former military regime.

INITIAL RESETTLEMENT

Haitians seeking asylum in the United States are generally young men and women who, if they had remained in Haiti and been employed, would have formed part of the primary sector of the labor force and the country's hope for the future. Cuban-Haitian Task Force (1981) statistics indicate that approximately 30 percent of the 1980–1981 arrivals were female and 70 percent male. Less than 10 percent were minors under the age of 18. Fifty-five to 60 percent were between 18 and 29 years old, and 25 to 30 percent were between 30 and 44. Approximately 5 percent were over 45.

A Cuban-Haitian Task Force (1981) sample showed that although the majority of the Haitian boat people were illiterate, many possessed rudimentary reading and writing skills, usually in French. Occupational data show that most male arrivals had most frequently been engaged in unskilled work, primarily field cropping, with a minority possessing such skills as tailoring and mechanical repair work. Haitian women arrivals had work experiences as seamstresses, domestics, vendors, farmers, and factory workers. (The majority of the Haitian arrivals listed themselves as single, but these data are difficult to interpret, as

common-law marriages may not have been included in the responses and because the question was also misinterpreted as having asked whether they arrived
in the United States alone.)

A large percentage of the Haitian boat people, approximately 85 percent,
settled in southern Florida, primarily in the Miami area. New York and New
Jersey received most of the remaining 15 percent of the arriving Haitians. Secondary migration has occurred among these areas since 1981, as Haitians have
become discouraged by employment and housing problems in Florida or find
the northern winters too harsh.

The main problems of the Haitians are underemployment and substandard
housing. Employment poses the most persistent problem for new arrivals, especially as they are unskilled, do not speak English or Spanish, and sometimes
are illiterate. Employment is often seasonal or temporary and low paying with
few benefits. Haitian men and women find work in service industries, factories,
construction, or as domestics. They must compete with other immigrant groups,
especially with Spanish speakers, whose language is an advantage in Miami.
Although statistics are not available, lack of employment has forced many Haitians to become agricultural migrant laborers, traveling along the eastern sea-
board to pick crops. Others have opted for a grueling life of cutting sugar cane
in Belle Glade or Immokalee, Florida; they are the poorest of the Haitian immigrants. Haitians also compete for agricultural jobs in Homestead, south of
Miami, and in Broward County, to the north. Opportunities for exploiting these
Haitians abound.

In Miami itself, most of the Haitians have settled in the Edison-Little River
section, now known as "Little Haiti." A poverty-stricken zone with substandard
housing, the area is the center for Haitian business, social, cultural, and religious
activities in Miami. Up to a dozen individuals, related or not, find themselves
living together in houses built for single families. The housing is expensive,
despite its delapidated state. Rats and other vermin create environmental and
health problems. The Haitians have formed a highly mobile population, individuals moving from one residence to another as required by circumstances.
Often, only a few members of a household are employed; their wages support
the others who are less fortunate.

A survey (Stepick and Portes 1986:338) of post-1980 Haitian arrivals in south
Florida provides evidence of the economic conditions faced by this group. The
random sample of 499 recent arrivals living in Little Haiti, Fort Lauderdale, and
Belle Glade showed an average educational level of less than elementary school
for both men and women. About two thirds had been employed in Haiti, but 80
percent of the women and more than one third of the men were unemployed in
Florida. This was a higher percentage of unemployment than that of Haitians
arriving in the United States between 1970 and 1980. It was also higher than
the level of unemployment for Mariel Cubans arriving in 1980.

In addition, many Haitians experienced downward mobility compared with
occupations in the homeland. Their incomes in Miami barely hovered above the

poverty line. Women arrivals were also at a greater disadvantage than men in finding employment and more likely to receive welfare assistance, mainly because of their children. Stepick and Portes (1986:346) found that key factors in finding jobs were knowledge of English and knowledge of the labor market. Even better-educated Haitians, however, faced high rates of unemployment and very low income.

Unlike Cuban arrivals who found work within the well-established and economically prosperous Cuban community in Miami, the existing local Haitian business community was neither large nor prosperous enough to offer a source of income for fellow countrymen (Stepick 1992). The Cuban community had been built for two decades by refugees with significant amounts of capital.

Social, educational, and health services were overwhelmed and unprepared to meet the needs of these particular arrivals. Agency personnel had little knowledge or understanding of Haitian cultural beliefs and social patterns; few Haitian Creole interpreters were available. Fear of detection by the INS also impeded access to health and mental health services (Spero 1985).

INTEGRATION

Social and Economic Change

Despite their problems, many of the Haitian boat people had the advantage of preexisting networks of kin and friends in the United States who eased the transition and adaptation process. A study of the boat people in the early 1980s showed that these Haitians had a remarkably positive outlook about their circumstances and prospects in the United States and were anxious to learn English and obtain an education (Stepick 1982). A follow-up survey in Little Haiti and Fort Lauderdale in 1986 showed some small improvement in Haitians' economic conditions. The improvement may stem from the ability of many of the Haitians to adjust their immigration status. However, the very low starting point ensured a continuing precarious economic profile (Portes and Grosfoguel 1994:67).

In the decade since the large influx of Haitians in 1980, a small Haitian business enclave has developed in Little Haiti with nearly 300 businesses. Most of these enterprises have been established by professional and middle-class Haitian-Americans who moved to Miami from the Northeast. The power to employ other Haitians is limited, as most Haitian businesses are small. Nevertheless, these businesses give Haitians a visible commercial presence in Miami and offer services and a sense of community to Little Haiti. An entire informal economy of child care, restaurants, and unlicensed taxi, repair, and construction services still offers Haitians an alternative route to making a living. More educated Haitians have gained a toehold in education, law enforcement, and the medical profession (Stepick 1992; Portes and Stepick 1993).

The educational system has been particularly responsive to addressing the needs of Haitian exiles. Haitians traditionally place a high value on education for its intrinsic worth and as an avenue of social mobility. Among the Haitian-born population in the United States, two in five have received some college education and only one in ten has less than eight grades of schooling (Miller 1994). Nearly 55 percent of the Haitian boat people interviewed in south Florida in the early 1980s had received some education in the United States, especially in English-language training (Stepick and Portes 1986:336). Although there can be no assertion about the Haitian boat people specifically, Miami-Dade Community College registered substantial growth in non-American black students, with the largest increase coming from the Haitian population (Vorp n.d.).

Ethnic Identity

For Haitians, the immigrant and exile experience has been strongly structured by issues of race and ethnicity. The issue of race hits Haitians squarely in the face on a daily basis, regardless of their social background. Phenotypically, and thus socially within American society, the majority of Haitians are perceived to be black. This categorization renders Haitian immigrants socially invisible within American society and subjects Haitians to the same kinds of discrimination faced by African-Americans. It also ignores a different system of complex social categorization within Haitian culture whereby skin color does not automatically translate into perceived social class status.

Haitians will proclaim their pride in being black and in being from the second free nation in the Western Hemisphere, a free nation of blacks. They do not deny their racial heritage. Thrust, however, into a dominant white culture where cultural characteristics can blunt ascription based on race, Haitians may use their cultural characteristics individually and collectively for access to resources and upward mobility. In the presentation of the self to white Americans, Haitians may draw upon the European side of their cultural heritage to engender more favorable reactions and treatment. By stressing French language and culture, as well as their willingness to work hard and their ambition, some Haitians try to combat the negative public perception of them as illiterate, impoverished people with nothing to offer the United States (Charles 1992; Fouron 1983; Woldemikael 1989).

The use of ethnicity and culture to minimize the negative connotations of race may distance Haitian immigrants from African-Americans, whose social position Haitians understand to be disadvantageous in American society. This stance causes tensions between Haitians and African-Americans. Although they often support each other on issues of racial discrimination, African-Americans and Haitians often share a negative opinion of each other based on perceived differences in culture. African-Americans are particularly wary of Haitians as competitors in the labor market and for community resources. The immigrant mentality of Haitians—their desire to make it in America and their resourcefulness—is viewed with considerable suspicion. At the same time, Haitians are largely unaware of the difficulties of the African-American experience. In Miami especially, where Cubans have achieved remarkable success, both Haitians and African-Americans are fearful of social and economic marginalization. They compete to avoid being on the lowest rung of the socioeconomic ladder (Stepick 1992).

The perceptions and attitudes of young Haitian exiles and especially of the American-born children of Haitian immigrants are reported to be strikingly different in this regard. Their identification with Haiti is relatively weak; it is an abstract homeland they do not remember or have never seen. Haitian high school students in Miami are reported to disguise their Haitian origins. The younger generation of Haitians in the United States identify as black, an identity they do not see as different from African-American. Haitian students model African-American cultural styles, in contrast to their elders' aspirations toward white American cultural styles. These differences in identity and style are an important part of the conflicts of assimilation that Haitian families have experienced (Woldemikael 1989).

At an organizational level, Haitians have leveraged various identities as ethnics, exiles, and blacks to gain access to resources made available to groups in American society on these bases. Haitian community-based agencies have been successful since 1980 as deliverers of social services such as translation, English-language classes and vocational training, employment counseling and placement, referral for local, state, and federal agencies, and legal advice. These centers have helped Haitian exiles to solve temporary and long-term problems associated with adaptation to American society. Even along the migrant worker routes, the Haitian presence had been addressed by agencies designed to meet their particular needs (Chierici 1991).

Definitions of self and community are also constantly informed and structured by Haitians' ongoing relations with their countrymen still at home. Haitians "of the diaspora" have an intense feeling of nationalism and investment in the future of their homeland. They are a significant force in the economy of Haiti through remittances to family members and through trade. Haitians abroad invest in Haiti as a hedge against their uncertain future in their countries of exile. Ties with Haiti are reinforced through visits, exchanges of audiocassettes, and news of Haiti reported in a variety of American-based Haitian newspapers. The Haitian-American press has both assisted with assimilation and maintained Haiti as an important focal point for its readership. Since 1986, many of these periodicals have taken on a new role since they are distributed in Haiti as well as in the United States.

The worlds of Haiti and the United States are not separate. Haitians live the reality of Haiti as well as of their daily lives in the United States. Both societies form the context of what it means to be Haitian. Jean-Bertrand Aristide made this link between Haitians inside and outside the country clear in his appeal for support and campaign funds from what he called the "Tenth Department," the community of Haitians living abroad. Regarding them as part of his constituency, Aristide spoke out strongly about issues affecting Haitians overseas, for example, being labelled as a population at risk for HIV (Richman 1992).

The few Haitian exiles admitted in the 1990s have not faced a warmer welcome than their compatriots who entered the United States in 1980. The image of thousands of ragged Haitians landing in barely seaworthy boats on the shores of Florida in 1980 is permanently etched in the minds of the American public. It is an image that repeatedly raised its head in the debate about U.S. policy toward Haitians in the 1990s, especially after the coup against Aristide. A beleaguered south Florida simply did not wish to receive another influx of people, either from Haiti or from Cuba. Public opinion, once again, did not favor the Haitians. A poll conducted in 1993 found that 65 percent of Americans thought that Haitians created problems for the United States; only 19 percent said that they benefited the country. Only Iranians fared as poorly as an immigrant group in the poll (Puente 1993).

Nevertheless, Haitians bring many strengths from the Haitian cultural heritage: a strong work ethic, fortitude, perseverance in the most arduous circumstances, deep religious faith, high self-respect, reliance on the extended family, and a tradition of sharing. These characteristics have enabled them to make a new life in the United States despite their problems and a welcome that has been less than open-armed.

CONCLUSIONS AND PROSPECTS

Haitians have faced enormous difficulties as exiles in the United States. Successive U.S. administrations have refused to recognize Haitians as legal refugees. Only strenuous legal battles have won for Haitians the right to have their cases for asylum heard by the INS. Having lost in court, three U.S. administrations have used other means for keeping Haitians out: turning them back at sea under a dubious arrangement with the Duvalier dictatorship or keeping them offshore to avoid U.S. constitutional responsibilities.

Two factors have generated U.S. policies toward Haitian exiles. The desire for political and economic control in a troubled neighbor has led to U.S. support for repressive regimes in Haiti. The fear of large numbers of Haitians needing public resources in the United States has made admitting Haitian immigrants politically expensive. These factors have resulted in denial that political abuses occur in Haiti and great ambivalence about the struggle for human rights there. American perceptions and attitudes about Haiti and its problems are unlikely to change. Haitians are not likely to be any more accepted as refugees in the future than they have been in the past.

Haitians in the United States, whether former boat people or long-term immigrants, continue to build their communities in spite of their lack of economic resources. Like other immigrant groups, they face questions of identity and cultural assimilation. Because of American notions of race and ethnicity, the issues faced by Haitians becoming Americans are particularly complex.

REFERENCES

Allman, James. 1981. Haitian Migration: Thirty Years Assessed. *Migration Today* 10(1): 7–12.

Buchanan, Susan Huelsebusch. 1979. Language and Identity: Haitians in New York City. *International Migration Review* 13(2):298–313.

Buchanan Stafford, Susan. 1987. The Haitians: The Cultural Meaning of Race and Identity. In *New Immigrants in New York City.* Edited by Nancy Foner. New York: Columbia University Press. Pp. 131–158.

Charles, Carolle. 1992. Transnationalism in the Construct of Haitian Migrants' Racial Categories of Identity in New York City. In *Towards a Transnational Perspective on Migration.* Edited by Nina Glick Schiller, Linda Basch, and Cristina Blanc-Szanton. *Annals of the New York Academy of Sciences* 645:101–123.

Chierici, Rose-Marie Cassagnol. 1991. *Demele "Making It": Migration and Adaptation among Haitian Boat People in the United States.* New York: AMS Press.

Cuban-Haitian Task Force. 1981. *Entrant Data Report* (May 31). Washington, D.C.

Farmer, Paul. 1994. *The Uses of Haiti.* Monroe, Maine: Common Courage Press.

Fouron, Georges. 1983. The Black Dilemma in the U.S.: The Haitian Experience. *Journal of Caribbean Studies* 3(3):242–265.

Leyburn, James G. 1966 (orig. 1941). *The Haitian People.* New Haven, Connecticut: Yale University Press.

Miller, John J. 1994. One Answer to the Haitian Dilemma: Let Them In. *The Wall Street Journal,* August 2.

Mitchell, Christopher. 1994. U.S. Policy toward Haitian Boat People, 1972–93. *Annals of the American Academy of Political and Social Sciences* 534:69–80.

Portes, Alejandro and Ramón Grosfoguel. 1994. Caribbean Diasporas: Migration and Ethnic Communities. *Annals of the American Academy of Political and Social Sciences* 533:48–69.

Portes, Alejandro, and Alex Stepick. 1993. *City on the Edge: The Transformation of Miami.* Berkeley: University of California Press.

Puente, Maria. 1993. USA Cool to Huddled Masses. *USA Today,* July 14. 1A.

Richman, Karen. 1992. A *Lavalas* at Home/A *Lavalas* for "Home": Inflections of Transnationalism in the Discourse of Haitian President Aristide. In *Towards a Transnational Perspective on Migration.* Edited by Nina Glick Schiller, Linda Basch, and Cristina Blanc-Szanton. *Annals of the New York Academy of Sciences* 645: 189–200.

Spero, Abby. 1985. *In America and in Need: Immigrant, Refugee and Entrant Women.* Washington, D.C.: American Association of Community and Junior Colleges.

Stepick, Alex III. 1982. *Haitians in Miami: An Assessment of Their Background and Potential* (Occasional Papers Series. Dialogue no. 12.) Miami: Florida International University Latin American and Caribbean Center.

———. 1992. The Refugees Nobody Wants: Haitians in Miami. In *Miami Now!: Immigration, Ethnicity, and Social Change.* Edited by Guillermo Grenier and Alex Stepick III. Gainesville: University Press of Florida.

Stepick, Alex, and Alejandro Portes. 1986. Flight into Despair: A Profile of Recent Haitian Refugees in South Florida. *International Migration Review* 20(2):329–350.

Vorp, Ronald. n.d. *Acculturation at Miami-Dade Community College, Fall Term 1981 through Fall Term 1991.* Miami, Florida: Miami-Dade Community College, Office of Institutional Research.

Wilkie, James W., and Stephen Haber, Editors. 1983. *Statistical Abstract of Latin America,* Vol. 22. Los Angeles: UCLA Latin American Center Publications.

Woldemikael, Tekle Mariam. 1989. *Becoming Black American: Haitians and American Institutions in Evanston, Illinois.* New York: AMS Press.

Chapter 13

Ethiopians and Eritreans

TEKLE M. WOLDEMIKAEL

Ethiopians and Eritreans are among the most recent groups of Third World refugees to come to the United States. Their number is small compared with other Third World refugees, such as the Vietnamese, Chinese, Cubans, and Haitians. The number of Ethiopians and Eritreans living in the United States was estimated to be between 50,000 and 75,000 in 1991 (USCR 1991a:11). Although the number of Ethiopians and Eritreans in 1995 could have reached to 100,000 people, the demographic impact of their presence is insignificant. They are, however, important symbolically. Since the end of the forced migration of Africans to the new world in the nineteenth century, Eritreans and Ethiopians represent the first African immigrants to come to the new world, especially the United States and Canada, in significant numbers. They are thus the first voluntary immigrants from Africa. Many other Africans want to immigrate to the United States voluntarily, but unlike Eritreans and Ethiopians, they have not had the opportunity to do so—although the number of other African refugees, mainly Somalis and Sudanese, began to increase considerably in 1992 (USCR 1994a: 12–13).

Until the passage of the Refugee Act of 1980, the U.S. government had no policy for allowing Africans to come to the United States as refugees. Ethiopians and Eritreans compose the first large group of Africans resettled in the United States. The first of these refugees to resettle in the United States were 169 refugees admitted in 1979 as seventh-preference immigrants (Koehn 1991:151; Scanlan 1980:105–106). After the enactment of the Refugee Act of 1980, the number increased dramatically. From 1975 to 1994, a total of 33,195 Ethiopians and Eritreans were resettled in the United States as refugees (USCR 1994a:10–11, 1983:5). In addition, between 1980 and 1994, 4,643 Ethiopians and Eritreans were granted asylum (USCR 1993a:12–13, 1994a:12–13; ORR 1993:A24). Of the 43,727 Africans allowed to enter the United States between 1982 and 1994 as refugees, the majority (around 68 percent) were Ethiopians and Eritreans. In the first ten years, from 1980 to 1991, Ethiopians and Eritreans constituted the overwhelming majority of African refugees in the United States. The data from 1982 to 1991 show that about 93 percent of the total number of African refugees were Ethiopians and Eritreans. However, from 1992 on, other Africans, especially Somalis and Sudanese, began to enter the United States as refugees in large numbers. The Somalis replaced Ethiopians and Eritreans as the largest group of African refugees to resettle in the United States in 1994. Out of the 5,856 Africans admitted in 1994, the Somalis constituted about 61 percent and the Sudanese around 21 percent, whereas the percentage of Ethiopians and Eritreans declined to about 5.6 percent (USCR 1994a:11–12).

The Ethiopian and Eritrean refugees came to the United States because of the terror, violence, torture, and persecution they experienced or feared they might experience in their country. This fear came from the hands of the provisional military government run by the Armed Forces Coordinating Committee, commonly known as the Dergue (meaning "committee" in Amharic), which ruled Ethiopia from 1974 to 1991. In February 1974, a popular uprising overthrew Emperor Haile Selassie's regime. The Dergue emerged to coordinate the activities of the various groups participating in the revolution and was expected to hand over power to civilians after stabilizing the nation. Instead, the Dergue took power into its own hands and unleashed a reign of terror for 17 years. During this period, it imposed on Ethiopia its own form of Marxist socialist program based on the Soviet model. The Dergue attempted to stamp out all opposition to its control and program. This included every person suspected of questioning the legitimacy of the provisional government or of having sympathies for Eritrean nationalist movements. Thus, the primary reason Ethiopians and Eritreans immigrated to the United States was political. Indeed, many of these refugees were relatively privileged and deeply attached to their home country. In a survey conducted in Washington, D.C., in 1984 (Koehn 1991:103–110), over half of the Ethiopian sample had high-level policymaking, professional, or managerial positions in their homelands, and 15 percent were primarily engaged in large-scale farming or other commercial activity. Approximately 80 percent of the Ethiopians, and 60 percent of the Eritreans, rated their personal or family income as "high" or "medium" at the time they left their country. Only 9 percent of the Ethiopians and Eritreans reported that their families' economic status or class position had influenced their decision to emigrate. Most came because of the dramatic political upheaval in their homelands and because of traumatic personal and family experiences, such as arrests and the death of relatives. Eritreans also cited fear that their nationality would be used to persecute them. Around 70 percent of the Eritreans stated that the failure to realize the objectives of a nationalist movement ranked as an important factor in their motivation to move to the United States.

The defeat of the Dergue army in May 1991 by a coalition of two opposition movements, the Ethiopian People's Revolutionary Democratic Front (EPRDF) and the Eritrean People's Liberation Front (EPLF), ended the Dergue's reign of terror. The EPRDF established a provisional government in Ethiopia and consented to the EPLF's demand that Eritreans be allowed to decide their fate through a popular referendum. In an internationally supervised referendum in April 1993, the overwhelming majority of Eritreans cast their ballots in support of an independent Eritrea. On May 24, 1993, Eritrea officially declared its independence from Ethiopia and soon afterward was admitted to the United Nations.

The emergence of an independent Eritrea and a nonmilitary government in Ethiopia have stemmed the tide of political refugees from Eritrea and Ethiopia. The slowing flow of political refugees was directly related to the end of the cold war. The Dergue was an unpopular regime propped up by the military and political support of the Soviet Union and the Soviet-influenced Eastern European countries and Cuba. With the implosion of the Communist block, external support to the Mengistu regime ended. Dergue power collapsed, and a new government emerged, led by the former liberation fronts of both Eritrea and Ethiopia. This has brought about major improvement in the political stability of the two countries. The exodus of refugees to neighboring Sudan and Somalia has slowed to a trickle. The United States stopped accepting applications for resettlement of Ethiopians and Eritreans who arrived in countries of first asylum after May 28, 1991, the date of the fall of the government of Mengistu Haile Mariam. As of November 21, 1991, the U.S. government officially stopped accepting new applications of Ethiopians and Eritreans to be resettled in the United States (USCR 1991a:10, 1991b:2). Thus, most of the refugees who were resettled in the United States between 1992 and 1995 were those who applied before November 21, 1991. By 1994, the annual number of Ethiopians and Eritreans resettled in the United States declined to 328 persons.

CONTEST FOR STATE POWER

The people of Ethiopia and Eritrea are a mixture of diverse cultures, religions, and races. The region was one of the earliest melting pots in the world. It was crisscrossed by people going from Asia to Africa, and vice versa, and saw widespread ethnic mixing, religious conversions, migrations, conquests, wars, and redefinitions of boundaries between states. The ethnic groups and nationalities that exist now are current labels, not natural groups that existed in isolation from one another in the past. Until the end of the nineteenth century, the core political unit in Ethiopia, then also known as Abyssinia, was a loose alliance of kingdoms (Moussa 1993:73). Because the majority of Eritreans and Ethiopians now in the United States spring from people who label themselves Abyssinians (Kiflu 1983), a brief description of the Abyssinians and their history is in order.

The Abyssinians are the core of the population in Ethiopia and a politically powerful group in Eritrea. They have considerable power in present-day Ethiopia and Eritrea. The Abyssinians are the product of a blending between indigenous Nilotic people, Cushitics and Semitic immigrants who came to the region presumably over three thousand years ago. The Abyssinians developed a unique culture that adapted Christianity to local conditions and created its own written language, called Geez, from which emerged many languages spoken in Ethiopia and Eritrea, including Tigrigna, Tigre, Amharic, Guragigna, and others. The Abyssinian political structure allowed for a fractured political order divided along provincial and regional lines but not among ethnic or cultural groups (Markakis 1987:12). A small segment of the Abyssinians, known as Jeberti, are Muslims.

Two regional and linguistic factions did compete for political supremacy: the southern Abyssinians, consisting of the Amharic-speaking peoples of southern and central parts of Abyssinia, versus the northern Abyssinians, consisting of Tigrigna speakers based in Tigray and southern Eritrea. The Abyssinians were united in their strong religious faith in Orthodox Christianity and in their fight against the competing Islamic powers in the region (Markakis 1987:12). They used the mythical history of the Solomonic Dynasty to announce that their kings could claim direct descent from the legendary King Solomon of the Bible. The throne was a basis for the unity of the state and was the most important institution in the country, next to religion. Throughout the history of Abyssinia, the throne was usually filled only after bitter internal strife and power struggles between various regional powers. The internal strife intensified between the seventeenth and the nineteenth centuries, a period known as Zemene Messafint (Age of the Princes), which led to fractured regional and provincial kingdoms. With the crowning of Teodros as emperor in 1855, the modern Ethiopian state, with its strong centralizing tendencies around southern Abyssinia, began. Following Teodros (1855–1868), three rulers fostered the centralizing process of the state. They claimed to be emperors of Ethiopia. They were Emperor Yohannes (1872–1889), Emperor Menelik (1889–1913), and Emperor Haile Selassie (1930–1974) (Tiruneh 1993:4). The last two emperors played important roles in shaping the recent history of Ethiopia and Eritrea.

Emperor Menelik of Shoa, a central province of Ethiopia, defeated several of his competitors. He marched north, south, east, and west of Shoa and colonized Oromoland and many eastern, southern, and western regions—thus establishing most of the state boundaries of present-day Ethiopia (Hassen 1990:198; Jalata 1993:50–74). Under Haile Selassie, the Ethiopian empire consolidated its control over the territories established by his predecessors. In an agreement to establish a federal state under his rule while maintaining Eritrea's administrative autonomy, he expanded the size of the country by acquiring the Ogaden in 1948 from the British, as well as Eritrea from the United Nations in 1952. A popular revolt in February 1974 against him ended the era of the Abyssinian throne and has come to be known as the Ethiopian Revolution.

Colonel Mengistu Haile Mariam led the Ethiopian Revolution and chaired the ruling committee, known as the Dergue. The Dergue eliminated not only the throne but the supremacy of the Orthodox Church. It declared Ethiopia a socialist Marxist state, eliminated private property and implemented land reforms, instigated large-scale resettlement into new areas of the country, organized urban populations into neighborhood associations known as *Kebeles,* enforced national service, and waged war against several nationalist and antiregime movements that challenged its power and policies. From 1977 to 1991, Colonel Mengistu Haile Mariam was the leader of the country. During his rule, Ethiopia was attacked by the Republic of Somalia and became entangled in several wars against Eritrean nationalists and the anti-Dergue Ethiopian movements. The political turmoil that ensued from the revolution wrenched the basic social fabric of the society. The major consequences of the upheaval were terror, death, and destruction waged on the whole nation. The people responded in one of three ways: (1) The majority chose passive resistance against the Dergue, (2) some joined the opposition forces, and (3) the rest fled to neighboring countries for safety and security.

The Ethiopian revolutionary state faced armed challenges in Eritrea, Tigray, and Ogaden (an area inhabited by Somalis and claimed by the Republic of Somalia) and from several resistance movements representing Oromos, Afars, and others. The conflicts caused large-scale destruction and displacement. The revolutionary government's attempt to centralize state power politicized the existing fissions along national and ethnic lines. This intensified the tensions to the point of armed conflict against the various national and regional movements representing Eritreans, Tigriyans, Afars, Somalis, Oromos, and others. This led to mass exodus of Eritreans and Ethiopians to neighboring countries including Sudan, Somalia, Djibouti, and Kenya. The next section of this chapter focuses on three such armed conflicts—the Eritrean Nationalist Front, the Ethiopian People's Revolutionary Democratic Front, and the Oromo Liberation Front—which have caused a massive influx of refugees into neighboring countries and are directly linked to the presence of Ethiopian and Eritrean refugees in the United States.

THE NATIONALIST WARS

The Eritrean Nationalist Front

Eritrea has an estimated population of 3.5 million, almost equally divided between Muslims and Christians, with nine different language groups. Eritrea was an Italian colony from 1884 to 1941. While Menelik was expanding his empire, the Italians consolidated their political control over the long strip of land shaped like a dagger along the Red Sea coast, north of Menelik's Ethiopia, and called it Eritrea (an ancient Greek name for the Red Sea). Italy attempted to expand its colony by attacking Menelik. In 1896, at the battle of Adua (a town in Tigray), Emperor Menelik and his army defended their territory by decisively defeating the Italian colonial army. The Italians and Menelik signed a peace agreement known as the Treaty of Ucciali in 1889, in which the Italians recognized Ethiopia's sovereignty, and the Ethiopians recognized the Italian occupation of Eritrea. Thus, modern-day Ethiopia and Eritrea were born at the same time.

After the Italians were defeated in World War II in 1941, the British colonial army established a military administration in Eritrea (1941–1952). Eritrea was federated with Ethiopia in 1952 by the United Nations, although there was considerable opposition from various segments of Eritrean society. From 1952 to 1962, the Ethiopian government slowly weakened the independent existence of Eritrea by suppressing the use of the Eritrean national languages, Tigrigna and Arabic, and replacing them with Amharic, the Ethiopian official language. The Eritrean flag was replaced by the Ethiopian flag. Local newspapers were censored. Political parties and trade unions were banned. Factories were closed and forced to relocate to Addis Ababa. The independent Eritrean police force was eliminated. The Eritrean parliament, under pressure from the Ethiopian government, voted to dissolve the federation in November 1962, and Eritrea was reduced to being the fourteenth province of Ethiopia. Although the act of federation was violated, the United Nations and most African nations tacitly accepted the dissolution, claiming this was an internal affair of an independent member of the United Nations and the Organization of African Unity (OAU).

The Eritrean armed struggle started in 1961 in western Eritrea, near the Sudanese border, with six men and five rifles in protest of the Ethiopian soldiers' encroachment upon their grazing and farming land. The protestors were primarily Muslims from the semipastoralist western Eritrea. In 1962, they linked up with members of the Eritrean Liberation Front (ELF), formed by Eritrean nationalists living in exile in Cairo and Saudi Arabia, and adopted the ELF for their guerrilla movement. The guerrilla movement grew in size and intensity from 1961 to 1966. In 1966, as more people joined the ELF, the leadership attempted to organize their fighting forces according to their regional and ethnic backgrounds. They created four regional and ethnic military units and added a fifth to accommodate to the increasing number of Christians from southern Eritrea joining the front. The five divisions led to a split of the movement along religious, regional, and ethnic lines. In 1970, a splinter group known as the EPLF emerged to challenge and compete with ELF's leadership. Between 1970 and 1973, a deep internal conflict between the two nationalist movements weakened the nationalist struggle. The ELF failed to eliminate the EPLF, which was gaining greater support from Eritrean workers; from urban-educated residents of Asmara, Addis Ababa; and from Eritreans exiled in Europe, the United States, and the Middle East (Woldemikael 1993:179–199).

During 1974–1975, the early stages of the Ethiopian revolution, the ELF and EPLF stopped their civil war, combined their forces, and controlled most of Eritrea except the capital city, Asmara, the ports of Massawa and Asab, and some smaller towns. In 1977, with strong Soviet and Cuban support, the Ethiopian government pushed the nationalist fronts back into their base areas in western and northern Eritrea. The two fronts resumed their internal conflict, and the bitter civil war intensified until the end of the 1970s, when it became the major killer of Eritreans. It ended with the EPLF defeating the ELF in 1981, pushing ELF forces from Eritrean land into Sudan (Woldemikael 1991:31–42). Some of the political refugees from Eritrea who entered the United States in 1980s were former ELF fighters.

The ELF never recovered from its defeat at the hands of the EPLF. It split into small groups, while the EPLF grew in size and strength. Between 1982 and 1984, the EPLF was severely weakened but not defeated when the Ethiopian government army waged "the Red Star" campaign. The government's goal was elimination of the nationalist movement by using all its firepower and military capability. The government army, receiving massive military support from the Soviet Union and Eastern Europe, included the combined forces of Ethiopian and Yemenese soldiers, with military advisers from Russia and Cuba. With the failure of the Red Star campaign, the defeat of the Ethiopian army became inevitable. On May 24, 1991, the EPLF defeated the Ethiopian army and captured Asmara, the capital city of Eritrea.

The Ethiopian People's Revolutionary Democratic Front

The EPRDF originated from another liberation front, the Tigray People's Liberation Front (TPLF), which was started by young students and ex-students, mostly from Tigray, in 1975. It aimed at eliminating the Dergue as well as gaining independence for Tigray. Although Tigray is the cradle of Abyssinian culture, it is one of the poorest provinces in Ethiopia. Haile Selassie kept it that way, so as to isolate and weaken the Tigrayans' sense of autonomy. The Tigrayans resented the Shoa-based Amhara rule. The majority of Tigrayans share the same culture, ethnic heritage, and religion of the highland Christians of southern Eritrea. The only difference has been the emergence of a new national consciousness among Eritreans who lived as a separate entity for over 60 years under Italian and British rule. During this period, generations of Eritreans grew up as colonized people with a sense of separate identity. The TPLF has had support and sympathy in Eritrea and a strong, though sometimes strained, relationship with the EPLF (Lefort 1981:106).

The TPLF grew in size and strength from 1975 to 1989, winning most of its battles against the Ethiopian army. In late 1989, it was estimated to have 20,000 fighters, with considerably more armed militia, and was the second-most powerful group in the region, next to the EPLF. In 1989, it captured Mekele, the capital of Tigray, and controlled the whole province. The same year, it formed the EPRDF, in coalition with other smaller Ethiopian groups. The TPLF and the EPRDF expanded their line of operations against the government army and took control of northern Ethiopia, including Wollo, Gojjam, Begemder, and finally the center of power, Shoa. On May 26, 1991, a few days after Mengistu

Haile Mariam fled the country, the EPRDF captured Addis Ababa, the capital city of Ethiopia. Immediately, it established a transitional government based in Addis Ababa. During the war, the Tigrayans suffered from famine as well as indiscriminate killing and torture at the hands of the Dergue.

The Oromo Liberation Movement

The third major group is the Oromo, who wish to establish an independent Oromo nation. The Oromos are believed to be more numerous than the Abyssinians. They are the largest ethnic group in the country, constituting almost 50 percent of the total population. They were first colonized by Abyssinian rulers. Menelik expanded the centralized control over the Oromos, and Haile Selassie consolidated it. Historically, they have been pastoralists specializing in cattle raising. A widely dispersed population, Oromos are found in every province of Ethiopia. They have adopted Amharic as their language as well as Amhara culture and traditions in many parts of Ethiopia. They traditionally worshipped an Oromo deity, but most of them converted to either Islam or Christianity (Jalata 1993; Markakis 1987:20). The most important Oromo movement has been the Oromo Liberation Front. It is based in Bale province in southern Ethiopia, a region bordering Kenya and Somalia. The Oromo nationalist movement was widely dispersed and lacked a strong organizational capacity like that of the EPRDF and the EPLF. Thousands of Oromos have fled to Somalia and Kenya to escape the war between the Ethiopian government and the Oromo nationalist movement in their region. The Dergue imprisoned and tortured Oromos suspected of supporting the nationalist aspiration of Oromo movements. The demand of Oromo nationalists for self-determination still persists and now poses a serious challenge to the legitimacy of the provisional government of Ethiopia.

ESCAPE TO AND REFUGE IN SUDAN

Most refugees from Ethiopia and Eritrea escaped to Sudan, Somalia, Djibouti, and Kenya. The estimated total number of refugees from Ethiopia and Eritrea to neighboring countries was about 1,066,300 people in 1991, with about 66 percent fleeing to Sudan and 33 percent to Somalia (USCR 1991b:33–34). With the termination of the nationalist wars in Eritrea and Ethiopia, a major cause of human displacement in the Horn of Africa ended. It also led to repatriation of some Eritrean and Ethiopian refugees to their homelands, and at the same time, it triggered new refugees to neighboring countries. At the end of 1994, there were still about 575,250 Eritrean and Ethiopian refugees (composed of about 67 percent Eritreans and some 33 percent Ethiopians) living in neighboring countries, mostly Sudan and Somalia. From 1991 to 1994, around 100,000 Eritreans were repatriated from Sudan and about 19,000 from Yemen, Ethiopia, and various Western countries. At the end of 1994, there were still about

380,000 Eritrean refugees in Sudan and 2,000 in Ethiopia, and 190,000 Ethiopian refugees in neighboring countries including 160,000 in Sudan, 20,000 in Djibouti, and 10,000 in Kenya (USCR 1995:56–57). The defeat of the Dergue sparked ethnic violence in southern Ethiopia, causing 80,000 Ethiopians to flee to Kenya during 1991–1992. A peace agreement between the fighting ethnic groups encouraged repatriation of most of the refugees with the aid of the United Nations High Commissioner for Refugees (UNHCR). By the end of 1994, some 10,000 refugees still remained in Kenya. An estimated 51,000 Ethiopian soldiers and their families who were based in Eritrea fled to Sudan after the EPLF took over all of Eritrea. Another 250,000 Ethiopian soldiers went south toward Addis Ababa after the EPLF captured Asmara. The UNHCR helped repatriate some of the ex-soldiers and their families from Sudan into Ethiopia (USCR 1992:42). In 1993 and 1994, some 26,000 Ethiopians repatriated from Sudan to Ethiopia (USCR 1995:58). About 100,000 Ethiopian Somalis, who had been refugees in Somalia following the Ethiopian-Somali war in the late 1970s and the subsequent civil unrest in the Ogaden region of Ethiopia in the 1980s, returned to Ethiopia, running from the civil war and famine in Somalia from 1991 on (USCR 1994b:53–54). During the nationalist wars, refugees from Eritrea, Tigray, and Wollo escaped to Sudan, while Somalis from Ogaden went to Somalia.

Throughout, Sudan has been the major destination of refugees and the major source of Ethiopian and Eritrean refugees resettled in the United States. Most of the Ethiopian and Eritrean refugees now resettled in the United States were in Khartoum, the capital city of Sudan, and the rest were scattered in different towns including Port Sudan, Kassala, Gedarif, and Wad Medani. In 1988, the UNHCR and the Office of the Sudanese Commissioners of Refugees (COR) estimated that over 250,000 refugees, mostly Ethiopians and Eritreans, lived in urban centers in Sudan (Kebbede 1992:111). They were mostly unemployed or living in poor conditions as domestics in Sudanese homes or as service workers for Sudanese families. They could not support themselves financially. They received help from remittances by family members abroad, from the offices of relief organizations, and from sharing resources among themselves. One study of 234 Ethiopian and Eritrean refugees in Khartoum conducted in 1988 found that slightly more than 50 percent of the sample was employed. Of those employed, only a third were full-time, and two thirds were relegated to low-paying service-type jobs or unskilled labor (Kebbede 1992:114). Another study of urban refugees, mostly in Khartoum, reported that in 1984, 20 percent of the urban refugees were unemployed, and an even higher percentage were underemployed in low-paying jobs. Two thirds of the sample reported that they received less daily income than was required to provide food, shelter, and basic necessities. Moreover, these urban refugees, who usually did not have identification cards allowing them to live in Khartoum, were subjected to exploitation by Sudanese landlords and employers. They were also subjected to arrest and involuntary relocation to other Sudanese towns and resettlement camps (Weaver 1985:152–155).

The economic plight of the refugees has to be understood in the context of the poverty of most Sudanese people and the limited economic development in the country. It is one of the poorest countries in the world. In early 1980, the International Labor Organization (ILO) estimated that in terms of satisfying basic needs of its people Sudan was close to the lowest in the world. In 1988, the World Bank estimated the per capita income of Sudan's 22.6 million population at $320 per year (Bernal 1991:24). What was unsettling about Sudan was that the government and the citizens used Ethiopian and Eritrean refugees as scapegoats for Sudanese economic and political crises. They were routinely refused credit, barred by law from owning fixed assets, and blamed for Khartoum's long-standing economic problems (Weaver 1985:154–155). They were accused of causing the shortage of housing, rising rents, pressure on public services, and insufficient supplies of consumer goods (Karadawi 1987:124).

In addition, the refugees were subjected to constant harassment and discrimination in public services. Refugees had difficulty obtaining, on their own, the identification cards required of every resident in Sudan; getting one required either the support of one of the major nationalist movements (which sometimes served as intermediaries with Sudanese officials, the government, and the voluntary agencies [Karadawi 1987: 121–122]), or bribing Sudanese public employees (Kebbede 1992:115). Government officials or anyone associated with the government could and often did threaten to send refugees to prison or have them deported to the borders of Eritrea or Ethiopia. To avoid being deported, refugees had to bribe public employees or those who posed as such, especially the police.

Refugees were advised to avoid the main streets of Khartoum or Port Sudan during times of "cleansing" (kesha, meaning "roundup" in Sudanese Arabic) of the cities from refugees, acts conducted several times a year. Those without identification cards were often loaded in military trucks and deported to a rural refugee community; ironically, most returned to the city within a few days' time on their own (Kebbede 1992:111–112). Even if a refugee possessed an identification card, Sudanese police and other government officials often ignored it and threatened to imprison him or her on any pretext. That way, they were able to extort money to augment their meager monthly income. Harassment of refugees, and targeting them for gaining money and other material or sexual favors, was an ongoing process obvious to the eyes of the Sudanese government and the international organizations.

The mistreatment and harassment often did not apply to Muslim Eritreans and Ethiopians, especially if they could create conversational intimacy in Arabic. The first thing the Sudanese would ask Eritrean and Ethiopian refugees was, "What is your name?" in order to find out their religion. Muslims were treated as acceptable foreigners rather than as undesirable intruders who were leading the society toward moral decadence and economic disaster. The worst harassment was directed toward Eritrean and Ethiopian women, who were seen as either prostitutes or potential prostitutes. Their Western-style dress or merely their walking unaccompanied by male friends or relatives exposed them to contempt from Sudanese men. Stones or other objects were thrown at them. Police officers often raped women refugees who were jailed for failing to produce an identification card. They were forced to disguise themselves to avoid recognition and the public eye. Still, many women were robbed and raped in their homes, and those who worked as domestics experienced rape and sexual assault at their workplace by their male employers or male members of the employer's family (Kebbede 1992:124–125).

The urban refugees stayed in the Sudan as a transitional place only until they could move to a third country. When an opportunity came for them to resettle in third countries in Europe or North America, most applied to the United States because they perceived the United States as the country that gives immigrants the greatest opportunities. Of the 1,656 Eritreans and Ethiopians resettled to a third country from 1981 to March 1983, for example, the largest number went to the United States (1,495), followed by Sweden (63), Germany (52), Canada (27), Switzerland (8), Somalia (5), the United Kingdom (4), Denmark (1), and Norway (1) (Kibreab 1987:12). In the 1984 Washington survey, the researchers found that around two thirds of the refugees interviewed had no expectations of migrating to the United States. This was especially true of Eritreans, 72 percent of whom had no expectation to migrate to the United States. A significant number of Eritrean refugees were ex-ELF fighters who became refugees when they lost their battle with the EPLF in 1981. They applied to come to the United States only because the opportunity to do so opened up while they were seeking refuge to a third country (Koehn 1991:161).

TRANSITION AND RESETTLEMENT

The passage of the Refugee Act of 1980 allowed Africans to enter the United States as refugees. The ceiling was set at 1,500 in fiscal year (FY) 1980, although only 955 persons were admitted that year. From 1981 to 1990, the ceiling fluctuated from a low of 2,000 in FY 1987 and FY 1989 to a high of 3,500 in FY 1986 and FY 1990. Yet the ceiling did not reflect actual admissions. For instance, although the ceiling for 1986 was 3,500, the actual number of refugees (1,315 persons) admitted in 1986 was lower than the actual number of refugees (1,994 persons) admitted in 1987 when the ceiling was set at 2,000 (USCR 1990:9). For 1991, the Bush administration made an increase to the African regional ceiling to 4,900, and this represented a 30 percent increase from 1990 actual admissions of 3,500 and a 70 percent increase over the original 1990 ceiling (USCR 1991a:4). In 1992 the ceiling went up to 6,000 persons, and in 1993 it was raised to 7,000. The ceiling remained at 7,000 for 1994 and 1995 (USCR 1994a:9). Despite these modest increases in the 1990s, the U.S. Congress has consistently set a low admission ceiling for refugees from Africa. There are several reasons: First, Africa had limited significance for the United States in the cold war. Second, in the early stages of the African refugee crisis of the

1980s, African governments, the OAU, the United Nations, and the UNHCR sought to repatriate or resettle Africans in African countries of asylum. They saw resettlement of Africans in third countries such as the United States as "unnecessary and counterproductive" (USCR 1981:4). Third, Africans do not have a constituency in the United States to advocate for the admission of Africans as refugees. Black Americans have ambivalent feelings toward admission of refugees because they fear that immigrants would compete with them for the scarce unskilled manufacturing and service jobs, and they see the plight of African refugees as an issue that does not directly concern them (USCR 1989:11). Fourth, racism exists in U.S. refugee and immigration policies with the U.S. Congress being slow in responding to the refugee crises of both Haitians and Africans. As Congressman Bruce A. Morrison stated, "The perpetuation of racism after slavery is a strain in American history, and we need to work hard to remove racist elements in U.S. immigration policies" (USCR 1989:11).

Compared with other Africans, Ethiopians and Eritreans have been relatively favored. For instance, in the first ten years, from 1980 to 1991, Ethiopians and Eritreans constituted the overwhelming majority of African refugees in the United States, and from 1982 to 1991 about 93 percent of the total number of African refugees were Ethiopians and Eritreans (USCR 1994a:11–12). By giving token refuge to Ethiopians and Eritreans who were fleeing a self-declared Communist country allied with the Soviet Union, the U.S. government effectively silenced its critics for not challenging Soviet power in the Horn of Africa. At the same time, this was a political gesture to the Sudan, next to Egypt, the closest ally of the United States in Africa in the 1980s, because Sudan blamed the refugees for being the primary threat to its political stability.

Yet unlike refugees from other Communist regimes, Ethiopians and Eritreans were the only groups not admitted in large numbers. Moreover, their transit to the United States took a long time. Most of the refugees spent one to five years waiting from the time they applied until they gained permission to enter the United States. Success in gaining entry depended on using appropriate admission strategy. The steps in the immigration process demanded a great deal of skill and luck. Convincing the screening agents—both the voluntary agency and the U.S. government person—that they were authentic and qualified refugees was a major hurdle for all would-be refugees. The most skillful individuals cultivated inside contacts and utilized their compatriots in community networks to find out and hone the stories that would secure the highest rate of acceptance. This meant that some denied participating in the antiregime political groups whose other members the U.S. government had refused admission on the ground that they were engaged in terrorist acts or the persecution of others. After an initial rejection, some would-be immigrants adopted a complete change of identity and tactics (Koehn 1991:167–201). Forged travel documents could be purchased on the black market for a fortune (Karadawi 1987:127; *New York Times,* May 26, 1987:6).

Once they arrived in the United States, most of the refugees were resettled and assisted by nongovernmental agencies. In the survey conducted in Washington, nongovernmental resettlement agencies were reported to have helped 85 percent of the Ethiopian and 95 percent of the Eritrean refugees. The largest numbers, 45 percent of both nationalities, were assisted by the U.S. Catholic Conference. Church World Service aided 18 percent of the Ethiopians and 10 percent of the Eritreans (Koehn 1991:201). The U.S. government and its authorized resettlement agencies followed the dispersal model in the resettlement of refugees from Ethiopia and Eritrea. The major concentrations of resettled Ethiopian and Eritrean refugees were in California, Washington, D.C., Maryland, Virginia, and Texas. Of the total 16,157 Ethiopian and Eritrean refugees resettled in the United States from 1983 to 1990, 22.3 percent were initially resettled in California, 12.5 percent in Texas, 6.6 percent in Maryland, 5.8 percent in New York, and 4.7 percent in Washington, D.C. (USCRa 1991:12).

After they were resettled, many Eritrean and Ethiopian refugees moved to major metropolitan centers where they could meet their compatriots. This secondary migration led to the concentration of the exiles in a few major urban centers—mostly Washington, D.C., Los Angeles, Dallas, and New York City. Washington, D.C., ranks as the number-one place of residence for Ethiopians and Eritreans in the United States. Since the 1960s, Washington, D.C., has been a hub for Ethiopian elites and their children, who were attending local schools. Around this core gathered other ex-students who came looking for jobs around Washington. The Ethiopian ambassador took an interest in the Ethiopian students in the United States and hosted the students during Ethiopian national and religious holidays. The reputation of Washington as the center of Ethiopian and Eritrean presence increased as it became the center of Ethiopian and Eritrean political activism. More and more students and ex-students joined their friends and families. Most students combined attendance at local colleges or universities with their work and political activism. The large service sector in the metropolitan Washington area provided ideal opportunities for jobs they could easily do in their spare time.

Ethiopian and Eritrean refugees had some unique demographic characteristics. The data on the refugees showed that those who arrived as political refugees were predominantly males. For instance, of the 2,929 Ethiopian and Eritrean refugees who arrived in 1992, 62 percent were males and 38 percent females (ORR 1993:10). Ethiopian and Eritrean societies are patriarchal and favor males over females in almost all spheres of public life, including education, employment, government, and business. Men predominate among those who were educated and employed in the modern sector. Thus, men in greater numbers than women met the complex criteria set by the U.S. gatekeepers in the refugee processing sites in the Sudan and in Europe.

In addition, contrary to the fact that the majority of the refugees in the Sudan were Eritrean Muslims, the resettled ones were Amharic-speaking Ethiopians and Tigrigna-speaking Eritreans, with some Tigrigna-speaking Ethiopians and some Oromos. Most of them were Christians, primarily Orthodox Christians.

Among Eritreans, large minorities were Catholics and Protestants. A few of the
Eritrean refugees were Muslims. The explanation as to why this happened is
complex. Those allowed in were Ethiopian and Eritrean immigrants whom the
U.S. government defined as able to integrate into the society faster and better.
This included those who were Christians, those not involved in nationalist movements, those who were better educated or young, and those who were deemed
to contribute most to the host society or had work experience in the modern
sector of the economy. The greatest influence in granting refugee status was the
refugee's educational background. For instance, while fewer than 5 percent of
the refugees from Ethiopia living in Sudan had attended a university, nearly 20
percent of the resettled household heads had attained this educational level
(Koehn 1991:169). The Shoa-based Amharic-speaking Ethiopians were the most
preferred for immigration to the United States because they had greater access
to educational and occupational resources in Ethiopia, and they were less feared
to be associated with "terrorist" organizations. They were mostly Christians as
well. Therefore, they were perceived as the most likely to integrate successfully
into U.S. society.

LIFE IN THE UNITED STATES

Economic Incorporation

Eritrean and Ethiopian refugees had been exposed to an idealized American
way of life as presented in the media. They aspired to that ideal and expected
to participate in it once they arrived. Their idealization of the American way of
life made them ideologically committed to the attainment of the "middle-class
lifestyle." Their desire was frustrated when they found themselves unable to
function in everyday life in American society. Except for some professionals,
who were employed as medical doctors, experts in international organizations,
or researchers and professors in higher education, the majority found employment that would place them on the lower rungs of the economic ladder in the
United States, mostly in unskilled service jobs. This created a sense of economic
dislocation or downward mobility and challenged their sense of identity, status,
and culture in the United States.

Generally, Ethiopian and Eritrean refugees faced difficulties in finding jobs
that matched their educational and occupational experience and qualifications.
They entered the U.S. economy as low-wage workers in the service sector. This
pattern started when Ethiopians and Eritreans were going to school in the late
1960s and early 1970s and working as parking lot and gas station attendants,
waitresses and waiters, busboys, taxi drivers, night guards, hotel and hospital
maintenance personnel, nurse's aides, and providers of other services. Most
hoped to return to their homeland and work in occupations based on their new
qualifications. They treated their stay and their work in the United States as
temporary until they finished their education or training. As the political crisis

in their encounters worsened and as new refugees arrived as permanent residents, their dream of returning home faded. Many continued in their previous jobs. The earlier residents helped the newcomers find jobs in the service sector. So there occurred a cultural division of labor, in which most Ethiopians and Eritreans specialized in low-paying service jobs that required only minimum interaction with the host society. A few who have saved enough capital have broken from this trend and opened their own businesses, including liquor and convenience stores, restaurants, gas stations, taxi cabs, real estate agencies, and computer and printing services. Like other Third World immigrants, such as the Chinese and Indians, many Ethiopians and Eritreans have succeeded in creating a niche for Ethiopian and Eritrean restaurants in most major American cities. They specialize in Abyssinian cuisine, a cultural practice shared by both Tigrigna-speaking Eritreans and Amharic-speaking Ethiopians.

In a survey conducted in 1986 in three urban areas of high Ethiopian and Eritrean concentration, including Dallas, Washington, and Los Angeles, researchers found that Ethiopian and Eritrean refugees were participating in the labor force at high levels. They reported that 93 percent were either working or actively seeking work in Dallas, 100 percent in Washington, and 75 percent in Los Angeles. In contrast, the labor force participation level for the U.S. population age 16 and above was 65.4 percent during the times of the site visits. However, the actual employment rates were much lower. Of those participating in the labor market, 92 percent of the Dallas sample were employed full-time, but 67 percent of the Washington sample and only 47 percent of the Los Angeles sample were working in full-time jobs. These rates showed a higher unemployment rate than the U.S. general population in the respective countries. Thus, Ethiopians and Eritreans were facing economic hardship in Los Angeles and Washington, while they were very successful in Dallas (Cichon, Gozdziak, and Grover 1986:30). Los Angeles in the West and Washington in the Northeast represent the economic crisis and job loss experienced by the major cities and regions in the West and Northeast United States, and their economic difficulties had a direct effect on the lives of the refugees.

The first jobs for the Ethiopian and Eritrean refugees in the sampled sites were entry-level positions in the service sector, including hotel housekeeping, dishwasher, and landscaping. Among the refugees in Los Angeles, there were more diverse types of jobs such as security guards, gas station and parking lot attendants, busboys, mail sorters, sometimes cashiers, waiters and waitresses, and restaurant hosts and hostesses. In the case of Dallas and Washington, they would obtain the latter types of employment only after some work experience in the initial jobs listed earlier. Los Angeles provided more time for the refugees to stay on public assistance than Dallas and Washington so that they could improve their language and work skills in training programs and thus enter the job market at a different level than those who went to Dallas and Washington. In the three-year period studied, 1983 to 1985, the refugees showed only slight advancement in pay, skill, and responsibility (Cichon, Gozdziak, and Grover 1986:31).

In terms of economic self-sufficiency, the Dallas sample was considered 100 percent self-sufficient, while in Washington 50 percent of the sample was considered self-sufficient and in Los Angeles only 41 percent. However, the earned income of the self-sufficient families showed a grim economic picture. Most of the refugees in all three cities were living below the poverty level. Their incomes varied from 62 percent of the poverty level to 308 percent of the poverty level. Most lived in poorer sections of the cities, sometimes in dilapidated buildings, alongside other minorities (Cichon, Gozdziak, and Grover 1986:33–34).

This limited income suggests the likelihood of receipt of public assistance by the refugees. In fact, there was wide variation among the three sites studied. In Dallas, there was almost no welfare receipt among the sample, while in Washington half of the sample received it at some point, and in Los Angeles, 36 percent of the sample reported receiving cash assistance at the time of the site visit and another 23 percent had received it at some prior time. Therefore, Ethiopians and Eritreans seem to use welfare when and where it is available in adequate levels (Cichon, Gozdziak, and Grover 1986:32) and when needed.

Social and Cultural Incorporation

Ethiopians and Eritreans are immigrants from predominantly agrarian and pastoral societies whose semifeudal social structure remained intact until the Ethiopian revolution of 1974. In the case of Eritrea, the feudal social structure was modified by 50 years of Italian colonialism (1889–1941) and a brief occupation by the British (1941–1952). The cultural incorporation of both groups in America has been particularly painful for them because they now have to function in a highly industrialized, urbanized, and bureaucratic society. They often find the work discipline of the capitalist system, and the regimentation and regulation of time and space, bewildering and difficult. As an Eritrean writer has noted: "Coming from a less developed part of the world to a nation of mass production and mass consumption where everyone has to run to make ends meet, a newly arrived immigrant finds the fast pace of American life exhausting" (Kiflu 1983:99).

Once in the United States, the refugees suffer a shift in their social position, from being members of the dominant majority groups in their own societies to being among the nondominant immigrant minorities. Most are from the politically dominant ethnic groups in their countries, including the Amharic and Tigrigna speakers in Ethiopia and the Tigrigna speakers in Eritrea. This creates a reversal of status and a consequent conflict in their identity. The identity conflict manifests itself in gender and family relations, race relations, and generational frictions. This means that Ethiopian refugees feel pressure to find a new sense of identity that blends their home-country-based sense of self with the self they construct in the new society.

Gender Relations

Ethiopian and Eritrean refugees come from highly patriarchal societies. In Ethiopia and Eritrea a person's status is determined mainly by the class and ethnic position of his/her families in society. Still, gender cuts across class and ethnic lines. Men receive more respect than women regardless of their class and ethnic position. Men's identity is public, requiring continuous affirmation from their male peers. "Achieving the male gender ideals of personal autonomy, masculine honour and prestige—all available for public scrutiny and evaluation—protects both respect for the individual man as well as the family's and group's reputation" (McSpadden and Moussa 1993:211).

Coming to the United States, men and women experience the new society differently. Eritrean and Ethiopian women gain greater financial and personal independence and security than they had back home. Women experience greater freedom and rights in the home and at work in the United States. Men, on the other hand, find their dominant position contested both at home and at work. They often resist changing their attitudes and behavior. They avoid helping their wives in the kitchen when visitors come to their homes, even if they do help when they are alone. Most single men do their own housework, including working in kitchens to survive. But once they get married, the gender roles tend to be sharply defined. They are mainly concerned about their culturally defined male image as the patriarch of the family (McSpadden and Moussa 1993:217).

Thus, the ideal of equality between the genders in the United States generates tensions within the refugee families and between males and females. The number of cases of wife battery has risen along with some divorce. The dilemma for a battered woman is that her husband or male partner is often the only person she knows in their new country. The fighting husband and wife often have no mediating community or family relations to which they can turn. The absence of trusted community elders and extended families to mediate marital problems increases the family tensions and the isolation of women and their male partners. In addition, marriage in Ethiopia and Eritrea represents the bringing together of two extended families. Thus, it is hard for a woman to imagine that she has the right to break the relationship on her own (McSpadden and Moussa 1993:214). In the short run, most of the refugee women, like the men, work in low-paying service jobs. The relative gender equality in the United States, however, compared to the glaring inequality in their homelands, gives them some hope of improving themselves and attaining the American dream of a secure middle-class lifestyle—with or without their male partners in the long run.

Race Relations

In the eyes of the first generation of refugees, the question of racial identity is not a major concern in their new life in the United States. They focus their attention on "making it" in the system in spite of race-based social divisions.

Race becomes a serious concern as they set up families and have children. They are aware of the racial divide in American society and the assumptions different racial groups have about each other. However, they do not publicly and collectively acknowledge that racial issues affect their own lives. Instead, they relegate the racial issue to a private and often secondary level of concern. This pattern continues even when the significance of race increases as their children grow up in a society that has "naturalized" racial identities and denied the existence of ambiguity in the meaning of race and ethnic identity. The first-generation refugees continue to focus on acquiring basic survival skills such as language, vocational and professional skills, and even higher education. They emphasize national and regionally based ethnic identity as a way of mitigating any racially based ascribed identity. They do not try to understand the meaning of such contested identities as race or class in the United States. At the same time, they do not feel they are entitled to speak on issues that affect native-born American minorities because they are not part of the historical legacy of U.S. society. Eritreans and Ethiopians thus focus on the well-being of their families, relatives, and friends, in exile and in their homelands, and consider racial issues secondary in their lives.

Communal Concerns

Some writers have remarked that Ethiopians and Eritreans in the United States are extremely isolated from the host society (Cichon, Gozdziak, and Grover 1986:41), and this leads them to depression, mental health crises, and a high suicide rate (McSpadden 1988; McSpadden and Moussa 1993). The study conducted by Cichon and others in 1986 showed that refugees found support within the rather sizable Ethiopian and Eritrean presence in three sites of research—Los Angeles, Dallas, and Washington. The earlier immigrants served as resources with whom they could socialize, eat their own food, listen to their own music, use their own language, and share their experiences. In spite of this, most refugees experienced loneliness and isolation because the total number of Ethiopians and Eritreans in the United States was small and dispersed in different parts of the cities. They were also divided along ethnic, political, and, in the case of Eritreans, religious lines. Most suffered from the absence of family support and elders with the authority to direct and advise them. The alienation was most severe with single males in their twenties (Cichon, Gozdziak, and Grover 1986:41–42).

The earlier 1984 survey in Washington differed in its findings and suggested that Ethiopians and Eritreans did not suffer from higher rates of mental health problems compared with other refugees. In fact, most Ethiopian and Eritrean refugees were reportedly competing effectively in the mainstream economy and were involved in large-scale organizations. According to the study, "Many live among U.S. nationals and are comfortable interacting frequently with them on a social basis. In short, they have friends in the dominant society. . . . Most members of the . . . communities interact socially with fellow migrants and feel closer to their compatriots than the U.S. national'' (Koehn 1991:334).

The apparent contradictory findings between the 1984 survey in Washington and the 1986 survey of Dallas, Los Angeles, and Washington can be explained by taking several factors into account. First, the 1984 survey was conducted among the first wave of refugees who were better educated and had more work experience than did the second wave immigrants. Second, Washington is a city where blacks are the majority. The presence of blacks as a majority in Washington might serve as a protective shield for the refugees from the full impact of being a racial minority in the United States. Third, because of the relatively high concentration of Ethiopians and Eritreans in Washington, the refugees could live almost entirely within Ethiopian and Eritrean circles for their social and cultural life. Refugees who live in Washington have informed me many times that they feel comfortable living there and even forget that they are living in exile because it is inhabited predominantly by blacks and because they work and socialize with their compatriots every day.

In most cities of the United States the refugees cope with their reversal of status by participating in all-Eritrean and -Ethiopian political and cultural organizations. These include support groups, either for the nationalist movements, in the case of the Eritreans, or for the anti-Dergue movements, in the case of the Ethiopians. They also can choose to participate in almost all-male soccer teams that have been active for over ten years in the United States. Other organizations, such as friendship circles and peer groups, meet and play and socialize on weekends. Many participate in ''Ekub,'' a traditional Abyssinian rotating credit association, by means of which individuals accumulate capital while also socializing with their compatriots. Very often, husbands and wives participate together in networks of friendship, family circles, and political organizations. Recently, there has been a growing interest in providing religious services for the adults and teaching Tigrigna and Amharic to the second generation.

Repatriation

The end of the nationalist and civil wars in Eritrea and Ethiopia in May 1991 made repatriation of the refugees to their homelands a distinct alternative and a widely discussed issue among the refugees. Since they defined themselves as sojourners who were waiting to return to their homes after the end of the wars, the refugees had to decide whether to go back home or not. From 1991 to 1995, most refugees visited their families and relatives in their homelands but then returned to the United States. The most dramatic visit was when 360 Eritreans departed the United States on July 30, 1991, only three months after the end of the Eritrean nationalist war, on a charter fight bound to Asmara, Eritrea, to visit their families and loved ones after having not seen them in many years or even decades.

There are very few of the refugees who have not gone home at least once in the last four years. Among Eritreans, those who have yet to set foot in an independent Eritrea include some Muslim Eritreans who feel alienated from the perceived Christian dominance of the new government and economy, and some former ELF supporters who still hold a strong animosity and resentment to the EPLF—the liberation front that defeated them in 1981 and whose leaders run the present Eritrean state. Among Ethiopians, a large segment of the Amharic-speaking refugees have refused to accept the legitimacy of the EPRDF-dominated Ethiopian government. They have organized themselves into several political organizations with their own publications and a radio station aimed at discrediting the new Ethiopian government in the eyes of the American government and public. Their dream is to create followers within Ethiopia by linking with some dissident groups inside the country and eventually toppling the EPRDF-led Ethiopian government.

The reasons why the refugees decided not to repatriate have been explored in a small-scale comparative study of Eritrean men in northern California and Eritrean and Ethiopian women in Toronto conducted among those who had already visited and those who intended to visit the home country. The study showed that men's and women's decisions were strongly influenced by what would enhance their social power as men and women, respectively. For men, this meant restoring their social power "congruent with the patriarchal Eritrean socio-cultural understanding of masculinity, based in education, employment, family responsibilities, and social status. Women in contrast look[ed] for a creative tension between maintaining aspects of their cultural identity which . . . [were] fulfilling and at the same time asserting their rights as women in an egalitarian and democratic sense'' (McSpadden and Moussa 1995:35).

The question of why most of the refugees decided not to repatriate after dreaming for so long about returning to their home of origin has to be explored in the context of the dilemma of being an exile or a person in diaspora. Many do not return home because the home they left does not exist after 30 years of war and destruction. The people they knew are old or dead or have also left. Those who stayed have been changed by the 30 years of rule of terror of the Dergue. The young children whom they left behind are adults with their own families now. Their neighborhoods and family homes have been changed, if not destroyed, during the war. New faces and new people live in the villages, towns, and places they consider home. Even the vocabulary and the expressions of language they spoke when they were young have changed. In addition, they find themselves alienated from the villages, towns, and cities they considered ''home'' because their experiences in exile in Sudan, in Italy, and in other places in which they lived before they were granted refuge in the United States have changed their sense of self and personhood. They find the society they left as too isolated, conformist, and critical of their statements, self-presentation, and behavior. The ''home'' they knew remains only in their imagination, where they can cherish and remember it while continuing to live in self-imposed exile.

FUTURE CONCERNS: THE SECOND GENERATION

The major long-term concern of Eritreans and Ethiopians in the United States has been how to continue their separate identity and pass on to their children their sense of connection to their homeland while also being full members of American society. Because of the strong assimilative mechanisms in the United States, the second-generation Eritreans and Ethiopians find it hard to follow their parents' cultural traditions. Their parents come from more communal and family-oriented societies. The parents' generation finds it hard to orient its children for coping with the demands of the competitive and individualistic U.S. society, which is also fractured along class, racial, and ethnic lines. They are often unable to control their children. When they try to use physical punishment or other authoritarian methods to discipline them, their actions draw public attention and they are then visited by police and government officials because of complaints of child abuse.

In the Eritrean and Ethiopian context, the older generation is respected because of their age and rank. Conversations follow a pattern in which the higher status is assigned to older men, followed by older women, followed by younger married men and married women, then the eldest sons, followed by the eldest daughters, and so on. In such gender- and age-based hierarchies, a child's or a young person's needs are hardly addressed. The children are forced to keep their mouths shut and pretend to conform to the wishes of their parents at home. But beyond the sight of their parents and outside their homes, they disregard their parents' wishes and hang around with youth in their neighborhoods and schools. Thus, the schools and neighborhoods where the children grow up play a significant role in shaping their identities and cultures. Families who live in poor minority neighborhoods, where gangs and drug-related criminal activities abound, find their children growing up exposed to such influences. As they grow older, they also become involved in gangs and drug-related activities. Children growing up in more affluent neighborhoods are more exposed to middle-class-oriented lifestyles and family life and thus are affected less by gangs and drugs.

There is no unique culture among the second-generation Ethiopians and Eritreans. The parental generation has been unable to pass its language, and to a large extent, its religious orientations, to the second generation. This failure to educate children about their faith and their language been a source of great anguish to them. Instead, the second generation has constructed and negotiated its own identity, blending its American and African cultural influences. The refugees' children are more individualistic and less nationalistic than their parents. Most of them confront American society as black persons with Ethiopian or Eritrean parents. What they become varies depending on their neighborhoods, their class backgrounds, and their own personal choice of friends and lifestyles. Some of them identify themselves as Eritreans/Ethiopians and Africans, and some as blacks. Many individuals assume different cultural identities depending on the social context. They use synthetic and racial identities as resources to manage socially challenging and often uncomfortable situations. When they apply to schools, they identity themselves as blacks. When they go to colleges, they participate in black-oriented associations, as well as African and international associations. They also take part in multicultural organizations. In the long run, the parental generation's strong pride in its national and ethnic heritage may help to give the second generation a strong basis for negotiating a meaningful collective identity for itself in the United States.

REFERENCES

Bernal, Victoria. 1991. *Cultivating Workers: Peasants and Capitalism in a Sudanese Village*. New York: Columbia University Press.

Bulcha, Mekuria. 1988. *Flight and Integration: Causes of Mass Exodus from Ethiopia and Problems of Integration in the Sudan*. Uppsala: Scandinavian Institute of African Studies.

Cichon, Donald J., Elzbieta M. Gozdziak, and Jane G. Grover, Editors. 1986. *The Economic and Social Adjustment of Non–Southeast Asian Refugees*. Dover, New Hampshire: Research Management Corporation.

Hassen, Mohammed. 1990. *The Oromo of Ethiopia: A History 1570–1860*. Cambridge: Cambridge University Press.

Jalata, Asafa. 1993. *Oromia & Ethiopia: State Formation and Ethnonational Conflict, 1868–1992*. Boulder, Colorado: Lynne Rienner Publishers.

Karadawi, Ahmed. 1987. The Problems of Urban Refugees in Sudan. In *Refugees: A Third World Dilemma*. Edited by John R. Rogge. Totowa, New Jersey: Rowman & Littlefield. Pp. 115–129.

Kebbede, Girma. 1992. *The State and Development in Ethiopia*. Atlantic Highlands, New Jersey: Humanities Press.

Kibreab, Giam. 1987. *Refugees and Development in Africa: The Case of Eritrea*. Trenton, New Jersey: The Red Sea Press.

Kiflu, Tesfai. 1983. Abyssinians in America: A Cultural Perspective. *The Mid-Atlantic Almanack: The Journal of the Mid-Atlantic Popular/American Culture Association* 2: 95–106.

Koehn, Peter H. 1991. *Refugees from Revolution: U.S. Policy and Third World Migration*. Boulder, Colorado: Westview Press.

Lefort, Rene. 1981. *Ethiopia: An Heretical Revolution*. Translated by A. M. Bennett. London: Zed Press.

Markakis, John. 1987. *National and Class Conflict in the Horn of Africa*. Cambridge: Cambridge University Press.

McSpadden, Lucia Ann. 1988. Ethiopian Refugee Resettlement in the Western United States: Social Context and Psychological Well-Being. Unpublished Ph.D. dissertation, University of Utah, Salt Lake City.

McSpadden, Lucia Ann, and Helene Moussa. 1993. I Have a Name: The Gender Dynamics in Asylum and in Resettlement of Ethiopian and Eritrean Refugees in North America. *Journal of Refugee Studies* 6(3): 203–225.

———. 1995. Power and Belonging: The Gendered Context for the Repatriation Decisions of Eritrean Refugees in North America. In *Selected Papers on Refugee*

Issues IV. Edited by Ann Rynearson and Jim Phillips. Arlington, Virginia: American Anthropological Association.

Moussa, Helene. 1993. *Storm & Sanctuary: The Journey of Ethiopian and Eritrean Women Refugees.* Dundas, Ontario: Artemis Enterprises.

ORR (Office of Refugee Resettlement). 1993. *Report to the Congress: Refugee Resettlement Program.* Washington, D.C.: U.S. Department of Health and Human Services.

Scanlan, John A. 1980. First Final Research Report Submitted to the Select Commission on Immigration and Refugee Policy. In *U.S. Immigration Policy and the National Interest.* Appendix C to the State Report. Washington, D.C.: The Commission. Pp. 105–106.

Tareke, Gebru. 1991. *Ethiopia: Power and Protest.* Cambridge: Cambridge University Press.

Tiruneh, Andargachew. 1993. *The Ethiopian Revolution 1974–1987.* Cambridge: Cambridge University Press.

U.S. Committee for Refugees (USCR). 1981. *Refugee Reports.* Washington, D.C.

———. 1982. *Refugee Reports.* Washington, D.C.

———. 1983. *Refugee Reports.* Washington, D.C.

———. 1984. *Refugee Reports.* Washington, D.C.

———. 1987. *World Refugee Survey.* Washington, D.C.

———. 1989. *World Refugee Survey.* Washington, D.C.

———. 1990. *Refugee Reports.* Washington, D.C.

———. 1991a. *Refugee Reports.* Washington, D.C.

———. 1991b. *World Refugee Survey.* Washington, D.C.

———. 1992. *World Refugee Survey.* Washington, D.C.

———. 1993a. *Refugee Reports.* Washington, D.C.

———. 1993b. *World Refugee Survey.* Washington, D.C.

———. 1994a *Refugee Reports.* Washington, D.C.

———. 1994b. *World Refugee Survey.* Washington, D.C.

———. 1995. *World Refugee Survey.* Washington, D.C.

Weaver, Jerry L. 1985. Sojourners along the Nile: Ethiopian Refugees in Khartoum. *Journal of Modern African Studies* 23(1): 147–156.

Woldemikael, Tekle M. 1991. Political Mobilization and Nationalist Movements: The Case of the Eritrean People's Liberation Front. *Africa Today* 38(2): 31–42.

———. 1993. The Cultural Construction of Eritrean Nationalist Movements. In *The Rising Tide of Cultural Pluralism.* Edited by Crawford Young. Madison: University of Wisconsin Press. Pp. 179–199.

Index

About the Contributors

MEHDI BOZORGMEHR is an assistant professor of sociology at the City College, City University of New York. He was project director of a survey of Iranians in Los Angeles (funded by the National Science Foundation) and has published extensively on Iranians in the United States—including entries in *Encyclopedia Iranica* and *Encyclopedia of American Immigrant Cultures.* He received his Ph.D. from the University of California at Los Angeles.

JOSEPH COLEMAN first participated in the Cuban refugee program when he worked in human services at the state and federal levels. Later, in 1975 he coordinated the Department of Health, Education, and Welfare's processing of Southeast Asian refugees arriving at Fort Indiantown Gap in Pennsylvania, and then spent the next 20 years with the federal refugee program, mostly at the U.S. Department of State. His major focus was on involving and informing refugee groups in both the domestic and overseas aspects of the program. From 1988 to 1993 he coordinated the roles of the federal agencies that were part of the private resettlement program of the Cuban American National Foundation—a program that he and the foundation developed. He is a graduate of Vanderbilt University.

FREDERICK J. CONWAY has conducted both academic and applied research on agriculture, health practices, and religion in Haiti, as well as comparative applied research in Francophone Africa. In 1980, he served as an adviser to the Cuban-Haitian Task Force in Miami and as acting director of the Krome South camp for unaccompanied Haitian minors. More recently, he has conducted research on immigration policy in California and currently teaches at San Diego

State University. He is a graduate of Yale University and subsequently received his Ph.D. in anthropology from American University in 1978.

PAMELA A. DEVOE has carried out research on culture change and cross-cultural interaction, including work with American Indians in the United States, American expatriates in Central America, and Taiwanese Chinese in Taiwan. In 1980 she began her involvement in refugee issues, conducting research in St. Louis, examining issues of refugee policy and program development, and contributing to the American Anthropological Association's Committee on Refugee Issues—of which she is currently the chair and formerly editor of its 1992 *Selected Papers on Refugee Issues.* Her Ph.D. is in anthropology.

TIMOTHY DUNNIGAN is an associate professor of anthropology at the University of Minnesota. His primary research interests are linguistic acculturation, cultural semantics, written translation, and oral interpretation—as well as language-based problems of ethnographic description. His published work focuses on both Native American and Southeast Asian cultures: specifically, the Pima, Ojibwa, Dakota Sioux, and Hmong. He received his Ph.D. from the University of Arizona.

STEVEN J. GOLD is an associate professor of sociology at Michigan State University and a senior fellow at the Wilstein Institute. He is the author of *Refugee Communities: A Comparative Field Study* (1992); has published numerous articles on immigrant adaptation, ethnic self-employment, and community development in both academic journals and edited volumes; and is the former president of the International Visual Sociology Association. Most recently, he has been involved in studies of Israeli immigrants in Los Angeles and Jewish philanthropy. He received his Ph.D. in sociology from the University of California at Berkeley in 1985.

ELZBIETA M. GOZDZIAK, a native of Poland, is an assistant professor at the Howard University School of Social Work and a lecturer at the Johns Hopkins School for Advanced International Studies. Her academic work covers displaced populations, research methods, and various aspects of Eastern European society and politics. She has also worked in policy analysis and project development, both on refugees in the United States and on development projects in Poland and Slovakia. Dr. Gozdziak is a cultural anthropologist by training.

DAVID W. HAINES is a social anthropologist whose involvement with refugee issues began in 1979 and has included policy-related work for the federal government and both small- and large-scale research projects on the adaptation of refugees. He is the editor of *Refugees in the United States* (1985) and *Refugees as Immigrants: Cambodians, Laotians, and Vietnamese in America* (1989). His academic writing includes Vietnamese social history, refugee adaptation, and

American culture and society. He received his M.A. in Southeast Asian Studies and his Ph.D. in anthropology from American University.

JULIENE G. LIPSON is professor of nursing and medical anthropology at the University of California at San Francisco (UCSF) where she teaches international/ cross-cultural and community health nursing. Since 1982, she has conducted research on the health and adjustment of immigrants and refugees to California from the Middle East and, since 1986, from Afghanistan. She is co-director of the UCSF-based health resource center for Middle Eastern immigrants and health and service providers. She also directs the Afghan Health Education Project, a community health assessment among the San Francisco area's Afghan community. She is an R.N. and received her Ph.D. in anthropology.

MILES A. MCNALL is a doctoral candidate in sociology at the University of Minnesota. His dissertation research concerns the adaptation of Eastern Europeans to emerging post-Communist social structures. In addition, he has published a number of articles pertaining to the adjustment of Southeast Asian refugees to life in the United States.

CAROL A. MORTLAND has been involved with research and programs with Southeast Asian refugees since 1981. She is the coeditor of *Cambodian Culture since 1975: Homeland and Exile;* her own published work deals with refugee patronage, refugee camp life, resettlement, and belief systems. She has also worked both as a director of local resettlement programs and as director of refugee programs for a national volunteer agency. Most recently, she has become involved in archaeological excavation in Cambodia. She received her Ph.D. in anthropology from the University of Oregon.

NGUYEN MANH HUNG is currently an associate professor of government at George Mason University and director of its Indochina Institute. Prior to leaving Vietnam in 1975, he was a professor at the National School of Administration and subsequently Deputy Minister of National Planning and Development for the government of the Republic of Vietnam. He has written extensively in both English and Vietnamese on issues relating to Vietnam and its foreign policy. He received his Ph.D. in international relations from the University of Virginia in 1975.

DOUGLAS P. OLNEY has conducted a variety of research on ethnicity, kinship, and refugee adaptation and currently works as a research consultant focusing on refugee issues. His major academic work relates to the development of Hmong self-help organizations in the United States. He received his Ph.D. in anthropology from the University of Minnesota in 1993.

PATRICIA A. OMIDIAN is a lecturer in the Department of Anthropology at

California State University at Hayward. Her major research focused on family conflict and life-course issues in an Afghan refugee community in northern California and reflected her more general concern with the formulation, production, and reproduction of identity among Middle Eastern and Central Asian immigrants and refugees. She has also worked directly as coordinator for both a community health resource center and an Afghan health education project. She received her Ph.D. in medical anthropology.

MARLINE A. SPRING is currently a research associate at the University of Minnesota's Community-University Health Care Center and a doctoral candidate in anthropology, also at the University of Minnesota. As an applied anthropologist, she has produced health education materials for Southeast Asian refugees and published articles on such health issues as the adequacy of reproductive services provided to Hmong patients.

SUSAN BUCHANAN STAFFORD is currently the director of Corporate and Foundation Relations for Queens College, City University of New York. Her major academic research focused on Haitian immigrants and refugees in the United States. She has worked for various branches of the federal government on Cuban and Haitian resettlement programs, for a refugee resettlement agency, and for a national advocacy organization on Haitian causes. More recently, she has been involved in grants and development in the area of higher education. She received her Ph.D. in anthropology from New York University.

JOHN K. WHITMORE, an historian of Vietnam, is currently a research associate of the Center for South and Southeast Asian Studies and an adjunct associate professor of the Department of History, both at the University of Michigan. He has published extensively on Vietnamese history—particularly the Lê dynasty—and was involved in a set of major surveys of Vietnamese, Chinese-Vietnamese, and Lao refugees in the United States, including coauthorship of *The Boat People* (1989) and *Children of the Boat People* (1991). He received both his M.A. in cultural anthropology and his Ph.D. in Southeast Asian history from Cornell University.

TEKLE M. WOLDEMIKAEL is currently an associate professor of sociology and anthropology at the University of the Redlands and also taught at the University of Gezira in the Sudan in the early 1980s. He has published articles on Haitian immigrants, ethnicity and nationalist movements in Eritrea, and ethnic relations in the Sudan and is the author of the 1989 volume *Becoming Black Americans: Haitians and American Institutions in Evanston, Illinois.* He received his B.A. in economics from Addis Ababa University and his Ph.D. in sociology from Northwestern University.